Street's Cruising Guide to the Eastern Caribbean

Puerto Rico, the Passage Islands, the US and British Virgin Islands

Books by Donald M. Street, Jr.

A Cruising Guide to the Lesser Antilles
A Yachting Guide to the Grenadines
The Ocean Sailing Yacht, Volume I
The Ocean Sailing Yacht, Volume II
Seawise

Street's Cruising Guides to the Eastern Caribbean:

Transatlantic Crossing Guide

Puerto Rico and The Passage Islands
U.S. and British Virgin Islands

Anguilla to Dominica
Including Anguilla, St. Martin, St. Barthélemy, Saba,
Sint Eustatius (Statia), St. Kitts, and Nevis,
Antigua, Barbuda, Montserrat, Redonda,
Guadeloupe, and Dominica

Martinique to Trinidad
Including Martinique, St. Lucia, St. Vincent, Barbados,
Northern Grenadines, Southern Grenadines, Grenada,
and Trinidad and Tobago

Venezuela
Including Isla Margarita and Adjacent Islands, Los Testigos,
La Blanquilla, La Tortuga, La Orchila, Los Roques, Las Aves,
Aruba, Bonaire, and Curaçao

Street's Cruising Guide to the Eastern Caribbean

Puerto Rico, the Passage Islands, the US and British Virgin Islands

Donald M. Street, Jr.

Sketch charts by Morgan B. MacDonald III

Imray-Iolaire harbor charts courtesy of Imray, Laurie, Norie & Wilson Ltd.

Topographical views by James Mitchell

W • W • NORTON & COMPANY

New York   London

Formerly titled *Street's Cruising Guide to the Eastern Caribbean, Volume II, Part One—Puerto Rico, the Passage Islands, the US and British Virgin Islands*

The text of this book is composed in Caledonia, with display type set in Bulmer

ISBN 0-393-03896-3

W.W. Norton & Company, Inc., 500 Fifth Avenue, New York, NY 10110
W.W. Norton & Company Ltd., 10 Coptic Street, London WC1A 1PU
1 2 3 4 5 6 7 8 9 0

Dedication

I first conceived of this cruising guide in 1963, and it was only through the hard work, perseverance, courage, and self-sacrifice of my late wife, Marilyn, that the original book got off the ground.

Fortunately for myself and my daughter, Dory, I met Patricia Boucher, now my wife, on the beach in Tyrell Bay. She has presented me with three active sons yet has had time to help in business, sailing *Iolaire,* and exploring. Although she had hardly sailed before our marriage, she has taken to sailing like a duck to water. Her love of sailing was largely instrumental in my decision to keep *Iolaire* when I was thinking of selling her to reduce expenses.

It is only because of Trich's hard work keeping our various enterprises going in my absence that I have been able to keep the third love of my life, *Iolaire.*

Iolaire has been my mistress for more than 30 years; at age 88, she is still the type of boat Michel Dufour would appreciate. She is "fast, beautiful, and responsive." She first arrived in the islands in 1947, remained for a few years, and cruised back to Europe in 1949, directly from Jamaica to England. In 1951, under the ownership of R.H. Somerset, she won her division's RORC Season's Points Championship at the age of 45. In 1952, she sailed from the Mediterranean via the Azores to New York to take part in the 1952 Bermuda Race. She then cruised back to Europe and the Mediterranean. In 1954, she returned to the islands, where I purchased her in 1957.

In 1975, we celebrated *Iolaire's* seventieth birthday by cruising to Europe via Bermuda, New London, New York, Boston, Halifax, and then a 15-day passage to Ireland. We cruised on to Cowes, took part in the fiftieth anniversary of the Fastnet Race, and then raced to La Rochelle, La Trinité, Benodet, and back to the Solent—four races, totaling 1,300 miles, in 21 days.

After Calais, we went up the Thames to St. Katharine's Dock in the Pool of London under Tower Bridge, then back down the Thames and up the Colne River in Essex, where we lay alongside the dock in Rowhedge—where *Iolaire* had been built 70 years earlier. Then we went to Plymouth, Glandore (Ireland), Madeira, the Canaries, and back across the Atlantic to Antigua in 18 1/2 days.

We arrived in Antigua seven months and seven days after our departure, having sailed 13,000 miles and raced 1,300 miles—all without an engine—and having visited all the places people had said we would never get to except under power.

We decided that *Iolaire* should celebrate her eightieth birthday in 1985 by retiring from round-the-buoys racing. Her swan song in that year's Antigua Sailing Week was wonderful—third in the cruising division (17 boats), first in the division of boats 20 years old or older.

Then we took *Iolaire* on a 12,000-mile, seven-month, double-transatlantic jaunt. In seven months, we visited Bermuda, five of the Azores islands, Ireland, Vigo (Spain), the Salvage Islands and the Madeiran archipelago, five of the Canary Islands, and three of the Cape Verde Islands. Then we rolled on home to the Caribbean in 14 days and four hours from the Cape Verdes to Antigua—not a record, but a good, fast passage for a heavy-displacement cruising boat.

We spent the winter of 1989-90 exploring Venezuela and crisscrossing the Caribbean, double-checking information for revisions of all volumes of this guide. After that, we sailed from Antigua directly to the Azores, then on to Ireland, down to Vigo, the Canaries, and the Cape Verdes—visiting all the islands we had not visited before in order to eliminate all secondhand information from *Street's Transatlantic Crossing Guide.* Again we did 12,000 miles in 12 months, without the aid of an engine. We did the Cape Verdes-to-Antigua leg of the trip in 14 days and 12 hours—with the spinnaker up the last five-and-a-half days. Not bad for an old girl of 85!

In 1990, *Iolaire* came out of retirement to sail in the new Classic Regatta and won her division! She is not about to race against her younger sisters, but she is still ready, willing, and able to take on the classic boats.

Iolaire has 11 transatlantic passages under her belt. I have sailed her at least 140,000 miles. Who knows how many miles she has sailed during her lifetime? There is little of the Caribbean that has not been furrowed by her hull—and, as some of my good friends will point out, there are few rocks that have not been dented by her keel!

To my three loves—Marilyn, Trich, and *Iolaire*—I dedicate this book.

Contents

List of Charts and Sketch Charts

Publisher's Note

Donald M. Street, Jr., a veteran Caribbean sailor, is well known as an author and the compiler of the Imray-Iolaire charts of that area. In addition, he is an international yacht-insurance broker who places policies with Lloyd's of London.

Street also serves as a design consultant on new construction and the rerigging of existing yachts, and he also helps find good cruising boats for people who want a proper yacht. His latest project is a sailing and seamanship video series with *Sailing Quarterly.*

Although Street is known mainly as a cruising skipper, he has raced successfully on *Iolaire* and other boats. *Iolaire,* now 90, has retired from round-the-buoys racing, but her skipper has not. He still participates in the various Caribbean regattas as an elder statesman — usually as "rock pilot." It is said he is excellent at this, as he has bounced off every rock in the Eastern Caribbean that is slightly less than *Iolaire's* draft of seven feet six inches.

His contributions to sailing in the Eastern Caribbean consist of his multivolume cruising guide and the 54 Imray-Iolaire charts that have replaced roughly 200 French, American, British, Dutch, and a few Spanish charts for cruising the Eastern Caribbean and the Atlantic islands.

The Street guides cover a vast area — equivalent to the distance from Eastport, Maine, to Cedar Keys, Florida; or Norway's North Cape to Gibraltar. No other yachting author has ever covered so much territory in such detail; Street spends every winter crisscrossing the Caribbean.

As an author, Street is prolific. His original *Cruising Guide to the Lesser Antilles* was published in 1966, *A Yachting Guide to the Grenadines* in 1970, and an updated and expanded *Cruising Guide to the Eastern Caribbean* in 1974, with continual expansions and updates since then. This has now become *Street's Cruising Guide to the Eastern Caribbean,* which covers a 1,000-mile-long arc of islands, plus the Venezuelan coast and the Atlantic islands. All of the individual volumes have been completely updated and rewritten regularly in the two decades since then.

Street has also written *The Ocean Sailing Yacht, Volume I* (1973) and *Volume II* (1978). *Seawise,* a collection of articles, came out in 1976. He continues working on a series of books — *Street on Sails, Street on Seamanship and Storms,* and *Street on Small-Boat Handling* — as well as *Iolaire and I,* the story of *Iolaire* and Street's lifetime of adventures and misadventures in the yachting world.

Street writes regularly for *Sail, Cruising World, Sailing, WoodenBoat, Telltale Compass, Yachting, Yachting World,* and *Yachting Monthly,* as well as for publications in Sweden, Germany, Italy, Ireland, Australia, and New Zealand.

For more than 20 years, Street owned land and two houses on Grenada, but, unfortunately, the houses are no more. They were taken over by the People's Revolutionary Army (PRA) in May 1979 to be used as part of its military base. The houses did not survive the United States "liberation" in 1983, when helicopter gunships targeted both of them. He hopes someday to rebuild on the old site.

Since Street's main occupation is yacht insurance, he and *Iolaire* appear at all the major gatherings of yachts in the Eastern Caribbean. In the fall, he is always at the St. Thomas and Tortola charter-boat shows. Then he proceeds eastward via St. Martin and St. Barts en route to Nicholsons Agents Week. Spring finds him at the Rolex and BVI Regattas, after which he heads to Antigua for the Classic Yacht Regatta and Antigua Sailing Week. Then it is south to lay up *Iolaire* beyond the hurricane belt. Formerly, *Iolaire* was laid up in Grenada, but her berth has been moved south and west to Centro Marina de Oriente in Puerto La Cruz, Venezuela. In July and August, Street is usually in Glandore, County

Cork, Ireland, skippering the family's 63-year-old Dragon, *Gypsy,* or trimming her sheets for his sons.

Street claims to be 38 and holding — as long as he can climb the mast without the aid of a bosun's chair; his wife still looks young enough to be his daughter. Street and his son Richard (plus a friend, Niall McDowell) took *Gypsy* to France in the summer of 1992 for the Classic Boat Festival in Brest. They sailed from Glandore (near Fastnet Rock) across the Irish Sea to the Isles of Scilly, then across the English Channel and on to Douarnenez. After the festival, they returned to Ireland — completing 700 miles in an open boat. In 1993, Street and his wife, Trich, sailed *Gypsy* out to Fastnet Rock to cheer on their sons Donald M. Street III and Richard around the rock.

As mentioned, Street is an insurance broker, and he has pointed out that many boats have trouble obtaining insurance coverage while in the Caribbean (and especially in Venezuela). So if you are having such difficulties, contact the author, c/o David Payne, Morgan, Wright & Coleman, 6 Alie Street, London E1 8DD, England (tel. 071-488-9000; fax 071-480-6917).

Preface

When I first bought *Iolaire* in 1957, I found on board what was then the only straight cruising guide to the Lesser Antilles—a mimeographed publication produced by the Coast Guard Auxiliary and edited by a Lieutenant Commander Buzby. Carleton Mitchell's *Islands to Windward,* published in 1948, was generally regarded as a good cruising yarn rather than a cruising guide, but it did have some basic cruising information in the back of the book. Unfortunately, by the time I started sailing outside the Virgin Islands in 1959, *Islands to Windward* was out of print. In 1960, *The Virgin Islands* by George Teeple Eggleston was published, the result of a one-month cruise aboard Eunice Boardman's 55-foot ketch *Renegade.*

In 1961, Percy Chubb III, after a cruise through the Lesser Antilles, produced the small, privately printed *Guide to the Windward and Leeward Islands of the Eastern Caribbean.* In 1964, Linton Rigg wrote *The Alluring Antilles,* a combination guide and cruising adventure of a half-year sail from Puerto Rico to Trinidad aboard the 45-foot ketch *Island Belle.*

Those books seemed to suffice for the small amount of Caribbean cruising done in those days, but the charter-boat business suddenly began to expand in the early 1960s, and many new boats arrived. It was Frank Burke of Island Yachts who inspired my entry into cruising-guide writing. Figuring that too many of the charter parties were missing the best spots in the Virgins because their skippers had not been in the islands long enough to get to know them intimately, he asked me to write a cruising guide to the Virgin Islands. I did so, and he had it privately printed. I received the magnificent sum of US$100—a veritable fortune for me in those days.

This small volume later formed the basis of the Virgin Islands section of my *Cruising Guide to the Lesser Antilles,* published in 1966 after I showed it

to Phelps Platt of Dodd, Mead, who encouraged me to expand it to cover the whole island chain. This was followed two years later by Tom Kelly and Jack van Ost's *Yachtsman's Guide to the Virgin Islands,* and then by Al Forbes's excellent *Cruising Guide to the Virgin Islands*—notable in that, unlike many guide authors, he had sailed the area for many years before he wrote his book.

In 1970, following eight years of cruising the Grenadines, I produced *A Yachting Guide to the Grenadines,* after which, in 1973, came Julius M. Wilensky's *Yachtsman's Guide to the Windward Islands,* which covered largely the same territory as mine. Also in 1973, Gordon C. Ayer produced an interesting small guide covering an island group that had never been detailed before—namely, the Passage Islands.

During the late 1970s and early 1980s, numerous guides to the Eastern Caribbean appeared. They covered individual areas such as the Virgin Islands; the northern Windward Islands; Anguilla, St. Martin, St. Barthélemy, St. Kitts, Nevis, and the Leeward Islands. Others keep popping out of the woodwork like mushrooms out of an old log.

It is very easy to write a guide to an area if someone else has previously done all the hard work—i.e., extensive exploring, producing charts, and bouncing off uncharted rocks. Most of the other guides have been written with an eye on the bareboat-charter market, so they concentrate on the well-known, popular anchorages and skip a tremendous number of excellent anchorages that are a bit out of the way.

As each year goes by, and more and more yachts cruise the Caribbean, the bareboat charter organizations are expanding exponentially. The area is now flooded with boats. But if you are willing to go off the beaten track, you can still have anchorages completely to yourself—or almost so.

My suggestion for finding this idyllic world of deserted (or almost-deserted) anchorages is to buy the other guides and then circle in red in my guide all of the harbors that are not listed in the other books. If you head for the anchorages circled in red, you will be able to avoid most of the other boats cruising the Eastern Caribbean.

To illustrate this, I would like to quote from a letter I received: "My thanks to you for your cruising guides. I have enjoyed my season down here in the Caribbean and the myriad of information in your books has really been a pleasant and informative education and made my cruise more safe, interesting, and fun. Just a brief example: I've begun to seek out the less crowded anchorages, and armed with your guides and eyeball navigation have visited Sandy Island, Grenada; Grand Bay, Carriacou (caught 10 lobsters there in 1 1/2 hours); Petit St. Vincent, north side (6 lobsters); Grand Bay, Canouan; World's End (some help from other sources). Always we were the only vessel anchored. Nifty—we loved it. Soon I'll be going around to Antigua with your guide in hand. Thank you for an excellent job. Great sailing and best wishes, Ray Bachtle, *Alchemist.*"

In *Street's Cruising Guide to the Eastern Caribbean,* I have tried to include all the information I have gleaned in some 40 years of cruising these islands. I have drawn not only from my own experiences, but, as you can see from the accompanying Acknowledgments, also from the experiences of old friends who are, in addition, good sailors. Thus, I feel I have described probably every cove in the Eastern Caribbean where one could possibly think of anchoring.

If you find one I may have missed, please let me know. I boldly asserted in my 1966 guide that the book would never become dated because rocks do not move. Little did I realize how eagerly island governments would actually start moving them—along with creating new islands, making islands into peninsulas, building low bridges, and so forth—as the development of the Eastern Caribbean boomed. Further, any guide is destined to go out of date simply because the idyllic, uninhabited spot of one year becomes a thriving hotel and cabaña settlement the next. Indeed, one of my readers once took me to task because he was using my original guide and expected to anchor off an island described therein as uninhabited. As he rounded between Pinese and Mopion, near Petit St. Vincent, he was greeted by a brand-new hotel ablaze with celebration, and he counted no fewer than 45 boats moored in the lee of Petit St. Vincent! Please . . . don't blame me!

I have largely stayed away from recommending restaurants and bars in the Eastern Caribbean, because these establishments—especially their cooks and bartenders—do change. A superb restaurant or bar one week can become rotten the next when the cook or bartender decides to move on to another challenge.

It is impossible for anyone to say he knows the Eastern Caribbean perfectly; even after three decades, I was still discovering new little anchorages. But then the time came to look to new fields—namely, Venezuela.

At various times, Venezuelan yachtsmen extolled the virtues of Venezuela and the offshore islands. I originally went to Venezuela to give a slide lecture to a yacht club and take part in a race. I then took *Iolaire* to eastern Venezuela for six weeks and later visited western Venezuela on *Boomerang.* There followed a month's cruise in 1978 and a two-week cruise in 1979. In the early 1980s, we seldom visited Venezuela, as it was the most expensive place in the Eastern Caribbean. In fact, Caracas was rated as the most expensive city in the world. But then came the collapse of the oil market—and the devaluation of the Venezuelan bolívar—in the 1980s. Suddenly Venezuela became the cheapest cruising area in the entire Eastern Caribbean. At first we were unable to take advantage of this, but since 1986, we have spent six to eight weeks (sometimes 10 weeks) every winter cruising there. The result is *Street's Cruising Guide to the Eastern Caribbean: Venezuela,* published in 1991 and covering the Venezuelan coast, its offshore islands, Aruba, Bonaire, and Curaçao.

With the aid of many veteran Venezuelan yachtsmen, plus yachtsmen from the Eastern Caribbean (see Acknowledgments)—and as a result of all my own cruises—I think Venezuela has now been superbly covered.

In 1975 and again in 1985, *Iolaire* and I made double transatlantic passages and explored the Azores, the Madeiran Archipelago, the Canary Islands, the Cape Verde Islands, and Bermuda. The information gained—combined with the information already in the first volume of *Street's Cruising Guide to the Eastern Caribbean*—came out under a new title: *Street's Transatlantic Crossing Guide and Introduction to the Caribbean,* the essential companion to my guides to the Eastern Caribbean. Not only does it contain transatlantic crossing information—plus cruising information on Bermuda, the Azores, the Madeiran Archipelago, the Canaries, and the Cape Verdes—but it also has important background information on the Eastern Caribbean: preparation;

wind, weather, and tides; universal tide tables; sailing directions; communications; provisioning and services; chartering; yacht clubs and racing; and lists of navigational aids for the Eastern Caribbean and the Atlantic islands. (The most recent edition of *Street's Transatlantic Crossing Guide and Introduction to the Caribbean* should be used in conjunction with the volume that covers the area where you are planning to cruise.)

Now I am extending the bet I first made years ago: If you can find any anchorage safe for a boat that draws seven feet in the Eastern Caribbean, the Atlantic islands, or along the Venezuelan coast that I have not mentioned in my guides, I will happily pay for an evening's drinks in exchange for the information on that unmentioned harbor. Also, I greatly appreciate the assistance that yachtsmen have been very willing to provide, so please do send suggestions for corrections, additions, or deletions to: D.M. Street, Jr., c/o David Payne, Morgan, Wright & Coleman, 6 Alie Street, London E1 8DD, England (tel. 071-488-9000; fax 071-480-6917).

Many cruising friends who knew the Eastern Caribbean in the early days have headed west to Belize, the Bay Islands, the River Dulce. They have been urging me to base *Iolaire* in that area for a few years and then write a cruising guide. I refuse to do that, as I do not feel you can cruise an area for a total of six to 12 weeks and then write a guide to it. It takes years to explore a cruising area adequately, and exploring is a young man's game. Those days are over for me; the "Old Tiger" has retired. It is time for one of the "Young Tigers" (daughter Dory or one of her three brothers, Donald, Richard, and Mark) to take over *Iolaire* and explore that new territory.

—D.M.S., Jr.

Foreword

The Lesser Antilles stretch southward from St. Thomas to Grenada in a great crescent 500 miles long, offering the yachtsman a cruising ground of unequaled variety. Some of the islands are flat, dry, and windswept, their shores girded by coral reefs and their land barely arable. Others are reefless, with jagged peaks jutting abruptly up from the sea, where they block the ever-present trades and gather rain clouds the year round; water cascades in gullies down their sides, and their slopes are well cultivated. The character of their peoples likewise varies—from the charming and unspoiled but desperately poor Dominicans to the comparatively well-to-do and worldly wise Frenchmen of Martinique.

Whether or not Puerto Rico to the north or Trinidad and Tobago to the south should be considered part of the Lesser Antilles is a question for the gazetteers to squabble over. For the purposes of this multi-volume guide, we welcome all three into the fellowship of proximity. (And, of course, the guide also covers Venezuela and the Atlantic islands.) Taken as such, the Antilles conveniently break up into a number of areas suitable for two- or three-week cruises. The starting and end points of a cruise will be governed by your own tastes and the availability of air transportation. The air services into San Juan and Trinidad are excellent, for example, but neither of these places is a particularly good spot to begin a cruise. San Juan is dead to leeward of the rest of the chain—unless, of course, you are planning to cruise the south coast of Puerto Rico or the wonderful undiscovered Passage Islands of Culebra and Vieques. Trinidad used to be a poor starting point, as the anchorage off the yacht club was so bad you would get seasick. Now, however, all this has changed, with new and convenient facilities. In addition, Trinidad Customs and Immigration offi-cials—who used to be the most difficult in the entire Caribbean—now are very helpful.

Unless you have a whole season at your disposal, it is foolhardy to attempt all the islands in a single cruise. Not only will you not make it, but you will fail to enjoy the slow, natural, and relaxed pace of life in these tropical islands. The first measure of a successful cruise is how soon your carefully worked out timetable gets thrown away.

Rule number 1 in the Antilles is: Don't make any plan more than a day in advance, since you will frequently—in fact constantly—alter your intentions to suit the pace and attractions of the locale.

Rule number 2: Each night before turning in, read the sailing directions covering your passage to the next area, and study the detailed description of your intended anchorage. In some cases, this will seriously affect the next day's plans—particularly the hour of departure. Remember, for instance, that when you are headed for the east coast of Martinique, Guadeloupe, Antigua, and Grenada, you must be in the anchorage by 1400 hours. Otherwise, the sun is in the west, directly in your line of vision, making it impossible to see any reefs until it is too late.

Rule number 3: Do not enter a strange harbor at night if at all possible. If necessary, stand off, heave-to, and wait for dawn!

Rule number 4: No chart can be absolutely accurate. In the Caribbean, knowing how to read the water is as important as knowing how to read a chart. Eyeball navigation is the key to safe and satisfying sailing in the islands.

To get to most Caribbean starting points, you must often rely on secondary local airlines with shuttle services. These vary from being fairly good from San Juan to St. Thomas and Tortola and the Venezuelan airlines, to downright disastrous with LIAT. LIAT's aircraft, pilots, and maintenance personnel are first rate, but the office staff has elevated the art of losing baggage and double-booking reservations to an exact science. There are various jokes about what LIAT actually stands for—some people claim it is an abbreviation for "Leave Islands Any Time," while others insist that it means "Luggage In Another Terminal." Still, it's all part of the adventure of a Caribbean cruise.

Which starting point you choose will say something of your tastes in cruising. If you prefer gunkholing and short jaunts between many little islands only a few miles apart, if you like snorkeling and little in the way of civilization, then it's the Virgins or the Grenadines for you. But you'd best hurry down, because real-estate developers and other sailors are fast making this situation a thing of the past. Mustique, for one example, was until recently a private estate in the hands of the Hazel family. But it was sold to a developer, who has worked it over at a pretty fast rate. Well-to-do Europeans have bought land and built houses, creating many new jobs for local labor but depriving the yachtsman of a wonderful hideaway.

For those of you who want to give boat and crew a good tuning-up for offshore racing, set out from St. Thomas up through the Virgins, then work your way across Anegada (Sombrero) Passage to St. Martin or Anguilla, and finish with a final leg up to Antigua. In doing so, you will gain a fair sampling of island diversity and of French, Dutch, and English colonial temperaments. The Anegada Passage is a nice, hard drive to windward, which should uncover any weak points in rig or crew.

Those interested exclusively in the pursuits of diving, treasure hunting, or snorkeling should steer for the low-lying islands of Anguilla, Barbuda, Anegada, Los Roques, and Las Aves. The reefs in these areas are vast and inexhaustible. Fortune hunters still flock to these islands, where innumerable offlying wrecks date back hundreds of years, some presumably still undiscovered. Consult the source books—but remember that these islands are low, flat, encircled by reefs, and hard to spot. The charts are based on surveys done mainly in the middle of the nineteenth century. Coral grows, and hurricanes have moved through the area a number of times; earthquakes have shaken the islands, and sandbars have moved. In short, you must be extremely careful. Do not let your boat become the next curiosity for inquisitive divers!

Saba and Statia (Sint Eustatius) are two attractive islands that are too seldom visited. Their anchorages are exceptionally bad, but when the conditions are right, they certainly are worth a go. Their close neighbors, St. Kitts and Nevis, are of historical interest, figuring as they do in the lives of Alexander Hamilton, Admirals Nelson and Rodney, and Generals Shirley and Frazer. St. Kitts is well worth a visit to see the beautiful restoration of the old fortress on Brimstone Hill. A number of the old plantation great houses have been restored and opened up as hotels and restaurants. Renting a car to tour St. Kitts is a good scheme.

If you like longer sails, the bright lights of civilization, and a variety of languages and customs, the middle islands—from Antigua to St. Lucia—should make you happy. The French islands of Guadeloupe and Martinique afford the finest cuisine in the Antilles. The local merchants offer an excellent selection of cheeses and meats from Europe and the best wines available outside France. The tourist shops are a woman's delight, and the perfumes are at about half the price charged in the States. Up until a few years ago, bikinis were so inexpensive (two for US$5) that the women bought them by the dozen. Regrettably, those days are gone—probably forever. There is still a fabulous collection of bikinis in Martinique, but the prices have gone up so much in France that the savings for an American no longer are substantial. Rough rule of thumb: The smaller the bikini, the more expensive it is. The string has arrived: its size—minuscule; its price—astronomical. One solution frequently used by the always economical French women was to buy only half the string at half the price. Others felt that even that was too expensive and sailed au naturel—not really showing off, just economizing!

The universal pastime of watching members of the opposite sex is alive and well in Martinique, and the visiting seafarer soon gets into the spirit of things. The women in Fort de France may not be the prettiest in the Caribbean, but they are far and away the most stylish. And the men, sitting at sidewalk cafés sipping their coffee or *punch vieux*, cut figures worthy of the boulevardiers of Paris. Newcomers, however, should take note: The *punch* will make a strong man weak-kneed and the coffee tastes not unlike battery acid.

The French and their chicory-laced coffee have distressed visiting foreigners for more than a century. A story is told of Count von Bismarck touring France after the Franco-Prussian War. At the close of a fine meal in a country inn, he called for the maître d'hôtel and offered to buy all his chicory at 10 percent over the market price; the maître d' agreed and sold him what he claimed was all he had. Again the count offered to buy any remaining chicory, this time at 50 percent over the market price;

the maître d' managed to produce a second quantity of the plant. For a third time, the count offered to buy any that remained—at double the market price—and the maître d' surrendered an additional small amount, insisting that this was indeed all that remained. Satisfied at last, the count concluded, "Very well, now you may prepare me a cup of coffee!"

H.M.S. Diamond Rock, off the south coast of Martinique, is the basis for many stories in folklore, most of them inaccurate. The story of Diamond Rock (now called Rocher du Diamant) is contained in *Her Majesty's Sloop of War Diamond Rock,* by Stuart and Eggleston.

Dominica is for the adventurous. A ride into the mountains by Jeep and horseback will take you to the last settlement of the Carib peoples. Here the natives fashion the distinctive Carib canoes that are also seen in Guadeloupe, Martinique, and St. Lucia. With nothing but a flour sack for a sail and a paddle for a rudder, the islanders set out in these boats against the wind to fish in the open Atlantic. Not an easy way to earn a living. Prince Rupert Bay, at the northern end of Dominica, should be one of the most popular anchorages in the Eastern Caribbean. It is well sheltered, has numerous small shorefront bars and restaurants, has a splendidly restored old French fort, and is a good jumping-off place for exploring the island. Also, it is the first good harbor north of Martinique for boats heading northward. In fact, it has everything going for it except that it has probably the most miserable group of boat boys (or perhaps I should say boat bums) in the entire Eastern Caribbean! I hope that by the time you read this, the government will have stepped in and sorted out the situation. If they have, I would certainly advise stopping there.

St. Lucia provides some superb anchorages at Pigeon Island, Marigot, and Vieux Fort, and the truly unbelievable one beneath the Pitons at Soufrière. The volcano and sulfur baths are an impressive spectacle, and it is well worth the expense to explore the island by car or Jeep—an adventure vividly recounted by George Eggleston in *Orchids on the Calabash Tree.*

St. Vincent, at the northern end of the Grenadines, is a high, lush island richly and diversely cultivated. The island has an intriguing history, highlighted by the almost continual warfare among French, English, and Caribs that lasted from 1762 until 1796, when the Caribs were expelled to Central America.

Bequia is the home of fishermen and whalers, an island where any sailor can explore, relax, and "gam"

for days on end. The harbor is beautiful and life is relaxed.

After cruising the entire Caribbean and getting to know all the islands intimately, many experienced yachtsmen declare Grenada to be "the loveliest of the islands." The highlands produce enough rain to allow the farmers to grow a large quantity of fresh fruit and vegetables, but the south coast is dry enough to allow the yachtsman to live and work on his boat. The island also has a dozen different harbors, providing 60 separate anchorages. Most of these harbors are only short, one- or two-hour sails from each other.

The town of St. Georges is picturesque; the main anchorage, in the lagoon, is only a short dinghy ride from supermarkets, cable and telephone offices, banks, and other services. The island has a friendly yacht club in an ideal location, with a small, do-it-yourself hauling facility. Other facilities include the Spice Island yacht yard at Prickly Bay on the south coast and a larger marina at The Moorings in Secret Harbour. Best of all, the island has a large population of very friendly citizens. In short, after some years of a topsy-turvy political situation, the island should, in years to come, reassert itself as the capital of Eastern Caribbean yachting.

Unfortunately, this will happen only if the government gets organized and persuades someone to buy out Grenada Yacht Services. Someone needs to bulldoze everything and completely redo the docks. Because of its harbor and location, GYS should be a major yacht yard, but political problems and poor management have thrust it into a state of utter disrepair. The economy of Grenada will never recover unless GYS is rebuilt and the island again becomes a yachting center. As of June 1994, nothing had been done; I hope that by the time you read this, the story will be different.

Barbados is relatively remote and seldom visited by yachts, except those that are coming downwind from Europe. If your plane stops there en route to another island, arrange for a layover of a day or two. It is undoubtedly the best-run island in the entire Caribbean and everything is clean and neat (by West Indian standards). The people are charming, speak with the most wonderful accent, and are solicitous and helpful to visitors. The old Careenage in Bridgetown should not be missed.

It is a shame that Tobago is seldom visited by yachtsmen. It is dead to windward of Trinidad, and from Grenada it is 90 miles hard on port tack. Even if you manage to lay the rhumb line from Grenada, it will be a long slog, hard on the wind. Current and sea will drive you off to the west. It is fairly inaccessible except from Barbados, from where it is an easy reach southwestward.

The American and British Virgin Islands have been described laboriously in the various tourist guides, but whatever the evaluation of shoreside life, a sailor can pass a very pleasant month cruising in this area. The Virgin Islands are only a few miles apart, and if you enjoy snorkeling and short sails, head for the Virgins or the Passage Islands. (The Grenadines and Puerto La Cruz, Venezuela, are also good locales for these pursuits.) If you are cruising the northern Virgins, take a side trip over to St. Croix. With luck, it will be a glorious, 35-mile beam reach. Christiansted is without doubt the most attractive town in the Caribbean, and you can make a side trip out to Buck Island, which divers consider one of the finest dive sites in the world.

The character of the various island peoples is apt to vary broadly within a very small area. Even among the former British islands, each has its own peculiar flavor, its own outlook and accent. (In fact, natives are known to complain that they can't understand the English spoken on neighboring islands.) For the most part, the people are quiet and law-abiding. Actually, the sort of racially inspired violence that periodically has troubled St. Croix and St. Thomas has been far less of a problem in the islands farther south.

As the years go by, the Eastern Caribbean becomes more crowded; hence, yachtsmen are beginning to head west to Venezuela. In the 1950s and 1960s, cruising in Venezuela was looked on as a hazardous pursuit—not because of unfriendliness to yachtsmen but rather because Fidel Castro was smuggling guerrillas ashore in small fishing boats. The Guardia Nacional and the navy frequently were guilty of shooting first and asking questions later, with the result that a number of yachts were ventilated by Venezuelan government agencies. All that is now a thing of the past. Although you may have to fill out a lot of documents, everyone is extremely friendly, and, to the best of my knowledge, there have been no nasty incidents involving yachts in Venezuela for many years.

Venezuela is a land of contrasts. The coast, with its mountains that rise directly from the sea to 9,000 feet, in some parts is dry and desolate like a desert; other sections, like the eastern end of the Peninsula de Paria, are covered with dense jungle. The easternmost tip of the peninsula rises 5,000 feet, with vertical slopes spilling into the Caribbean on one side and into the Golfo de Paria on the other. From the Golfo de Paria, one can visit Angel Falls and the Orinoco Delta, take excursions into the jun-

gle, and see unbelievable wildlife right from the boat. This area is the original primeval jungle, occasionally visited by powerboats but seldom by sailing yachts. The windswept offshore islands provide some of the finest fishing, snorkeling, and diving in the Eastern Caribbean. They have not been fished out and they are generally uninhabited.

Los Roques, a 355-square-mile cruising area off the north coast, is almost as large as the American and British Virgin Islands, and at least 50 percent of it is unsurveyed. Venezuelan yachtsmen and a few Americans (such as Gordon Stout) have crisscrossed this wonderful place and spent as long as a week cruising here. This area would be ideal for a bare-boat organization, and perhaps one will take advantage of the opportunity. It will be interesting to see what develops here in years to come.

Yachting has taken hold in Venezuela, and modern marinas now can be found at Caracas (five, in fact), Cumaná, Puerto La Cruz (three), Puerto Cabello, and Morrocoy National Park. Furthermore, there are hauling facilities in all of these harbors. In addition, at Centro Marina de Oriente, in Puerto La Cruz, you will find a brand-new yacht yard, repair facility, and marina—specifically built to cater to the needs of cruising yachtsmen. Without a doubt, it's the most modern facility east of Miami.

Because of the devaluation of the bolívar, most things in Venezuela are inexpensive. Hauling and repair costs, for example, are considerably less than in the Eastern Caribbean, so more and more yachtsmen now are sailing to Venezuela for repairs and refits. This is especially true in summer, when boats head there for refitting and at the same time escape from the hurricane belt. Everyone remembers the devastation caused by Hurricane Hugo in 1989, and one way to avoid being "Hugoized" is to head for Venezuela. (See Reflections on Hugo, below.)

Once you get away from the major population areas, you will seldom have more than one or two other yachts in your anchorage—and the only time you are likely to encounter many boats is on the weekends. My advice is to arrive at a marina on Friday night as the Venezuelans are all departing and berths become available. Stay for the weekend, enjoy sightseeing, etc., on Saturday, go out on the town Saturday night, sleep late Sunday morning, and depart Sunday afternoon prior to the return of the Venezuelan yachts.

Unfortunately, the great welcome that the Venezuelan private clubs used to give visiting yachtsmen has cooled. As more and more sailors go to Venezuela, the behavior of some has been such that the door has been slammed shut against the rest of us in most private Venezuelan clubs. If you know a Venezuelan yachtsman, write to him ahead of time and he probably can get the door opened specifically for you.

Close to Venezuela are the ABC islands of Aruba, Bonaire, and Curaçao. Low and windswept, they vary from the quiet, simple, and slow-moving Bonaire to the hustling, bustling, and very cosmopolitan Curaçao.

Fighting your way eastward along the north coast of South America is rough—especially once you pass Cabo de la Vela. By the time you reach the Golfo de Maracaibo, you are dead exhausted and would love to stop. It used to be a matter of pushing on to reach Aruba, but a few years ago I discovered (via the Venezuelan Hydrographic Office) that there is a small naval base at Los Monjes with a passable anchorage between the islands. Here you can stop, rest for a day or so, and then fight your way to Aruba.

Aruba used to be just a low, flat island covered with oil refineries, but now the refineries have been dismantled, tourism has taken hold, and the island is covered with hotels. A new marina in Oranjestad offers all the amenities a yachtsman could want, although it is very crowded, and dock space must be reserved in advance.

Bonaire is low, flat, and sparsely populated. Its shores rise so steeply from the sea bottom that it is almost impossible to anchor in its lee. But the anchorage problem has been solved with a new marina. Adequate supplies—fresh, frozen, and canned—are available. The people are very friendly and Bonaire has some of the best diving in the world—with topnotch support facilities right at hand.

If you want to connect up with the outside world from the ABC islands, go to Curaçao, which has excellent air communications and first-class hotels. Curaçao also has superb harbors and all kinds of supplies.

WHEN TO COME

The weather patterns in the Caribbean—and especially the northern end of the Caribbean—have changed drastically in the last three or four decades. When I first came here some 40 years ago, the fronts coming out of the Bahamas would stall in Hispaniola. We heard about them, but they didn't affect our weather. Come the 1960s, they pushed on through the western end of Puerto Rico, and the main effect in the Virgins was that the trades would die out once in a while and come in very light from the northwest. In recent years, fronts have pushed farther and farther east—through Puerto Rico and down to the Passage Islands. In 1993, when we were anchored at Buck Island in St. Croix, the wind was blowing 15 knots from the west!

From November to July, winds will be 15 to 20 knots from the east. These are referred to as the northeast trades, but that is a misnomer. In early winter, they are generally east to east-northeast, sometimes crawling around to northeast or north-northeast. Traditionally, the weather report reads, "East-northeast to east-southeast, 10 to 15 knots, higher in gusts." Some of us feel that this is a recording put on in early November and played until April. Then it is replaced by a recording that reads, "East to southeast, 10 to 15 knots, higher in gusts." When fronts come through, it will blow 20 to 25 knots, sometimes for a week or more.

The normal Eastern Caribbean trade winds are influenced by the island of Puerto Rico—which, of course, has a much greater mass than the other islands to the south and east. Exactly how much influence it exerts depends on the strength of the trades. If it is blowing 20 or 25 knots—or above 30, as it sometimes does—the land breeze from Puerto Rico will have little effect on the trade winds. But as the trades ease off to 10 or 15 knots, the land mass drastically affects them.

It is worth noting that as long ago as my first cruising guide (1966), I pointed out that the best sailing of the year occurs in May, June, and July—when the wind blows at a steady 12 to 15 knots day after day, and no fronts come blasting on through.

RAIN

The rainy season is the same as the hurricane season—roughly July to October (although hurricanes have occurred in June and November). Even then, it very seldom rains day after day but rather a maximum of three hours a day. The rest of the day is sunny. However, at times the rainy and dry seasons reverse themselves, confusing everyone. In 1993, for example, during the "dry season," our longest stretch without rain was only 36 hours. So be sure to have on hand a raincoat or a foulweather jacket. Trousers and boots are not really necessary, as the air is warm enough, but you will get tired of having a wet tail, so if you have a full-length raincoat with a hood, you won't be sorry.

Amazingly, however, the best months for sailing the Eastern Caribbean are May, June, and July—the weather patterns tend to be more stable.

SUN

Despite the fact that you might have spent time in Florida or the Bahamas and not suffered from sunburn, that does not mean that you will be safe when you get to Puerto Rico and the Virgins. Remember that Florida is 26°N; the Virgin Islands are 18°30′. You will get a tan in the Virgins even if you keep all your clothes on. Be sure you have a broad-brimmed hat, at least one long-sleeved white shirt, long cotton trousers, and plenty of sunblock. And use it all! If you have a tiller-steered boat, be especially careful to put sunblock on the tops of your hands and the tops of your feet. Men's cotton pajamas or doctors' scrub suits make good coverups to keep you from getting too much sun.

WHAT TO WEAR

Travel light. If you can't fit everything into the standard duffel (generally measuring 26 inches long by 12 inches in diameter), you have too much gear. Dress in most places is casual. In town, women should wear a skirt and blouse or long shorts and a blouse; bare midriffs and bikinis are not acceptable. For a fancy night out, women may want a long dress and men may want a jacket and tie. Plus, if you go to any of the mountaintop restaurants in Puerto Rico, St. Thomas, or Tortola, be sure to take along a jacket or light sweater; you lose a degree of temperature for every 150 feet of altitude. The temperature can easily be in the upper 60s (and feel quite chilly) at one of these aeries. On the south coast of Puerto Rico, where the cold air comes down off the mountains at night, the temperature drops quickly to the 60s.

For sitting out on deck at night, you may discover that a sweater is comfortable, and if you do any night sailing, you'll want a woolen hat for night watches.

On the trip down, carry some clothing in your hand luggage—a bathing suit, a hat, and a change of clothes—in case your baggage doesn't arrive at the same time you do. There is nothing worse than walking around San Juan or St. Thomas or Tortola wearing your winter duds.

CUSTOMS AND IMMIGRATION

When you enter or leave either the United States or British Virgin Islands, it is necessary to clear Customs and Immigration. The USVI stations are in Charlotte Amalie (St. Thomas), Cruz Bay (St. John), and Christiansted (St. Croix). The BVI stations are in West End and Road Town (Tortola), Virgin Gorda Yacht Harbor, and Jost Van Dyke.

If you are a foreign-registered vessel entering US waters, it is essential that you clear Customs and Immigration with the entire crew. If you are anchored off St. John, it is legal to leave one crew member on board, but that person should be a US citizen; otherwise, he or she will have to go in and enter after the rest of the crew has cleared.

When departing, no matter whether you are US- or foreign-registered, someone will have to go down to Customs and Immigration and obtain clearance papers for your next port. If you have foreigners on board who have had cards dropped in their passports, those cards must be left off at Immigration.

Everyone entering US waters must have identification. US citizens can use a passport, a voter registration card, or a birth certificate; a driver's license is not acceptable. Non-US citizens must have a passport. Even though Canadian citizens are accustomed to crossing the US-Canada border without a passport, they must have a passport when entering the US Virgin Islands. They can encounter massive problems if they try to enter the USVI without the correct papers.

When entering the British Virgin Islands, all yachts must clear Customs and Immigration. The skipper (or a representative) should be able to do it, but we have had difficulty with that at times. He or she must go ashore carrying proper papers for everyone on board. That means passports from everyone, or, in the case of US citizens, a voter's card or birth certificate.

When departing the BVIs for any other area, it is necessary to clear both Customs and Immigration, and your clearance is only good for 12 hours. This setup is absolutely ridiculous—if you are heading east for Virgin Gorda and also want to stop at Anegada, it is not legal to do so. I hope that by the time you read this, those regulations will have changed.

Most of the Customs and Immigration officials you will meet will be cordial and helpful, but some seem to go out of their way to make life difficult. I wish they would keep in mind that tourism is vital to the island economies, and a bad greeting at the Customs or Immigration office sets the tone for a whole stay. No amount of subsequent goodwill can compensate for an initial surly encounter.

PROVISIONING

Gone are the days when bareboat charterers would fly down from the States carrying a cooler full of frozen food packed in dry ice—sometimes it worked, sometimes it didn't. All too often, baggage would go missing for two or three days, and by the time it arrived in the Virgin Islands, the dry ice had evaporated and all the expensive goodies had gone bad. Today you can purchase (admittedly at higher prices) a tremendous variety of food in Puerto Rico and the Virgins, and the quality is as good as in most Stateside or European markets. (The only place in the Eastern Caribbean where you can provision for less money than Puerto Rico is Venezuela.)

FISH POISONING

I have no idea how to avoid the fish poisoning known as ciguatera, although it's easy to find people who will give you advice on the matter. I have never heard reports of anyone dying of ciguatera, but people have said that it makes you feel so terrible you wish you were dead!

One of the problems is determining what fish are likely to be poisonous. What's poisonous in one area is not necessarily so in another area. In St. Croix, barracuda is consumed by the ton. In the northern Virgins, on the other hand, no one eats barracuda because it is alleged to be poisonous if found on the northern side of the islands and nonpoisonous if found on the southern side of the islands. How do you tell whether you have caught a traveling barracuda?

One recommendation is to cook fish with a silver spoon; if the spoon stays shiny, the fish is fine. Well, we tried that once on *Iolaire.* Four of us ate the fish, with mixed results. Our West Indian cook ate a lot and was very sick; two American friends, Marv and Carol Bernning, ate a moderate amount and were moderately sick; I ate a little and did not get sick. On another occasion, when we were given a fish, part of the crew went to a friend's house and cooked half of the fish. Some of them were fine, some slightly sick, some violently ill. Aboard *Iolaire,* where five of us ate the other half, we were all fine. Who can figure it out?

In St. Barts, the advice is to cut out the fish's liver and put it down for the ants; if the ants eat the liver, the fish is fine. If they don't eat it, you shouldn't either. Some suggest offering some of the fish to a cat and waiting 24 hours. If the cat is fine, go ahead and eat the fish; if the cat gets sick, throw out the rest of the fish.

The best advice is to check with the locals. In general, if they would be willing to eat it, you should be too.

COMMUNICATIONS

Communications are no longer a problem. Via VHF, you can contact WAH on St. Thomas. Its transmitter is so high on Crown Mountain that the broadcasts reach the US and British Virgin Islands, Puerto Rico, and the Passage Islands (except for a few small blank spots caused by mountains here and there). They can put you through to a phone service anywhere in the world. Cellular phones are also available for rent from most of the major charter operators.

From telephone booths in Puerto Rico and in the US and British Virgin Islands, you can reach AT&T, which enables you to call anywhere in the world. St. Thomas, St. John, Tortola, and Virgin Gorda have communications offices (Vitelco in the US Virgins, Cable & Wireless in the British Virgins) that have fax machines and also mail and courier services. In the British Virgins, you can use an AT&T credit card for USA Direct Service, or a Visa card for Cable & Wireless, which can connect you to any spot in the world. All of the marinas in Puerto Rico have fax machines and will send and receive mail for you, but be sure to make prior arrangements before having mail forwarded to a marina.

RENTAL CARS

Cars are available for rent everywhere in Puerto Rico, as well as on virtually every Caribbean island that has roads. Shop around, as the rates and the quality of the vehicles vary widely.

TIDES

Tides are minimal in the Lesser Antilles, and a single tide never rises or falls more than 18 inches. Because of the variation in heights from winter to summer, there can be a three-foot difference between high high water in winter and low low water in May, June, and July. You can predict the tides in Puerto Rico and the Virgins if you refer to *Street's Transatlantic Crossing Guide and Introduction to the Caribbean,* chapter 6. It should be noted that the tides in Puerto Rico can be two or even three feet, while the tides in Trinidad's Gulf of Paria can vary from four to six feet.

GROUND SWELLS

Ground swells are produced by storms in the North Atlantic and have absolutely nothing to do with local weather. They used to arrive completely unannounced, but now the weather reports from Puerto Rico usually predict them. Each year, ground swells put at least one boat up on the beach. Anytime you see an especially beautiful sandy beach, you know the ground swells have done their bit to create it. Throughout this volume, mention is made when an anchorage is subject to ground swells. In such a case, be sure to use a Bahamian moor (see *Street's Transatlantic Crossing Guide and Introduction to the Caribbean*), or your boat may be the one up on the beach.

BUOYAGE

The buoyage system in Puerto Rico and the Virgin Islands is IALA System B, the same as the United States—red/right/returning. The major buoys put out by the BVI government and the US Coast Guard are fairly reliable, but don't rely on them totally, because if one goes adrift, it takes a while to be replaced. (The US Coast Guard buoy tender visits Puerto Rico and the Passage Islands only twice a year!) Throughout the islands, there are privately maintained buoys that frequently go adrift and are frequently altered. This volume mentions places that are likely to be privately buoyed, but the privately maintained buoys are not marked on the charts, because they are too subject to change. Basically, anywhere there is likely to be a buoy, you should be able to use eyeball navigation. Judge depths by the color of the water: Brown is reef, white is shoal water, light green usually is deep enough to sail in, and blue is deep water. A good test of your skill is to try to guess the depth of the water and then turn on the fathometer to check.

Don't sail at night; enter all harbors when the sun is still fairly high. When heading eastward, you can enter as late as 1700, because the sun is behind you, but if heading westward, you should be in harbor by 1600 at the very latest. Similarly, before leaving a harbor in the morning, take a good look around. Check the access to the channel and the bearing to the sun. In the morning, the sun may be right in your eyes, making it hard to see anything, so you may have to delay your departure until 1000 or 1100.

LIGHTS

Despite what other guides say, the lights in the Caribbean are NOT all reliable. In the French islands, the lights are excellent and reliable; in the American islands, they are good and fairly reliable, but not absolutely; in the British (and ex-British) islands, it looks as though the lighting and buoyage system was established to keep harbor pilots, shipwreckers, and salvagers from starving to death. DO NOT RELY ON THESE LIGHTS.

DIVING

Puerto Rico and the US and British Virgin Islands have dive operations too numerous to list here. Check when you arrive. If you are chartering, the charter-boat management will be happy to steer you in the right direction. You can contact all of the dive operations via VHF and arrange for them to pick you up at your boat and take you diving. Of course, the king of divers in this part of the Caribbean is Bert Kilbride of Saba Rock, near Virgin Gorda, still going strong in his late seventies.

REFLECTIONS ON HUGO

The entire Caribbean is hurricane territory, and hurricanes are more frequent than most people realize. The Virgin Islands, for example, have been hit or sideswiped by 32 hurricanes since 1871. In 1916 alone, there were three hurricanes. In 1889, 1891, and 1979, there were two hurricanes in the same year.

Puerto Rico has been hit by 34 hurricanes, of which three were in 1916 and two were in 1891, 1898, 1899, 1901, and 1979. The Antigua/Guadeloupe area has had 32 hurricanes (three in 1933), plus the area has been sideswiped by 10 or 12 tropical depressions. The Martinique/St. Lucia area has had 44 hurricanes, plus about a dozen tropical depressions.

The frequency of hurricanes in St. Vincent and the Grenadines is much lower than farther north, BUT there are really no hurricane holes in the area. The first hurricane hole south of St. Lucia is all the way down on the south coast of Grenada—an area that has had only about five hurricanes in its history.

Amazingly, Isla Margarita in Venezuela has been hit by two hurricanes in the last 120 years, even though no hurricanes have struck the Venezuelan mainland.

In light of the above, one must figure on a major hurricane every four to five years, no matter where you are in the Caribbean. For the best odds, head for Grenada, Trinidad, or mainland Venezuela—and I urge that underwriters offer discounts to boats that arrange to be in those areas between July and November.

Nowadays, the Eastern Caribbean is overpopulated with boats. The hurricane holes are so overcrowded that all you need for disaster is one or two boats that are anchored improperly and start dragging. (Of course, I well remember being told in prep school that all general statements are suspect, and even the statement—"all general statements are suspect"—is suspect!) Undoubtedly, there are a few hurricane holes that are not overcrowded or that people do not know about. Witness Ensenada Honda Vieques, off Puerto Rico. To the best of my knowledge, almost no boats went to Vieques in 1989 during Hurricane Hugo; like lemmings, they all poured into Ensenada Honda Culebra—whereas Ensenada Honda Vieques, which is a better hurricane hole, had relatively few boats tucked up into the mangroves.

Further, throughout the Caribbean, anywhere there are bareboat fleets, the hurricane season creates what the local yachtsmen refer to as "bareboat bombs"—so called because the bareboat operations do not have enough labor to put a crew on every boat to ride out the hurricane, tend lines, or shift anchors, and the vessels become potential lethal weapons. Few bareboats are equipped with more than two anchors, and those may be sufficient for a 30-to-40-knot blow, but nothing more. Once one of the "bareboat bombs" starts dragging down on you, you have a problem. You may be lucky, and he will just bounce off you and do no damage, but it could be a disastrous situation. The bareboat hooks your anchor, pulls you loose, and you both end up on the beach, high and dry.

One of the tragedies of this sort of situation is that the bareboat companies are all insured. The underwriters pay off the damage done to the bareboats, but all of the courts consider the hurricane as an "act of God." If you are insured and a "bareboat bomb" drags down on you and your boat is damaged or lost, it is not fine and dandy, but at least it is not a complete disaster, as your insurance company will cover your loss. If, however, you are NOT insured, your chances are minimal of finding an admiralty lawyer who will entertain a case against a boat dragging down on you in a hurricane. Even if you find one, you will need to put up US$5,000 or $6,000 before he will even consider taking the case. This is just another good reason why cruising yachts should be insured. Insurance is particularly essential for cruising yachtsmen who have retired and are living aboard, with everything wrapped up in their boat. (See *Street's Transatlantic Crossing Guide and In-troduction to the Caribbean* for information on insurance.)

In light of the damage done by Hugo, what is the solution to the hurricane problem? Go to sea! This sounds very drastic—going to sea in the face of a hurricane—and it is if you do it at the last minute. But it is a viable option if you do it 48 to 72 hours before the expected arrival of the hurricane.

The situation with hurricanes has changed radically over the years. Until the early 1950s, the hurricane warning system in the Caribbean was very poor. Hurricanes originated out in the Atlantic, and unless they were spotted by a passing ship that sent in a report, the Eastern Caribbean did not realize a hurricane was en route until the barometers started falling. And then the barometers usually dropped so fast that the bottom fell out, and there was little time—perhaps 18 to 24 hours—to prepare. Seamen could only hunker down in the nearest hurricane hole, lash everything down, and hope for the best.

In the early 1950s, however, the old B-36s were converted to weather planes and became hurricane hunters. For more than a decade, they spotted most of the hurricanes, tracked them, and provided fairly good warnings. But they did not find them all. Once, when one popped up just east of St. Barthélemy, the St. Barts people called St. Thomas to tell them a hurricane was on the way. St. Thomas said they had received no warning, and how did St. Barts know it was a hurricane? St. Barts replied, "Because our radio tower is about to blow down," and then they went off the air. Recognizing the danger, St. Thomas went into action and the warnings went out. The St. Thomas charter fleet (which, luckily, was quite small in those days) tried to get out and head to Hurricane Hole in St. John—a dead beat to windward. A few of them made it, but most of them were blown back into the harbor in St. Thomas, where they rode out the hurricane.

Each year, the hurricane tracking system has improved, and now, with sophisticated satellites, it's well nigh perfect. Normally, there is plenty of warning; it is only the freak hurricane, such as Klaus in late 1984, that catches the islands unaware. Klaus popped up just south of Puerto Rico, went northeast, and was very late in the year. Klaus was one of only three hurricanes in 100 years that tracked northeast below 22°N!

Today, there is at least a three- or four-day warning of an approaching hurricane. The US government publication *Tropical Cyclones of the North Atlantic Ocean* (US Department of Commerce—NOAA—1871 to 1980, with an update to 1993) shows the tracks of all the known hurricanes. You'll notice that, with very few exceptions, hurricanes follow a definite and predictable pattern as they approach the islands of the Eastern Caribbean. Admittedly, once they reach Puerto Rico, Haiti, and the Dominican Republic, they can execute a 180-degree turn, or a 360-degree one, or a right angle, or anything in between. They are not predictable once they pass through the islands. Thus, many experienced seamen have concluded that if you have a decent boat of 40 feet or more, well equipped, with an engine so you can power, and if there are light airs in front of the hurricane, the solution is to pull up the anchor and go to sea. With a two-day head start, you certainly can be 250 to 300 miles from the storm center. Thus, you could expect a large (possibly huge) ground swell, but no more than 40 knots of wind. (In any case, if you don't have a boat that can handle 40 knots of wind, you should not be out sailing.)

The boats in English Harbour, Antigua, survived Hugo with relatively little damage, but many seamen figure they were just lucky. If the hurricane had followed a route 30 or 40 miles farther north, English Harbour would have been a disaster area, because even though it is beautifully sheltered, there were plenty of untended, poorly moored boats that could have become absolute bombs and destroyed the other yachts.

Three days before Hugo passed south of Antigua, it was easily predictable that the hurricane would hit Guadeloupe or Antigua or pass close to the north of Antigua. Thus, any boat in Antigua could have hoisted anchor and headed due south 48 hours before the storm was supposed to hit. They could easily have been 300 miles to the south, down near Grenada, by the time the storm arrived in Antigua, and they would have experienced nothing more than 30 knots of wind.

Similarly, the United States and British Virgin Islands, Puerto Rico, and the Passage Islands had plenty of warning. It was obvious that the hurricane was going to pass south of or through the Virgins, and the boats could have hauled anchor and headed due north (or, possibly better, northeast), thus being 300 miles from the brunt of the storm.

Bill Skokl, of the 42-foot double-topsail, gaff-rigged schooner *Media,* took off southward, singlehanded, from Isleta Marina in Fajardo, on the east coast of Puerto Rico, 48 hours before Hugo hit. He experienced no more than 30- to 40-knot gusts of wind, huge but long swells, and no damage whatsoever to his boat. When he returned to Isleta Marina, he found nothing but utter destruction. Go to

sea; don't try to ride out a hurricane in an overcrowded harbor.

Another solution to the hurricane problem is to sail south to Grenada and spend the hurricane season doing your repairs and refitting there. Grenada has only been hit three times by hurricanes, and even though many of them have passed fairly close to the north, the hurricane holes on the south coast are so sheltered (until yachting increases even more and produces the same kind of crowded conditions that exist in the Virgin Islands) that you should be safe in any of the hurricane holes there. The only glitch in this solution is that even though Grenada has enough hurricane holes to shelter the island's entire yachting fleet, the charter companies in Martinique have taken to sending large portions of their fleets to Grenada to avoid hurricanes. The result is overcrowding and a flock of potential "bareboat bombs." Be forewarned! If you are in Grenada and it appears that a hurricane is going to pass too close to the island, you can always pick up anchor and head a hundred miles south to Trinidad, thus avoiding even the edges of the storm.

To be absolutely safe, of course, go to Venezuela, which is out of the hurricane area. Just north of Venezuela, a few lows have developed, blowing 40 to 50 knots, that later turned into hurricanes when they reached the Western Caribbean, but, to the best of my knowledge, Venezuela has never had a bad hurricane and has only suffered heavy rain and massive ground swells from storms passing through the region.

But what about boats stored ashore? Yacht yards that have onshore storage facilities in the Eastern Caribbean are doing very well. People are storing boats on shore for a number of reasons: to avoid having their boat stolen by someone who wants to make a quick drug run and then pull the plug; to allow the bottom to dry out, thus minimizing the chance of osmosis. Finally, some boats are stored ashore in the misconception that a boat is safer there in a hurricane. This is a very erroneous assumption. Admittedly, if a hurricane just brushes an island, relatively few boats are damaged ashore. If it comes close, there is considerable damage. But if the hurricane hits dead-on, the boats all topple like pins in a bowling alley—a few in a near-miss and almost all in a direct hit. The marinas on the east coast of Puerto Rico were pretty well cleaned out by Hugo, with the exception of Puerto del Rey Marina, which survived with an acceptably low level of damage.

As a result of Hugo, not only have boatowners who had their boats stored ashore suffered, but the underwriters have been taken to the cleaners. The only ones that came out on top were the boatyards doing the repairs (often the same yards that made money by storing the boats).

It has been recommended that underwriters should not cover boats stored ashore north of Grenada unless the mast is removed. Further, if the boat has a deep-keel, fin-and-separate-rudder configuration, you should dig two holes and chock up the boat a foot or two off the ground, with the rudder and the keel in the holes. Chocked up this way, with the rig out, the boat should survive the hurricane. I realize this is an expensive procedure, but it is a hell of a lot cheaper than rebuilding your boat.

Probably the most important chapter in this book is chapter 1—Sailing Directions—and you should read and study it carefully. Consult it regularly before finalizing each day's plans. While the navigational features and anchorages of the individual islands are described in the chapter concerned with that island, the routes between the islands are detailed in chapter 1.

Remember: Always be alert and cautious. Almost every place in the Eastern Caribbean where a yacht can anchor has been described or at least mentioned in the Street guides, but not all are easy to enter. Many of these anchorages can be used only in good weather and perfect visibility. Besides, some boats are handier than others and some sailors are more skilled than others. Thus, you must evaluate each anchorage for yourself before entering. The time of day, the weather, your abilities, the weatherliness of your boat—all influence the final decision.

Some advice to readers who operate bareboat charter fleets: Study this book carefully, make your judgments, and mark on the charts in the book the anchorages you want your charterers to avoid.

Finally, before you sail anywhere in the Eastern Caribbean (and particularly if you are going during hurricane season), I advise you to take to heart the advice that appeared above.

Acknowledgments

Yachtsmen who cruise the Caribbean should be thankful to Phelps Platt of Dodd, Mead, who saw my original draft of what was then going to be a privately printed guide to the Virgin Islands and liked it enough to encourage me to write a complete guide to the other islands. Yachtsmen should also thank Bernard Goldhirsh, founder of *Sail* magazine, who published the 1974 updated and expanded cruising guide.

Thanks are now due to Eric Swenson of W.W. Norton and Company, who not only agreed to publish a completely updated guide but also agreed that it should be expanded to include Venezuela, its offlying islands, and Aruba, Bonaire, and Curaçao, plus tremendously enlarged sections on "Getting There" and "Leaving." The guide has become so comprehensive that we have produced it in an ever-expanding series.

Special thanks should go to Harvey Loomis—a good literary editor and an excellent sailor. When he took over my manuscripts, I finally had an experienced editor who has cruised in the Caribbean and understands the problems of sailing—and racing—in the Caribbean. For eight years, he labored hard as editor of these guides, and he was a tremendous help in rewriting the sailing and piloting directions to make them clear. Both I, the author, and you, the reader, owe Harvey a vote of thanks.

I must also thank the many yachtsmen who have helped me with valuable information. Augie Hollen of *Taurus* (the only person I know who cruises in a genuine Block Island Cowhorn), Carl Powell of *Terciel,* and Ross Norgrove, formerly of *White Squall II,* all deserve a special vote of thanks for helping me update the Virgin Islands section. Jon Repke of Parts and Power—refrigeration expert, electrician, mechanic, sailor, and pilot—solved many of the mysteries of St. Martin/St. Barthélemy/Anguilla by spending the better part of a day flying me through

that area. Carl Kaushold supplied an excellent chart and information on the Salt River. Ray Smith of Grenada was most helpful in his suggestions on tides and weather patterns in the Caribbean, and in compiling the list of radio stations and radio beacons. His brother, Ron, solved the mystery of the whereabouts of Tara Island, off the south coast of Grenada, which is marked improperly on the chart. Carl Amour of Union Island's Anchorage Hotel solved the great mystery of the rocks off Scotts Head, Dominica. Dr. Jack Sheppard of *Arieto,* the late Dick Doran of *Laughing Sally,* and Carlos Lavendero of several boats made possible the inclusion of the information on Puerto Rico and the Passage Islands. Gordon Stout of *Shango* and Peter Lee of *Virginia Reel* made possible the inclusion of Tobago. Jerry Bergoff of *Solar Barque* and Sylver Brin of St. Barthélemy were most helpful in clearing up some of the mysteries of the eastern end of St. Barts.

Pieter van Storn, formerly of Island Waterworld, and Malcolm Maidwell and Peter Spronk, both of the Caribbean Catamaran Centre, were most helpful in the Sint Maarten area. Hans Hoff, from the 90-foot ketch *Fandango,* is one of the few people who has won a bet from me on anchorages. The standing bet is that I will buy a drink for anyone who can find a good, safe anchorage with six feet of water in it that has not been mentioned in this cruising-guide series. I expect to be nabbed once in a while by a small boat, but not by the skipper of a 90-foot ketch! Hans found an anchorage inside the reef on the north coast of Anguilla. Where the chart showed nothing but solid reef, Hans managed to find himself inside the reef with 40 feet of water!

John Clegg, formerly of *Flica II,* Dave Price, formerly of *Lincoln,* and Gordon Stout have popped up continually with wonderful odd bits of information that they have gleaned on their cruises from one end of the Lesser Antilles to the other.

Numerous other skippers have, over the years, given me a tremendous amount of help. In the Antigua area, they include Desmond Nicholson, of V.E.B. Nicholson and Sons, English Harbour, and Jol Byerley, skipper of *Morning Tide* (and former charter skipper on *Ron of Argyll, Mirage, Etoile de Mer,* and *Lord Jim*), to name but two. For finer points on the exploration of the east coast of Antigua, I am deeply indebted to David Simmons of the little racing/cruising sloop *Bacco.* David is former head of Antigua Slipways and the senior marine surveyor in the Eastern Caribbean. Thanks should also go to Simon Cooper and David Corrigan, both of whom unfortunately have left the islands; Morris Nicholson of *Eleuthera;* Simon Bridger of *Circe* and other boats; Peter Haycraft and George Foster, harbor pilots and yachtsmen based in Tortola; Martin Mathias of the sportfisherman *Bihari;* Bert Kilbride, diver extraordinaire of Saba Rock, British Virgin Islands; and the Trinidadians Doug and the late Hugh ("Daddy") Myer of *Rosemary V* and *Huey II.* I want also to thank Arthur Spence of *Dwyka,* Marcy Crowe of *Xantippe,* Andy Copeland of various boats, Mike Smith of *Phryna,* Ken McKenzie of *Ti,* Dave Ferneding of *Whisper,* Chris Bowman of *Water Pearl of Bequia,* and others whose names I may have forgotten to include.

The Venezuela volume was made possible with the help of a tremendous number of Venezuelan friends and yachtsmen—most particularly Dr. Daniel Camejo, Daniel Shaw, Peter York, Otto Castillo, Pedro Gluecksman, Humberto Contazano, Rolly Edmonds, and especially Peter Bottome, who at various times lent us aircraft so we could fly over the areas we describe in the guide. Sailing is a wonderful way to explore, but a plane allows vast areas to be covered in a matter of hours. This was particularly true for the Los Roques area, a huge archipelago that is mostly listed as UNSURVEYED. Trying to explore it in a yacht would be almost impossible, but from the air we were able to obtain a very clear view of the layout of the unsurveyed area.

Jim Young of Dive Tobago provided reams of information on Buccoo Reef at the southwest corner of Tobago, on Tyrrels Bay at the northeast corner, and on many coves in between. The Tobago charts in the Venezuela volume could not have been done without his help. Molly Watson, her son Eddie, and all the members of the Trinidad Yachting Association have done a great deal to help get out the word on Trinidad. Curaçao yachtsman Dick Nebbling was most helpful with the Netherlands Antilles section.

Other yachtsmen in the Eastern Caribbean who helped with Venezuela information were Hank Strauss of *Doki,* Richard and Barbara Weinman of *Naranja,* and Mike Jarrold of *Lily Maid.*

Thanks are also due to all the West Indian crews and mates who have helped me over the years. In many cases, they started off as apprentice crew and ended up as mates sailing *Iolaire* from island to island in my absence. Special thanks should go to Selwyn Nimblet, Alston Blackett, Leslie Duncan, and many of their friends who helped out at various times as temporary crew—George "Bees," Scott, Frenchie, and Luckie/Winston/Tonton Sam, a fellow with THREE nicknames.

Another sailor who deserves a big vote of thanks is Timi Carstarphen (son of the late Captain Jack Carstarphen, one of the founders of the St. Thomas charter-boat fleet). Timi has sailed with me aboard *Iolaire* on and off since 1957. When Timi was a kid of seven, I paid him 25 cents a day to polish the brass, and I didn't find out until 20 years later that two kids were paying *him* 10 cents a day each for the privilege of helping *him* polish the brass! Timi was making a fortune of 45 cents a day at the age of seven.

It is only with the help of experienced yachtsmen such as these that a book of this type can be written.

A special vote of thanks must go to my nephew Morgan B. MacDonald III, who labored hard for three months in Grenada putting together the sketch charts contained in two of the volumes in this series. Thanks to the staff of Imray, Laurie, Norie & Wilson, especially the late Tom Wilson, who decided to produce the Imray-Iolaire charts; his son, Willy Wilson, who is carrying on his father's efforts; and Alan Wilkinson, their cartographer, who has labored long and hard to draw the charts for all of the volumes of the Street guides and who also draws all of the Imray-Iolaire charts of the Eastern Caribbean. Thanks also go to my son Richard, who worked hard with Alan Wilkinson during the summers of 1993 and 1994, almost completely redrawing all the sketch charts originally done 30 years ago by Morgan MacDonald. Richard also has produced sketches of the Puerto Rican racing sloops. Thanks go to Jim Mitchell, who has done a superb job of drawing local watercraft and preparing topographical views.

Admiral Sir David Haslam, retired head of the British Hydrographic Office, and his successor, Rear Admiral R.O. Morris, have been most helpful in supplying information and giving permission for material from the British Admiralty charts to be incorporated in this book. These appropriations have been made with the approval of the controller of

Her Majesty's Stationery Office and the Hydrographer of the Navy.

I also want to thank Patricia Street, my sister Elizabeth Vanderbilt, her husband Peter, and their son Jay, for their help in rechecking many facts.

Finally, a special round of thanks:

Maria McCarthy of Union Hall, County Cork, Ireland, labored long and hard during the summer of 1978 typing corrections and inserts on an early edition of the *Martinique-to-Trinidad* volume. Audrey Semple spent the winter of 1978-79 doing a magnificent job of cutting, gluing, correcting, typing, and fitting it all back together again. Geraldine Hickey, my secretary during the winter of 1979-80, did similar work in times of trying circumstances.

Aileen Calnan of Glandore, County Cork, not only worked with me in Ireland but also came on board *Iolaire* in the winter of 1983 as typist, secretary, crew, sometime babysitter, and sometime cook. She stayed through the summer of 1988, then went on to bigger and better things, working in a bank in New York. Her replacement came on board, started learning the ropes, and was beginning to do a very good job when she fell in love with our Venezuelan interpreter/expediter and departed in January 1989 with 24 hours' notice. Needless to say, we were up a creek without a paddle, but we were saved by Nick Pearson, an ex-British Army telegrapher who was wandering through the Caribbean on boats. He became our "hairy-legged" secretary and labored hard through the winter of 1989. Not only did he bang away on the typewriter, but he also was our number-one man for jumping overside in shoal water, grabbing the anchor, carrying it onto the beach, and burying it.

In January 1990, Cheryl Tennant came on board, worked extremely hard as secretary and also helping train Venezuelan crew, but, unfortunately for the skipper, she fell in love with a crew member and got married. Aileen Calnan returned in the summer of 1991 to help me put together the complete rewrite of the *Martinique-to-Trinidad* volume.

In the winter and spring of 1992, Nancy White made possible the rewrite of the *Anguilla-to-Dominica* volume. Sophie Munroe worked hard as secretary during the winter and spring of 1993 to help me put together the *Puerto Rico, Passage Islands, and Virgin Islands* volume.

I am also grateful for the help of Dale Mitchell, who sailed as mate on *Iolaire* from December 1991 through June 1993, helping us explore all sorts of places *Iolaire* had never before visited. In April 1993, when I was ashore in St. Martin, Dale and Sophie and Caroline Schmidt did a magnificent job of sailing *Iolaire* out of Marigot Harbor when an unexpected northwest squall blew in and swung her stern toward the breakwater. Dale hoisted the main, Sophie dropped one anchor line and cut the other, and Caroline backed the mizzen. *Iolaire* fell off and gathered way when the stern was only 10 feet from the breakwater. They managed to save her from massive damage. The squall was so sudden that three boats with engines, anchored near us, ended up on the breakwater!

Thanks should also go to Diane O'Connor, production editor at W.W. Norton, who has fought all the guides through the editors, copyeditors, and printers. Finally, when she could no longer stand my bad typing, and manuscripts glued together with last-minute additions, she recruited Kathleen Brandes to do a combination job—copyediting and keyboarding all the guides on computer. Kathleen has done a wonderful job, and, unlike other editors I have suffered through and fought with, she knows and understands both sailing and the Caribbean. The Street guides have finally entered the computer age!

The help of all these devoted friends of the Street family and of *Iolaire* has been invaluable to the production of this book and the other volumes in this series.

Charts

REMEMBER: DO NOT ENTER STRANGE HARBORS AT NIGHT!

I used to carry on board *Iolaire* about 200 American, British, French, Dutch, and a few Spanish charts— all of which were out of date; that is, even though they were new charts, the various government offices had not accurately corrected and updated them. The British Admiralty will correct charts of a foreign area *only* if the government concerned officially notifies the Admiralty. Much worse, US charts are corrected only when a whole plate is corrected; if you buy a new chart of Puerto Rico and it is a 12-year-old edition, no corrections will have been made on that chart since the date of the edition 12 years earlier!

Furthermore, BA and US charts often are on the wrong scale for inshore navigation by a yacht. The charts covering Grenada, the Grenadines, and St. Vincent are 1:72,000, while the famous old Virgin Islands chart is 1:100,000, which is even worse. You need a magnifying glass to find small anchorages and coves. In addition, it cuts Virgin Gorda in half. Several of the US and British charts break up the St. Vincent and Grenadines area in odd splits not conducive to use by the average yachtsman. The US chart of the Grenadines has an excellent enlarged insert for the Tobago Cays, but it does not have tidal reference points. The British chart does have this valuable information. Furthermore, the US and BA charts are based on surveys made in the 1890s. The latest NOAA and Admiralty charts have new deepwater information but retain the old inshore errors.

As a result of all these difficulties, I signed a contract with Imray, Laurie, Norie & Wilson (usually known simply as Imray)—which traces its ancestry back to 1670—to produce updated and accurate charts specifically tailored to the needs of the yachtsman. Our information has been gathered from US National Ocean Survey (NOS) and Defense Mapping Agency (DMA) charts, British Admiralty charts, French and Dutch charts, plus unpublished US and British Admiralty surveys, topographical maps, and aerial photography, backed up by the information I have gathered in some 40 years of exploring the Eastern Caribbean. Information also has been supplied to me by other experienced yachtsmen. Although it may be true that I know the Eastern Caribbean as a whole better than any other yachtsman, there are people who know individual islands and areas much better than I do. These yachtsmen have been tremendously helpful in sharing their expertise (see Acknowledgments).

Our charts come in one standard size, 25 inches by 35 1/2 inches, and three colors. Blue denotes deep water; white denotes water five fathoms or less; yellow indicates one fathom or less. Detailed harbor charts are inserted in the margins of the general charts. Useful ranges (transits) are shown to guide the mariner clear of dangers. Various overlapping coverages and often contradictory information found in the various French, US, Dutch, and British Admiralty charts have been eliminated.

We have now also introduced half-size planning charts (25 inches by 18 inches) for those who wish to plan a cruise before arriving in the islands, or just to mark off a cruise after the fact. These charts are suitable for wall mounting. Half-size versions are available for the following charts: US and British Virgins (A-231 and A-232); Anguilla/St. Martin/St. Barthélemy (A-24); Anguilla to Dominica (A-3); Martinique to Grenada (B-5); and St. Vincent to Grenada (B-3).

Imray-Iolaire charts are kept up to date through careful attention to the British Notices to Mariners, my own observations, and comments sent by users of these charts and readers of these cruising guides.

Important corrections are inserted by hand at Imray prior to shipment; all corrections are logged in on the master sheet so that even minor corrections are included in new editions. Seldom do we go more than six months between printings of a chart. (A complete list of the annual corrections to all of the Imray-Iolaire charts can be ordered directly from Imray, Laurie, Norie & Wilson, Ltd., Wych House, The Broadway, St. Ives, Huntingdon, Cambridgeshire PE17 4BT, England; tel. 0480-462114; fax 0480-496109. The list is available about mid-September each year.)

All of the charts are now being reprinted on waterproof paper. In addition, charts of certain island groups—Virgin Islands (A-231 and A-232), Antigua (A-27 and A-271), Guadeloupe (A-28 and A-281), and Martinique (A-30 and A-301)—have been printed on both sides of the paper, so that each of these areas is covered on a single chart.

As of this writing, 54 Imray-Iolaire charts cover the entire Eastern Caribbean. Further, we have expanded the scope of the charts to cover the Atlantic Island groups: Azores, Madeiran Archipelago, Canaries, Cape Verdes, and Bermuda. There is also a transatlantic planning chart that covers the Atlantic Ocean north of 8° north latitude—a useful chart for yachtsmen making passages either eastward or westward across the Atlantic.

The Imray-Iolaire charts have become the accepted standard; the US Coast Guard, as well as the St. Vincent and Grenada Coast Guards, use Imray-Iolaire charts rather than government charts. Very few chart agents in the Eastern Caribbean continue to stock the government charts.

Most of the harbor charts in this volume have been taken from the relevant Imray-Iolaire charts. The few sketch charts included here are just that—sketches. They are as accurate as I can make them, but they are *not* official publications, so they should be used only in conjunction with *reliable* navigational charts, common sense, and eyeball observations.

NOTE: Keep in mind that the sea level in the Eastern Caribbean is roughly 12 to 18 inches lower in May, June, and July than it is the rest of the year. Imray-Iolaire chart soundings are based on this low, low datum. Other charts may not be.

It must be remembered that positions obtained via modern electronic navigation are likely to be more accurate than chartwork. Once you get within three or four miles of an island, however, you must switch from electronic navigation to radar or visual navigation—backed up by soundings obtained electronically or by throwing the leadline.

Electronic navigation seems to work fairly well in the Caribbean, with the exception of St. Vincent and Grenada and the Grenadines, which show up roughly half a mile west of their charted positions. Elsewhere in the Caribbean, the differences between the chart datum and the WGS 84 datum (to which most GPS models are calibrated) is so slight that an offshore course the width of a pencil line will vary, depending on the scale of the chart, anywhere from 300 or 400 yards down to 30 or 40 yards. On large-scale charts, the line width is greater than the offset. Thus, GPS positions can be plotted directly on the chart.

If you are using the individual harbor charts and plotting GPS positions on them within the region covered in this volume—Puerto Rico, the Passage Islands, and the US and British Virgin Islands—the positions will be slightly out in latitude and approximately 150 feet out in longitude. A GPS is not accurate to within 10 meters (11 yards); about 100 meters (109 yards) is really the best accuracy you can expect. At times, the GPS can be as much as 300 yards out. Inshore, be sure to remember this warning. For inshore navigation, however, be sure to use the Imray-Iolaire charts, because they are updated and corrected regularly, whereas the US and UK charts are not.

The charts that cover the area between Anguilla and Grenada—whether NOAA, DMA, BA, French, or Imray-Iolaire—are based on ancient datums, so none of the information is dead accurate. All of the islands are misplaced to a greater or lesser degree. In this area, be especially cautious when using electronic position fixing. Electronic navigation may indicate that you are in deep water when you are in fact high and dry on Cade Reef! Electronic navigation is a wonderful tool, but it must be used with caution and intelligence.

NOAA, DMA, the British Hydrographic Office, and Imray-Iolaire are trying to get all their charts onto WGS 84. By the time you read this, we will have sorted out the Imray-Iolaire charts so that the new ones will be able to be used with confidence with GPS. If you have old Imray charts, you will be able to obtain correction tables from our chart agents. However, despite the claims of the GPS manufacturers, the ultimate reliability of a GPS, as I stated above, is a circle 300 meters (or about 328 yards) in diameter.

No chart can be absolutely accurate, but I feel that the Imray-Iolaire charts are the most accurate ones available. They can be kept that way only if experienced yachtsmen continue to feed information to us so we can correct the small errors that may still exist or to update charts where the topography has been changed by hurricanes, earthquakes, or dredging.

Please send information regarding chart corrections to: D.M. Street, Jr., c/o David Payne, Morgan, Wright & Coleman, 6 Alie Street, London E1 8DD, England (tel. 071-488-9000; fax 071-480-6917).

Street's Cruising Guide to
the Eastern Caribbean

*Puerto Rico, the Passage Islands,
the US and British Virgin Islands*

1

Sailing Directions for Puerto Rico, the Passage Islands, and the US and British Virgin Islands

Before planning any passage to the Eastern Caribbean from the East Coast of the United States or from Europe, be sure to consult *Street's Transatlantic Crossing Guide and Introduction to the Caribbean.* It is the essential companion to each of the other volumes in this series.

The Lesser Antilles stretch east and south from Puerto Rico and St. Thomas in a great crescent. The entire sweep is best shown on Imray-Iolaire (II) Chart 1, which illustrates the Eastern Caribbean in a scale suitable for planning a cruise. (Use Imray-Iolaire Chart A for planning your cruise in Puerto Rico, the Passage Islands, and the Virgin Islands.) As you develop your itinerary, remember that the northeast trades are a misnomer; they vary continually, sometimes crawling all the way around to the north—and, more often, especially in the late spring and summer, favoring the southeast to south quadrants.

A bit of advice for cruising the Lesser Antilles: Instead of making plans in the morning after breakfast (thus getting a late start and arriving at the next anchorage at dusk or after dark—a dangerous practice), it is better to drag out the charts, the cruising guide, and the travel books the evening before departure. Study them well, and be sure to read the sailing directions for the area likely to be covered. Make your plans and then turn in, prepared for the next day's adventures.

When working to windward, from the northern islands, eastward toward Antigua, be sure to remember that there is an average of one knot of foul current; thus, your speed to windward may be discouraging. Once you turn the corner at Antigua and head south—and, similarly, on your northbound courses from Martinique—remember that the current usually will be on the weather beam at approximately one knot, or often more. This will set you to leeward at a considerable rate. If you are sailing at four knots, a one-knot current on the beam will set you to leeward roughly 15; if you are sailing at five knots, the set will be 12; at six knots, it will be 10; at seven knots, it will be 8.

It must be pointed out, however, that no rules about currents in the Antilles are hard and fast. Changing tidal influences, varying wind strengths, and local topographical peculiarities all affect the movement of Caribbean waters. As a generalization, though, it is fair to say that the current runs to the west; consequently, when cruising in the Lesser Antilles, it is a good idea to stay to windward of the rhumb line between any two points. There are exceptions to this rule, but they are few and far between.

Remember also that the southern islands are far enough apart that the next island is not always visible when you start off. Thus, you should lay off your rhumb-line course, set your actual course to allow for the current, and then continually take back bearings on the island astern to make absolutely sure you are not set to leeward of the rhumb line. This is where the hand-bearing compass can earn its keep.

The sailing directions in this chapter apply primarily to passages from island to island. Once you approach an island, be sure to refer to the specific directions and descriptions in the chapters that follow.

Proceeding East

Most skippers coming from the Miami or Fort Lauderdale area end up island hopping through the Bahamas and then cruising along the north coast of Hispaniola. This, however, is a long, time-consuming trip with many reefs to hit and some potential political hazards in Haiti and the Dominican Republic.

My advice is to go to Grand Bahama Island and wait for a norther. After it hits Florida, take off just as it is reaching the Bahamas—the wind will be out of the north, coming straight off Grand Bahama, and the sea will be smooth (or relatively so). It will blow you out through the Northeast Providence Channel, with eased sheets.

Instead of heading on a rhumb-line course to Puerto Rico, try to head due east or on a course as close as possible to east—in order to get a good turn of speed. Hold this course until the western end of Puerto Rico bears 180° magnetic, then bear off and head for Mayagüez. Enter Mayagüez, resupply, and then head south along the west coast to Puerto Real, Boquerón, and then eastward along the south coast of Puerto Rico, taking advantage of the nighttime calm or northerly shift. The wind frequently will come right out of the north, giving you a beam reach eastward. As you will see in chapters 4 and 5, the anchorages (or at least harbors of refuge) are never more than 20 miles apart—and frequently 15 miles—so you can work your way eastward in easy jumps and have a wonderful time doing so.

Ignore the north coast of Puerto Rico. The San Juan Trench, 1,000 fathoms deep, is only a few miles offshore, and the huge Atlantic swell, coming up against this vertical wall, makes Puerto Rico's north coast very lumpy. Needless to say, that accounts for why marinas have been built on the east coast of Puerto Rico rather than in San Juan—no one likes

the 40 miles from San Juan around the corner to Fajardo.

If you are heading to San Juan and can't quite make it, you can stop at Arecibo (see chapter 6), but only in desperation. When you reach San Juan, there are two marinas: Club Nautico, a private club that probably will be full, and San Juan Bay Marina, operated by Bill Bachman, member of a longtime Puerto Rican family.

One of the advantages of stopping at the San Juan Bay Marina is that you are within walking distance (or a short taxi ride) of charming Old San Juan and the magnificent El Morro fortress—both worth half a day each.

WEST AND SOUTHWEST PUERTO RICO

From Mayagüez south to Puerto Real and Boquerón is no problem. Unless you have a deep-draft boat, hug the shore and sail on southward. (See chapter 3 before entering these harbors.)

Keep in mind that the southwestern tip of Puerto Rico is relatively low, so even though the cool air does come down off the mountains during the night, the land breeze/sea breeze effect is nowhere near as noticeable as it is farther north near Mayagüez or farther east near Ponce. The wind will tend to be light in the morning and come in out of the west or south.

Be warned, however, that as you reach Cabo Rojo, the wind will definitely come out of the east. Thus, when heading south from Boquerón, favor the inshore side. If the wind moves to the south, do not let yourself be driven offshore. If you are off to the west trying to make Cabo Rojo and suddenly the wind comes from the east, you have thrown away two or three good miles of windward work. Stay close inshore.

The water west and north of Punta Aguila is, as they would say in the Bahamas, "a little bit tin," and that does not refer to 10 feet; it means "thin"—the bottom is close to the top!

Between Punta Aguila and Cabo Rojo, there is not much water; in Bahía Salinas, it is strictly a case of eyeball navigation in good light (a two-foot spot there will stop you hard!).

Once you are south of Cabo Rojo, stand inshore to get in the smooth water provided by Arrecife Margarita and Arrecife Laurel.

You can beat to windward inside of Arrecife Laurel with seven and a half feet of draft—we did it on *Iolaire*. The only problem was that we became careless when our fathometer disagreed with the soundings on the charts. I figured that the one-fathom spot wasn't there, but it was—*Iolaire* slid up on it. We were parked—not aground—for about five minutes, and then we sailed her off and anchored. The reason we had become careless is that even though the chart shows a two-fathom maximum in this area, we found a bunch of holes that were anywhere from 20 to 30 feet deep. In general, however, the bottom throughout this area is about 12 feet, shoaling to eight or nine feet.

It should be noted that on the older Imray-Iolaire charts, no water is shown in the gap in the northeast corner of Arrecife Laurel. In fact, even though the gap is narrow, there is a full 24 feet of water. Under power, that gap can be used, but there is not enough room to tack; it's better to use the gap north of Arrecife Laurel, where you can even tack a long-keeled boat like *Iolaire*.

LA PARGUERA TO PONCE

When you depart La Parguera, leave early. If you have an engine, pass up through Puerto Quijano, then out to sea between Arrecife Enmedio and Arrecife Romero. But if the sun is high enough so you can see (there are numerous shoals in this area), you can continue eastward, north of Romero, passing all the way (if you draw six feet or less) to Cayo Don Luis, where you can exit. That means you will have been in calm water all the time.

If you are sailing, you can pass either north or south of Arrecife Enmedio. If passing south, as soon as you clear Arrecife Enmedio, tack back in toward Arrecife Romero in order to stay in smooth water. Short-tack up the beach until you just clear Punta Jorobado. Under power, you can motor eastward inside Arrecife Baul, or, if you have a good eyeball navigator, you can short-tack up inside Arrecife Baul and stand off to clear Punta Brea. If the light conditions are not right and you feel you are not skilled enough to sail up inside Arrecife Baul, clear the eastern end of Arrecife Baul and immediately tack back inshore to Punta Brea.

East of Punta Brea, it is not all deep water. Due east of flashing red buoy number 4 is Corona La Laja, where the chart shows least depth of eight feet. It might even be less, and with any sort of sea running, you could bottom out, so stay clear of it. If proceeding eastward, stay inshore on the shelf to keep out of the current, but be careful of the reefs and islands east of Guánica. If it begins to blow hard, duck into the excellent anchorages around Punta Jacinto (see chapter 4) and wait until morning.

East of Punta Ventana, stay inshore to obtain shelter from current and sea provided by Arrecife Guayanilla. When heading eastward from Arrecife Guayanilla, be sure to use the detailed insert in Imray-Iolaire Chart A-12. While passing Cayo Maria Langa and Cayo Caribe, stay on your toes and keep your wits about you. Keep the chart and the hand-bearing compass in front of you, as carelessness could easily get you into trouble on the reefs east of Cayo Caribe. Once clear of Cayo Caribe and its offlying reefs, stay inshore. We found a full 11 feet along the shore between Punta Cucharas and Cayo Arenas, giving us smooth water. East of here, be careful, as it is difficult to spot Cayo Viejo and Las Hojitas.

PONCE TO PUERTO PATILLAS

Proceeding eastward from Ponce (see chapter 5), again leave very early in the morning with the northerly wind and stay close inshore. There you will be sheltered from wind and sea by Punta Petrona and Cayos Cabezazos. Tack back toward shore as soon as possible. You can sail between Cayos de Caracoles and Cayo Alfenique, but again tack back toward shore as quickly as possible in order to get shelter from the sea. If conditions are right, shoal-draft boats can pass between Punta Petrona and Cayos Cabezazos, staying slightly north of midway between the two. There is a straight stretch of channel—about seven feet deep—with shoals on either side.

Tack inshore into Bahía Rincón and stop at Salinas. Or, if proceeding eastward, continue inside all the islands into Bahía de Jobos.

Proceeding eastward from Bahía de Jobos, again stay as close to shore as possible until you reach Punta Ole Grande.

Beyond Las Mareas, tack offshore to clear Arrecife Mareas, but once clear of that reef, tack back inshore. If the light is not good, however, do not get into shoal water, as there is an unnamed five-foot spot southwest of Arrecife Algarrobo, plus Arrecife Corona. All of these can be spotted when the sun is high and the light is good, but caution is still essential in this area.

Stay inshore to Punta Figuras, then tack offshore to clear the headland. In this area, carefully consult the inset on Imray-Iolaire Chart A-13. Note that off Punta Figuras there is an eight-foot spot, which would certainly bring deep-draft boats to a sudden stop. Make sure you stay far enough offshore to avoid this shoal, but be sure to stay inside the unmarked Arrecife Guayama. Stay inshore in the bay of Puerto Patillas.

EAST AND NORTH FROM PUERTO PATILLAS

From Puerto Patillas (see chapter 6), leave very early in the morning to take advantage of the cold air coming down from the mountains to produce a northerly wind (or at least to minimize the trades). If you depart later, you will be slogging your way eastward. As you work your way to the east, assess the situation and make your decision about staying inshore or going offshore. If you stay on the shelf, you will be out of the current, but you may encounter short, steep seas because of the big Caribbean swell coming up on the shelf. You may decide that it is better to stand offshore in the deep water fighting the current in order to gain smoother seas.

Whether you go inside or outside Arrecife Sargent is debatable (see the pros and cons in chapter 6).

Once you have cleared Punta Yeguas and bypassed Puerto Yabucoa, with any luck you should be able to lay a course up the coast to Cayo Santiago and stop there for the night. However, if the wind is south of east, you should be able to get to Isla Cabras (clearing Punta Puerca), then run off to Pasaje Medio Mundo and anchor behind Isla Piñeros.

If you have stopped at Cayo Santiago to grab your breath before beating on up the east coast, stay close inshore, as the sea is much smoother in behind the headlands and on the shelf. Plus you are out of the current; it can be setting southwestward up to a knot and a half, which will negate your windward-going progress. When passing Punta Lima, be very careful of Arrecife Lima. The day we passed it in 1993, we could not spot it, so take careful bearings.

Work your way eastward across the shelf south of Ensenada Honda by Punta Cascajo, and pass Cabra de Tierra; tack out to clear Isla Cabras, then tack back into Bahía de Puerca to get shelter. Stand on past Punta Puerca until you pick up the ranges for Pasaje Medio Mundo.

I have been told that you can pass between Isla Piñeros and Isla Cabeza de Perro, but do not attempt this passage unless the conditions are ideal. In March 1993, we noted a boat piled up on the reef on the eastern side of the passage. Obviously, every boat does not make it through. In April 1994, Bob Lamson took us through this passage in his

sportfisherman. There is plenty of water, but there is also a very strong current with powerful eddies.

The sailing directions in the older Imray-Iolaire charts have the wrong range for entering the channel.

If you carefully adhere to the sailing directions that follow, a full 13 feet can be carried through the entire Pasaje Medio Mundo. When coming from the south, going north: Pass northeastward of Punta Puerca, bringing the buildings of Gaviota Estates to bear 330° magnetic. Stay on this range until Isla Cabeza de Perro disappears behind the southwest tip of Isla Piñeros, bearing 100° magnetic. Then head up to bring Cabo San Juan light one-third of the distance from the western side of Isla de Ramos to the eastern side. Then you will be absolutely in the channel.

Once north of Punta Figuera (the point of land just south of Puerto del Rey Marina), bear off to course 350° magnetic until Cabo San Juan light lines up with the low western building of Isleta Marina in Fajardo. Stay on this range, 015-195° magnetic, until into Isleta Marina anchorage.

Coming from the north (heading south from Isleta Marina) the directions are as follows: Depart from Isleta Marina, put Cabo San Juan light above the low western building in Isleta Marina, 015-195° magnetic. Hold that range until Cayo Ahogado is abeam. (Take bearings; the islet was submerged by Hurricane Hugo in 1989 and now is about one foot underwater.) Then steer 170° magnetic until Cabo San Juan light is one-third of the distance from the western side of Isla de Ramos to the eastern side. Stay on this range until Isla Cabeza de Perro appears from behind the southwest tip of Isla Piñeros, bearing 100° magnetic. Then alter course to 150° magnetic, keeping the buildings of Gaviota Estates bearing 330° magnetic. Hold this course or east of this course until Punta Puerca is aft of abeam.

PUERTO RICO TO ST. THOMAS

When departing Fajardo, on Puerto Rico's east coast, stay to the south but close to the islands and reefs that stretch between San Juan and Culebra to get shelter from the Atlantic swell. Then head east or southeast to Culebra to get shelter from the sea. Once you have departed from Culebra, stand east or southeast until you reach Sail Rock. Then go over to starboard tack and go in behind St. Thomas to get to smooth water. In daylight, there are no dangers; if you can't see it, you can't hit it. Stand right over to the St. Thomas shore, then short-tack up the shore through

South West Road, staying in smooth water. Pass outside buoy number 3, proceed through West Gregerie Channel, and then go between Water Island and the "mainland." If you draw eight feet or less, you can get through Haulover Cut (between Hassel Island and the "mainland"). If you draw more than that, go around Hassel Island to the main harbor entrance.

Instead of beating all the way into St. Thomas Harbor, you have two choices of anchorages where you can enjoy your last night of solitude before returning to civilization. The best anchorage is behind Saba Island, where you are almost guaranteed to be alone—except on weekends. (Do not try to get into this anchorage if conditions are not good.) Or you can anchor north of the runway in Brewers/Airport Bay (see chapter 9).

It is important to note, when passing the end of the airport runway, that there are two small white buoys marking the airport approach pattern. You must pass west of those buoys or you will be subject to a nice, fat fine.

If approaching St. Thomas at night, the safest method is to stay offshore and use the main entrance channel, but beating up outside Saba Island and Dry Rocks puts you in rough water. The alternative is to get inshore. Since there is deep water right up to the St. Thomas shore, you can tack along the coast, anchor north of the runway in Brewers/Airport Bay, and wait until dawn to enter St. Thomas Harbor via the back door.

Working your way up to South West Road, Savana Island is easily spotted because of its light, but take careful bearings and be sure not to get involved with Kalkun Cay, or with Saltwater (or Money) Rock in Savana Passage. In this area, you might encounter a strong southeast or northwest current—if it is running southeast, it will lift you up to windward; if it's going northwest, stay away from Savana Passage, as it will suck you off into the Atlantic like a big vacuum cleaner.

Once you are safely east of Savana Island, Kalkun Cay, and Saltwater (Money) Rock, there are no problems. Just sail close to the St. Thomas shore, where the water is so deep you can practically put your bowsprit ashore. There is no danger of running aground. Keep working your way eastward in smooth water until you reach Brewers/Airport Bay.

ROUTES FROM ST. THOMAS

Generally speaking, there are seven islands that offer good jumping-off spots for further cruising: St. Thomas, St. Martin/Sint Maarten, Antigua, Martinique, St. Lucia, Grenada, and Trinidad. They all provide air communication to the United States, plus convenient harbors, shipyards where your boat can be minded in your absence, and stores and markets where you can resupply to continue your trip.

Despite its being fairly far to leeward, St. Thomas still is the port from which most extended cruises begin, so let's consider a few of the possible routes to the east and south:

St. Thomas through the Virgin Islands, island hopping to Antigua, 210 miles to windward, with possibilities of stopping and resting at various islands.

St. Thomas to Martinique direct, 337 miles, course 143° magnetic; there is some possibility of laying the course.

St. Thomas to Martinique via Necker Island Passage, course 152° magnetic.

St. Thomas to St. Lucia direct, or from Virgin Gorda via Necker Island Passage—the same course as that to Martinique, except that the distance will be somewhat greater.

St. Thomas to Grenada direct, 423 miles, course 163° magnetic. Once clear of St. Croix, you can lay the course.

St. Thomas to Grenada via Necker Island Passage, about 400 miles, 170° magnetic; an easy reach from Necker on down.

The Virgin Islands stretch out to the eastward from St. Thomas, making a cruise through them a dead beat to windward. But this is not a difficult beat, since the islands are close together and, although the wind may blow hard, you'll have to contend with nothing more than a large chop. You can easily spend a pleasant week to 10 days cruising the Virgins.

When departing from St. Thomas and proceeding eastward, leave Rupert Rock to port. While sailing along the shore toward Muhlenfels Point, you will have a good chance to tie in a reef. The high hills block the wind, and, once clear of the point, you will feel the full force of the trades and their attendant swell. If you have a vessel that draws less than seven feet and don't mind tacking or are proceeding under power, you can pass inside the triangular area off Muhlenfels Point. Beat to windward along Morningstar Beach, past the low house with a large white roof on the edge of a low cliff, and stay close aboard the western shore of Green Cay. This will not necessarily save you time, but it will keep you out of the sea for the first few miles of beating to windward. Once you have tacked far enough offshore to clear Green Cay, it usually is best to tack back in toward shore. Work your way alongshore in short tacks, and you will avoid most of the ocean swell.

Be careful, however, of two dangers. There is an eight-foot spot 800 yards east of Green Cay that is on the direct line from the south end of Green Cay to Long Point. The other hazard is Packet Rock, which is very dangerous, since it has only one fathom of water over it. Despite the fact that a nun marks the rock, it is difficult to spot, because the buoy usually is about 40 yards southeast of it.

Stand inshore on starboard tack toward the western shore of Long Point. Tack offshore and continue offshore until you are sure you can lay Cas Cay and Jersey Bay. Do not cut it close, because if you have to tack, there is always a bad sea in this area. This is no place to be caught in stays with a dead lee shore.

Directly east of Cas Cay is an eight-foot spot that will bother only larger boats. Once clear of Cas Cay, stand into Jersey Bay until you can stick your bowsprit ashore. On the next tack, you may be able to weather Cow and Calf Rocks. If so, continue on until you can lay Current Hole, then tack. If you can't weather Cow and Calf, tack back inshore rather than continuing to seaward, since you will find calm water in behind Great St. James.

When passing through Current Hole, you can pass either east or west of Current Rock. The eastern passage is the widest and deepest—deep enough for any yacht. The high hill to the east of the passage blocks the wind, so it is quite possible that you will have to turn on the engine if you have a foul tide. The western passage is shoal, but evidently the controlling depth is eight feet, as I have sailed *Iolaire* (seven feet six inches) through this pass for years and have never touched. On the western side of Current Rock, you do not lose your wind, but you must be careful, since there is barely room to tack.

When using the western pass, remember that the axis of the tide through this pass is northeast-southwest. If there is a foul tide and the wind is well north of east, do not attempt this passage, because a strong weather bow tide will sweep you toward the rocks on the lee side. However, if you are able to head northeast or east of northeast, you have nothing to fear, even with a foul tide, since you will be able to lee-bow the tide. Under these conditions, even if you are not quite laying the passage, a quick luff will present your lee bow to the tide, and it will push you to the weather side of the channel. A fair tide makes this passage simple. The tide is so strong that, once you are in the pass, it will carry you through, no matter what the wind.

Once through Current Hole, continue on starboard tack across Pillsbury Sound, but be sure to clear Cabrita Point with room to spare. Off Cabrita Point is Jumping Rock, which, fortunately, is now marked by a buoy, because a number of boats have come to grief on it. (If for some reason the buoy is not there, give Cabrita Point a wide berth.) The high hills of St. John produce radical wind shifts, especially when the wind is south of east.

Always stand across Pillsbury Sound on starboard tack until you are east of Stevens Cay, because the tide creates a swell from the south between Stevens Cay and Great St. James. If you tack to the south, you will have this sea dead on your nose. It is so short and so steep that you will make no progress. In the old days, this area was known as the Graveyard—probably a reference to the number of overloaded Tortola sloops that met their end here. In more recent times, the area has swallowed a number of dinghies being trailed astern. As you cross Pillsbury Sound between Stevens Cay and Great St. James, check your tide; in this area, it runs northwest-southeast, which is at right angles to your course. By adjusting your course to compensate for this tide, you will save considerably in distance sailed. Lay your course for the northern end of Stevens Cay.

When you pass the end of Stevens Cay, either harden up for Cruz Bay or continue eastward without easing sheets, because you probably will be headed in the neighborhood of Lind Point. As you reach Caneel Bay, the wind usually becomes more northerly, heading you. The passes between Lovango Cay and Hawksnest Point have strong tides, so be watchful. I prefer to use the pass between Hawksnest Point and Durloe Cays. By hugging the shore, you may be able to find a back eddy that will give you a fair current even though the tide is against you. The water appears to be smoother on the St. John side of the channel.

The only danger in this area is Johnson Reef, easily spotted since it usually is breaking and there are buoys off its north and south ends. There is plenty of room to tack between Johnson Reef and Trunk Bay if you exert normal caution.

Another method of working your way eastward from St. Thomas is to stop for the night at Christmas Cove, on the west side of Great St. James Island. The next morning, you can sail through the passage between Little St. James and Great St. James and head east toward the numerous wonderful anchorages on the south coast of St. John, where you can spend a couple of quiet, easy days in uncrowded coves. If you decide that you want to sail directly up the south coast of St. John and on to the British Virgins, short-tack inshore and stay out of the sea and current. However, once you have cleared Ram Head on St. John's southeast coast and are standing over to Sir Francis Drake Channel, be especially alert to avoid going up on Eagle Shoal. (Sketch Chart 44 shows the ranges for avoiding this hazard.)

When proceeding eastward to the Drake Channel, the most logical route appears to be through The Narrows, but I recommend passing to the north of Great Thatch Island. My old *Sailing Directions to the Caribbean*, published in 1867, when wind and tide were important to a mariner, describes a much better method of getting into Drake Channel. When clearing Windward Passage, stand north and pass north of Great Thatch. Then stand out into the sound between Jost Van Dyke and Great Thatch or Tortola. Tack to fetch the western end of Tortola. Pass the rocks on the western end of Tortola close aboard, then stand over to the Little Thatch Island shore. Do not tack until the very last minute. With luck, if you get one good lift, you will weather Little Thatch and pass on into Drake Channel. At worst, you will need only two quick tacks to clear the eastern end of Little Thatch. This will save making 10 or 15 tacks in The Narrows, and, if the tide is foul, it will save hours.

Once you are clear of Little Thatch, stand over to the St. John shore and tack only at the last minute. Your next tack should allow you to weather Frenchman's Cay, and now, if you work your way along the Tortola shore, you will be out of the worst of the tide. The remainder of Drake Channel is straightforward, except that you should avoid the southeastern tip of Beef Island. There is a tide rip, and the high cliffs create a back eddy and disturb the flow of wind.

ANEGADA (SOMBRERO) PASSAGE

Once you leave the Virgins through Necker Island Passage or Round Rock Passage, there is little between you and Africa. The seas sweep across 3,000 miles of open ocean, and, as they enter Anegada (Sombrero) Passage, they are influenced by the tide ebbing and flowing into the Caribbean. The islands on both sides of the passage disturb the natural flow of the waves, creating an area that is always rough and uncomfortable. When the trades really begin to pipe up, the passage is difficult for large boats and well-nigh impossible for smaller ones.

In Anegada (Sombrero) Passage, the wind is generally east, and the current flows west to northwest at one to one and a half knots—in other words, a dead slog to windward with a foul current all the way. There is, however, some room for play in this passage, which I will try to explain with close reference to the chart.

The north equatorial current—which runs northwest as it passes Nevis, St. Kitts (St. Christopher), Statia (Sint Eustatius), and Saba, swings toward the west between St. Croix and the other Virgin Islands. A strong eddy holds almost due north around the west end of St. Martin and Anguilla, then northwest along Horse Shoe Reef (Anegada Reef) and the eastern shore of Anegada. Once it reaches the northern end of Anegada, it goes westward, with a strong back eddy looping eastward below the island on Virgin Bank. This eddy has been attested to by fishermen and pilots who have spotted large accumulations of sargasso weed between the westerly current and the easterly eddy, and by the surprising number of wrecks on the western reefs of Anegada.

A boat crossing Anegada (Sombrero) Passage will be favored by the northerly current on its lee bow. Since this northerly tendency becomes less pronounced the farther off to the south you fall, you should stay well to the north. If you allow your course to sag off toward Saba, you will find the current right on your nose the rest of the way east to St. Martin. (As a general rule, if you can't see Sombrero Light, you are too far off to the south.)

For example, if the wind is well in the north, work your way eastward within the shelter of the Virgins before heading out through Necker Island Passage and standing across to St. Martin. However, if the wind is east or east-southeast, work your way much farther north before venturing out into the passage. Take advantage of the easterly eddy hooking around Anegada, and lay a northerly course so that you pass close aboard the west end of Anegada. Stand far enough north to clear Anegada and Horse Shoe Reef in one tack. As you proceed southeastward on port tack, you should have an increasingly strong lee-bow current, lifting you favorably. In short, my advice is to stay to the north, granting that there are exceptions to every rule. In the 1973 St. Thomas–St. Martin Race, one boat took a flyer from the rest of the fleet. He stood southeast to Saba Bank, then tacked, beating all his competitors by a country mile and confounding the local sailing authorities.

In years past, there wasn't much reason to stop in Anegada, but that has changed: Among other attractions, there are three hotels that serve excellent lunches and dinners. Needless to say, arrive around noon so that the light is good for finding an anchorage. Enjoy an afternoon on the beach and a good dinner ashore, then take off the following day. This reduces the pain of crossing Anegada (Sombrero) Passage, as the distance from the western end of Anegada to Dog Island (where you begin to get shelter) is 71 miles as the crow flies. (Of course, with the current against you on a beat to windward, you are likely to sail 110 miles to cover that distance.) Once you reach Dog Island, it is a relatively easy 10-mile sail to Road Harbour, Anguilla, or a 15-mile passage to Marigot, St. Martin.

Yet another recommendation for tackling Anegada (Sombrero) Passage comes from Dr. Robin Tattersall, owner of the 36-foot Herreshoff Nereia ketch *Galatea*. Based in Tortola, Dr. Tattersall regularly used to go to Anguilla for a few days to perform surgery. Rather than fly over, he liked to sail across Anegada (Sombrero) Passage. Thus, he has had plenty of experience driving his boat to windward— which has stood him in good stead during the many races in which he has competed.

His method is to proceed first to Eustatia Island, north of Virgin Gorda. This considerably shortens the distance across the passage, since it is 75 miles on a rhumb-line course of 115° magnetic from Eustatia to Road Harbour, Anguilla, with the possibility of a stop at Sombrero or Dog Island.

To Sombrero Island, the rhumb-line course is 090° magnetic, while the distance is 54 miles; the course is 110° magnetic to Dog Island, a distance of 62 miles. You could also take off from the anchorage behind Necker Island.

The great advantage of starting at either Eustatia or Necker Island is that each affords a good daytime anchorage, good snorkeling, and an excellent beach. You can relax under the awning, have a decent lunch and a snooze, and then take off early in the afternoon, well fed and rested. You can reach both islands without slogging to windward in the open ocean, as you would have to do if you left Drake Channel farther west at Cooper or Ginger Island. You can beat up behind Virgin Gorda and enter Gorda Sound (if you draw six feet or less) through the Western Passage between Mosquito Island and Anguilla Point. Next, you beat to windward across Gorda Sound in calm water, pass between Saba Rock and John O Point, sail on into Eustatia Sound, and then anchor behind Eustatia Island or continue north through the reef to Necker Island.

Dr. Tattersall advises leaving Eustatia or Necker at about 1500 or 1600. Once clear of Eustatia Sound or Necker Island (watch out for the Invisibles, half a mile east of Necker Island), stand to the north about four miles, keeping a careful check on your position in relation to Horse Shoe Reef. If the wind is in the north, Dr. Tattersall advises going back to port tack as soon as you can. Lay Dog Island, keeping in mind that if you are able to lay 120° to 110° magnetic, you will have a lee-bow current lifting you to windward. With any luck and a good boat, you should be off Dog Island at dawn. There you can drop the anchor, have a good breakfast, swim, walk on the beach, and then continue on to Anguilla, arriving in late afternoon.

In the spring and summer, however, when the wind is in the southerly quadrant (and provided the ground swell is not running), it's best to stand off on starboard tack once clear of Horse Shoe Reef. Aim for Sombrero—rhumb-line course 100° magnetic, distance 44 miles. The advantage of this course is that long before you lose the lights on the top of the hill on Virgin Gorda (given decent visibility), you will pick up the lights of Sombrero, where it is calm enough to anchor in normal weather. (If the ground swell is running, forget it.) In the lee of Sombrero, you can get the better part of a good night's sleep, enjoy a good breakfast, a walk ashore, and a swim prior to hoisting the anchor and continuing on to Anguilla or another island. (See chapter 15 for details about anchoring off Sombrero.)

It should be noted here that despite all our talk about the rough conditions of Anegada (Sombrero) Passage, it is not always that way. In November 1977, *Iolaire* broad-reached across the passage from the Virgin Islands with the spinnaker before a light southwesterly. Similarly, many years ago, the late Bill Taylor, editor of *Yachting*, went south to sail with friends across Anegada Passage, about which he had heard horrendous tales all his life. He was most disappointed to have to motorsail across in light airs.

Aboard *Iolaire*, we have had so many rough trips across Anegada Passage that my wife regards it as the local equivalent of Cape Horn. Yet almost every time we make the trip without Trich on board, we have an easy passage. The trouble is that she refuses to believe the stories we tell her.

In 1993, we had a rather odd trip across Anegada (Sombrero) Passage. We took off from the northwestern point of Anegada, and despite the fact that the weather report said the wind was southeast, it was so far in the south that the first part of the trip we had a glorious sail along the north coast of Anegada, heading 130° magnetic. The wind slowly lifted us, and the current set us to the north, but except for about two hours on port tack (we were nursing our way through a series of violent rain squalls), we were on starboard tack all the way to Sombrero, with the wind quite light the last 25 miles.

As we reached Sombrero, the St. Martin radio station said the wind was east to southeast, but the wind went around to the southwest and we were lifted to a course of 180°. Amazingly, after days of heavy weather, the current reversed itself and set us east, so we could not quite lay Prickly Pear Cays. We had to throw in a short tack to get east of Seal Island Reef and Prickly Pear Cays, and then it was an easy reach into Road Harbour, Anguilla. The passage was not overly swift, but it was very comfortable.

ANTIGUA WESTWARD

From Antigua, you are in a position to lay just about any island passage. A course can be set southward to Montserrat or slightly north of west to Nevis and on to St. Kitts, St. Eustatius, St. Barthélemy, or St. Martin—all easy jumps from one island to the next.

One word of warning, however, about night passages between the St. Barthélemy–St. Martin–Anguilla area and Virgin Gorda: The current sets strongly to the northwest through here, at times as much as two knots. Some yachts and commercial vessels bound from this area for Virgin Gorda or Round Rock Passage have received the surprises of their lives on Horse Shoe Reef (Anegada Reef). The current changes erratically from day to day, and there is no predicting how it will be running when you get out there.

In years past, I preferred to leave Anguilla or St. Martin in the evening after a good dinner and lay a course midway between St. Croix and St. Thomas. Both of these islands would be visible by dawn, at which time I could alter course accordingly. In the 1970s, there were no lights in the British Virgins visible from the east, but that has all changed. Now, the loom from Road Town on Tortola can be seen for miles. On Virgin Gorda, the house lights along the road that leads over the hill between Biras Creek and Little Dix Bay are bright and high enough on clear nights to be visible 30 or 40 miles to the east.

Nowadays, I lay a course off the Ginger Island light, allowing for a northerly set in the current. I figure that even if Ginger Island light or Pajaros Point light is out, I will see the lights of Virgin Gorda before I get into trouble. Then I decide which passage to take into the British Virgins. Don't opt for Necker Island Passage unless the sun is high—you could pile up on the south end of Horse Shoe Reef. If you do use this passage, be sure not to stray north of the line of bearing of 280° magnetic from the north side of Necker Island. If you are going into Sir Francis Drake Channel and Road Town, the best route is Round Rock Passage, between Round Rock and Ginger Island. If you choose another route, be careful—you may encounter some unmarked rocks.

Another problem to consider is that in heading westward from Anguilla or St. Martin, you usually will be dead before the wind. I have seen boats rolling and slatting endlessly, their jibs alternately filling and collapsing, their mains threatening to jibe, the sun directly overhead frying the crews' brains out. Don't do it this way. Instead, wing the jib on a whisker or spinnaker pole, guy the main boom forward, come down hard on the boom vang, and rig a cockpit awning that can be left up under sail. Then relax. Life will be a dream.

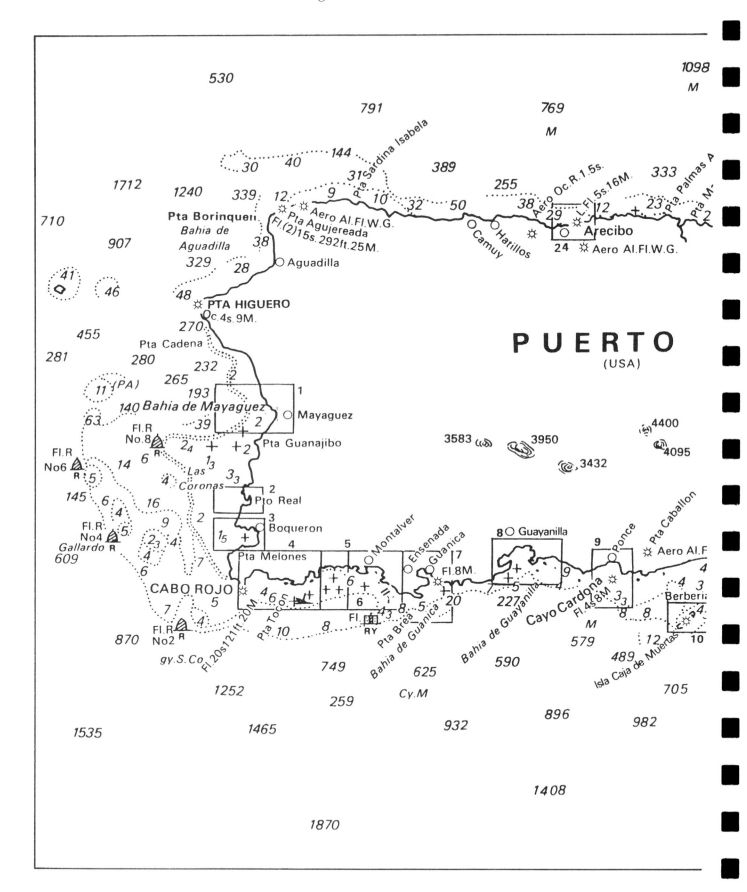

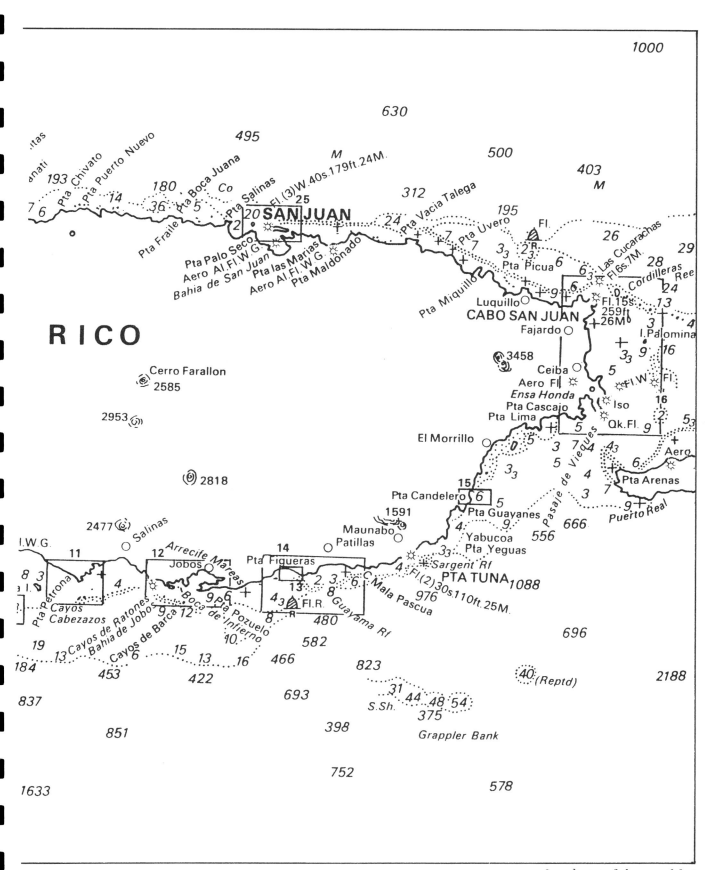

1000

630

495

500

403
M

M

itas

193 Pta Chivato

Pta Puerto Nuevo

180

Pta Boca Juana

Co

Pta Salinas

Fl.(3)W.40s.179ft.24M.

312

Pta Vacia Talega

195

Fl.

26

Las Cucarachas

29

anati

7 6

14

Pta Fraile

36

5

Pta Maldonado

Pta las Marias

Pta Palo Seco

Aero Al.Fl.W.G.

Bahia de San Juan

Aero Al.Fl.W.G.

2

20

25

SAN JUAN

24

Pta Uvero

7

7

3 3

2 3

R

Pta Picua

6

6 3

Fl.6s.7M.

28

Cordilleras

Ree

24

Fl.15s

259ft

26M

0

13

3

4

Luquillo

9

CABO SAN JUAN

R I C O

Fajardo

I.Palomina

3 3

9

16

Cerro Farallon
2585

3458

Ceiba

5

Fl.W

Fl

Aero Fl

Ensa Honda

Pta Cascajo

Iso

16

2

2953

Pta Lima

5

Qk.Fl.

9

5 3

El Morrillo

0

5

3

7 4

4 3

Aero

2818

3 3

5

5

6

Pta Arenas

15

4

3

7

2477

Salinas

Pta Candelero

6

5

Pasaje de Vieques

9

Puerto Real

I.W.G.

11

12

Arrecife Mareas

Jobos

14

Pta Figueras

1591

Maunabo

Patillas

Yabucoa

Pta Yeguas

4

9

666

556

8 3

Pta Petrona

4

Boca de Jobos

9 Pta

6

13

2

3

8

6

C. Mala Pascua

4

3 3

Sargent Rf

PTA TUNA 1088

Fl.(2)30s.110ft.25M.

Cayos
Cabezazos

Cayos de Ratones

9

12

Pta Pozuelo

10

4 3

8

Fl.R.

R

976

480

Guayama Rf

19

13 Cayos de Barca

6

15

13

16

466

582

696

184

453

422

823

40 (Reptd)

2188

837

693

31

44

48 54

S.Sh.

375

851

398

Grappler Bank

578

752

1633

NOTES

2

Puerto Rico

(Imray-Iolaire Charts A, A-1, A-11, A-12, A-13, A-131, A-14, A-2)

To speak very briefly of a large island, Puerto Rico offers rich opportunities to the cruising yachtsman. The south coast abounds with small coves and deserted anchorages, sandstone caves, and white-sand beaches. With all the wonderful cruising on the south coast of Puerto Rico, it's really not necessary to carry on to the increasingly crowded anchorages in the Virgin Islands. The charter boats out of the Virgins should be heading west to Puerto Rico and the Passage Islands rather than east to the overcrowded US and British Virgin Islands.

The major harbors in Puerto Rico are well buoyed; the smaller harbors and coves are not buoyed, so it is strictly eyeball navigation. This area is NOT WELL charted by the standard NOAA charts, as we discovered when exploring back in the early 1980s. We thought that since we were dealing with US waters and NOAA charts, they would be accurate and right up-to-date. Nothing could be further from the truth. After we had run aground several times and found many errors in the charts, we visited NOAA to report these problems—only to learn that the basic surveys for Puerto Rico and the Passage Islands had been done in the early twentieth century, right after we captured the islands from the Spaniards. Except for major harbors, the charts have not been updated since then!

As of 1993, the NOAA charts still did not have corrections for the errors I had reported. Thus, I strongly advise using Imray-Iolaire charts. They basically followed the NOAA charts but have been updated regularly. Our two months exploring the area in 1993 confirmed the accuracy of the Imray charts.

Sailing directions for the west, south, and east coasts of Puerto Rico appear in chapter 1.

The sightseeing on the island is varied, rewarding, and—with more than 3,000 miles of paved roads—convenient. To tour the interior, you can rent a car or use the excellent and inexpensive *público* system. The topography of the island varies dramatically—areas that are arid and desertlike, as well as lush mountains and rain forests. Most notable in the eastern end of the island is the 28,000-acre Caribbean National Forest (the El Yunque rain forest), with well more than 200 species of trees. In the western half of the island is Rio Camuy Cave Park, where you can take a guided tour of a fascinating network of more than a dozen spectacular caves. Many old coffee plantations up in the hills have been converted to attractive hotels—they are high enough in altitude that you'll need a sweater at night, and you're likely to find the guests gathered around a roaring wood fire.

On the south coast, be sure to visit Ponce, as the island's second city has been restored magnificently. Attractions in San Juan include the fortress of El Morro, Old San Juan, and the Plaza Las Americás shopping center (a stupendous complex that will leave a major dent in your wallet).

There are hotels and nightclubs for everyone's taste—from fancy international ones to small and unpretentious Puerto Rican establishments.

The Puerto Ricans are polite, helpful, and friendly. At times, however, language can be a problem. Members of the upper class speak English, but Spanish is the basic language among the poorer people. Usually you can find an interpreter without too much effort. Amazingly, however, you can find seemingly out-of-the-way places where everyone speaks English—such as La Parguera, on the island's southwest coast.

For many years, Puerto Rico's yachting was limited primarily to powerboating—and some pretty reckless powerboating at that. Woe betide the hapless dinghy that got in the way. Puerto Rico is still powerboat heaven, but sailing now has a very firm foothold in the island. Further, among the powerboaters, there are two distinct categories: One group roars off to the nearest beach for huge parties, while another group includes very avid and skilled sportfishermen. Some of the sportfishing boats are incredible, with outriggers that cost at least as much as a new spar for a J-24!

Yachting used to be hampered by the lack of marinas—in the early 1970s, yacht brokers had customers very willing to buy boats as long as the brokers could guarantee them a slip. But getting a boat into a slip in those days was like trying to break into the gold vaults at Fort Knox. During the 1980s and early 1990s, however, marina development exploded. Now, for instance, Ponce has 100 berths, La Parguera has 50, and Boquerón has 105. Club Nautico in San Juan is expanding from 70 to 120. The San Juan Bay Marina has 150 slips, Marina de Salinas has 80, Puerto del Rey Marina has 750, Villa Marina has 300, Isleta Marina has 265, and Marina Puerto Chico has 275. Visiting yachtsmen no longer have any problem finding slips—rather, the marinas are having trouble filling the slips they have! In addition to these, there are a number of small marinas catering to powerboats and sportfishermen.

The Puerto Ricans have joined the ocean-racing circuit with a vengeance, and the winning boats in the regattas always include some from Puerto Rico. The circuit continues all year, but the biggest events are the Don Q Regatta in late March, just before the BVI Regatta and the Rolex Regatta—forming the Caribbean Ocean Racing Triangle (CORT), a hotly contested PHRF series. A few of the best Puerto Rican sailors continue eastward after the above series to race in Antigua Sailing Week, in late April/early May.

Boardsailing has also taken Puerto Rico by storm, and many of the island's top boardsailors are of international caliber. Surfing on the north coast of Puerto Rico is excellent whenever the northwest ground swell comes in. It does this completely independent of the weather conditions, so you are likely to have a northwest ground swell together with a southeast wind—which aficionados tell me makes for perfect boardsailing.

The marine-supply situation is excellent in Puerto Rico, and there are a number of marine-supply stores in San Juan. The biggest and best is Marine Dream, a relatively new store with a tremendous inventory. Its location (in Old San Juan, across the street from the Capitol) is convenient, as it is situated over a propeller-rebuild shop and under a sailmaker's shop. They can all put you in touch with electronics technicians, diesel mechanics, or whatever other specialists you need.

The new San Juan Bay Marina, operated by Bill Bachman (from an old Puerto Rican family that has owned boats here since the late 1920s), has a 60-ton Travelift and is equipped to do most repairs. They insist that they can call in an outside contractor for anything they cannot do. Since Bachman is a third-generation Puerto Rican, he certainly knows the ropes and has the right contacts.

In the Fajardo area, you can find anything you want or need. Among the facilities are the Skipper Shop in Villa Marina, Able Marina (just north of Puerto del Rey Marina), the chandlery in Puerto del Rey, plus the independent contractors that operate out of the various boatyards along the east coast of Puerto Rico. What cannot be obtained on the island can be shipped in by courier within three or four days.

Making landfall in Puerto Rico is a relatively easy matter, since it can be spotted from great distances. A high mountain range runs the length of the island, and the well-lighted cities and towns provide ample warning for approaching mariners. The industrial complexes on the south coast are visible 30 miles at sea.

Many of the island's out-of-the-way spots are likely to be very overcrowded with day-trippers on weekends. I advise using Puerto Rico's small, secluded anchorages and coves only on weekdays. Spend your weekends in the major harbors, taking on provisions and fuel and savoring the local culture.

It is important to remember that even though Puerto Rico is a US commonwealth, it is beyond the US Customs jurisdiction, so if you are arriving from the US or the US Virgin Islands, you must go through Customs formalities. If you are arriving from anywhere else, you must check in at both Customs and Immigration. Ports of entry for yachts are San Juan, Fajardo, Ponce, Guánica, and Mayagüez, plus Ensenada Honda in Culebra and Isabel Segunda in Vieques. Boats coming to Puerto Rico from the east are advised to enter at Culebra. If you don't stop there, enter at Fajardo. Boats coming from the south should enter at Ponce or Guánica, but the latter is strictly a commercial harbor, so Ponce is better for yacht clearance. If you are coming from the west, enter at Mayagüez; Customs officials in Mayagüez do not appreciate boats going into Puerto Real or Boquerón before they have cleared in Mayagüez.

The Puerto Ricans are very strict about Customs regulations. All foreign-registered vessels must enter and clear at every major Customs port. If you do not have a cruising permit, you must go through the entire routine of Customs and Immigration at every major port. If you have obtained a cruising permit, either upon entry into Puerto Rican waters or prior to entry, you need to inform Customs and Immigration via telephone that you have arrived.

By the time you read this, regulations may well have changed again, so be sure to check before going. For relatively minor infractions of Customs laws, Puerto Rican Customs officials have been known to slap very substantial fine on yachts, particularly in Ponce.

Important note: The Puerto Rican law is very strict on guns. Not only must they be declared to Customs, but they must also be registered with the police in Puerto Rico, no matter where else they are registered.

Potential Dangers in Puerto Rican Waters

1. In Boquerón (chapter 3), Roca Velasquez has a wreck with only five feet of water over it. My old friend Augie Hollen reports that when he was there in the summer of 1992, boats were hitting it with amazing regularity.

2. Bahía de Guánica (chapter 4) has little to attract yachtsmen, and it has several hazards, among them Corona La Laja, half a mile due east of channel buoy number 4. It has only eight or nine feet of water over it and is completely surrounded by deep water, so deep-draft boats could easily come a cropper on it as they work their way eastward under sail.

3. In Bahía de Ponce (chapter 5), the water is murky around Cayo Viejo and Las Hojitas, and they are very hard to spot.

4. East of Ponce (chapter 5), there is an eight-foot spot one and one-fourth miles south of Cayo Berberia, and I have not figured any good ranges to avoid it.

5. Puerto Arroyo (chapter 5). There are numerous eight-foot spots here.

6. Approaches to Fajardo (chapter 6). If coming from the north or the northeast, Bajo Laja has less than eight feet over it, and is unbuoyed. When coming into Isleta Marina, leave C3 to port and feel your way in. Eyeball it around the end of Isleta Marina to the anchorage or dock.

7. On the north coast of Vieques (chapter 7), one and a half miles west of Punta Mulas (Isabel Segunda) and one mile north of Punta Martineau, there are seven-foot spots surrounded by 13 to 15 feet of water on the south and east and 30-plus feet of water on the west and north. Deep-draft boats, beware.

NOTES

3

West Coast of Puerto Rico

(Imray-Iolaire Charts A, A-1, A-11)

Keep in mind that many of the harbors on the west coast of Puerto Rico—Puerto Real and Boquerón are exceptions—are open to the ground swell that comes in from the northwest due to storms in the North Atlantic. (These storms have absolutely nothing to do with the local weather pattern. See *Street's Transatlantic Crossing Guide and Introduction to the Caribbean* for more information on weather patterns.) Thus, from November through April, even though you may be sheltered from the wind and the trade-wind sea, the ground swell may come rolling in from the northwest to such a degree as to make anchoring difficult, uncomfortable, and possibly dangerous. So if you are coming from the Bahamas, are tired, and are seeking peace in the lee of Puerto Rico, ascertain first whether the ground swell is running. If it is, you won't find comfort in any of the anchorages on Puerto Rico's west coast.

AGUADILLA

(II A, A-1, A-11)

In the summer, when there is no threat of a ground swell, this anchorage is fairly comfortable. However, in the ground-swell season (November through April), it is untenable for yachts.

Aguadilla is a well-preserved old Spanish town well worth exploring. Powerboats en route from the Bahamas to the Dominican Republic will put in here to fuel up alongside the steamer dock. If the anchorage is choppy, proceed southwest around Punta Higüero to Mayagüez, Puerto Real, or Boquerón.

RINCON

(II A, A-1, A-11)

Here you'll find a beautiful white-sand beach, many attractive vacation cottages, and some small restaurants and bars—a wonderful place to stop for a hearty meal. Bear in mind that the beach traces its origin to centuries of ground swell, so anchor accordingly. Make sure you anchor on the shelf, since the bottom drops off abruptly from one or two fathoms to 36. The holding on the shelf is excellent. Surfing is a major pastime of Rincón in the winter months. Even in calm weather, the waves break onshore, so care must be taken when landing in a dinghy. Basically, unless you are a surfer, Rincón is only a summer anchorage.

MAYAGÜEZ

(Chart 1; II A, A-1, A-11)

Mayagüez is the main entry port on the west coast of Puerto Rico. US-registered yachts arriving from foreign territory should be able to do their clearance officially by phone (tel. 831-3342 or 3343). Foreign yachts will have to go through full Customs procedures. If you have done this, be sure to obtain a cruising permit. If you don't, you will have to enter and clear Customs every time you move the boat. The cruising permit allows you to clear by phone, but this can be a movable feast. We had a cruising permit on *Iolaire,* and in Fajardo all they wanted to know was the name of the boat, the registration number, and the name of the owner and the skipper. In Mayagüez, on the other hand, officials insisted that I read off to them over the phone the full list of

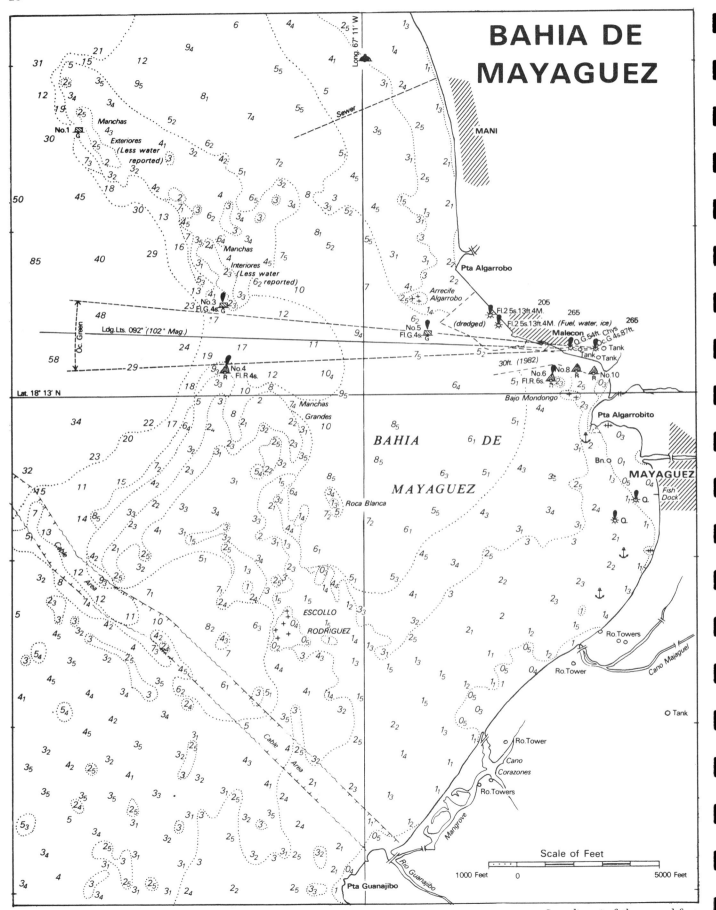

BAHIA DE MAYAGUEZ

CHART 1 Bahía de Mayagüez

Soundings in fathoms and feet

crew, along with names, birthdates, and passport numbers. So, good luck to foreign yachts!

Foreign yachts should not go into Puerto Real or Boquerón without first clearing Customs in Mayagüez.

Any yacht with firearms on board should call the police department, declare the weapons, and register them. Even though Puerto Rico is alive with guns and the number of people who legally carry them is incredibly high, there is a mandatory jail sentence of a couple of years if you have them on a boat and don't declare them (even if you have a license). Over the years, a number of yachts have been snagged on this, because Customs officials do not ask anything about guns during clearance procedures. Be forewarned!

The entrance to Mayagüez Harbor is well buoyed and well lighted, but remember that in the winter months the ground swell comes in from the northwest and will break on shoals of two and 2.5 fathoms. So follow the buoys and stay in deep water while approaching the port. On the eastern end of the main dock is a lower section where yachts can tie up for short periods to clear and to take on water and supplies. If you do this, though, be sure to place a breasting-out anchor to the south so that you can pull the boat away from the dock if the ground swell comes in. It is said on the south coast of Puerto Rico that you can always spot a yacht that has been lying alongside the Mayagüez dock, because all of the lifeline stanchions on the port side are bent inward.

All in all, it is probably best to place a bow anchor to the south and tie up stern-to. Run your water or electricity lines over the transom. You will be beam-to the wind, but if the ground swell comes in, it will be much easier to get out of there without damaging the yacht. While alongside the dock, take on water. If you draw more than six feet, I suggest you also take on fuel, as once you leave the commercial dock at Mayagüez, your fueling options will be few and far between. Salinas reportedly has seven feet alongside its dock, and the Yacht Club at Ponce has six feet. Other than those, the next possible fuel stops are on the east coast at Palmas del Mar (which allows a maximum draft of eight feet) and Puerto del Rey Marina (which has no limit on draft).

There is no fuel per se on the dock at Mayagüez, but when we talked to the crew on *Miss True,* they said they went alongside the dock in March 1993. There was a flat fee for the dockage (US$25), plus US$3 for all the water they could use. An English-speaking Puerto Rican with a pickup truck came by and asked if they needed fuel. When they said yes, he left and returned an hour later with two 55-gallon drums full of diesel fuel. He charged them US$1.30 a gallon—not a bad deal considering they drew eight feet and would have had trouble getting fuel before reaching the east coast of Puerto Rico. The same gentleman is likely to be able to obtain fuel for you if you need it.

I suggest that you anchor southwest of Punta Algarrobito, since you can row the dinghy ashore there and tie it up at the small dock just west of the fishing-club dock. (The latter was wiped out in Hurricane Hugo and has not been rebuilt.) Dinghies seem to be safe there, as the local fishermen have boats tied up here and their outboards are not locked on. Also, we met a friendly fisherman who noted that a westerly wind was blowing and insisted on towing *Iolaire's* dinghy full of groceries (plus her skipper) back to the mothership. During the early 1950s, the fisherman had sailed to the United States in a boat about the size of *Iolaire.* He had worked in tuna clippers and also spent some time as a New York taxi driver.

To stock up on cooking gas, go over by the baseball field and use the pay phone to call the taxi service (tel. 832-1154 or 1115). Ask for an English-speaking driver. The dispatcher spoke no English when we did this, and he insisted there was no English-speaking driver, but the driver who showed up (taxi number 8) knew a fair amount of English. Ask the driver to take you and your gas bottles to Tropigas, out of town to the south. They will fill them while you wait. We paid US$4 for 10 pounds. Then go to the open-air market and buy as much as you can handle. The fresh fruits and vegetables there are much less expensive and of much better quality than what you can find in the supermarket. Next go to the huge Mayagüez Mall, where you will find the Xtra Supermarket—the largest and best one I have ever seen. It has everything—peaches, pears, grapes from California, a meat counter that must be 75 yards long, with meat fresh and frozen. Obviously, if you are stocking a boat—and especially if you speak Spanish—speak to the manager, and I am sure the butchers will cut meat to order.

The yacht *Miss True* had a big freezer and an icebox that were pretty much empty when we met the crew, since they had just arrived via the Bahamas, Haiti, and Santo Domingo. I suggested they go to the supermarket and buy enough to fill their freezer to the top, as it would be the cheapest shopping and the widest selection they would find until they reached Venezuela. And the meat is even better than what's available in Venezuela.

Any boat in Venezuela heading north to the

United States or Europe should stop in Mayagüez. It should be an easy reach from any port in Venezuela. Stock up in Mayagüez and continue onward.

Once you have stored everything aboard, you can find excellent block ice at Modal's Ice, on the corner of Simon Carlos and McKinley Streets, right in town. Also, if you don't want to go to the super-supermarket, Pueblos is closer and has a good selection, even though it doesn't compare to the Xtra. Besides, the Mayagüez Mall has about every type of service and retail firm you might need, plus six different cinemas. The one thing you will not find in Mayagüez—unless you are a very good detective—is English-language magazines and newspapers (other than the tabloid trash). Keep an eye out for a Walgreen's drugstore, as it is the most likely to have English-language publications.

Mayagüez is pretty much a modern commercial Puerto Rican city—that is, it's not too attractive. But when you have beaten to windward through the Bahamas, where fresh food is scarce and expensive, the prices and selection of food available in the markets of Mayagüez will put you in seventh heaven.

In the Mayagüez area, the wind direction and velocity are somewhat different from what you can expect to encounter in the rest of Puerto Rico. You are in the easterly trade-wind belt, but the trades are drastically affected by the size and height of Puerto Rico. In periods of strong trades, you will experience the normal easterly winds, but in periods of light trades, as the land behind Mayagüez heats up, it begins to pull the cooler, over-water wind from the west. Thus, in the late morning you will encounter a westerly wind that increases during the day—to the point that at 1600 to 1700 you may find a 15-to-20-knot westerly onshore breeze and a considerable chop. Come sunset, however, the cold air will start falling down from the mountains, fighting the sea breeze, which will die out and be replaced by a light, cool, offshore breeze. This breeze will then continue through the night and into the early morning, picking up if strong trades push their way through,. In periods of weak trades, the easterly will die out and be replaced by a westerly sea breeze.

When heading south from Bahía de Mayagüez, be careful of Escollo Rodriguez, which is not only a bunch of lumps of coral but also has shoal water extending well out from the reef in both directions. Head directly for Punta Guanajibo until you are well by Escollo Rodriguez. Go southwest until you are clear of the point. Then turn south. It should be noted that the water is murky in this area; you must rely on visual bearings, the leadline, or the fathometer—eyeball navigation is not enough.

CLUB DEPORTIVO

Club Deportivo marina is covered by no charts, and I have only sailed by it, so I do not know the availability of berthing space. Gauging from the sizes of the spars, I would estimate that seven to eight feet of draft might be squeezed inside.

South of Punta Ostiónes are the shoals and offshore rocks of Cayo Fanduca, which you must pass outside. Once you are beyond them and going toward Puerto Real, head southeast, making sure you stay in at least two fathoms of water.

PUERTO REAL
(Chart 2; II A, A-1, A-11)

The only chart I have ever discovered of Puerto Real is based on a 1901 survey. However, we sailed in there in *Iolaire* in March 1993. Because of shifting winds, we sailed around and covered almost all the harbor. The best water appears to be about one-third of the way across the channel toward the entrance from the southernmost point. There we found 12 feet of water, and inside nowhere shallower than 10 or 12 feet, with mud bottom. I wonder about the one-fathom spot shown in the center of the harbor. It may be a hard piece of rock, but luckily we didn't hit it. We anchored southwest of the fishermen's piers in 10 feet of water, and we had no problems.

Puerto Real is an old town that exists for fish. I wonder, in fact, whether or not you could even buy meat here. Rosa's Dock is where the action is—depth alongside the fuel pumps is about six feet, maybe seven feet at high tide. Electricity can be rigged, and there is a pay phone that may or may not work. Facilities include a laundromat, good block ice right on the dock, and some groceries and marine supplies. The showers are not fancy, but they are free to anyone who wants to use them. Walk up the dock about 50 yards to Panderia, which the locals claim makes the best bread in all of Puerto Rico. If you arrive at 0630 or 0700, you can grab hot bread just as it comes out of the oven. Continue another 100 yards and you will find a small grocery store that stocks the essentials but little fresh fruit.

Continue up the road to a fork, where you bear left. Go about 200 yards to the fishermen's cooperative hauling facility. There's a 30-ton Travelift, but, judging from its condition, I would say it could haul 15 or 20 tons maximum. Draft is limited to six feet. Nonetheless, this is the cheapest haul anywhere in the Caribbean outside of Vene-

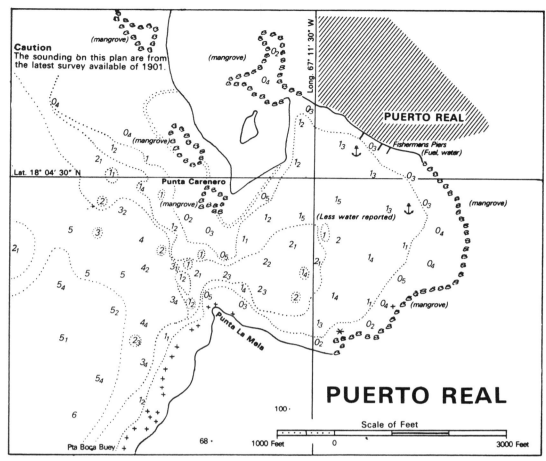

Caution
The sounding on this plan are from the latest survey available of 1901.

PUERTO REAL

Fishermens Piers (Fuel, water)

(Less water reported)

(mangrove)

PUERTO REAL

Punta Carenero

Punta La Mela

Pta Boca Buey

Long. 67° 11' 30" W
Lat. 18° 04' 30" N

100 ·
68 ·

Scale of Feet
1000 Feet   0   3000 Feet

CHART 2   Puerto Real

Soundings in fathoms and feet

zuela, and it may even be cheaper than that! You can do your own work here, or hire local labor to help out. The yard boss, Tiki, has a reputation for being able to get anything fixed by going out and finding the right subcontractors. He has done fiberglass repairs, and he will locate shipwrights, machinists, plumbers, electricians, diesel mechanics, and so on. It's no problem getting an outboard repaired, as there are 30,000 boats registered in Puerto Rico. Every one of those has an outboard engine, either on the stern or on the dinghy, so there is no scarcity of outboard mechanics. One skipper told me they hauled their boat, were out of the water for five days, and paid a total of US$120 to repair a 36-foot boat. You can't beat that!

There is no post office or bank, but you can take a *público* to Mayagüez or Cabo Rojo, or down to Boquerón. (A *público* is a private car operated like a bus that follows a set route.)

The security situation in Puerto Real has gone up and down like a yo-yo. A number of years ago, Puerto Rican yachtsmen told us it wasn't safe to leave a boat there. Then, in the late 1970s and early 1980s, yachtsmen said the Puerto Real fishermen were the most honest in the world and everything was completely safe. When Benjamin Brown (of Schafer and Brown in Boquerón) arrived on the west coast with his boat in 1990, he felt everything was so safe that you could go off and leave your boat unlocked for a day or two and not worry about a thing. Unfortunately, drugs have become available, and young people have started playing around with them. Even though the hardworking fishermen of Puerto Real earn a good living, it is not enough to support a drug habit, so when anyone gets hooked on drugs, he or she starts breaking into unoccupied houses or unattended boats.

It's no problem leaving a dinghy alongside the dock during the day, but it's wise to lock it. As long

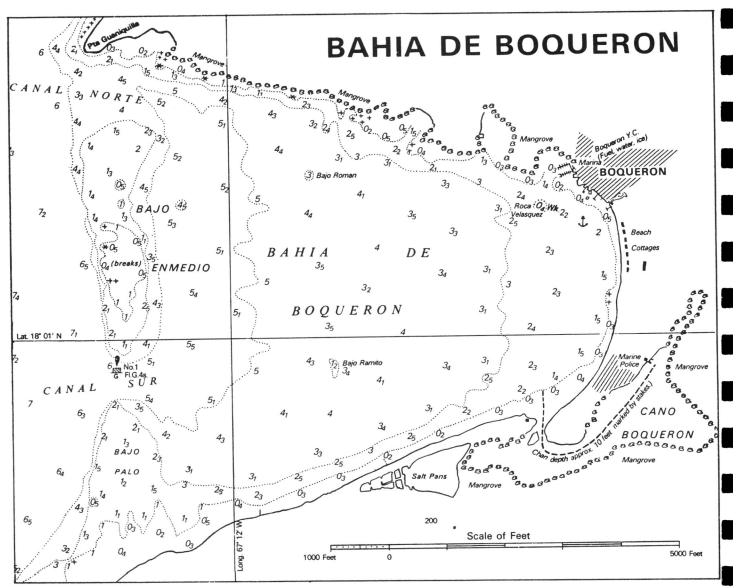

CHART 3   Bahía de Boquerón   Soundings in fathoms and feet

as people are going back and forth to your boat at night, everything should be all right. If the boat is unattended, however, it might be robbed.

BOQUERON

(Chart 3; II A, A-1, A-11)

The next bay to the south of Puerto Real has become the yachtsmen's Mecca. In 1982, there were about three yachts anchored off. In March 1993, we counted 60 boats at anchor and I was told that throughout the year there are anywhere from 40 to 60 boats anchored in Bahía de Boquerón.

The entrance to Boquerón is easy, either north or south of the shoal Bajo Enmedio. The southern entrance is marked with a buoy, but it is a matter of eyeballing the northern entrance.

The anchorage is in the northeast corner of the harbor. Where you decide to anchor will be dictated by the number of visiting yachts. Be warned, however, that Roca Velasquez, which the chart shows as having 11 feet of water over it, does not: There is a sunken wreck on top of the rock! The wreck has only five feet of water over it, and since the wreck is unbuoyed, you'll need to proceed with caution—particularly if you are trying to get to the docks at the Boquerón Yacht Club.

Fuel and water are generally available at the yacht club. About six feet of draft can be squeezed in at high tide, but check with the yacht club to make sure that fuel is actually available. Water is five cents a gallon on the honor system, but unfortunately that will probably end soon, as all too many yachtsmen are not that honest. (Are they yachtsmen or just "water people"?) These rascals have a habit of coming in at 0600 or 0700 with their water jugs, taking 20 or 30 gallons of water, and not paying for it. This may not sound like much, but when it is multiplied over a period of time, it means that the Boquerón Yacht Club is being shortchanged—literally.

Cube ice is available virtually everywhere. There are four small supermarkets with an amazing variety of food; check with the local yachties about which locations offer the best deals. In 1993, I obtained a wonderful six-page guide to Boquerón compiled by Peg Congdon of the yacht *Elizabeth*. It gives you every piece of information you might need about shoreside activities in Boquerón. Copies are available at local shops.

Cruising yachtsmen will want to know about the availability of showers. Walk across a little bridge in the south end of town to the beach cottages, where you can have a shower with unlimited fresh water for the extremely reasonable price of 25 cents.

There are no hauling facilities in Boquerón, but the supply situation is quite good. Basic necessities can be purchased at Boquerón Marine, which is run by Ivan Carlo. His wife is the office secretary and his daughter is the assistant. They carry Imray-Iolaire charts and Street guides. Adjacent to the store (which is also the local Esso station) is their outboard repair shop, which has gained an excellent reputation for good work at a reasonable price.

If you have diesel problems, contact either Ivan Carlo or Ben Brown at Schafer and Brown. Ben Brown has the training and background to take good care of yachtsmen. He was born and raised in Puerto Rico, joined the navy at 18, and ended up as a quartermaster on submarines. Later he worked for more than seven years in the electronics repair shop in the Puget Sound Naval Shipyard, after which he and his wife sailed their boat from Puget Sound to Puerto Rico. He has told me some horror stories about the passage from Panama to Puerto Rico, saying, "The less said the better; it's a trip I'd like to forget." Then first set up shop in Puerto Real but then realized that more transient yachts were pass-

ing through Boquerón, so they moved there. Ben takes care of radio and electronics repairs, watermaker repairs, and is the agent for a great many electrical suppliers. He has a fax machine and can arrange for shipments via Federal Express, DHL, and so on. In addition to all this, he maintains satellite systems for hotels in the entire area between Mayagüez and Ponce. Thus, if you have electronics problems and are not in Boquerón, you can telephone Ben at 255-2351 or use VHF channel 16 or 72. On channel 72, you can talk as long as you want, as he has a legal shoreside VHF license. His wife, Barbara, stocks Imray-Iolaire charts and Street guides.

Boquerón has a post office but no bank. For that, you have to go to Cabo Rojo by *público*, which departs from the triangle in town. Boquerón has a travel agent who can arrange car rentals, plane flights, and accommodations in the island's government-run inns known as paradores.

The VHF party line in the harbor is channel 72. There are two laundromats in town, as well as two bakeries—both reputedly good. Dinghies can be taken to the T-shaped dock by the main square. There's no need to lock them up during the day, but it's best to secure them after dark. Do not leave any trash on the dock; walk about 150 yards to the dumpsters at the far end of the plaza. You can have your gas bottle filled by taking it to Colmado Rodriguez, near the triangle; ask for directions. If you drop off the bottle before 0900, you probably can get it back the same day. Otherwise, it will be overnight service. In any case, be sure that your bottle is well marked. You can buy kerosene for the stove, as well as stove alcohol, at Ferreteria Sin Nombre at the triangle.

Restaurants in Boquerón are too numerous to mention. The plaza by the dinghy dock is the gathering area where everyone sits around outside the bars for afternoon refreshments. Roadside vendors offer oysters collected from the mangroves; the vendors will pop them open for you with amazing speed. Be wary of these, however. Having had hepatitis, and knowing the level of pollution in various parts of the Caribbean, I am a bit suspicious of these shellfish. But the locals insist that they have never heard of anyone becoming ill from Boquerón oysters. They claim the public health department regularly checks the oysters—but perhaps this is because they are worried about them.

The Puerto Ricans are much better at harvesting tree oysters than the West Indians because they pull the oysters off the branches. The West Indians, on the other hand, go in with machetes and cut off a chunk of mangrove along with the shellfish. This is particularly common in Carriacou, where two friends developed worse cases of hepatitis than I had. Evidently, during the rainy season, outhouses above the mangroves dump their waste into the mangrove swamps, with the result that the oysters there could easily consign you to the graveyard.

You can explore the lagoon behind the beach in your dinghy. If you hear a hurricane warning, this is a perfect hurricane hole. The 12-foot channel behind the mangroves is marked by stakes. Line up the stakes on a course of 190° magnetic entering the lagoon, then follow the stakes around to port, favoring the western side of the lagoon. A 12-foot channel leads up to the marine police station and the University of Puerto Rico nautical station, which keeps several powerboats here. A good person to get to know is the station's captain, German Acusta, who is familiar with every inch of the west coast, in addition to being an avid fisherman and skin diver.

A word of warning before you go into the lagoon to escape a hurricane: Be sure to read Reflections on Hugo in the Foreword to this volume. With the many yachts that are pouring into the Boquerón area, this hurricane hole could become a disaster area if too many yachts try to squeeze in. Further, Augie Hollen offers the reminder that you might escape the hurricane undamaged, but the subsequent flooding could do you in. A tremendous current comes pouring out of the lagoon after a hurricane, and it can easily break out anchors and pile yachts on top of each other. If I were in Boquerón and heard about an approaching hurricane, I would depart northward or southward 48 to 72 hours ahead of the storm. Better yet, spend the hurricane season in Venezuela.

As in so many of the more secluded anchorages in Puerto Rico, the lagoon is a great place for clamming, fishing, and birding among the mangroves.

Boquerón is an ideal base for hiring a car and exploring the towns of Mayagüez, San Germán, Maricao, and Sabana Grande. The *público* system also serves these areas, but it can be complicated to figure out. Once you understand it, though, it's an inexpensive way to get around Puerto Rico. It certainly can be entertaining, providing fascinating glimpses of island life. For an extra fee, most *público* drivers will swing off their standard routes and drop you off at a specific location.

I am told by Puerto Rican friends that San Germán and Maricao are musts for visitors to Puerto Rico. One interesting idea—especially if you have just slogged down from the Bahamas—is to leave half the crew on board and send the other half up into the hills of San Germán and Maricao to stay in one of the government-sponsored paradores. These are old coffee plantations that have been converted to guest houses. The price is low and the hospitality is superb. Instead of rocking on a boat, worrying about mosquitoes, and suffering from the heat, you are high in the hills and sleeping in a four-poster bed underneath a heavy blanket.

San Germán was the second town established in Puerto Rico, but it has been bypassed by modern commercial development, so it is extremely well preserved. Among its treasures are the seventeenth-century Porta Coeli Church and the oldest university in the Western Hemisphere. My wife, Trich, visited San Germán in 1982 and was extremely impressed.

Maricao is another wonderful old coffee town largely bypassed by development. It is in these towns—not San Juan—that you will find the real Puerto Rico. I recommend that you hire a car and drive up into the mountains, where the roads are narrow and there are dozens of switchbacks. You can drive for hours and discover that you have not gone very far. Of course, this is not for the fainthearted. You can also stop at one of the old coffee plantations and spend the night, then continue your drive the next day.

Another inland destination is Rio Camuy Cave Park, where there are miles of limestone caves filled with stalactites and stalagmites. Guides take you through the maze of caverns and underground streams.

If you want to get away from it all and still be in the shelter of Bahía de Boquerón, sail along the southern edge of the harbor and anchor halfway down to the entrance. Anchor bow-and-stern, parallel to the beach. There you will be undisturbed, sheltered from the east by the land mass of Puerto Rico and with little chance of being bothered by the northerly swell, because the harbor entrance, I am told, breaks the swell.

Again courtesy of Augie Hollen, I understand that Boquerón explodes with tourists in the summer. All the beach cottages and rental accommodations are overflowing—not to mention the sewer system. During the night, they pump out all the sewage that the purification system cannot digest, so it comes out raw. For that reason, many people do not swim in the harbor during the summer. They sail out of the harbor and down the coast to Punta Moja Casabe, where they anchor off the very pleasant beach at El Combate.

South of Boquerón, there are no all-weather anchorages, but in settled weather, one can enjoyably daysail down the coast and find some good beaches. Bahía Salinas is not a good anchorage, although the large salt factory there makes a convenient landmark. On the south side of the bay, there has long been a restaurant that many claim is itself worth the sail down from Boquerón. I began hearing reports about the food here as long ago as the 1970s. The restaurant is named Agua al Cuello, meaning "water up to the neck," which gives an idea of the shoal situation. The restaurant is in a small house off by itself at the southern end of the bight. It serves the crispest, tastiest tostones you will find in the Caribbean. (Tostones are made with green plantains smashed into thin cakes and fried until crisp. They are absolutely delicious and understandably renowned.) Anchor off, row ashore, and try the tostones. If they are still good, drop me a note.

Reference to the chart of the west coast of Puerto Rico will show the shoaling tendency of this entire shore. The combination of the currents running north-and-south and the periodic activity of the ground swell tends to move the sand around a good deal. Sandbars and shoals are likely to extend much farther to the west from the points of land than the chart indicates. Don't be put off by this, but be cautious; keep the leadline or depth sounder working and post a sharp-eyed lookout. Only the careless will run aground.

When sailing along the west coast of Puerto Rico, watch out for Arrecife Tourmaline, Escollo Negro, and Las Coronas—marked by buoys numbered 8, 6, and 4, respectively. They form a rough triangle that should be avoided at all costs. The various hurricanes that have swept across Puerto Rico have moved the shoal spots around to the degree that no chart of this area can be absolutely trusted. Stay well outside this shoal area, or hug the coast and sail along the Canal de Guanajibo which is well marked by buoys.

Islands off the West Coast of Puerto Rico

Between the Dominican Republic and the west coast of Puerto Rico are two islands owned by Puerto Rico that should be mentioned—one very briefly.

ISLA DESECHO
(II A, A-1, A-11)

This is no more than a pinnacle rock rising 700 feet out of the sea. There is no anchorage off the island and no dinghy landing; in other words, there is no possibility of getting ashore.

ISLA MONA

An oval island that is flat and roughly six miles in diameter, Mona is composed largely of limestone, with countless caves. The north and east coasts are lined with white cliffs more than 150 feet high, making landings from the sea quite impractical. The best anchorages are found off the lowland on the south and west coasts. Playa de Pájaros is the best anchorage during the winter and during settled summer weather. In a stiff blow, the entrance can become very difficult, if not downright dangerous. This spot is adequate for use by yachts of no more than 40 feet with a maximum draft of six feet.

To enter Playa de Pájaros when coming from the east, head for the lighthouse at Cabo Este, running southwest along the coast off the barrier reef until you spot a large white streak on the cliff resembling an exclamation mark without the period. The marking has been made by the Coast Guard to designate the entrance, and it is the only such mark on the cliff. Bring your vessel abeam of it, make about a 90-degree turn, and sail roughly 315° magnetic directly toward the mark. As soon as you spot a diamond-shaped wooden post on the beach, align yourself with the range made by it and the mark on the cliff. Adhere to the range closely, since there are coral heads on both sides of this channel. Having established the range, do not sail a compass course, since the current and sea will be setting you to the southwest at an appreciable rate. The channel is narrow and should be attempted only when the sun is high—and never in rough seas. Keep a lookout. Once across the main body of the reef, turn sharply toward the small pier on shore. Watch the rock off the starboard corner of the reef, round up, and anchor according to your draft. If no boats have arrived before you, you can tie up to the mooring. This is securely attached to some 40 feet of heavy chain, and the chain is attached to a large engine block. You can also tie up to the four-foot-square concrete slab with a heavy metal ring in its center. This has been put there by the Coast Guard for the workboats that used to make runs between Mona Island and Puerto Rico. When you want to leave, it is simply a matter of slipping the line from the ring and off you go. This is an extraordinarily beautiful spot, one that is highly praised as an overnight anchorage by yachtsmen bound east from the Bahamas to Puerto Rico.

The water here is crystal clear over white sand. A narrow beach runs along the shore. Nearby are a few wooden buildings belonging to the Coast Guard.

Behind the dock is a road leading to the lighthouse two miles away. If you want to make the trip to the lighthouse, start early in the morning, since the sun can become oppressively hot by midmorning. The view from the lighthouse over Mona Passage and the rest of the island is splendid.

Isla Mona is nothing short of a spelunker's paradise. Supposedly there are so many caves that you can work your way underground from one side of the island to the other. The island supports a variety of wildlife, including iguanas up to five feet long, hundreds of wild goats, and wild boars with huge, white tusks. And, at certain times of the year, the island has large populations of doves that have flown over from Hispaniola.

When leaving Playa de Pájaros, stay on the range. Put a lookout forward to watch for coral heads and another on the cabintop facing aft and giving hand signals to the helmsperson to maintain the range. If the sea begins to build up and break across the entrance, under no circumstances attempt to leave. Rather, double up your line and wait for the weather to moderate. It may get uncomfortable inside the reef, but at least it won't be dangerous.

On the south coast of Isla Mona, there is a good anchorage at Playa del Uvero for boats drawing no more than three feet. The approach through the reef must be eyeballed. The south coast is quite beautiful, with woodlands stretching all the way down to the beaches.

On the west coast, Sardiniera is primarily a summer anchorage; during northerly winter weather, it is frequently untenable. The range to guide you into the anchorage will not be apparent until you near the reef. From there, you will be able to spot some concrete houses, a partially destroyed pier, and the entrance through the reef, which is marked by two rocks, one on each side. The entrance is deep, but the anchorage itself will allow no more than six feet of draft. The bottom is hard-packed sand over a rock slab. If the sea begins to make up, get out right away, since an anchor will not hold against the surge. Ashore are four small concrete houses and the decrepit dock. No services are available in this picturesque, lonely spot.

When departing from Isla Mona for the Puerto Rican "mainland," your objective should be to avoid the heavy going in Mona Passage. The wind usually begins to blow by 0900 or 1000, picking up as the day progresses and reaching its peak about 1700. The best time to depart is late afternoon, when the wind is abating, in order to motor or sail across in less trying conditions. According to information I received from Dr. Jack Sheppard of *Arieto*, Mona Passage has a deservedly bad reputation. Boats bound east for Puerto Rico will be dead against the wind. The current flows northwest through this passage at a rate alternately reinforced and diminished by the tide. Puerto Rican yachtsmen recommend holding south of the rhumb line, since the current usually will push you northward at a rate greater than the half knot listed on the chart. The west coast of Puerto Rico is well lighted, so it should be no problem to approach at night across this passage. As long as the ground swell is not running, it is feasible to anchor anywhere along the southwest corner and to wait until dawn before making a final approach.

NOTES

NOTES

4

Southwest Coast of Puerto Rico

(Imray-Iolaire Charts A, A-1, A-11, A-12)

Puerto Rico is such a large land mass that it creates its own land and sea breezes. As the sun sets, the cold air begins to fall down from the mountains and creates a breeze off the land. On the east coast of Puerto Rico in the winter, even the hard easterly trade wind dies off, so that by late in the evening or early in the morning, the wind is blowing *west* on the *east* coast. On the south coast, the trades are overcome even sooner, so that by 1800 or 1900, the wind is blowing from the *north*—an offshore breeze along the south coast. On the west coast, it merely diminishes and becomes cool, but the breeze continues out of the east.

If you choose to stay close inshore during the night on the southwest and south coasts, you will frequently carry a north wind all night and into the early hours of morning. As the trades pick up in the morning, they are still influenced by the north wind, so that close inshore the wind is from the northeast rather than from the east.

By making use of the land-and-sea breeze on the entire south coast of Puerto Rico, you can work eastward much more easily than on the north coast.

As the land heats up, it will start sucking the wind in from the cooler sea, so it will shift to the east, then often to the southeast. As you get headed on port tack, it's time to tack back inshore, and sometimes the trades will go to the southeast as the land heats up. If they do, this will allow you to take very long boards along the shore.

Remember, though, that as all this happens, the wind velocity will increase—15 knots at 1200, 20 knots by 1400, and 25 knots by 1600. By 1900, you will find flat calm or a light northerly. Thus, it is well worthwhile to leave before dawn, have breakfast underway, reach the next harbor by noon, and anchor before it really starts blowing.

In the spring of 1993, *Iolaire* worked her way along the south coast by taking advantage of the above-mentioned wind shifts. We anchored by noon and were amused each evening as we overheard crews on boats that left their anchorages at 0900 and arrived at 1700 very battered and bruised and talking about the gale they had just weathered. So start EARLY.

The best plan is to start in the evening or *early* morning; around noon, when the trades are starting up against you, duck into a cove and wait, lie about, swim, snorkel, or fish until the wind again goes around to the north. Or anchor for the night and head out again early the next morning.

CABO ROJO
(Chart 4; II A, A-1, A-11)

Judging from the chart, the cove east of the light on Cabo Rojo, in the southwest corner of the island, appears to be excellent. However, I have been told that it is not at all good and should be avoided. The same holds true of Bahía Sucia.

Proceeding eastward from Cabo Rojo, it is essential to be cautious. The yellow bluffs east of Punta Molino should be read as a danger signal. Just before the place where they end and the mangrove begins is a group of houses known as La Pitahaya.

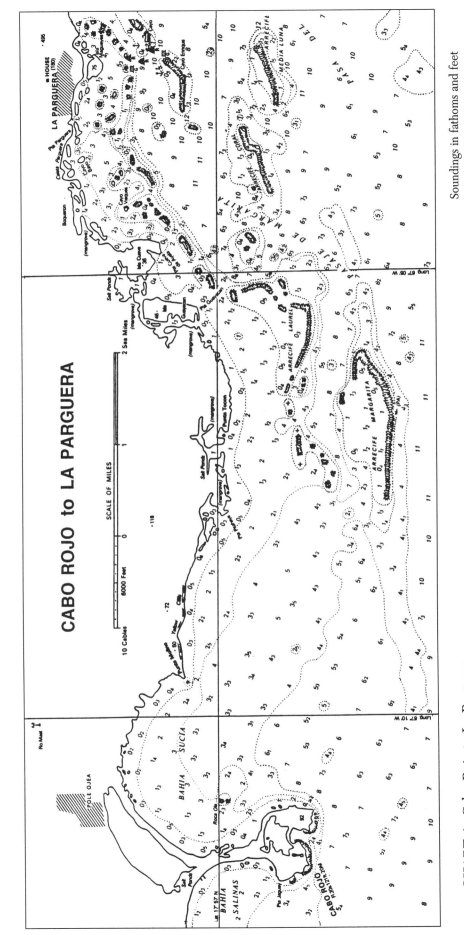

30

CHART 4   Cabo Rojo to La Parguera

Soundings in fathoms and feet

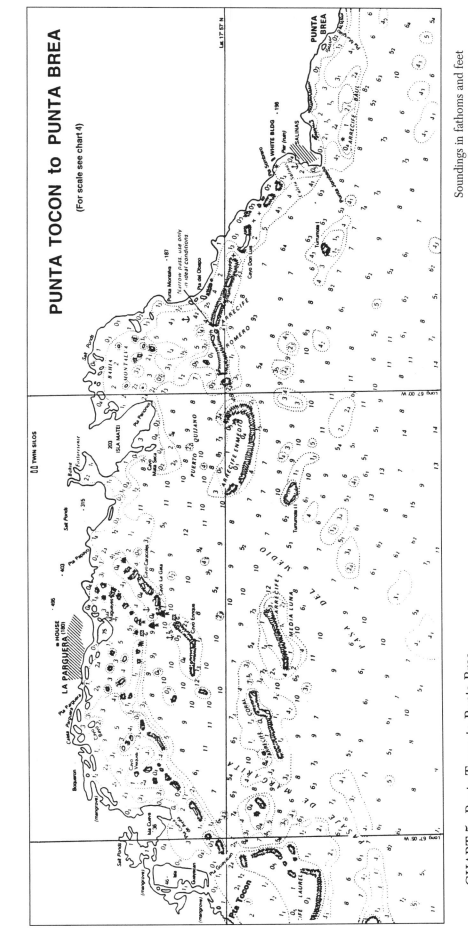

Soundings in fathoms and feet

CHART 5 Punta Tocon to Punta Brea

These are almost due north of the western end of Arrecife Margarita (*arrecife* is "reef" in Spanish). Here you must decide whether to leave the reef to port or starboard. The outside route is safer but rougher. Inside, the water will be calm, but you must proceed with the greatest caution. I recommend standing inshore to get into the smooth water provided by Arrecife Margarita and Arrecife Laurel. (See chapter 1 for sailing directions along this coast.)

Arrecife Laurel varies in height from a few feet to as much as six feet above water level. It breaks the sea completely, and the eyeball navigator can work in behind the reef and anchor in total safety and comfort. The only wind that could disturb you would be a hard westerly, which occurs very seldom.

Once through the gap at the north end of Arrecife Laurel, you can short-tack up in the blue water until you pick up the main channel buoy. Then you have several choices. You can anchor anywhere between Cayo La Gata and the islands northeast of Cayo La Gata and Cayo Caracoles. That area is sheltered from all directions.

If you want to get closer to town, you can sail through the gap to the inner harbor; there is enough water, but be careful. Do this only in good light, as there are numerous unmarked shoals. Anchor anywhere, or head for the marine biological research station on Isla Magueyes. Keep close aboard this large island, sail westward close aboard the next two cays, then round up and anchor right off the hotel in 10 feet of water. This is a great anchorage, and very convenient—except on weekends, when you will be buzzed continuously by outboards, Jet-skis, and other noisy craft.

When doing this operation, however, be sure to keep your eyes open in the area near the mangrove islands. A hundred yards to the southwest of the islands is a coral shoal marked with a stake, plus an unmarked six-foot spot known to the locals as the "booby trap."

LA PARGUERA

(Charts 4, 5; II A, A-1, A-11)

Because of the scale of the charts, it is impossible to show all the shoals and coral heads in the white area in the vicinity of La Parguera, so it is strictly a matter of eyeball navigation. If you are good at eyeballing, it is possible, with a boat drawing six feet or less, to enter behind the islands in the gaps east of Arrecife Laurel. The first two gaps approaching from seaward would be very difficult; forget about them. The third gap due south of Cayo Vieques is

the widest, clearest, and deepest, but once inside the white area on the chart, proceed with caution. Do not take a boat drawing more than five feet inside the mangrove cays, or you will be parked with great regularity.

The village of La Parguera does not look like much, but it is interesting. There are a number of small restaurants and a couple of small hotels that make up in hospitality for what they lack in style. It is not unusual to encounter there a yachtsman who was heading for the Virgin Islands, reached the La Parguera area, and is still there a couple of years later.

La Parguera is very much the weekend colony of Puerto Rico; it is absolutely flooded on weekends. I recommend that if you arrive in La Parguera on Friday, head for one of the outer anchorages, and stay there until Monday. Almost everyone in La Parguera speaks English—in sharp contrast to Mayagüez, where we found almost no English spoken. There was very little English spoken in Puerto Real, and a little more in Boquerón.

La Parguera has a small supermarket, a laundromat, and numerous bars, in addition to the hotels and restaurants. Gas and diesel are available at the fuel dock at the western end of town, but depth alongside is only four and a half feet. If the fuel dock appears closed down when you arrive, look behind the shack, where you are likely to find the proprietor relaxing in his hammock. Water is free, but the pressure is so low that it takes all day to collect it.

Cube ice is available everywhere, but there is no bank or post office (both are in Lajas, a 15-minute *público* trip away). At the dock in the main square are bins for dumping trash.

If you want to visit the outer anchorages for snorkeling or diving and your dinghy is not up to the trip, the best idea is to rent one of the local boats for US$12 an hour (including gas). These are good, heavy dinghies with brand-new outboards. We chartered one for three hours and were able to do a tremendous amount of exploration we would not have been able to do in the deep-draft, engineless *Iolaire*.

Via *público,* you can also visit Maricao, the old coffee center high in the hills (described in chapter 3). La Parguera is a very good base from which to explore the southwest corner of Puerto Rico.

There are numerous wonderful anchorages in the La Parguera area—as long as you are good at eyeball navigation and have a boat that draws six feet or less. These beautiful, windswept anchorages are protected by reefs or land on all sides, so a secure anchorage can be had in all normal conditions. West of

La Parguera, near Arrecife Margarita, an anchorage can be had anywhere on the shelf. This also is true for the northeast corner of Arrecife Laurel and the northwest corner of Arrecife Enmedio. In each instance, ease your way in very slowly, as the bottom comes up from 50 feet to nine feet in a couple of boatlengths, then slowly shoals to five feet. When you are far enough in to run aground, drop your anchor and back her down. Make sure your anchor is really well set, then take out the dinghy and set an anchor in a Y well to the north. I recommend this because if you drag the least bit, you will be trying to get your anchor to hold on the back side of a slope, which is impossible. The anchor off to the north will keep you from swinging around on your main anchor if the wind dies during the night and a northerly comes in. These anchorages are all quiet— far from the regular haunts of the powerboats and Jet-skis.

Below are three detours along the route between La Parguera and Punta Brea.

PHOSPHORESCENT BAY (BAHIA FOSFORESENTE)

(Charts 5, 6; II A, A-1, A-11)

This is the bay northeast of Isla Matei—seven feet of water over a mud bottom. It is considered one of the most brilliant phosphorescent bays in the Western Hemisphere—second only to the Golfo de Santa Fe on the coast of Venezuela.

The best way to visit the Phosphorescent Bay is to take the dinghy into La Parguera and board the tourist launch that goes to the bay. Be sure to go on a night when there is no moon, because moonlight destroys it all.

PUERTO QUIJANO/BAHIA MONTALVA

(Charts 5, 6; II A, A-1, A-11)

These bays, lying east of La Parguera, are completely accessible to the average yacht by using eyeball navigation. With care, you can work your way three miles eastward from La Parguera completely in the shelter of the reef; how far east you go depends on your skill and your guts. If you have a shoal-draft boat (six feet or less) and want to go as far as Arrecife Romero, you can enter the ocean just west of Cayo Don Luis. Or anchor behind any one of the reefs forming the south side of the bay. You will find yourself with plenty of breeze and com-

pletely undisturbed by other yachts. Needless to say, when anchoring here, remember that the wind will shift and come off the land at night.

The distinctive house on the 180-foot hill behind La Parguera forms an excellent landmark. Take bearings on this house and on the conspicuous white building at Caleta Salinas, and you will be able to fix your position accurately.

CALETA SALINAS

(Charts 5, 6; II A, A-1, A-11)

A tolerable anchorage can be had in Caleta Salinas. Work your way inshore until the point south of the bay bears 185° magnetic, drop your hook in 12 feet of water, then moor bow-and-stern facing south. Hobbyhorsing up and down is preferable to lying with only one hook and rolling all night long.

This bay is easily spotted from afar by the large white building on the beach. The town is not much—merely a village—but it has a nice white-sand beach; it is an excellent rest stop before beating your way farther east.

When leaving this harbor, be particularly careful of the tidal current. (See the chapter on tides in *Street's Transatlantic Crossing Guide and Introduction to the Caribbean.*) We discovered that with springtides, we were set very quickly to the east and had to alter course well to the west to clear Punta Jorobado.

If beating westward at night, en route to Caleta Salinas, be sure to stand well offshore to clear Arrecife Baul. When the sun is high, or when you are headed east under power, you can go inside Arrecife Baul, but I would be very loath to do this unless conditions were ideal.

BAHIA DE GUANICA

(Chart 7; II A, A-1, A-11, A-12)

This bay is easily entered through the buoyed channel, but I don't see much to recommend stopping here unless you need it as a hurricane hole. (Even in that situation, be sure to read Reflections on Hugo in the Foreword to this volume.) The bottom is mud, which is good holding, but there are no yachts to speak of.

Corona La Laja, half a mile due east of channel buoy number 4 has only eight or nine feet of water over it and is completely surrounded by deep water, so deep-draft boats beware.

The lighthouse on the cliff on the eastern side of

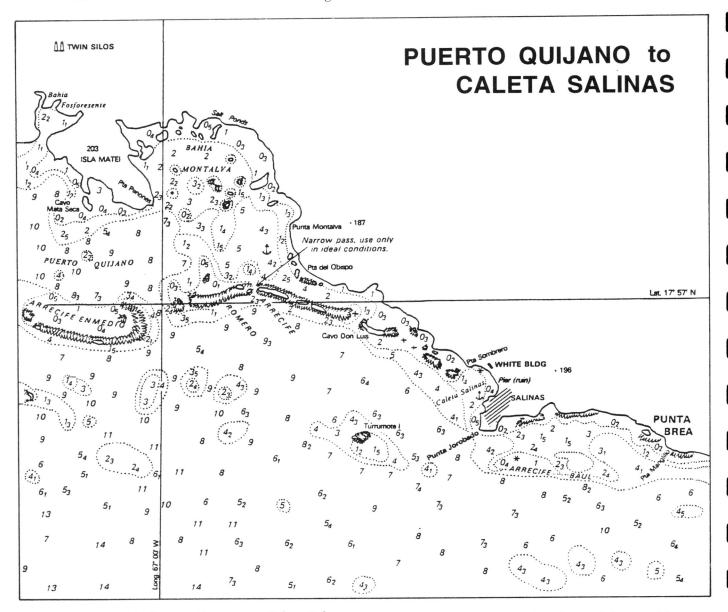

CHART 6   Puerto Quijano to Caleta Salinas   Soundings in fathoms and feet

the entrance is visible for eight miles. There is no need to worry about the cable across the entrance—there is a full 150 feet underneath. Stand due north beyond the commercial pier, keeping your leadline or depth sounder working all the while, since the water is not clear enough to eyeball. As soon as the bottom starts shoaling, anchor in nine or 10 feet. On a mud bottom, it is best to use a heavy plow on chain—certainly more effective than a light Danforth. The shoal water extends well offshore of Playa de Guánica. Do not venture into the northwest arm of the bay, since this is the commercial sector.

A dinghy can be taken ashore to the north end of the harbor, and from there a taxi will take you into town, where you can buy supplies. If you walk the half mile to the hill east of the harbor, you will find an abandoned fort in excellent repair. It commands an impressive view of the area; take your camera. Guánica holds a place in American history as the location of the first landing of American troops in the Spanish-American War.

When sailing out of Guánica, keep in mind that the easterly wind hooks around the high land on the eastern side of the harbor and blows from the

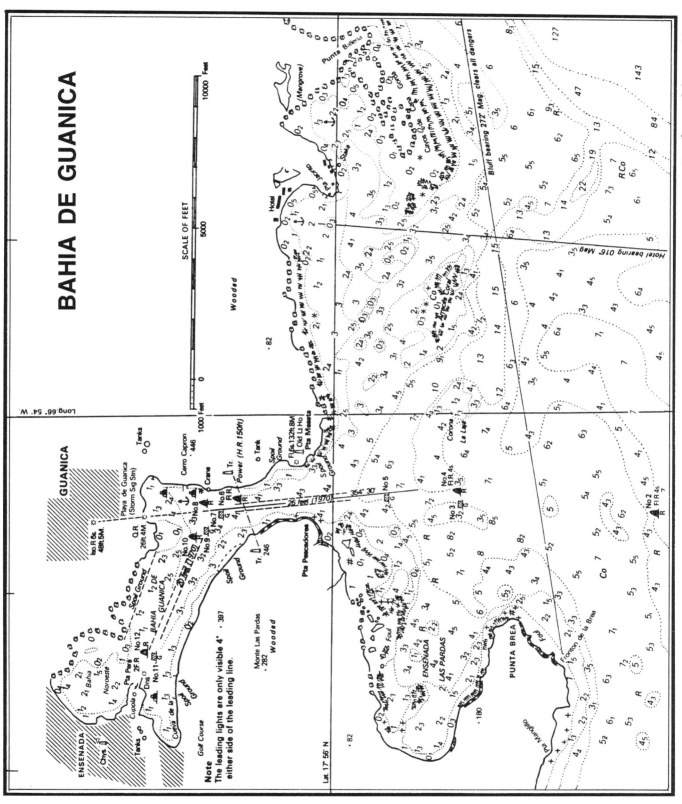

BAHIA DE GUANICA

SCALE OF FEET

Feet

5000

0

1000 Feet

10000 Feet

Long. 66° 54′ W.

Lat. 17° 56′ N

Note

The leading lights are only visible 4°
either side of the leading line.

Soundings in fathoms and feet

CHART 7   Bahía de Guánica

south, so you will be short-tacking out of the channel.

East of Guánica is a rather attractive anchorage on both sides of Punta Jacinto. The western anchorage off the hotel is fine, and sheltered in all normal conditions, but it is a little rocky and rolly. Even with her mizzen up and despite her heavy displacement, *Iolaire* still managed to roll here (although not badly). A modern light-displacement boat might be rather uncomfortable. However, east of Punta Jacinto and north of Cayos de Caña Gorda is a superb anchorage that is completely sheltered, so you won't roll.

There are two ways to enter these anchorages: (1) You can come directly from the west, favoring the shore, as there are a number of coral heads offshore. This should be attempted only by experienced reef navigators and only when the light is good. (2) The easier entrance is to sail east outside the reefs until the westernmost building of the hotel (the peak-roofed bar) bears 020° magnetic. Then run in on this line of bearing. There are breaking reefs on either side, but as you pass the eastern reef, there is a shoal that does not break just west of this line of bearing. Eyeball navigation is necessary. As you approach, either head up or bear off, as the bearing leads over a three-foot spot (we were unable to find it last time we were there). Anchor off the hotel in two fathoms, with the dock for the launches to the beaches at Cayos de Caña Gorda bearing approximately due east.

The Copamarina Beach Resort has recently been redone, and it has all the amenities—bar, restaurant, tennis courts, swimming pool, and so forth. The management is very friendly to yachtsmen and encourages use of its facilties. Introduce yourself at the manager's office. It is an excellent hotel, but a bit on the expensive side. Landing a dinghy there can be rather difficult, because the water is only two feet deep for 50 yards offshore. Instead of trying to haul your dinghy onto the beach, it is easier to carry a dinghy anchor, drop it in 30 or 40 feet offshore, and wade ashore. The hotel has just obtained permission to build a 275-foot dock, which will extend into seven and a half feet of water. The management plans to have water, ice, showers, and cold drinks available at the end of the dock.

On the eastern side of the harbor are the launches that shuttle back and forth to Cayos de Caña Gorda. At the head of the island's dock is Gilligan's Island— a restaurant and bar with a pool table, ice, and 25-cent showers. (The bar serves a good piña colada.) Cayos de Caña Gorda is inundated on weekends with day-trippers, and sometimes even on weekdays, but this is all during the daytime. You can have the place completely to yourself in the mornings and evenings. The dock is on the western end of the main cay; on the eastern end of the main cay is a very nice little beach that is accessible with a boat drawing six feet. Be careful, however.

The old Imray-Iolaire charts are wrong; hurricanes and storms have scoured out deep channels in the easternmost mangrove cays. If you are careful, you can carry nine feet through the easternmost channel. The water is absolutely crystal-clear. Stick your bow up on shore, bury the anchor, run out a stern anchor, and you will be in a bugless, wind-swept, reef-protected anchorage with crystal-clear water and white-sand bottom. What more could you want? You are far enough away from the day-trippers so you won't be disturbed, and if someone has beaten you into this channel, all is not lost. Between the main cay and the first small cay to the west of the main cay, there is a six-foot channel similar to the one mentioned above.

Be sure to keep in mind that when entering and leaving the anchorage, the best range is 020° magnetic on the peak-roofed building on the western end of the hotel. Proceed with caution lest you hit the charted three-foot spot 300 yards west of Punta Jacinto. Even though we haven't been able to locate it, it could be solid coral head.

BAHIA DE GUAYANILLA
(Chart 8; II A, A-1, A-12)

This is a major commercial port, a fueling station with smokestacks spilling pollution into the air. Obviously, the anchorage is to be avoided by yachts, although it could be entered day or night in an emergency. At night, the burnoff from the refinery illuminates a wide area that appears as a beautiful— if somewhat ghastly—landmark 30 or 40 miles to the south.

When sailing toward Guayanilla from the west in 1993, short-tacking along the shore, we discovered some interesting features. As we came in on Punta Verraco, we saw a distinctive and intriguing natural bridge that was probably 70 feet high. We tacked close inshore, then tacked back behind Arrecife Guayanilla and spotted a sand island about three feet high. The light conditions were not good, it was blowing hard, and we did not have time to stop, but we were convinced that a yacht could work its way up behind Arrecife Guayanilla's sand island and anchor. Further, after looking at the chart (unfortunately, the detailed insert on the old Imray-Iolaire

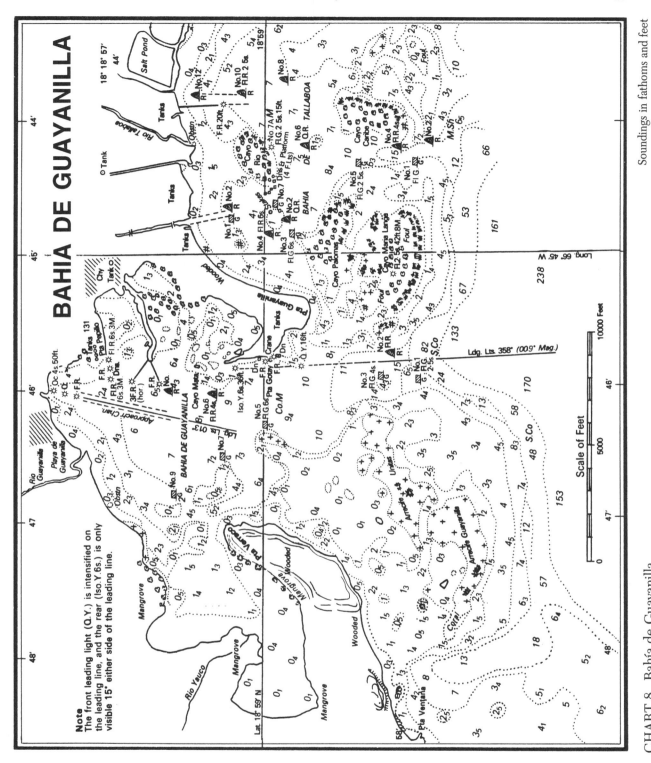

BAHÍA DE GUAYANILLA

Note
The front leading light (Q.Y.) is intensified on the leading line, and the rear (Iso.Y.6s.) is only visible 15° either side of the leading line.

Soundings in fathoms and feet

Ldg. Lts. 358° (009° Mag.)

Scale of Feet

CHART 8 Bahía de Guayanilla

chart does not go far enough west to show the western entrance of Arrecife Guayanilla), we were pretty convinced that you could eyeball your way inside Arrecife Guayanilla and anchor between Arrecife Guayanilla and Arrecife Unitas. (The US chart shows a deepwater channel between the two reefs, but I would not consider running down into a channel that is this tight. Besides, the US charts of Puerto Rico are based on surveys done between 1901 and 1911. Only the major harbor areas have been updated since then.) I think you could work your way up from the west or sail in the main entrance channel, turn west around port-hand buoy number 5, and run west and then southwest inside Arrecife Unitas. Once inside the reef, you probably will find a fantastic anchorage. The water is crystal-clear; the reef is to windward and would break any swell; and the land to leeward has no roads on it. You would be guaranteed perfect solitude. (By the time you read this, the Imray-Iolaire chart will be revised to show this area.)

NOTES

NOTES

5

Ponce to Puerto Patillas (South Coast)

(Imray-Iolaire Charts A, A-1, A-12, A-13)

PONCE

(Chart 9; II A, A-1, A-12)

Ponce is Puerto Rico's second city. In the days when sugar was king, it rivaled San Juan in both wealth and culture. However, as sugar ceased being the backbone of the island's economy, Ponce declined dramatically. Since the early 1980s, however, Ponce has seen a rebirth, and the economy has rebounded.

When coming from the west, especially if it is blowing hard, a good eyeball navigator can pass inside Cayos de Ratones and Punta Arenas. Favor the inside ("mainland") side of the passage. *Iolaire* sailed through this passage in March 1993 and found 11 feet of water in the entire stretch—much to the amazement of the local yachtsmen, who did not think there was that much water there. A daytime anchorage can certainly be had in settled conditions behind Punta Arenas or Cayos de Ratones. In both cases, you will find uninhabited sand islands that are not frequented by any day-trippers.

As you work eastward toward the Ponce Yacht Club, take bearings carefully and make sure you do not hit Cayo Viejo or Las Hojitas. These shoals are hard to spot, as the visibility in the harbor is none too good. Take careful bearings on the large crane in the commercial harbor.

If you are beating to windward and coming from outside these islands, a bearing of 071° magnetic on the big container crane, if you can lay it, will lead you to windward of Cayo Viejo and Las Hojitas and to leeward of Isla de Cardona. If you cannot lay this course or if the visibility is poor, I recommend that you stay outside Isla de Cardona and proceed to the main ship range that passes eastward of buoy number 5, and stay in very deep water.

The basin of the Ponce Yacht Club is sheltered in all weather, although it can be very windy in the afternoon when the sea breeze picks up. Remember that after sunset, the sea breeze probably will die out; the wind will come in light out of the north, so anchor accordingly. Further, I advise anchoring as far east as possible, but stay clear of the permanent moorings. There used to be a fish factory here with an awful stench, and even though that has gone, there is still an aroma in the area. If you are anchored east of it, you are safely to windward of it.

The anchorage is sheltered in all weather and the bottom is mud. The holding is not all that good, as we found out during our 1993 cruise. Our anchor dragged in the usual 25-knot evening blow. When anchoring, make sure you do not anchor in a way that will foul permanent moorings.

The dock on the north side of the channel is mainly used for promenades and as a berth for a ferry that operates only on weekends, carrying day-trippers back and forth to Isla Caja de Muertos.

If you are a foreign-registered yacht that must clear Customs at every official port of entry, be sure to do so here. The US Customs officials in Ponce have been extremely strict on enforcing the letter of the law on all yachts. If you complain to Puerto Rican yachtsmen about the treatment of yachtsmen by Customs and Immigration officials, they point out that they are treated even worse because they speak Spanish. So be forewarned—do everything legally and by the book.

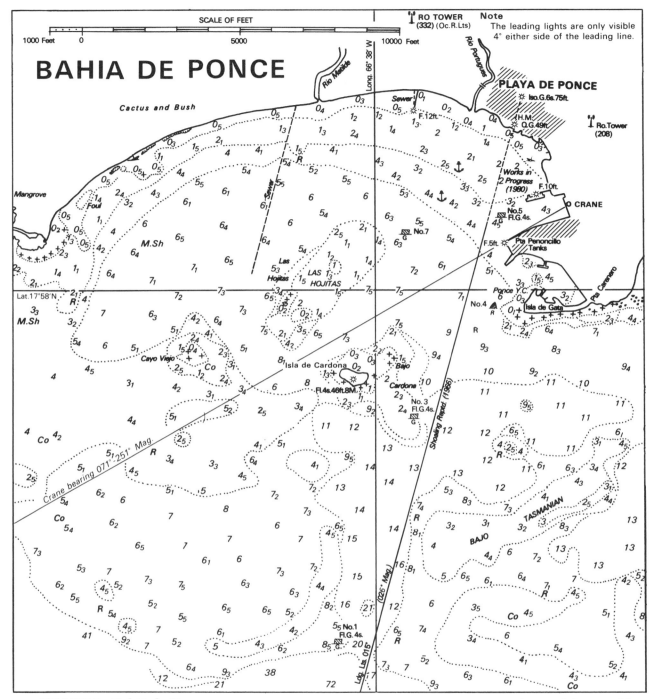

CHART 9   Bahiá de Ponce

Soundings in fathoms and feet

Anchor north of the Ponce Yacht Club and then check in with the management of the club to arrange a guest card. (Be sure you are carrying your membership card from your home yacht club.) At the yacht club, pick up the guide to Ponce, which lists activities of interest to visiting yachtsmen. Prepared by club members, this guide is so complete

that I see no need to go into great detail about what you should see and do. It's all in their book!

Call a taxi (the club will give you the number) and go to the main plaza, where you will find banks, shops, a magnificently restored nineteenth-century firehouse, and the cathedral. Just across from the cathedral is Casa Armstrong-Poventud, which houses the tourist office and a museum of Puerto Rican culture. Even if the museum is closed, walk in the side door, turn left, and go up the stairs. At the top, turn right and then left to find the tourist office. There you can collect a large stack of brochures on all of the attractions in Ponce and the surrounding area.

Down in the plaza, trolley-buses offer free tours of the center of Ponce. The tours last 20 to 50 minutes, depending on the traffic situation.

On your way into town, not far from the yacht club, you will have passed the Cash and Carry market. Just across the road is the Ponce Marine Center, which carries basics but not a wide array of marine items.

Some marine supplies are also available in the chandlery at the Ponce Yacht Club. Other facilities at the hospitable club include showers, a swimming pool, a restaurant/bar, and a 30-ton Travelift. The lift can handle six-foot draft with no problem, but if you have more than seven feet, forget it. Once hauled, it's a do-it-yourself situation; there is no yard contractor. Fuel and water are available alongside the dock, but the depth at the fuel dock is only six feet. For water, anchor out, run stern lines, and connect two or three hoses together.

Ponce is an excellent place to stock up on food and cooking supplies. There is a covered open-air market, you can have your gas bottles filled, and block ice is available. There is a laundry in town, and the above-mentioned yacht club guide lists where you can obtain electrical supplies, diesel and outboard engines and repairs, and more. Ben Brown of Schafer and Brown in Boquerón usually ends up in Ponce about once a week, so you can contact him to work on your electronics. You can leave your dinghy at the new dock owned by the fishermen's cooperative and then take a *público* to anywhere you want to go.

If you must go to San Juan, the *público* costs only US$12 and takes two hours. At that price, why rent a car? You can sit back and enjoy the magnificent mountain views because you are not doing the driving.

ISLA CAJA DE MUERTOS

(Chart 10; II A, A-1, A-12)

Seven miles southeast of Ponce, this is a popular weekend destination for members of the Ponce Yacht Club. It was formerly owned by the Wirshing family; the late Tito Wirshing was the generous host of some of the most spectacular yachting parties ever to shake the islands. He claimed never to understand how those giant Americans could collapse into such wet rags after a few hours of rum punch. The ability of Puerto Ricans to consume the island rums in unlimited quantities with no apparent effect is a wonder to behold. I can only prescribe a hearty meal of milk and cream cheese to anyone en route to a Puerto Rican outing. Isla Caja de Muertos ("Coffin Island") was presented to the Ponce Yacht Club as a tribute to the irrepressible Tito Wirshing. The island is now owned by the Puerto Rican Parks Department, which runs large ferries out there every weekend. I recommend avoiding the island on weekends, as it is inundated with day-trippers. Visit during the week, when the island is deserted.

On the lee side of the island, near the smaller of the two promontories, is an old pier where you can tie a stern line, anchoring the bow in deep water. This would appear to be the ideal anchorage, but an experienced yachtsman told me that a better one is roughly west to northwest of the lighthouse; anchor bow-and-stern, facing northeast. The beach is not as good there, but there is much less roll, so the anchorage is more comfortable. A path leads up to the lighthouse and a commanding view of the whole south coast of Puerto Rico.

CAYO BERBERIA

(II A, A-1, A-12)

In settled conditions, a good anchorage can be found west of the cay off the mangrove-lined beach. The reef on the eastern shore is prime for shelling and diving.

PLAYA DE SANTA ISABEL

(Chart 11; II A, A-1, A-12)

Except in settled conditions, this is not a particularly good anchorage, but some of the shoal-draft boats that really know the area squeeze in behind the mangroves east of the jetty, anchoring in four or five feet of water for perfect shelter in all weather. A new dock and restaurant, the Aquarium, has been established here.

Inside Cayos Cabezazos, there is reputed to be a narrow, deepwater channel, but there are no ranges. The channel supposedly is roughly U-shaped—running southeast, east, and then northeast. I have never been through this passage, but Fred Long, who is in the salvage business in Puerto Rico, insists that it no longer exists. Yet I have spoken with other experienced yachtsmen who maintain that it does exist. I would not enter this channel without having sounded it first with a dinghy. If you do it, please write to me about it.

BAHIA DE RINCON

(Chart 11; II A, A-1, A-12)

There are several reefs through here, so this is a good place for a daytime anchorage and for swimming and snorkeling in good weather. Do not spend the night. The best anchorage is northwest of Arrecife Media Luna ("Half-Moon Reef"), where there is an excellent beach with lots of shells.

PLAYA DE SALINAS

(Chart 12; II A, A-1, A-12)

Playa de Salinas has become a very popular yachting stop, as the harbor is sheltered in all weather.

Entrance is from the south; our fathometer found 10 feet all the way in, but because of the state of the tide, I would not take anything drawing more than eight feet into this harbor without first sending in a dinghy. If you run aground, however, it is very soft mud, so you will be able to back off.

The Marina de Salinas has fuel, water, and electricity; the outer docks have eight feet of water, but the fuel dock only has a guaranteed six feet. People report that boats drawing eight feet have managed to get in, but I can't imagine how. Dockage is US$10 per boat, which entitles you to unlimited use of hot showers, a 20 percent discount in the bar and restaurant, and use of the swimming pool. Not a bad deal. The marina also has a small chandlery.

If you are anchoring out, do not get too close to the eastern side of the harbor; there is a very noisy nightclub that is likely to play its music at full volume until the early hours of the morning.

In the gap between Punta Salinas and Cayo Mata are a couple of small, mangrove-covered islands with beautiful white-sand beaches. These are great places

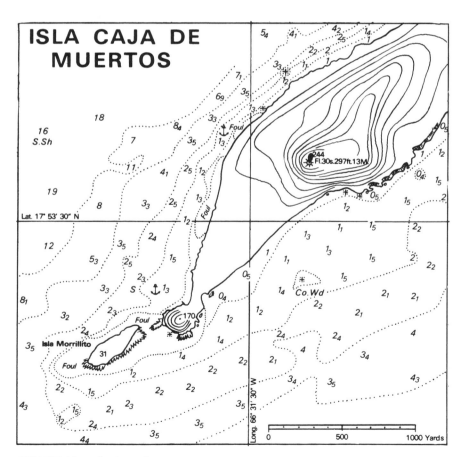

CHART 10 Isla Caja de Muertos   Soundings in fathoms and feet

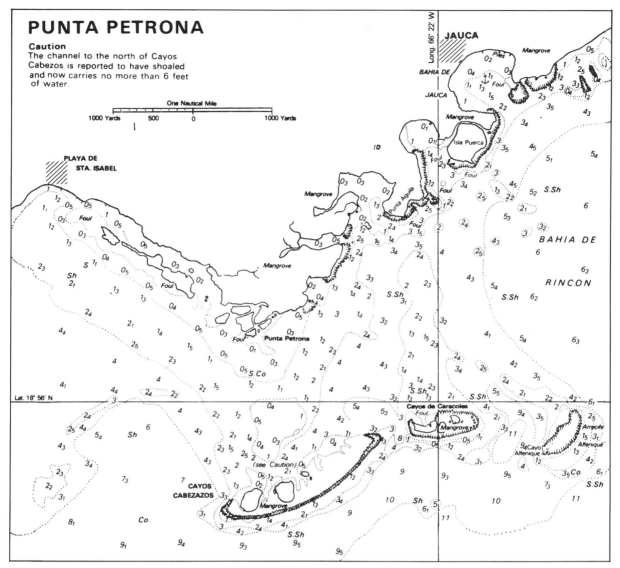

CHART 11   Punta Petrona

Soundings in fathoms and feet

to bask in the sun, but they are not particularly good for swimming, as the bottom is mixed sand and grass, with sea urchins lurking in the grass.

The town of Salinas is a mile from the marina. Walk or borrow a bike, or hitch. In town you will find a good supermarket, post office, and banks, plus taxis, *públicos,* and buses to everywhere.

On our last visit, we saw two of the local 20-foot racing sloops hauled up near a waterfront bar. Called *Chalanas,* they are real racing machines, rather like a Star, with a thin keel, hard chine, and a big modern rig. Apparently they race on certain holidays on the south coast. One yachtsman told of being up in Puerto Patillas on a weekend when they

were racing. They used him as a turning mark. He said there were about 15 boats, and the races were hotly contested.

Another interesting thing we discovered was that the small boys in Salinas build beautiful sailing models about 18 inches long. Extremely modern in design, they look like the naval architect's dream of the IMS round-the-world racer, complete with what looks like the bulb-shaped Scheel keel. It seems that the local kids have been building and racing these boats for years. This was all very interesting to me, because the only other place I have seen this phenomenon—young boys building and racing topnotch sailing models—is in Bequia, 500 miles away. Salinas

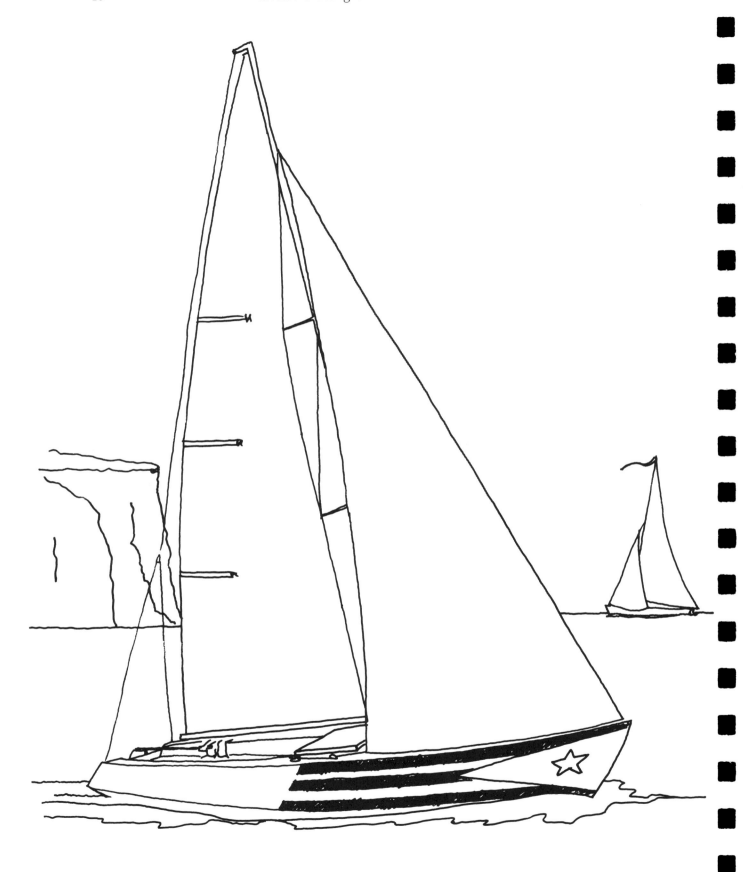

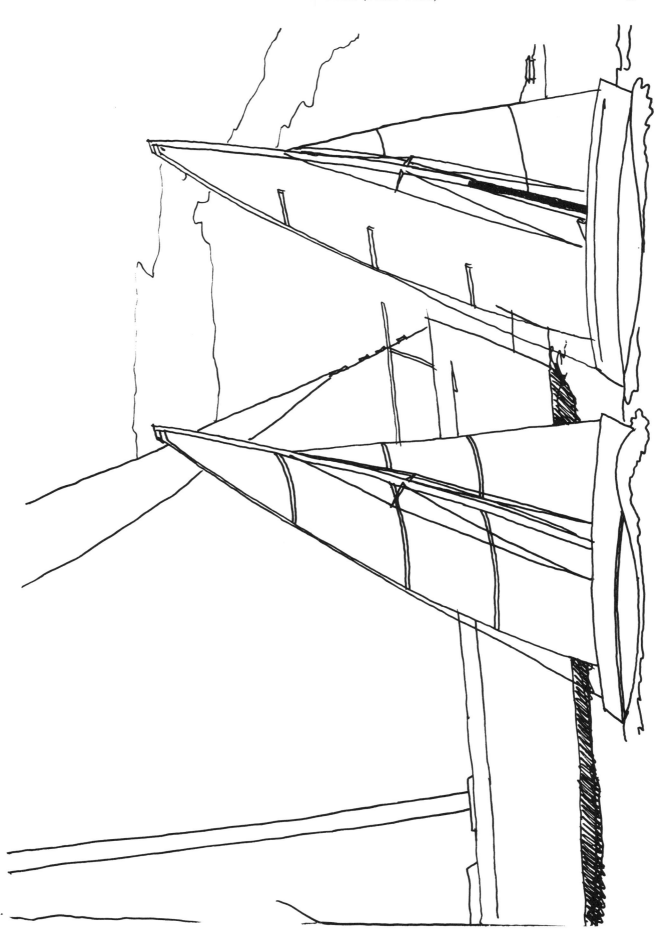

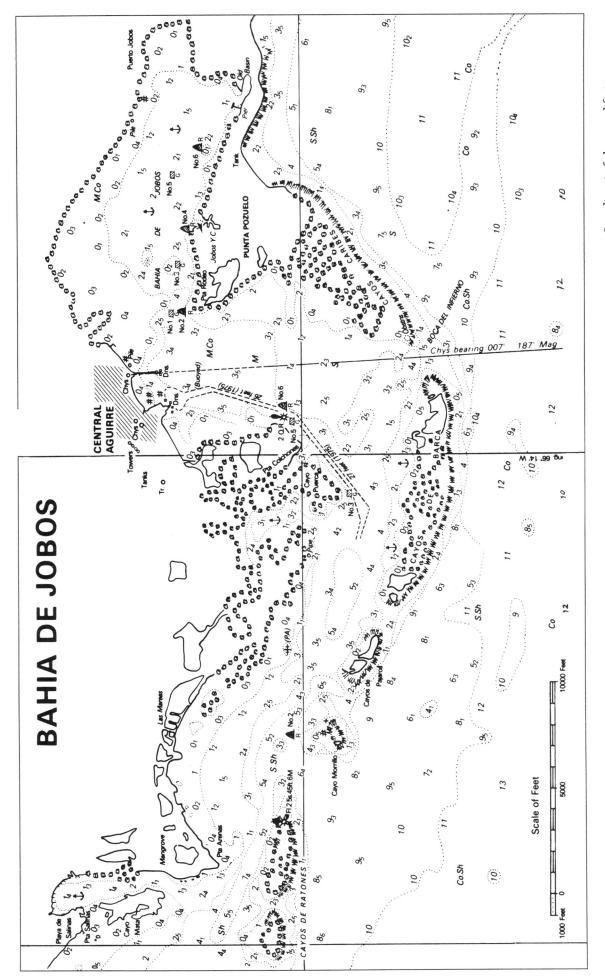

BAHIA DE JOBOS

Soundings in fathoms and feet

CHART 12 Bahía de Jobos

is very much cruising-yacht territory; why and how the boys developed these extreme racing models is beyond me.

Kirsti, a young Danish woman, has a shop in town where she does sail repairs and canvaswork, operates a book exchange, and runs a lending library. Her place obviously is a gathering place for all the visiting yachties, and you are also likely to run into some of the young modelmakers trying to bum offcuts of sailcloth to make sails for their boats. A fellow named Charlie runs a dive operation out of the same shop, and Kirsti can tell you how to find David Morgan's shop, Nitica del Mundo, where you can buy Imray-Iolaire charts. She also recommends the small grocery owned by Junior Rodrigues; he is local, speaks excellent English, and is very helpful. (He also arranges and encourages races for the small boats.) Besides, his small grocery store has an amazingly varied inventory, and what he doesn't have, he can dig up for you.

BAHIA DE JOBOS

(Chart 12; II A, A-1, A-12)

Although in the past I have recommended skipping this harbor, I no longer feel that way. Bahía de Jobos is an excellent place to stop, since there are numerous anchorages away from the smoke and smell of Central Aguirre. Also, it is an ideal jumping-off spot when you are going east. From Bahía de Jobos eastward, there are no real harbors until you reach Puerto Patillas, which I call a harbor of refuge because it is sheltered but rocky and rolly.

An added advantage of the Jobos anchorage is that if you run into one of those spells where the hinges are blowing off the gates of hell, you can keep yourself amused inside Bahía de Jobos by moving from one anchorage to another.

Coming from Salinas, you can enter Bahía de Jobos by passing inside Cayos de Ratones; if you are coming from offshore, pass between Cayos de Ratones and Cayo Morrillo. There are two other passages: one between Cayo Morrillo and Cayos de Pajaros, the other between Cayos de Pajaros and Cayos de Barca. The first of these passages is buoyed; the other two are not. It's strictly a matter of eyeball navigation.

The easiest entrance is directly from the south of Boca del Infierno, with the chimneys of Central Aguirre bearing 008° magnetic. In extremely heavy weather conditions, it might be unwise to enter through this gap. However, I think it would require a really bad gale to pile up the sea so that this entrance would be unsafe. On entering, favor the starboard side of the channel, since that is the deepest part; both sides are very steep-to.

Anchorages can be had north of any of the cays previously mentioned. When entering from the south, you can round up and anchor immediately inside the gap west of Cayos Caribes. When deciding on any of these anchorages, remember that the wind will most likely switch to the north during the evening; anchor accordingly.

There is an excellent small, secluded anchorage behind Cayo Puerca—ideal for fishing in the mangroves, although I wonder about the mosquito population. Once inside the mangroves, get in the dinghy and you can explore to your heart's content. Depths are not given on the Imray-Iolaire chart, as the scale does not permit it. Besides, the only survey available was done before 1911, so how accurate can the figures be today? Do not rely on the figures that appear on the NOAA chart, as they are from the uncorrected early twentieth-century survey.

When local yachtsmen discuss channels through the mangroves, they offer all sorts of conflicting information as to how many feet of draft can be carried up to the inner edges of the trees. All agree, however, that the mangroves would provide an excellent hurricane hole, as they give plenty of protection, there is ample room, and, most important, this area is not inundated with yachts, as is the case in the Virgin Islands.

You may want to sail up to the eastern end of Bahía de Jobos and check out the yacht club. It has slips for members, and perhaps some additional space. I have checked it out from the air and figure that you probably can get seven feet in there. Yacht club members tell me that the club is extremely hospitable to visiting yachtsmen, but remember that you would be out in the middle of nowhere if you stayed here. By dinghy, Central Aguirre is about two miles from the club; by car, it is about seven miles.

If you spend the night at Salinas or one of the other anchorages in Bahía de Jobos and plan to leave very early to take advantage of the northerly breeze, I do not recommend leaving via Boca del Infierno unless you have a shoal-draft boat. You will not be able to see the chimneys of Central Aguirre to take a back bearing. There is coral on both sides of the channel, so taking this route without good light is a poor idea. Rather, depart between Cayos de Pajaros and Cayos de Barca, as the channel there is deeper and wider. It is two miles in the wrong direction, but it is a lot safer. If you are leaving from Salinas before dawn, exit west of Cayos de Ratones.

During daylight hours, when you can get a back

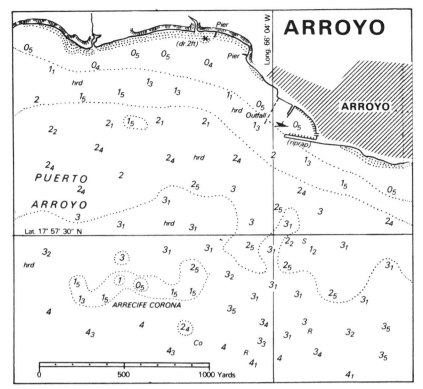

CHART 13   Arroyo   Soundings in fathoms and feet

bearing on the Central Aguirre chimneys, it is entirely possible to exit via Boca del Infierno.

LAS MAREAS

(II A, A-1, A-12)

This is another harbor that should be avoided, since it is exclusively an oil port and of no use to the yachtsman except in an emergency.

PUERTO ARROYO

(Charts 13, 14; II A, A-1, A-12, A-13)

This is strictly an emergency stop for shoal-draft boats fighting their way eastward. There is a sunken fishing trawler in the middle of the harbor entrance, so be careful. Nine feet of water has been reported off the entrance, five feet inside the breakwater. If you are hugging the coast in this area—to stay in smoother water—keep a close eye on the chart and put a crew member in the rigging to spot the many unnamed shoals.

PUERTO PATILLAS

(Chart 14; II A, A-1, A-12, A-13)

When approaching Puerto Patillas, I would definitely favor the shore side. Stay to the north of the shoals marked on the US chart (remember that the chart dates from 1901-11) and note that the four-foot spot is almost impossible to identify; the other reefs break, so they are visible. In March 1993, we found 10 feet of water with the white-painted spot on the big retaining wall bearing 030° magnetic and the southeastern point of the harbor bearing 125° magnetic. We also discovered that if we had gone another 50 yards to the southeast, we would have run aground. so be forewarned.

Puerto Patillas provides an excellent rest stop when it is blowing hard. If you leave from Bahía de Jobos and go directly to Palmas del Mar, the distance is 32 miles—a hard go if you are beating to windward. Plus, if it is blowing particularly hard, you may not even want to go into Palmas del Mar (see chapter 6). If you decide Palmas is too rough, it is five additional miles to a more sheltered anchorage (Cayo Santiago).

If you stop at Puerto Patillas, it is only 17 miles east of Bahía de Jobos or 20 miles east of Salinas.

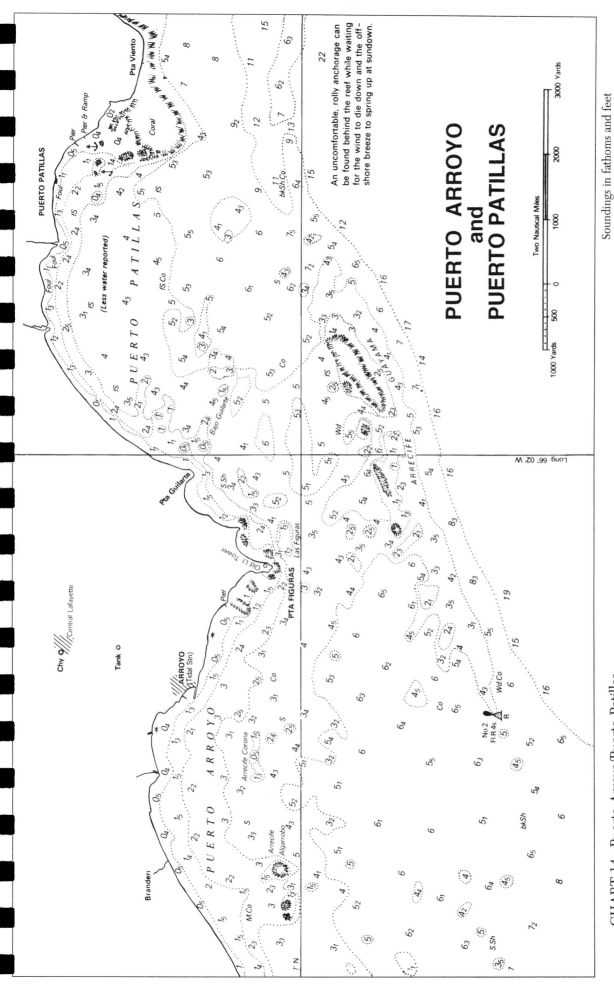

An uncomfortable, rolly anchorage can
be found behind the reef while waiting
for the wind to die down and the offshore breeze to spring up at sundown.

PUERTO ARROYO
and
PUERTO PATILLAS

Soundings in fathoms and feet

CHART 14 Puerto Arroyo/Puerto Patillas

This makes it far closer to Palmas del Mar (or Cayo Santiago). If the wind is in the southeast, you have a good chance of reaching all the way up to Pasaje Medio Mundo.

The anchorage here is rolly because the sea hooks all the way around the reef and swings in from the southwest. Even *Iolaire* rolled with the mizzen up. To prevent the roll, rig a flopper-stopper or leave the mizzen up or anchor bow-and-stern facing southwest. If it is blowing hard, make sure your anchors are well dug in, as you will have the wind on the beam when it comes in from the southeast.

Ashore in Puerto Patillas, you will find numerous docks and charming people. We rowed ashore to a dock where there were about four powerboats and asked some onlookers if it was public. They said, "No, it is private, but since you have a good-looking dinghy and two nice ladies with you, it is public for you. What can we do to help you?" These friendly fellows told us that Puerto Patillas is the home of a number of Puerto Ricans who have made their money, retired, and now spend their time fishing and drinking and having a good time.

There are plenty of restaurants here, plus a small grocery store with the basics, a few vegetables, and cube ice. At the north end of the village is a public beach. As soon as I heard there was a good beach, I became a little suspicious of the anchorage. A good beach usually means there has been something to produce the sand—such as a ground swell.

We did not have a chance to dive on the reef, but it must be a fairly good dive spot, because fishing is big here. There must have been 40 fishing boats pulled up on the beach, and the reef was littered with fish pots. (Be sure to keep your propeller clear of the fishing gear.)

Puerto Patillas is the gathering place for the 20-foot racing sloops we saw in Salinas, but no races were scheduled when we were last there.

When leaving Puerto Patillas, head northwest until you feel you have cleared the four-foot spot. Then head southwest until you are absolutely sure you have avoided the hazard. After that, you can head for the western edge of the reef, which is steep-to. The sea will be coming directly out of the south and be very steep, so again be forewarned.

NOTES

NOTES

6

East and North Coasts

(Imray-Iolaire Charts A, A-1, A-13, A-14, A-2)

The east coast of Puerto Rico and Vieques Sound is not as bad as it may appear from the charts, and with some careful piloting, the area should present no undue difficulties.

PUNTA TUNA

(II A, A-1, A-13)

Punta Tuna has a very bad reputation for rough seas—it has even been described as the Puerto Rican equivalent of Cape Horn. Within a couple of hundred yards, the bottom comes up from 1,000 feet to ankle-deep water. Needless to say, in heavy weather, a large Caribbean swell comes in and meets on this vertical wall; it humps up and bounces back and makes a godawful sea condition. In early March 1993, sailing downwind, we ran in behind Arrecife Sargent close aboard Punta Tuna. Outside it was very rough, but in the shoal water it was calm, only a small chop. If I had had a boat that went to windward and tacked well, we would certainly have come up inside Arrecife Sargent and tacked up to Punta Yeguas. Then we would have stood offshore to get well outside the shelf and the rough water.

Just west of Punta Tuna, the US chart lists "Puerto Maunabo." I don't think this is a real port. It certainly is not a harbor, but it is a stopping place. When we went by, we discovered a few small local fishing boats moored there in calm water, despite the fact that it was blowing a solid 20 to 25 knots. Further, we noticed the same phenomenon behind Punta Yeguas.

Punta Tuna and Puerto Maunabo could be harbors of refuge if the wind were northeast, but neither would be tenable if the wind were east or southeast.

PUERTO YABUCOA

(II A, A-1, A-13)

This is a commercial port only; pass it by except in an emergency.

PALMAS DEL MAR

(Chart 15; II A, A-1, A-13, A-2)

On Imray-Iolaire Chart A-13, at Punta Guayanes, pinpoint Punta Fraile, which forms the base of the breakwater that creates the north side of the harbor. If approaching from the northeast, be careful to avoid the conspicuous rocks off Punta Fraile. Leave the rocks to starboard, since there is a shoal patch between the rocks and the breakwater. Continue southwest until you pick up the outer buoy, then head approximately northwest, following the privately buoyed channel into the outer basin. The draft in the outer basin is 14 feet at the southern end, shoaling to eight feet at the northern end.

The management of the extensive Palmas del Mar Resort warns that there is a steep swell in the entrance channel, so that powerboats feel comfortable coming in a little faster than normal to reduce the chance of broaching. It sounds rather like running a New Jersey inlet; entering and leaving under sail may be more than a little difficult.

The entrance to this harbor is both buoyed and lighted by privately maintained buoys under the normal American buoyage system—easily understood when approaching during daylight hours. Anyone who approaches and attempts to enter this harbor at night dead downwind before the easterly swell needs his or her head examined.

Palmas del Mar once was a home base for one of Steve Colgate's sailing schools. The school's boats

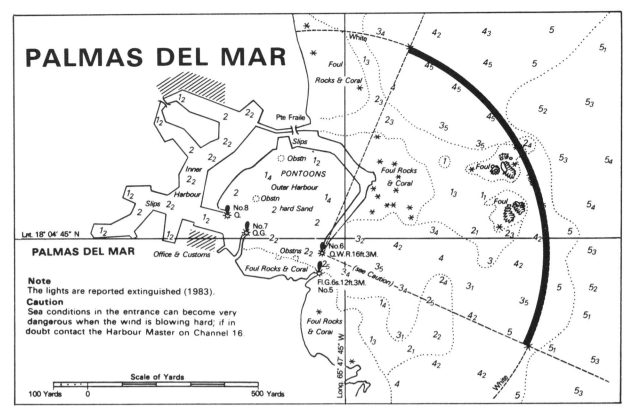

CHART 15   Palmas del Mar   Soundings in fathoms and feet

entered and left under sail regularly, but remember that these were responsive, easily handled Solings.

We are told that depth is 10 feet into the inner harbor, except that there is an eight-foot rock in the middle of the channel to the inner harbor. If you draw seven feet or more, hug either the starboard or the port side of the channel.

The harbormaster's office and operations center is on the port side when entering the harbor. If it is really blowing, I urge that you contact the harbormaster on the radio before trying the entrance.

There are 140 slips here, but the size of boat you can squeeze in depends on your maneuvering skills; I would say no more than 60 feet. Gas, diesel, and holding-pump outlets are available, and an anchorage can be had in the outer harbor. However, despite the narrow entrance, there is still a rock and roll at the anchorage. The problem with anchoring in Palmas del Mar is that you are out in the middle of nowhere. This is an expensive resort, and it has any resort-type amenity you could want (18-hole golf course, casino, tennis courts, fitness center, and more), but it doesn't have a supermarket or any other place to stock up on food. The restaurants are excellent, but, as you should expect, pricey. If you

want to spend some time tied up here, you might be able to arrange a long-term rental by contacting a condominium owner who doesn't have a boat.

The boatyard at Palmas del Mar has a 50-ton Travelift, but it's a two-hour drive from here to San Juan to buy supplies. Hauling fees are incredibly reasonable, so this would be a great place to rebuild a wooden boat if you have the skills to do it yourself, because there is limited skilled local labor. If you want to do this, however, you should arrive with all your tools and parts, because otherwise you will use up a vast amount of time, money, and energy commuting to and from San Juan. When I was here in February 1993, there was very little activity, and the marine store stocked only the basics.

CAYO SANTIAGO

(II A, A-1, A-13, A-14, A-2)

Cayo Santiago, six miles northeast of Palmas del Mar, is not the world's greatest anchorage, but if it is blowing a gale and you are tired, it is a good place to throw the hook and get some rest. The island is only 600 yards long, north to south, but the wind hooks around the southern end and becomes southeast even when it is really east. If the wind is north and north of east, Cayo Santiago has pretty good shelter. Anchor halfway down the island; it becomes shoal as you near the northern end. Anchorage is in mixed sand and grass. If the wind is south of east, forget it.

If the wind is southeast, you should be on a close reach and easily able to reach Pasaje Medio Mundo and anchor behind Isla Piñeros.

If you are beating northward against a howling northeasterly or a northerly, you know that once you get in behind Cayo Santiago, you will have shelter. This is locally known as the "monkey island," as it was a monkey experimental station for many years. The station has now been closed down, and the monkeys are wild, so be cautious. I have been told that the monkeys are less than friendly and tend to bite.

PUERTO DE NAGUABO

(II A, A-1, A-13, A-14, A-2)

This is not a particularly good anchorage, as you can surmise by looking at the nice, long, sandy beach. Evidently the swell does not get too bad, though, because local fishing sloops (the beautiful racing ones) anchor here. If the wind is well in the northeast and you decide you want some shoreside civilization, you can find a tolerable anchorage in the harbor. Go ashore in the dinghy and you will find some good fish restaurants that are off the beaten track and therefore not tourist-oriented.

BAHIA LIMA

(II A, A-1, A-13, A-14, A-2)

West of Punta Lima, Bahía Lima is a fair anchorage sheltered from northeast winds. The land to the east is low, guaranteeing cool breezes.

ENSENADA HONDA (ROOSEVELT ROADS)

(Chart 16; II A, A-1, A-13, A-14, A-2)

Northeast of Punta Lima and locally called "Rosie Roads" (actually Roosevelt Roads), this is the location of a US Navy base. As such, it is well charted and buoyed. It should be left to starboard when entering. The naval-base yacht club is in the northernmost corner of the harbor, outside the dredged area. Proceed with extreme caution, since boats go aground regularly entering and leaving the yacht

club. In fact, having heard a large number of horror stories of people going aground, I would anchor just north of buoy C, take the dinghy ashore, and obtain firsthand directions for avoiding the shoal and the wrecks.

The yacht club is restricted to naval personnel, either active or retired, and their friends. If you are nonmilitary, you may go to the yacht club and anchor there only if the friend who has invited you is on board your vessel or at the yacht club at that time.

Small Islands Off the Coast

These provide a wonderful selection of anchorages, all very close together. Many are secluded and uncrowded, except on weekends. The east coast of Puerto Rico is well covered by Imray-Iolaire Charts A-13 and A-14. I would definitely not use the US charts, because they are not well laid out and they have a number of errors—we know, because we went aground using them.

ISLA PIÑEROS

(Charts 16, 17; II A, A-1, A-13, A-14, A-2)

There is an excellent anchorage between this island and the "mainland." The water is clear and absolutely calm in all conditions, so this is a wonderful place to snorkel, swim, and sail without fear of being blown out to sea.

If the wind is south of east, a good anchorage can be had on the north side of Isla Piñeros.

ISLA DE RAMOS

(Chart 16; II A, A-1, A-13, A-14, A-2)

An excellent anchorage can be had west of Isla de Ramos. There are beautiful white-sand beaches, completely deserted except on weekends. Exactly what the legal position is for landing, I'm not sure, but I gather that in Puerto Rican waters you are not trespassing as long as you stay on the beach. I think the average yachtsman who behaves properly and stays on the beach will be welcomed on most Puerto Rican islands and beaches.

But do not go off exploring ashore unless invited. The buoys with lines in between them off the beach are not so much to keep people from landing as to keep high-speed motorboats—of which there are

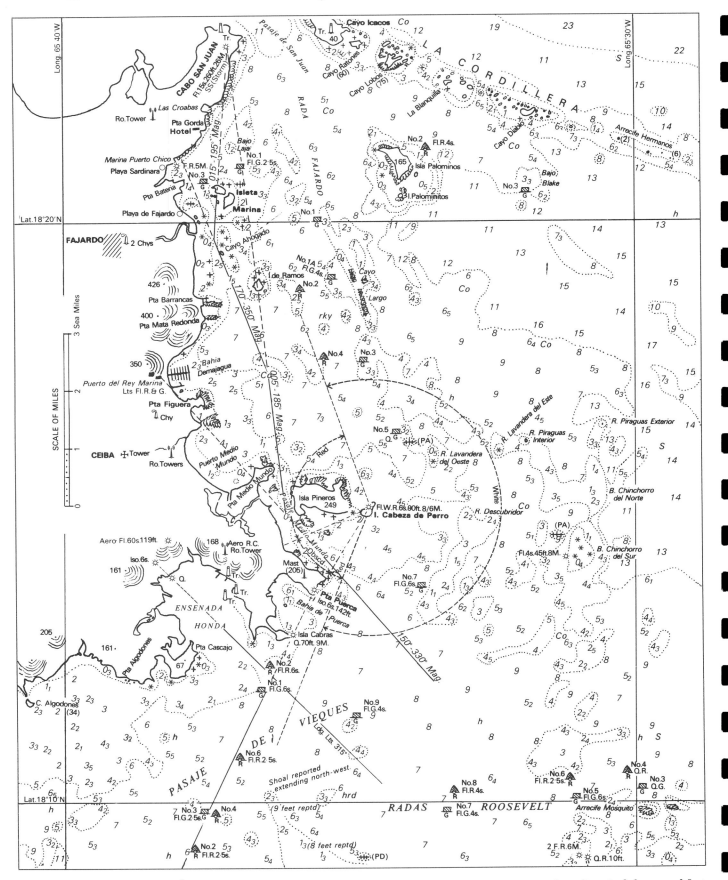

CHART 16   East Coast of Puerto Rico   Soundings in fathoms and feet

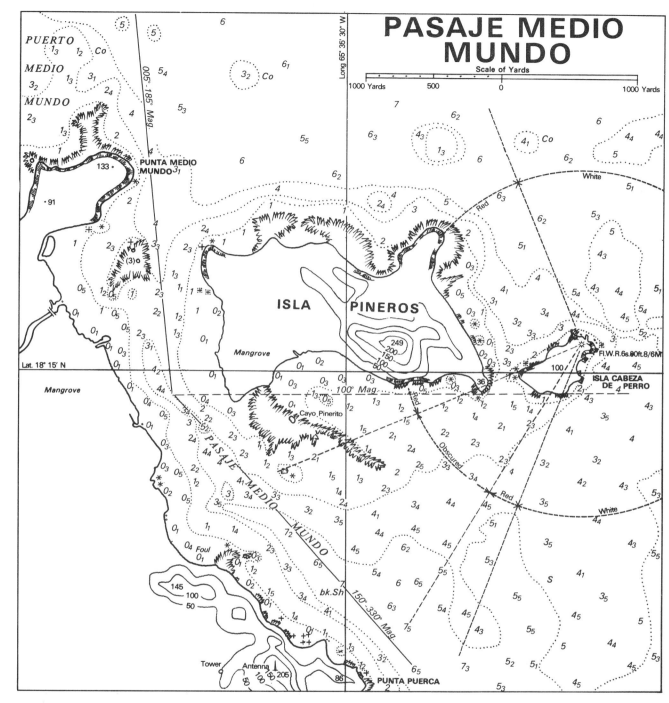

CHART 17   Pasaje Medio Mundo   Soundings in fathoms and feet

many in Puerto Rico—from running too close to the beach and chopping up the swimmers.

There is a landing strip on the island so that the owner can beat Puerto Rico's weekend traffic jams. The 10-minute flight saves a two-hour car trip plus a launch ride!

CAYO AHOGADO

(Chart 16; II A, A-1, A-13, A-14)

This used to be an absolutely perfect deserted island—pure white sand, no vegetation, and only a huge timber 30 feet long and 18 inches in diameter, evidently washed up in some storm. A later storm

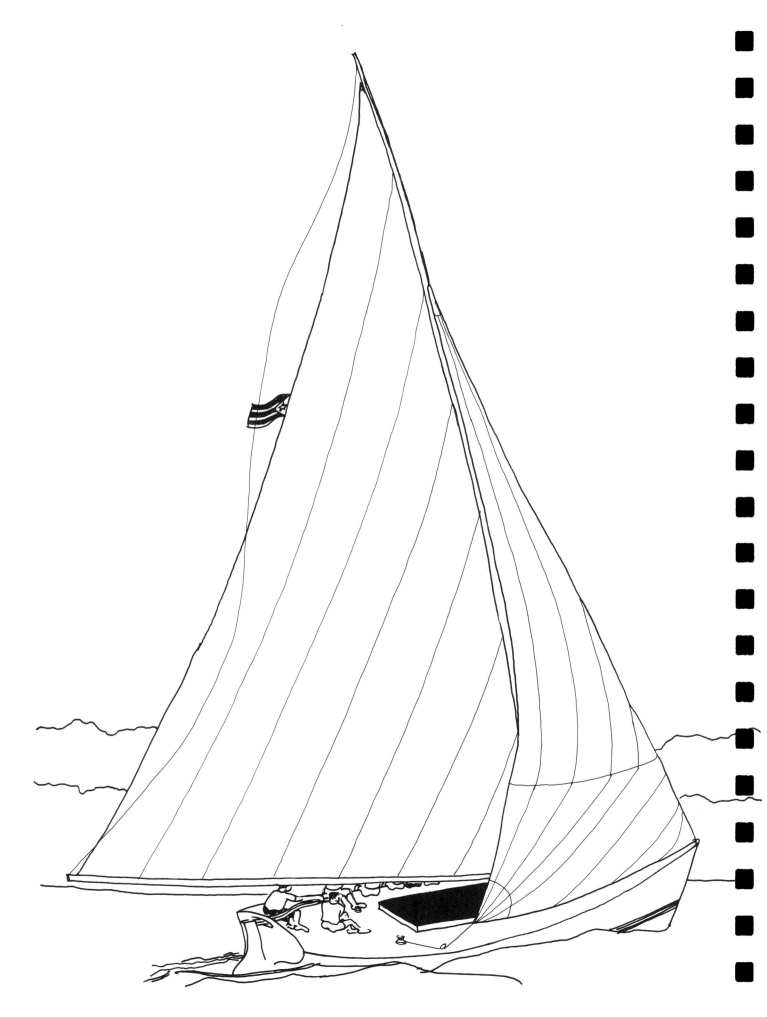

did it in, however—Hurricane Hugo submerged it, and now it is only breaking reefs. We can only hope that someday it will reappear.

CAYO ICACOS

(Chart 16; II A, A-1, A-13, A-14)

Given the right conditions, this island and the reefs to the east of it offer fascinating exploring, diving, and fishing. Between November and April, with the ground swell up, the area can be a little treacherous, but it is ideal during the summer. Cayo Icacos is large enough to provide adequate shelter. When the wind is southeast, anchor in the island's western bay; when it is northeast, anchor hard by the ruined pier on the south side. The island is brush-covered and mostly uninhabited.

CAYO RATONES

(Chart 16; II A, A-1, A-13, A-14)

This is definitely not an anchorage, but if you are anchored over at Cayo Icacos, take the dinghy around to Cayo Ratones, anchor at the little cove on the south side of the island—stern anchor out, bow line to the seagrape tree. Walk over to the eastern side of the island, where you will find beautiful rock pools almost as warm as a Jacuzzi. With sea breaking on the rocks, and plenty of shells, this is a great place to be off by yourself.

CAYO LOBOS

(Charts 16, 18; II A, A-1, A-13, A-14)

An anchorage can be had here in normal conditions, but eyeball navigation is necessary. Ease your way in between the reefs and anchor bow-and-stern. This is a private island, and you probably won't be allowed ashore. Thirty years ago, there was a private club here—a hideaway for Puerto Rican businessmen and their girlfriends. Times have changed, however, and Puerto Ricans nowadays think nothing of taking girlfriends off for a day of fishing or cruising, so the club is no longer necessary. A large hotel was built here at one point, but it went belly-up, after which a single family bought the island.

ISLA PALOMINOS

(Charts 16, 19; II A, A-1, A-13, A-14)

This anchorage, frequented by weekending Puerto Rican yachtsmen, is approachable only during the daytime—two coral peaks surrounded by deep water are located due west of the island's highest land. The peaks rise to within three to five feet of the surface.

The best way in is at the northwestern end of the island, at Punta Aguila. Eyeball your way southeastward, staying close to the shoal water. You will be safe, since the water drops off quite steeply through here. Continue south until the dock roughly bears east. Anchor to a Bahamian moor between the dock and the shoal to the west.

An alternate anchorage is just south of Punta Aguila. Remember, however, that the current runs extremely strong here north-and-south, so you must be tucked right up close to shore to anchor. Upon rounding Punta Aguila, stand eastward until Las Cucarachas disappears behind Punta Aguila. Drop a stern anchor, pay out plenty of line, and sail on until the bow is in three or four feet of water. Then drop the bow anchor, slack off its side, and take up on the stern anchor so that you are moored bow-and-stern within swimming distance of the beach. If the wind

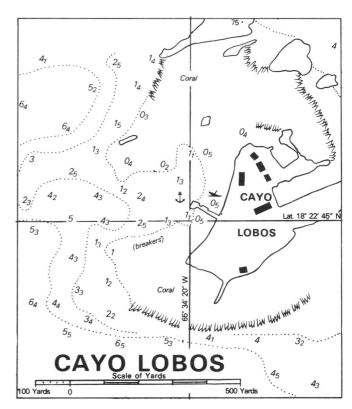

CHART 18 Cayo Lobos   Soundings in fathoms and feet

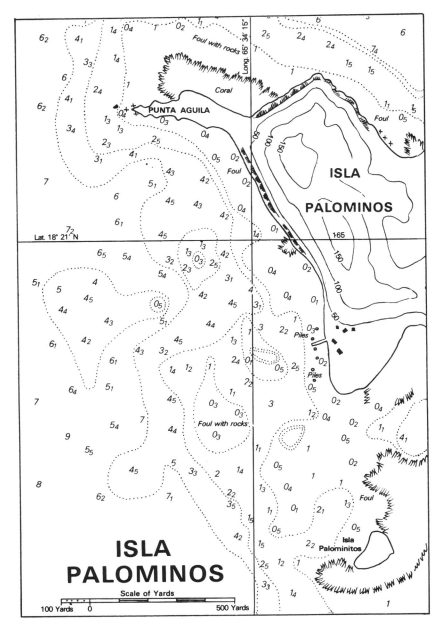

CHART 19   Isla Palominos   Soundings in fathoms and feet

is south of east (in the summer), a good anchorage can be had on the north side of Punta Aguila.

The Bachman family, owner of the island, has given a long-term lease to the Japanese owners of the old El Conquistador Hotel in Las Croabas, which is being massively expanded to 1,000 rooms. However, the Bachmans have retained the northwestern point, where they have built a dock and plan to build a large house for their extended family. Needless to say, their privacy should be respected.

Isla Palominitos, a few hundred yards south of Isla

Palominos, has a good sheltered anchorage on its west side. Eyeball your way in and anchor with the island breaking about southeast. The reefs to the east of Isla Palominitos completely break the sea but not the wind. During the week, the island is deserted—a wonderful spot for a picnic or an evening barbecue. Unfortunately, many picnickers have left their trash behind—here and on other Puerto Rican beaches. Any yachtsman who wants to do the world a favor can carry a shovel ashore on a Puerto Rican beach, dig a hole, and bury the garbage that has been left by others.

LA BLANQUILLA and CAYO DIABLO

(Chart 16; II A, A-1, A-13, A-14)

There is always a very strong current around La Blanquilla, so it is impossible to anchor, but you might try taking a dinghy into shallow water and diving around it.

Cayo Diablo is a good daytime anchorage for diving only, provided the wind is well in the north; it is no good if the wind is east or south of east.

Along Puerto Rico's east coast, marinas are sprouting like weeds—to the point where they are having trouble filling their slips. So you'll have no problem finding a berth—it's only a matter of deciding where you want to tie up.

EL CONQUISTADOR MARINA

(Chart 20; II A, A-1, A-13, A-14)

The elegant old El Conquistador Hotel has been through several incarnations. After it went bankrupt, it was picked up by an evangelical church group, which itself went belly-up. Now it has been sold to Japanese businessmen, who are busy doing a massive expansion. How much they will expand the marina is questionable, but I suspect the marina will be restricted to boats connected to the hotel, so space will not be available for visiting yachts. Too bad, because this would be a good spot for visiting yachts—the road to Fajardo is circuitous, so it's easier to get there by dinghy than by car.

LAS CROABAS

(Chart 20; II A, A-1, A-13, A-14)

In years gone by, the harbor in this well-known fishing village was filled with small fishing sloops like those formerly found in Tortola. They were a dying breed until recently, when the sport of racing fishing sloops became big business, with plenty of money being bet on sponsored entries. Now these noble sloops are being built strictly for racing. The boats used to have big, old, straight wooden spars, but then some of the racing types installed light aluminum poles, which greatly increased stability. After Hugo, damaged rigs could be bought for almost nothing, so many of the Puerto Rico racing sloops now sport modern spars from cruising boats or racing machines.

My old friend Bob Lamson, who has lived in Puerto Rico for more than 30 years, told me that one of the oldest boats in the racing association is still going strong and still winning more races than any other boat.

When not racing, some of the boats are used for fishing and others are used for day charters. The fishermen make a lot more money handlining and pulling pots than they would if they were taking tourists on day trips.

You used to be able to haul here inexpensively if you drew six feet or less, but the owners of the local restaurants complained about the noise and dirt when sailors ground down paint. So now no power tools can be used—and the hauling operation has pretty much collapsed.

Las Croabas is so crowded that I would never take my boat in there unless it was under 30 feet. The harbor is easy to get into but difficult to leave under sail. And there is little room to anchor once you are in. However, if you want to see an authentic traditional Puerto Rican fishing village, it's worth going to Las Croabas. Don't use a car, as it's a long, circuitous road that takes about 25 minutes from Villa Marina or Marina Puerto Chico, whereas it's only 15 minutes from Isleta Marina by dinghy—or less if your dinghy is fast.

In Las Croabas, you'll find every kind of restaurant—tiny ones for working fishermen, larger ones for successful fishermen, others for Puerto Rican businessmen. None are geared to the North American tourist. I recommend choosing whichever one draws the most locals. That's bound to have good food and good value for the money.

I do not advise running over to Las Croabas at night and trying to find your way into the unlighted channel (or, worse, trying to get out through the channel at 2300 with a good dinner and some drinks under your belt). I suggest you head over around noon, admire the local sloops, have a long lunch, and then get back to your boat in daylight.

ISLETA MARINA

(Chart 21; II A, A-1, A-13, A-14)

This was the first marina built on Puerto Rico's east coast—a marina with a good vertical lift for up to 100 tons and facilities for side-tracking. For many years, it had the only side-tracking facility in the Eastern Caribbean, so it supported itself very well. Now there is also a 60-ton Travelift. There is ample room to work on boats, but there is inadequate space for long-term storage. The only place in Puerto Rico where there is enough long-term storage is Puerto del Rey Marina (see below). Isleta Marina is sheltered in all normal conditions, but when

64

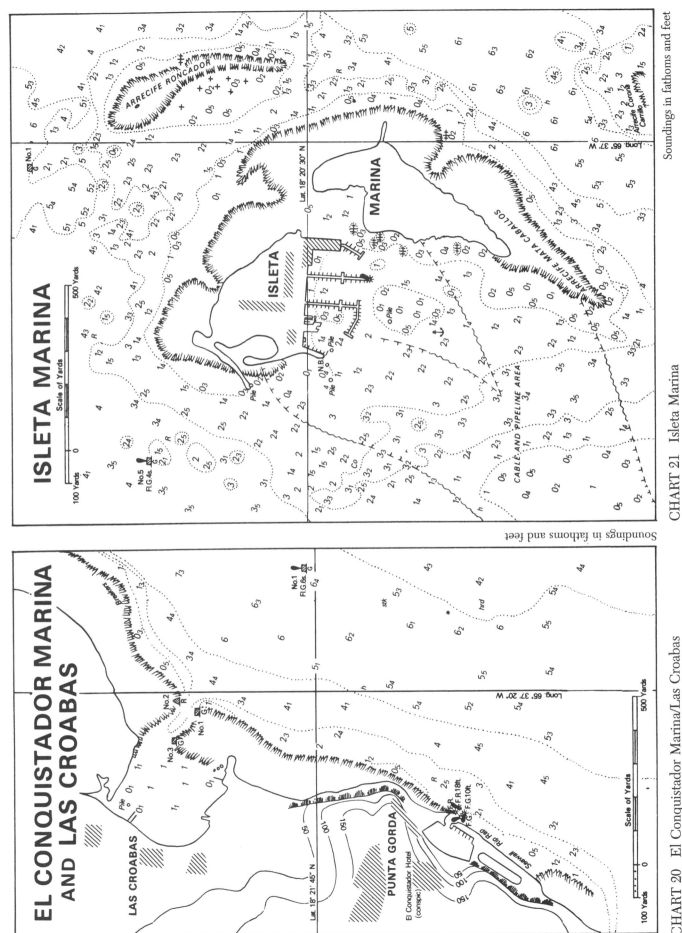

Soundings in fathoms and feet

ISLETA MARINA

Scale of Yards

500 Yards

100 Yards

0

ARRECIFE RONCADOR

Lat. 18° 20' 30" N

Long. 65° 37' W

Arrecife Corona
Arrecife Carrillo

MARINA

ISLETA

ARRECIFE MATA CABALLOS

CABLE AND PIPELINE AREA

No.1
G

No.5
Fl.G.4s.

Pile
O.N.B.
Pile

CHART 21   Isleta Marina

Soundings in fathoms and feet

EL CONQUISTADOR MARINA
AND LAS CROABAS

Breakers

No.1
Fl.G.6s.
G

No.2
R
No.1
G
No.3
R

Pile

LAS CROABAS

Lat. 18° 21' 45" N

Long. 66° 37' 20" W

Scale of Yards

500 Yards

100 Yards

0

PUNTA GORDA

El Conquistador Hotel
(conspic)

F.R.18ft.
F.G.10ft.

Rip Rap

Seawall

CHART 20   El Conquistador Marina/Las Croabas

Hurricane Hugo came through in 1989, it was completely flattened. (See Reflections on Hugo in the Foreword to this volume.)

At Isleta Marina, the crew can do all of the normal work, and difficult jobs can be subcontracted out.

As the marina expanded, condominiums were built on the island by a separate corporation, and now there is a crazy situation: Both organizations operate high-speed diesel launches back and forth from Isleta to town, and usually they are only one-third full. It's a shame that they haven't been able to combine launch services, saving a tremendous amount of money and fuel and also reducing power-boat wash. If you are tied to the dock or hauled, you will receive a complimentary pass for the marina's launch service. Otherwise, you must use the condominium launch service, which can become expensive. If you use either launch service, check the schedule carefully, because if you miss the last boat, you will be sleeping on the beach or looking for a hotel room. Except in calm conditions, there is no suitable place to tie a dinghy in Fajardo, as the boat will beat itself to death against the dock unless it is well fendered and held off with a good stern anchor.

Facilities include a commissary with basic supplies, laundry facilities, showers, water, electricity, and pay phones (which leave a bit to be desired).

Isleta Marina is the only place on Puerto Rico's east coast where you can anchor off. There is space for 20 to 30 boats. If you are at the western edge of the fleet, be forewarned that there is a very strong reversing current that runs north-south up to the maximum of two knots. The best anchorage (if there is space) is on the eastern side of the harbor, tucked up behind the reef.

VILLA MARINA

(Chart 22; II A, A-1, A-13, A-14)

This operation is primarily for powerboats, but there are a few sailboats. There is a 60-ton Travelift, plus shops that will do practically any work you might need. Fajardo Canvas is the local North agent, and the Skipper Shop has an excellent inventory of marine supplies, including Street guides and Imray-

CHART 22 Marina Puerto Chico/Villa Marina

Iolaire charts. The complex has other boutiques and shops too numerous to mention.

Be careful entering here, as the channel goes dead to windward, and the slips are a tight squeeze when you bring in a sailboat.

MARINA PUERTO CHICO

(Chart 22; II A, A-1, A-13, A-14)

This is almost the same as Villa Marina, but it seems to have more slips available and caters more to sailboats. Although Villa Marina and Marina Puerto Chico are both sheltered, the latter does not have the backup facilities of the former. But no problem—just jump in your dinghy and make the five-minute trip over to Villa Marina.

Although these two marinas are both sheltered in normal weather, they were complete death traps during Hurricane Hugo. Not only were the docks

and sheds destroyed, but almost all of the boats in them were demolished. A complete disaster. The metal-covered sheds have now been replaced with metal framework covered with awning fabric. The assumption here is that if another hurricane blows through, it will tear away the fabric and leave the framework. I wonder . . . .

PUERTO DEL REY MARINA

(Chart 23; II A, A-1, A-13, A-14)

This is Puerto Rico's newest and largest marina, with 750 slips and long-term storage space for any size yacht. In fact, it is the largest marina on the east coast of North or South America. They have good bunkering facilities, but who supplies the cheapest bunkering in the Caribbean? They all claim it—it's just a matter of checking with everyone. In April

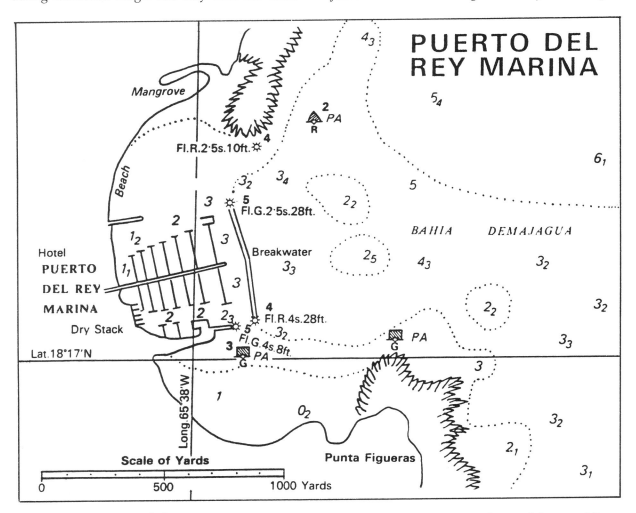

CHART 23   Puerto del Rey Marina   Soundings in fathoms and feet

1994, Puerto del Rey Marina's bunkering was 85 cents a gallon.

Opened in the late 1980s, the marina is still not completed—perhaps because of Hurricane Hugo's interference—and it may not be finished for several years.

When approaching Puerto del Rey Marina from the north, once you have passed Isleta Marina, stand southeastward behind Isleta Marina until Cabo San Juan light comes in over the top of the buildings of Isleta Marina, 015°-195° magnetic. Follow this bearing until you spot the reefs of Cayo Ahogado. Steer approximately 170°-350° magnetic until Isla de Ramos is abeam. Turn south and then southeast. The ends of the reefs at Punta Barrancas and Punta Mata Redonda are marked with stakes; once past them, head southwest for the northern end of Puerto del Rey Marina's breakwater. From there, you are home free.

If approaching from the east, come in on a line of bearing of approximately 270° magnetic, which will take you south of Cayo Largo. You should pick up buoys numbered 3 and 4—remember that these are north-south buoys for the deepwater channel leading to Roosevelt Roads, and they can be disregarded by normal-size yachts. Then head for the north end of Puerto del Rey Marina's breakwater.

A few warnings are in order about entering this marina. (1) Beware of the six-foot rock due east magnetic from the post in the reef marking the starboard side of the channel. The reef is privately buoyed, and the buoy was gone in March 1993 (the chain rusted thin), but it was scheduled to be replaced in a few days. Favor the breakwater side of the channel. (2) The marina's docks are quite high, and we had trouble with *Iolaire* alongside the outer docks. We sailed in, luffed alongside the dock, and made what we thought would be a perfect landing—fenders all rigged and the boat just where we wanted to be. The wind was blowing us about 10° onto the dock, and suddenly the whole thing became a shambles. The dock was so high that our fenders were touching nothing, and our lifeline stanchions were jamming underneath the dock's wooden rubstrake. The inner docks are somewhat lower, but even modern, high-freeboard boats have problems, so be forewarned.

The marina does, however, have all kinds of facilities: hot showers, small commissary, wreck bar, barbecue on the beach, and two restaurants, one of which serves fancy French cuisine. There is a marine store, but when we were there in early 1994, it was more like a boutique with a few marine supplies. I have been told, however, that what they don't have, they will get within 24 hours.

A few miles up the road is Able Marine, run by Tony Able, who is also in the salvage towing business. He can be reached 24 hours a day on channel 16. In Fajardo, 15 miles away by car, there are numerous marine supply stores, as well as laundromats and various independent marine contractors who do woodwork, fiberglass, refrigeration, electrical repairs, hauling, painting, and so on.

In April 1994, there was a 70-ton Travelift in operation, plus shops for carpentry, fiberglassing, sailmaking, engine repair, and refrigeration—all housed in 40-foot containers. The local planning authority had just granted permission for the marina to expand its hauling operation onto the adjacent 12-acre site, so plans were underway to erect two large buildings—one for all the shops and service industries, the other to provide all-weather shelter for boat maintenance and repair. On order were a 300-ton (yes, 300 tons!) Travelift, plus an 80-ton Broward hydraulic trailer. Obviously, the Marina del Rey management expects to become one of the major hauling facilities in the Eastern Caribbean.

In 1994, there was only 10 feet of water in the hauling bay and alongside the fueling dock. This, of course, will have to change if they want to offer such a broad range of services.

Water, electricity, telephone, and TV hookups are available at every slip, but if you are out at the end of the dock, it is a half-mile walk to the office. Even the head is a quarter-mile walk. You can call on channel 71 for an electric cart, which will come and pick you up, but you might have to wait 10 or 15 minutes. Getting messages to these little carts is problematic and can be frustrating. I have urged that they install a VHF in each cart so you could call the cart directly instead of relying on a paging service.

To avoid all of this frustration, I wish the marina management would take a cue from the Jolly Harbour Marina in Antigua and rent bicycles to visiting yachtsmen. (Notice that the megayachts always carry several bikes for this very purpose.) When you send a crew member to buy a bolt or two at the marine store, you may not see him or her again for an hour! Bikes would solve that problem nicely, although the management here says that fear of lawsuits has kept them from offering bicycle rentals.

Whereas the other marinas in the Fajardo area were virtually wiped out by Hurricane Hugo, Puerto del Rey Marina came through in relatively good shape—I was told that damages were roughly 30 percent, with very few total losses. Was the marina just lucky? Or was it because of the big breakwater and strong (but too high) docks? The boats most damaged were in the northern slips. Even in normal weather, the farther you can be from the northeastern entrance the better. Even though it was not uncomfortable on *Iolaire,* there certainly was a bit of a bobble.

The marina's latest plan for minimizing the surge and providing support for fenders is to install plastic skirting from the top of the dock to two feet underwater. Let's hope that proves adequate.

Navigational Warnings: East Coast of Puerto Rico to Culebra and Vieques

When navigating between the western coasts of Culebra and Vieques and the eastern end of Puerto Rico, be very careful in the western part of this triangular patch of water. All of the buoys are set up for passages in and out of Roosevelt Roads, the big naval base; they are not set up for yachtsmen passing east or west. It is essential to keep the chart in front of you and your eyes open, as there are numerous well-charted but unbuoyed rocks that you can pile up on. If you do go aground, you will not be the first.

Also in this area, when heading for the northern passage to Isleta Marina, Marina Puerto Chico, or Villa Marina, there are numerous unmarked dangers. Shoal-draft boats have no problem, but boats drawing more than six feet can easily hang up on the unbuoyed shoal Bajo Laja, bearing 315° magnetic to Punta Gorda, 210° magnetic from the buildings at Isleta Marina, and north magnetic to the lighthouse on Cabo San Juan. If coming from the north, the best way to avoid this is to favor the Puerto Rican shore until you reach C3. Then feel your way to Villa Marina or Marina Puerto Chico. Or, if heading for Isleta Marina, leave C3 to port and feel your way in. If coming from the east, pass C1 close aboard to port, continue west until C3 bears south—do not head directly for C3, or you can clip the shoal that extends north of Isleta Marina—then jibe around and head south.

North Coast of Puerto Rico

The north coast of Puerto Rico offers but one usable harbor for the cruising yachtsman—San Juan. Otherwise, this coast is to be avoided. The Atlantic swell often comes rolling in out of deep water and runs up on the steep incline of the Puerto Rican shelf, making the offshore region rough and unpredictable.

PUERTO ARECIBO
(Chart 24; II A, A-1)

The only possible stop west of San Juan is Arecibo—and that is feasible only when the ground swell is down and the wind not too far around to the north. I can't imagine planning a visit to Arecibo—it is not very attractive—but it is a spot to keep in mind for an emergency. Feel your way in and tuck into the northeast corner, where you should be able to find at least a moderate degree of shelter.

I have never anchored here, but my inspection of the anchorage by car in February 1993 confirmed that it is definitely a desperation anchorage. The dock is rundown and barred and bolted. There is no chance of getting ashore via the dock—it's strictly a matter of taking the dinghy to shore. And even when you get there, it's still three or four miles away from the town.

There is a small fishing club on the beach from which the members launch their small boats; up the narrow river is a larger club where the sportfishermen have their boats shoehorned into slips.

SAN JUAN
(Chart 25; II A, A-1, A-14, A-2)

This major port presents no difficulties for the average yacht; rather, it is the large steamers that have trouble when a ground swell builds up. The ships, of course, have the right-of-way at the channel entrance, so give them room for maneuvering. A near tragedy happened here a number of years ago. The day the law went into effect giving a large ship right-of-way over everything else in a restricted channel, the late Dick Doran was sailing into San Juan on Dave Dana's catamaran *Barefoot* with about 30 tourists on board. As they passed under El Morro, the wind died and the outboard failed to start. Coming up the channel astern of them was a US Navy submarine, which plowed right through the catamaran, breaking it into little pieces and dumping everyone into the water. Amazingly, none of them drowned. Dick and Dave tried to sue the US government, and had the accident happened one day earlier, they might have won the case. But with the new law in effect, they had no recourse. Be forewarned that you are likely to lose your wind under El Morro, so make

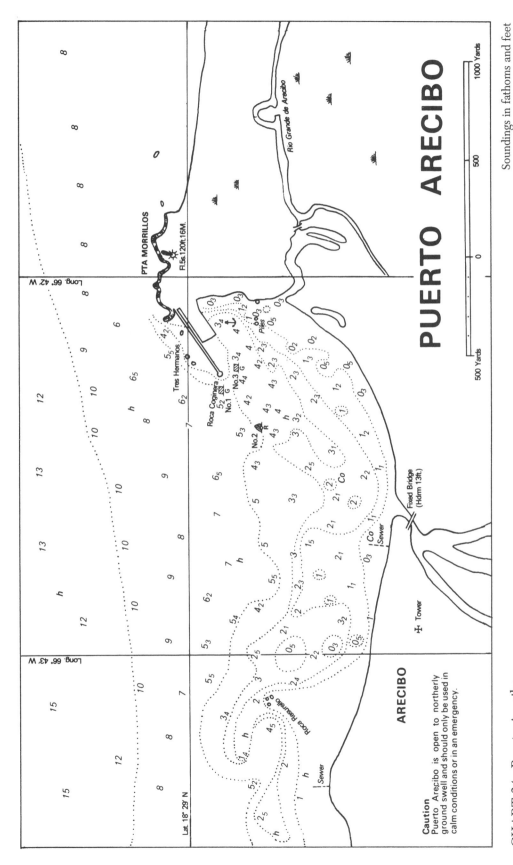

PUERTO ARECIBO

Soundings in fathoms and feet

Caution
Puerto Arecibo is open to northerly ground swell and should only be used in calm conditions or an emergency.

CHART 24 Puerto Arecibo

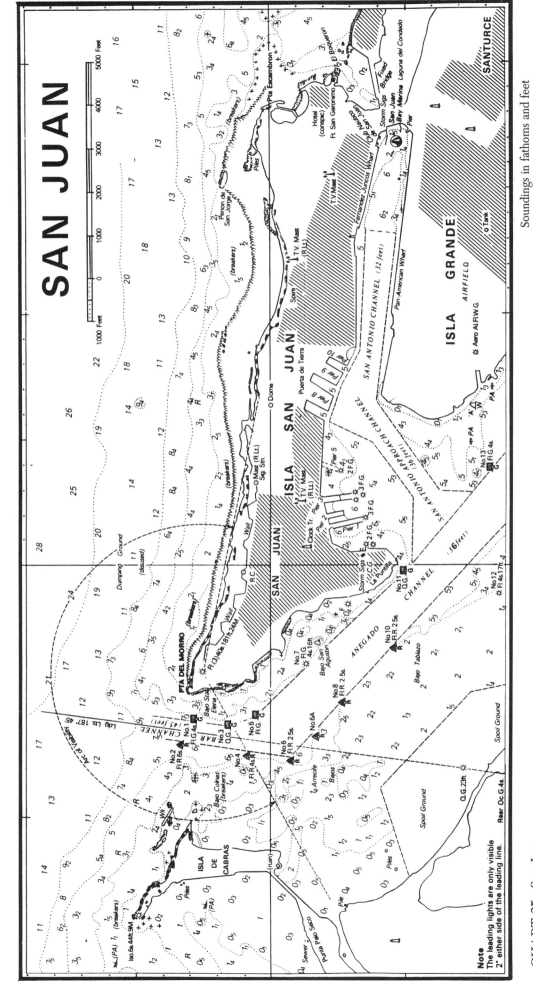

70

SAN JUAN

Soundings in fathoms and feet

Note
The leading lights are only visible
2° either side of the leading line.

CHART 25 San Juan

sure the engine is running to allow you to get out of the way of commercial traffic.

Once past El Morro, swing southeast on Anegado Channel, then swing up into San Antonio Channel. At the end of San Antonio Channel, on the north side, is Club Nautico of San Juan, a private club that sometimes has slips available for visiting yachts. On the starboard side is the new San Juan Bay Marina, with 150 slips. When approaching the south side of the marina dock or the hauling bay, favor the north (pier) side of the channel, as the south side, near the retaining wall, is shallow. The marina has a 60-ton Travelift, and all slips have hookups for electricity, water, and telephones. By the time you read this, each slip will also have a fueling point, so you won't have to move your boat to fuel.

At the head of the dock are a commissary and a marine store, but for restocking, you'll want to hire a taxi and go to a shopping center (ask the marina staff which one is best for your needs). The marina is within walking distance (a mile and a half) of Old San Juan. It's well worthwhile to spend at least a day exploring the old city and the El Morro fortress.

The Bachman family, which runs the marina, has been in the boat business since the 1930s, so they can arrange for anything that needs to be done on a yacht. There is an excellent marine supply store—Marine Dream—opposite the Capitol building in Old San Juan. This is one of the better-supplied marine stores in the Eastern Caribbean, and certainly the best in Puerto Rico. Armstrong Sails is directly above Marine Dream, and underneath it is a propeller and machine shop. They can also line up an electrician if you need electrical repairs.

When leaving San Juan Harbor, the only option is to sheet her flat and bull your way east and south against wind and current to the Fajardo area.

NOTES

NOTES

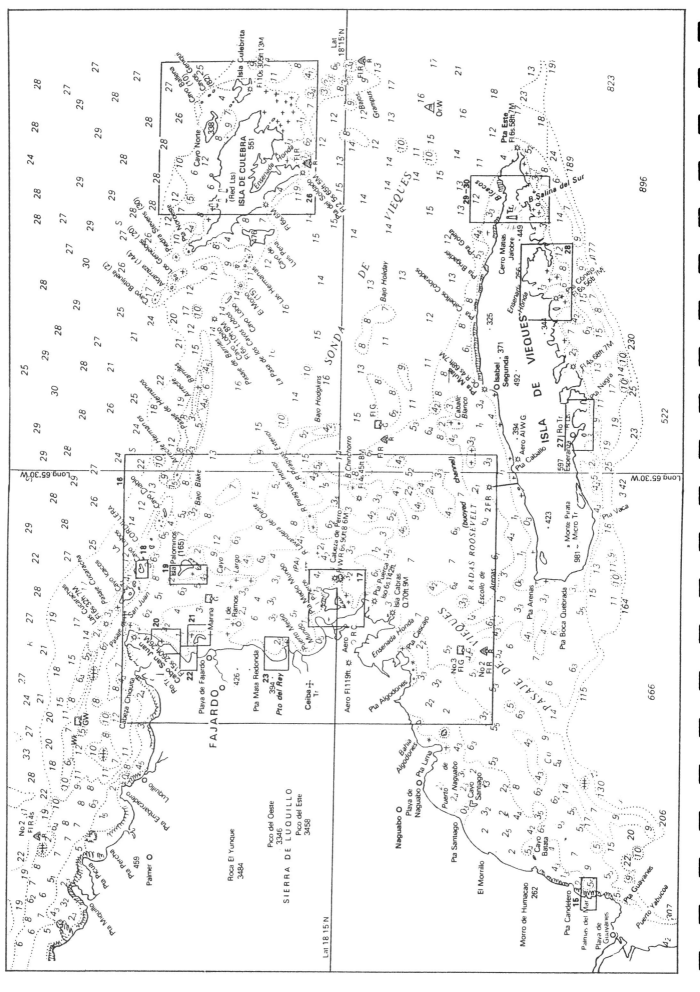

7

The Passage Islands

(Imray-Iolaire Charts A, A-1, A-13, A-131, A-14, A-141, A-2, A-23)

The Passage Islands of Vieques, Culebra, and Culebra's offlying cays can justly be described as the undiscovered jewels of the Caribbean. They have always been there, of course, but because they used to be under the control of the US Navy, they have been almost totally bypassed by cruising yachtsmen, and particularly St. Thomas charter boats.

Culebra is particularly unspoiled. Until the early 1970s, the US Navy owned most of the island and used it as a major training base for amphibious operations. When the Navy moved out, the locals regained control of their island, but development has been very slow. When we arrived there in 1993, Trich and I were reminded of Carriacou in the 1960s.

Culebra received notoriety more recently when Hurricane Hugo came through in 1989. Ensenada Honda in Culebra had long been regarded as a hurricane hole for boats from St. Thomas, and it definitely is a good spot for 30 or 40 boats to tuck up into the mangroves. However, when the alarm went out about Hugo's imminent arrival, more than 300 boats tried to pack themselves into a harbor that is only two miles long and half a mile wide—a harbor that is open to the southeast and does not have particularly good holding. A recipe for disaster.

After the hurricane, there were 111 boats piled on top of one another, plus 75 to 100 scattered around the corners of the harbor in various states of damage—minor, major, and total loss. (For more information on this, read Reflections on Hugo in the Foreword to this volume.)

Until the late 1980s, two-thirds of Vieques was a US naval base, used for bombing drills. Later, the bombing and shelling activity was confined to the eastern tip of the island. Finally, with the end of the cold war, training exercises have become infrequent,

and it is possible to visit the area—provided you obtain prior clearance. (See below for information on how to do this.)

Both Culebra and Vieques have numerous small coves and anchorages that are extremely attractive. In almost every case, they are totally undeveloped or have only one or two houses ashore. The only beach with a hotel on it is Flamingo Beach, on the north side of Culebra, but the anchorage there is usable only in summer, when the ground swell is not running.

If I were asked to name the 10 best anchorages in the Eastern Caribbean, three of them would be in the Passage Islands: Bahía de Almodovar in Culebra, and Bahía Icacos and Bahía Salina del Sur in Vieques.

The St. Thomas charter fleet fights its way eastward to the crowded and "described-to-death anchorages" of the British Virgin Islands. In contrast, from St. Thomas Harbor, it is only 18 miles downwind to Culebra and 25 miles to Vieques. As far as I'm concerned, both islands beat the British Virgin Islands 16 ways to Sunday. Having lived in the Eastern Caribbean for 40 years, I think I know whereof I speak. Why spend your time visiting crowded anchorages when a short sail westward will take you to an area of tranquil anchorages and tremendous hospitality?

Needless to say, if you are seeking bright lights, big crowds, fancy hotels, and expensive boutiques, avoid Culebra and Vieques. However, if you are looking for the Caribbean as it was three decades ago, head west for Culebra and Vieques!

Most charterers arrive in St. Thomas and pick up their boats either in the main harbor of St. Thomas or at Redhook. The anchorages in these areas are not particularly pleasant, so it is better to provision the boat, check out, drop off the docklines, and head for one of the nearby anchorages with crystal-clear water.

From Redhook, it is a mile and a half to Christmas Cove, which undoubtedly will be crowded, but Buck Island is only four and a half miles downwind. Round up close aboard the northwestern point of Buck Island, work your way right up into the cove, and drop your hook in two fathoms of water to a rock-and-gravel bottom, a couple of lengths off the old ruined dock. There is no white-sand beach, but you'll find clear water, a calm anchorage, and little chance of other boats being there for the night (except on weekends).

If you leave from St. Thomas Harbor and do not want to go hard on the wind the three miles out to Buck Island, head west through Haulover Cut and Gregerie Channel between the "mainland" and Water Island. Two choices then lie before you.

(1) Swing around Red Point (making sure to stay outside the black can that marks a dangerous reef), head north, swing around the end of the 1,800-foot runway extension, and anchor in the newly created Airport Bay. Here you'll find a sand bottom, clear water, white-sand beach, and a good breeze coming across the lowland. The only disadvantage is the noise of the planes landing at the airport. The prime advantage is that if you need to go back into town for last-minute shopping or errands, it is a short walk from the beach to Virgin Islands University, where you can pick up the bus—a cheap but circuitous and slow ride to town—or call a taxi.

(2) If you don't like the noise of jets, you can lay a course from Water Island to Saba Island, only two and a half miles distant—a broad reach or a run all the way. There is an excellent anchorage tucked in behind the sandbar that separates Saba Island from Turtle Dove Cay; you'll have only a slight roll. It is crowded only on weekends. Set a stern anchor so that if the wind dies during the night, the swell will not swing you around toward the sand beach. The wind will sweep across the low sandspit, guaranteeing you a cool and bug-free night.

Culebra

From any of the above anchorages, it is an easy 16-mile downwind sail to Culebra, which is well covered by Imray-Iolaire Chart A-131. (Since the area around the island was so heavily used by the US Navy, it has been surveyed and resurveyed many times, so the American charts are also accurate here.)

When approaching Culebra, especially from St. Thomas, note that the shoals north of Bajos Grampus are only three to four fathoms deeper. They are not shoal enough to cause the average yacht any problem except in periods of heavy weather. When the ground swell is rolling in, seas will hump up over these shoals and occasionally break, making it a very rough passage.

If you are leaving your boat, you can reach Culebra by air or ferryboat from Puerto Rico. The ferry makes one round trip daily between Fajardo and Culebra; the one-way trip takes about one hour.

ENSENADA HONDA
(Chart 26; II A, A-1, A-13, A-131, A-14, A-2, A-23)

Culebra's main harbor is well lighted and well buoyed, but be aware that the range marks that blew down during Hurricane Hugo in 1989 still had not been replaced by February 1993. Let's hope they will be in place by the time you read this!

When approaching Culebra en route to Ensenada Honda, be very careful to stay south of the buoys that mark the reefs and shoals east of the island. It is all too easy to find yourself in the shoal water south of Arrecife Culebrita. The course from St. Thomas is approximately 260° magnetic. If the weather is good, you can pick up buoy number 2 and follow the numbered buoys straight up into the harbor. If conditions are bad, however, I recommend continuing southwestward until you have left to starboard the flashing red buoy marking Bajo Amarillo. Then lay a course of approximately 030° magnetic toward buoy number 8. Pick up the outer channel, which has an axis of 334° magnetic, and run in between the buoys and on up to the town of Culebra (formerly called Dewey).

If you are approaching from St. Croix, no problem. Lay off a course for the Bajos Grampus buoy, allowing for the westerly set of current, which will become more northwesterly as you near Culebra. Take cross bearings on Savana Island off St. Thomas, which will give you a good indication of when to start looking for the Grampus buoy. When you pick it up, don't be confused. It is number 2, the same buoy number as the one at the south end of Arrecife Culebrita. Is this numbering system just a booby trap to catch the unwary mariner? If conditions are good, head for buoy number 2, then Canal del Este. If conditions are bad, head for the southeast corner of Culebra, pick up the flashing red buoy marking Bajo Amarillo, turn to about 030°, head north, and

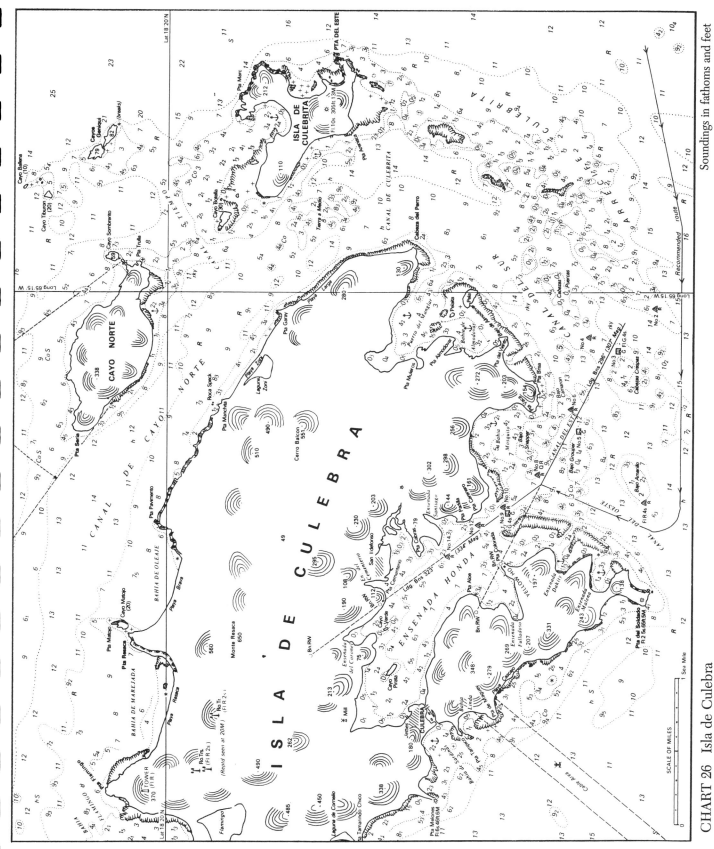

CHART 26 Isla de Culebra

Soundings in fathoms and feet

pick up the entrance buoys to the missing inner-channel range marks.

When leaving Ensenada Honda through Canal del Este and turning northeast into Canal del Sur, pay attention to the buoys and do careful eyeball navigation, because the area is littered with coral heads.

In all normal conditions, Ensenada Honda is an excellent harbor. You can anchor anywhere you want to, and you will be fine. Of course, many boats want to be close to the town of Culebra, so they will anchor near Cayo Pirata. If you wish to be farther away from town, you can anchor in other corners of the harbor. Be forewarned that you won't be able to sleep late if you anchor in Ensenada Honda—the commuter flights start arriving and departing at dawn.

Clearance in Culebra is dead simple, with the nicest Customs and Immigration officer I have ever met—Señor Silvestri, who holds forth at the airport. Give him a call; he will tell you to come and visit him. The easiest way to get there is to take your dinghy to one of the derelict docks in the northwest corner of the harbor and tie up the boat. Then walk two minutes to the main road and another five minutes to the airport for a quick, painless clearance. On the return trip, you might want to make a quick stop at the Happy Landings bar, home of the best sandwiches in town.

There are a number of small restaurants scattered around the harbor. Ownership changes frequently, so check them out when you get there. In the town hall is a small tourist office where you can pick up brochures with considerable information on Culebra.

One of the appealing features of Culebra is that most things are accessible via dinghy. When you anchor in Ensenada Honda and head for the canal between Ensenada Honda and Bahía de Sardinas, you'll see the Dinghy Dock restaurant about 100 yards to the east of the canal. If you tie up here, be sure to use your dinghy anchor to hold your stern off. The Dinghy Dock is a great place to tie up if you want to join in the Friday- and Saturday-night barbecues. Everything operates on the honor system: "You gets your drinks, you grabs your food, and when the time comes to leave, you goes and tells them how much you had and they figure out the bill." Similarly, above the water hose on the dock is a box with a sign over it: "Water, 5 cents a gallon." You fill your jugs on the honor system and drop in the right amount of money.

On the port side, behind the little mangrove island, is a fuel stop where you can pick up diesel, gasoline, and good kerosene; on the starboard side is

Mamacita's—excellent for breakfast and lunch (closed evenings). There is only four feet of water alongside the fuel dock, and the channel is very narrow, so I would not take a 40-foot boat in there. At the southwestern entrance of the canal is another fueling spot, but the hoses are not long enough to reach the end of the dock! Unless you draw four feet or less, refueling in Culebra is a matter of loading jerry cans into the dinghy and carting them back to your boat.

There is a lifting bridge over the canal, but it has only lifted once—the day it was inaugurated. When they lifted the bridge, it jammed, so there was no way to get a car from one side of the canal to the other. Reportedly it was stuck in the up position for several days, so when they finally got it back down, they decided never to raise it again. And that was more than 30 years ago!

Food shopping is none too good here. There are three small grocery shops, but sometimes if you ask for something you don't see, they may turn it up from the back room. We even managed to find birthday candles and birthday cards!

Fresh supplies come in every Tuesday night on the ferry from Puerto Rico. What is not sold Tuesday night is available in town on Wednesday morning, but all of the good stuff goes very quickly. When my mate Dale and my son Mark went to the ferry dock one Tuesday night, they returned two hours later, having met almost everyone on the island. It's rather like an Old West town, where everyone congregated when the once-a-week stagecoach came through.

On the northeast side of the village of Culebra is what purports to be a dinghy dock, but whoever designed it must have been an engineer sent down from the States to mess up the local economy. When we were there in February 1993, the height of the dock made it almost impossible to climb onto it from a dinghy. Even if you had had a 40-foot boat, the topsides would slide under the dock, the fenders would be useless, and the lifeline stanchions would be pulled right out. By February 1994, a wooden skirting had been attached to the dock, minimizing (but not eliminating) the problem. At least it was possible to climb onto the dock from a dinghy. There were electrical outlets, too, but they were not connected, and a padlocked chain extended across the inner end of the dock. On top of all that, no one seemed to know who was in charge!

Up the hill on the right is a little house with a sign that says, *Se Vende Hielo*—"We Sell Ice." Not only does he have cube ice, but there is also good, hard block ice at a reasonable price. The block ice is round—frozen up in plastic buckets.

Cube and block ice are also available at the fish factory in the dinghy pass between the two halves of Culebra. Next to the factory is a place that sells some marine supplies—not much stock, but enough to carry you over in an emergency. Amazingly, this is the only place in the Caribbean that I have seen selling well-made, nine-foot oars and bronze oarlocks.

You can buy kerosene (bring your own container) at the gas station on the west side of the channel near the fish factory. To fill gas bottles, hop in the dinghy and go to the head of the harbor. Pass the baseball field, then the big white house, and stop at the next dock, where you will find a fisherman who fills gas bottles from 100-pound cylinders. It's not too efficient, but it beats sending them over to Fajardo.

Throughout the Caribbean, getting a good breakfast at an early hour is a lost cause. The above-mentioned Mamacita's can take care of you for breakfast, but the best place in Culebra used to be the Hard Luck Cafe ("a sunny place for shady people"). Unfortunately, when we were there in February 1994, it was closed—let's hope it will reopen before long.

At the southern entrance to the channel between the island's two halves is a building with four laundry machines that you can plug full of quarters. Unfortunately, there are no dryers. We had no success finding showers, so you'll just have to go for a swim and dump a bucket of fresh water over your head.

There is a bank, but it is not open every day. When we went looking for a photocopy machine, we found out that there is only one on the island, and it wasn't working. When we asked about a fax machine, we discovered that Mr. Cortez who works in the post office has one at home. For a fee, he is happy to send and receive faxes for you. (This whole experience reminded us of life in Tortola 30 years ago!)

There are few phones; local calls are only 10 cents, and calls to Puerto Rico are just under a dollar. You can, however, plug into AT&T and USA Direct lines.

Cars are available for rent, but the island is so small (seven miles long), why rent a car? Bicycles are also available for rent.

Henry Gabriel Canovos, owner of Martez el Fresco—a small hotel, restaurant, and delicatessen—is an interesting fellow who is full of information about the island's past, present, and future. He moved here from Puerto Rico 25 years ago to teach in the little school but then gave up teaching and built a dock to cater to Puerto Rican fishermen who came visiting on weekends. Like many others, he was wiped out by Hurricane Hugo, but he has rebuilt in concrete rather than wood.

Due south from Cayo Pirata appears to me to be the best anchorage within Ensenada Honda. It is readily accessible to town, the water is clean (but not clear), yet it is far enough offshore not to have a bug problem. Farther to leeward, the water begins to run out. The farther west you go, the greater the fetch and chop when the wind pipes up. It is interesting to note that the wind funnels between the hills on both sides of the harbor and increases in velocity as you get farther into the harbor. It blows five knots more off Cayo Pirata than it does behind the reef southeast of Punta Colorada.

Some boats like to anchor behind Cayo Verde, which means that if the wind is north of east, you are getting good shelter from Cayo Verde. However, this puts you farther from town. Boats looking to get away from heavy weather are likely to stick up into Ensenada del Coronel and Ensenada del Cementerio (the real hurricane holes are up by San Ildefonso, north of Punta Cabras). This is where Herb Payson, owner of *Red Shoes* and author of the humorous book *Blown Away,* anchored during Hugo. He survived, but after examining the area, I cannot believe that more than 30 boats can tuck into that corner.

Needless to say, if you examine the chart, Ensenada Santiago also provides a place where you can tuck a boat in. Ensenada Honda is not a good hurricane hole, because you need to be absolutely up in the mangroves. If you are not in there when the hurricane passes by, the wind clocks around and you can end up having as much as five miles of fetch. That much fetch, backed up by 100 knots of wind, guarantees that no anchor will hold. Plus, with the number of boats that will have crowded into the harbor, someone is bound to be dragging down on you. So forget it.

One of the best anchorages in Ensenada Honda is between Punta Colorada and Ensenada Dakity. There you have absolutely calm water, as the reef to windward breaks the swell and the wind comes whistling across the top of the reef. The water is crystal clear, the bottom is white sand, the holding is excellent, there are no bugs—this is certainly one of the better anchorages in the Caribbean.

The entrance to Ensenada Dakity is from the north, by Punta Colorada. In February 1993, when we scouted the eastern entrance from the dinghy, we reached the conclusion that you might be able to power out through there with a good engine, but only a madman would run downwind through that entrance. It is possible to go from Ensenada Dakity to Ensenada Malena inside the reef in a shoal-draft (three feet or less) boat. There is good swimming and snorkeling in the area between the two harbors.

Ensenada Malena is not as great as it appears on the chart. The entrance is wider than that of Ensenada Dakity, so it does not give enough shelter. Plus, around the shores of Ensenada Malena are numerous small houses, whereas there is nothing except a few boats in Ensenada Dakity.

West Coast of Culebra and Islands to the West

Due north of Punta del Soldado, in an unnamed bay, is an excellent anchorage. The beach is gravel rather than white sand, but as long as the wind is in the east or north of east, it should be fine. (*Iolaire* did not anchor here, but we explored it by dinghy.) As you continue northwest from Punta del Soldado, you can anchor almost anywhere on the shelf. There are shingle beaches, but no sand beaches until Punta de Maguey.

Behind Bahía Linda is a small anchorage where only one or two boats could squeeze in. On the eastern side is a small sand beach.

BAHIA DE SARDINAS
(Chart 26; II A, A-1, A-13, A-131, A-14, A-2, A-23)

This bay on the south side of the town of Culebra (Dewey) provides a good anchorage in two fathoms of water. Be careful of the detached rock northwest of Punta Tampico. You can get from here into Ensenada Honda, but it is strictly a dinghy passage. It has been dredged out several times, but each time it has filled in again. This is the commercial port for the ferry that connects Culebra and Puerto Rico. On the south side of the bay are some attractive sand beaches—not completely isolated, however, as there are houses along the shore.

PUNTA MELONES
(Chart 26; II A, A-1, A-13, A-131, A-14, A-2, A-23)

Just north of Punta Melones is a good anchorage with a white-sand bottom. The small beach is very crowded on weekends, when Puerto Ricans arrive in droves, but during the week, you should find it deserted.

BAHIA TAMARINDO
(II A, A-1, A-13, A-131, A-14, A-2, A-23)

This excellent anchorage is likely to be better in winter and early spring than in summer. When the wind goes to the southeast in summer, it probably will funnel up between Culebra and Cayo de Luis Peña.

North of Punta Tamarindo Grande, I haven't visited the anchorages, but Alan Maubery, who runs a dive boat out of Puerto del Rey Marina, reports that the little cove north of Punta Tamarindo Grande has a beautiful white-sand beach and room for three boats. It is an excellent anchorage, but only in summer, as it is open to the winter ground swell.

CAYO DE LUIS PENA
(II A, A-1, A-13, A-131, A-14, A-2, A-23)

During summer, when the brown boobies are nesting here, access is restricted. In winter, there are a number of good anchorages. One of the nicest is the cove in the southeast corner of the island. Sail in between the reefs, but only if you are a good eyeball navigator and have a fairly small boat (30 feet or under). Or go in under power, round up, and anchor behind the south reef. Only one or two boats can fit in here. You'll find excellent reef snorkeling and a good beach. A short walk to the western side of the peninsula (be sure to wear shoes) takes you to a glorious sand beach. There is also an anchorage off the beach—mixed sand and rock. Be sure to anchor in the sand.

On the west side of Cayo de Luis Peña, north of Punta Cruz, is another anchorage. During the summer, there are excellent anchorages on the northwest side of the island. During the winter, however, anywhere along the northwest shore is open to the ground swell. Most boats anchor on the southern side of the northwest cove, but Alan Maubery highly recommends anchoring in the northernmost corner of that cove. Alan has confirmed all of the anchorages in the islands west of Culebra, and we have checked them out from the air.

CAYO DE AGUA
(II A, A-1, A-13, A-131, A-14, A-2, A-23)

Half a mile west of Cayo de Luis Peña, Cayo de Agua provides good shelter in normal conditions, when an anchorage can be had in the cove on the south side of the island. Depth is two fathoms; use two anchors and dive to make sure they are secure;

if you drag off the shelf, the anchor will be hanging straight down.

CAYO LOBO

(II A, A-1, A-13, A-131, A-14, A-2, A-23)

In stable conditions, when it is not blowing hard, an anchorage can be found in the cove on the southwestern side of Cayo Lobo. Again make sure you are well anchored—if you drag off, your next stop will be Puerto Rico!

CAYO LOBITO

(II A, A-1, A-13, A-131, A-14, A-2, A-23)

In late spring and summer (NOT in winter), an anchorage can be had in 18 feet, sand bottom, between the cove on the north end of Cayo Lobito and south of Cayo Tuna. On the western side of the island, due west of the light, there is also an anchorage. Again, be sure you are properly anchored. Diving is excellent around the island.

North Coast of Culebra

BAHIA FLAMINGO

(II A, A-1, A-13, A-131, A-14, A-2, A-23)

Surfers flock here, where the Flamingo Hotel has its base. In winter, the bay is open to the ground swell, but it is big enough so that you can anchor well out in the middle and still have swinging room if the ground swell came in. However, you are likely to spend a rocky-and-rolly night. Come summer, you can anchor in the head of the harbor and be sheltered from all directions except right out of the north—which is extremely uncommon that time of year.

BAHIA DE MAREJADA/BAHIA DE OLEAJE

(II A, A-1, A-13, A-131, A-14, A-2, A-23)

These bays are totally useless as anchorages in the winter, when they are glorious for surfing. In the summer, however, when the wind is in the south and it hasn't been blowing hard, you probably could anchor in these bays and enjoy vast stretches of pure white sand and little habitation.

Southwest Coast of Culebra

BAHIA MOSQUITO

(Chart 26; II A, A-1, A-13, A-131, A-14, A-2, A-23)

As long as the wind is north of east, this is a good place to anchor away from it all. There is nothing much in the way of beaches, but there should be good snorkeling behind Punta Vaca. We have explored Bahía Mosquito in *Iolaire's* dinghy, and the shelter appears to be good. The anchorage is in sand and grass, so holding may not be too secure. A couple of handsome houses overlook the beach. One could have been pulled out of Aspen, Colorado, and dropped in the tropics; the others are of typical West Indian design, with big porches.

Behind the beach is a salt pond, which makes me suspect that Bahía Mosquito is well named, so do not anchor close to shore. Try to find some clear sand for good holding.

PUERTO DEL MANGLAR

(Chart 26; II A, A-1, A-13, A-131, A-14, A-2, A-23)

There is an anchorage on the north side of Puerto del Manglar, but it is exposed to the easterly swell, with a good fetch. A couple of boats are on permanent moorings there, and the dock is nice, but the head of the dock has a huge sign, "Private Property. No Trespassing."

The head of the bay is shallow and surrounded by mangroves, while the western side has a cove called Punta Muleros, completely enclosed by mangroves—among the largest I have seen outside of Las Aves in Venezuela. Unfortunately, most of these giant trees are dead. There is a good five feet of water almost all the way up to the head of Puerto Muleros; this ought to be a good spot for fishing fans.

Entering Puerto del Manglar is dead simple. Just sail by the entrance, heading north or south, and the entrance will open up. Run on in. If heading southwest into Bahía de Almodovar (see below), jibe over and pass between the red and green stakes marking the two sides of the channel. Pass midway between them. This channel carries about 12 feet. Once inside, anchor wherever you desire.

BAHIA DE ALMODOVAR

(Chart 26; II A, A-1, A-13, A-131, A-14, A-2, A-23)

Without doubt, this is one of the finest anchorages in the entire Eastern Caribbean—clear water, white-sand bottom, and a reef to windward that breaks the sea. We were lying there in 20 knots of wind with nothing but a small chop! During the week, the anchorage is most likely to be deserted.

There is excellent snorkeling on the reef to windward. Tiny Isla Pelaita has a couple of quiet little beaches, ideal for skinny dipping, but stay away during the summer, when it is a bird refuge. (Signs are posted.) Brown boobies fly all the way from the Galápagos to nest in huge flocks in the small islands around Culebra and Vieques.

The "islands" northwest and northeast of Isla Pelaita are in fact reefs that only break the surface at low, low water in the summer. (The older Imray-Iolaire charts and the NOAA charts used to show these as islands.)

Leaving Bahía de Almodovar is no problem, but if the wind is in the southeast, be prepared to throw in three or four quick tacks as you leave Puerto del Manglar. A fair-size bobble can build up at the entrance to the harbor, making tacking a bit difficult if one is not prepared.

You can take a dinghy southwest around Punta del Viento to an unnamed bay where there is good snorkeling, but there is absolutely no anchorage in this bay. The water is much shallower than most of the old charts indicate.

Islands to the East

CAYO NORTE
(Chart 26; II A, A-1, A-13, A-131, A-14, A-2, A-23)

I have not visited this little island, but I have flown over it, and it looks as though there should be a good anchorage on the shelf in the southeast corner of the island in late spring and early summer—as long as the wind is east or north of east. Further, in summer, when there is no danger of the ground swell, there also should be a good anchorage behind the southeast corner of Cayo Sombrero (between Cayo Sombrero and the shelf between Cayo Sombrero and Cayo Norte). However, I definitely advise a bow-and-stern anchor in case the current runs to windward over the shelf at the change of tide. These anchorages should be strictly for reef pilots who are interested in exploring.

CULEBRITA
(Chart 26; II A, A-1, A-13, A-131, A-14, A-2, A-23)

A protected anchorage may be found in the cove on the northwest side, but it is completely exposed to the ground swell in winter, so it can be very uncomfortable. Be sure to anchor bow-and-stern so that if the ground swell comes in, you will not swing around and end up on the beach. If you equip yourself with shoes, long-sleeved shirt, long pants, hat, and machete, you can cross the low land to a beautiful beach on the windward side of the island. In March 1994, while flying low over the area in Jon Repke's plane, we spotted the path. Whether it was made by goats or humans, I don't know, but a path does exist.

The best anchorage is off the ruined docks due west of the lighthouse. The bottom comes up very steeply here—from 16 feet to 70 feet—so make sure you don't drag off the shelf. Use two anchors and dive down to be sure they are well buried. This anchorage is sheltered from all directions except due south or southwest—uncommon wind directions—and is best if the wind is east or north of east. It gets a little lumpy if the wind is south of east.

A climb to the lighthouse is well worth the effort, since you get spectacular views westward to Culebra and Puerto Rico and eastward to the Virgin Islands. It is a hot climb, so take water. Go early in the day, since the Culebrita mosquitoes come out the minute the wind dies.

West of Culebrita is a shoal called Tierra a Medio, which has great fishing. Row the dinghy out, anchor, and dinner will be forthcoming.

Vieques

Like Culebra, Vieques is one of the undiscovered islands of the Eastern Caribbean, with many fine anchorages. Not realizing that the US Navy no longer uses the island for target practice, many yachtsmen still avoid the island. Only the area east of Cerro Matlas is still used by the military. The rest of the island can be visited anytime. The only thing I have been warned about is that low-flying jets may scare the living daylights out of you as they make their approaches to and take off from the eastern tip of the island. The navy's observation post is so brilliantly lighted that it can be seen 20 miles off, making it a perfect reference point for navigating through the area between Puerto Rico and St. Thomas.

On the south coast of Vieques, with Puerto Real, Ensenada Sun Bay, Puerto Mosquito, Puerto Ferro, Bahía de la Chiva, and Ensenada Honda, there is enough cruising to keep a yachtsman busy for weeks. In Ensenada Honda alone, up among the mangroves, are enough hurricane holes to hide the entire St. Thomas charter-boat fleet with room to spare.

There is a daily ferry from Fajardo, plus commuter flights from Puerto Rico.

ISABEL SEGUNDA

(II A, A-1, A-13, A-131, A-14, A-141, A-2)

When approaching Vieques from the east, it will be necessary to gain entrance to Puerto Rican waters at Isabel Segunda. The town harbor is a good anchorage when the wind is in the southeast, but the combination of a northerly wind and the ground swell will make it uncomfortable. The anchorage, which can be rocky and rolly, is off the small pier between Punta Mulas and the commercial pier. The town is nothing spectacular. There is a fuel dock that sells diesel and gas, reputedly with 10 feet alongside. Gas bottles can be filled at the Esso garage, and cube ice is available. A few grocery stores carry the basics, but this is no place to reprovision.

Overlooking the town is a star-shaped fort—the last bastion built by the Spanish in the New World. Construction began in 1843, but I have no idea why it was built where it is. There are higher hills around it, so it is hard to spot from the sea, which should have made it very vulnerable. Reputedly, it was so costly that the Queen of Spain asked if the bricks were made of gold. Nowadays, the fort houses a museum of art history and the Vieques archives.

Punta Mulas lighthouse is undergoing restoration and will also become a museum. (Spanish lighthouse architecture was absolutely superb.)

CABALLO BLANCO

(II A, A-1, A-13, A-131, A-14, A-141, A-2)

Northwest of Isabel Segunda, this islet appears to be a good daytime anchorage. We did not stop here, because we were in something of a hurry, but we hove-to on *Iolaire* and looked it over. It has a beautiful reef and a white-sand beach—all deserted. It's definitely off the beaten track and a worthwhile day stop. It might even be a good overnight anchorage in calm conditions—as long as you were rigged to get out in a hurry if you had to.

If you are approaching Vieques from the north, be very careful of the extensive reefs—Escollo de Arenas—to the northwest of Isabel Segunda. You can avoid them by sailing with chart in hand and taking careful bearings on the numerous buoys in the area. Keep a watchful eye until you are clear of the naval pier. West of the pier, it is clear sailing. Boats drawing five feet or less can sail across Escollo de Arenas, and deeper-draft boats can also do it if they are navigated skillfully. The current scours the sand and moves the channels in this area, so the charts must be read with appropriate caution. The water is not clear, so eyeball navigation is not reliable. If you draw more than five feet, I recommend that you go around the northwestern corner of Escollo de Arenas and then turn south toward Punta Arenas.

Western End of Vieques

If heading westward from Isabel Segunda, follow the buoyed channel or wait until the sun is directly overhead and proceed with careful eyeball monitoring. There are numerous shoals and coral heads just under the surface.

There is a good and very popular anchorage south of Punta Arenas and just west of the tanks—a favorite weekend destination for the yachts from Roosevelt Roads Yacht Club. During the week, the anchorage is likely to be deserted. The beach is beautiful—all white sand.

The NOAA charts and the old Imray-Iolaire charts show a reef south of Punta Bermudes, but Ed Saari (a first-rate refrigeration expert in Puerto Rico) tells me that there is no reef and that it is an excellent anchorage when the northern end of the beach is crowded.

Alan Maubery reports excellent anchorages (for boats drawing six feet or less) a mile southeast of Punta Boca Quebrada. The chart shows a reef sticking out, but Alan says you can go in behind the reef as long as the conditions are good and you understand eyeball navigation.

South Coast of Vieques

PUERTO REAL

(Chart 27; II A, A-1, A-13, A-131, A-2)

Ten feet can be carried into this anchorage. Do not trust the NOAA charts for this harbor, since one of them clearly shows 10 feet between Cayo Real and Vieques, when in fact the depth is five feet. We found this out the hard way when we came up to the shoal hard on the wind on the port tack. My mate, Alston, said the water looked "tin," and he wasn't referring to a depth of 10 feet—he meant it was looking thin! I agreed, but I felt we were heeled

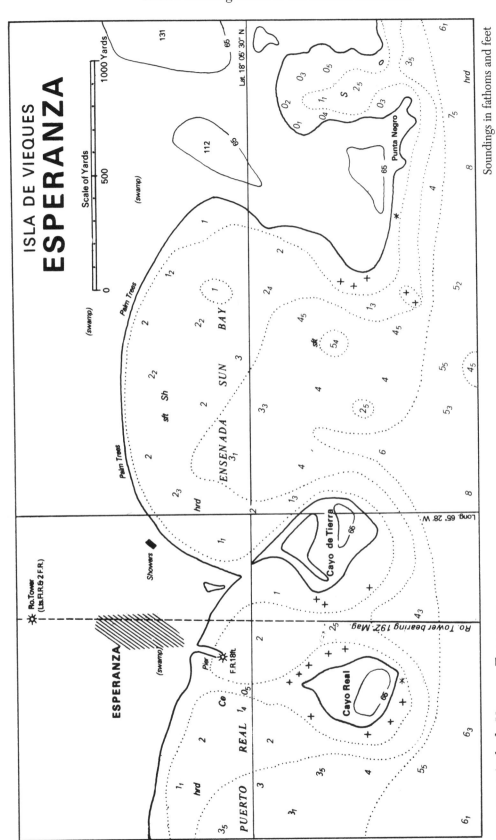

CHART 27 Isla de Vieques, Esperanza

over far enough so that even if the chart were slightly inaccurate, we could still skim over the shoal. I was wrong. We ground to a halt right at the top of the falling tide.

It might be interesting to tell how we got off—it wasn't easy. We ran an anchor out ahead and pulled it home. Then we ran another anchor out ahead and pulled that home. Then we got mad, tied one anchor line onto the other, and ran the line over the bow to a dock piling. We rigged a block and tackle on the anchor line, ran the fall to a big winch, and cranked away. The anchor line became taut—but *Iolaire* did not move. Then Charlie Connelly arrived in his sportfisherman, and he added his 230 hp of Caterpillar diesel. Still nothing. In desperation, we took the spinnaker halyard to Charlie's boat, and he slowly put a strain on the halyard to heel us down until the lee rail was well under. Suddenly we floated off, shooting forward like a rocket when the stretch came out of the line.

It turned out to be a very propitious grounding for us, because Charlie came aboard, had a beer, and wanted no salvage payment. We discovered that he had a Boston Whaler and had spent 20 years on the island diving and fishing, so we made a deal with him to give us a guided tour of the south coast of Vieques early the next morning. This we proceeded to do, and all the yachtsmen who use this guide and the Imray-Iolaire charts for the island of Vieques owe a great deal of thanks to Charlie Connelly.

Note: I reported this chart error to NOAA when I visited the Washington office in 1982, and it still had not been corrected in 1993!

There are two anchorages off Puerto Real. One is west of the shoal, sheltered in all normal weather but not as calm as the one east of the shoal. Boats drawing five feet or less can swing over the top of the shoal and anchor in the eastern bay. Boats drawing more than five feet should continue east, south of Cayo Real, until the radio tower bears 192° magnetic. Then run in on this bearing between Cayo Real and Cayo de Tierra, round up, and anchor in a convenient location. This is a beautiful anchorage: good swimming, good beaches, and the pleasant small town of Esperanza. There are numerous good and inexpensive restaurants along the shore, a few small grocery stores, and an excellent dive shop run by a former navy officer.

ENSENADA SUN BAY
(Chart 27; II A, A-1, A-13, A-131, A-2)

This is a fair anchorage with a long, white-sand beach that is likely to be mobbed in the summer and during the Christmas and Easter holidays; it has average-size crowds on weekends. During the week, however, it is yours to enjoy. There are showers that you are supposed to pay for, but we couldn't find out how and where to pay for them, so we had them for free. There is more water pressure than I have seen anywhere—the shower almost blasts you through the floor. If you are anchored in Puerto Real and want a fine beach, merely take your dinghy to the sandspit between Cayo de Tierra and the "mainland," pull it up on the beach, and walk across the spit to Ensenada Sun Bay.

Sun Bay is a bit rocky and rolly—which goes hand-in-hand with a white-sand beach—but it is passable as an anchorage in the right conditions.

PUERTO NEGRO
(II A, A-1, A-13, A-131, A-2)

Charlie Connelly did not think too much of Puerto Negro when he was showing us the south-coast harbors, but in future years, when Vieques begins to become crowded, this small harbor may be a good spot to get away from it all.

PUERTO MOSQUITO
(II A, A-1, A-13, A-131, A-2)

This bay has a number of anchorages. The outer anchorage on the starboard hand on the way in, right behind the reef, is the kind I like. Northwest of the reef is a beautiful, windswept anchorage with good snorkeling and some small sand beaches. But if you like to fish with a rod and reel and want complete shelter, you can continue up through the channel. You can squeeze six feet into this harbor at high water. Proceed very slowly—no real danger, since it is all soft mud—but hug the western side of the channel going in. Once inside, you can anchor anywhere and enjoy complete shelter, excellent fishing, mangrove oysters, solitude—and splendid displays of phosphorescence on dark nights.

PUERTO FERRO
(II A, A-1, A-13, A-131, A-2)

The entrance to Puerto Ferro is very easy to find, since there is a modern light on the point west of Puerto Ferro. Just north of the light is a wonderful old Spanish lighthouse, a magnificent building with a fantastic view looking right out into the trades.

And right below the lighthouse is a beautiful white-sand beach.

One danger on this coast is a breaking rock 100 yards offshore, south-southwest of the light. Do not get close inshore in this area.

When entering Puerto Ferro, hug the starboard side of the channel and anchor when well inside the harbor. Seven feet can be squeezed in with care. Once anchored, get in your dinghy, get out the rod and reel, and have some fun fishing among the mangroves. (Needless to say, with the presence of the mangroves, Puerto Ferro makes an excellent hurricane hole.)

Warning: There is also an unbuoyed reef southeast of Bahía Corcho with only two feet of water over it. Make sure you spot this reef when working your way eastward. There is plenty of water inside and outside of it, but no water over it.

BAHIA CORCHO/BAHIA TAPON

Forget about these two. There are nice beaches but no anchorages in Bahía Corcho; Bahía Tapon has no water inside.

BAHIA DE LA CHIVA

(Chart 28; II A, A-1, A-13, A-131, A-2)

This bay provides two good anchorages—one northwest of Isla Chiva, the other east of Isla Chiva, right up under Punta Conejo. Do not try to pass between Isla Chiva and the "mainland," since there is only three feet of water. This is strictly a dinghy passage.

ENSENADA HONDA

(Chart 28; II A, A-1, A-13, A-131, A-2, A-23)

Here is the pièce de résistance of the south coast of Vieques. You can spend days exploring this bay. There is complete shelter inside and passages up into the mangroves with 10 or 15 feet of water. In hurricane conditions, there is room to hide hundreds of boats, and there was little or no damage to the 30 or 40 boats that tucked in here during Hugo in 1989.

Around the edges of the harbor, use a leadline or sounding pole and feel your way around—there are countless nooks and crannies.

To enter Ensenada Honda, approach from the south, steering a course of about 345° magnetic and favoring the lighthouse side of the entrance. As you enter the harbor, start swinging around to the north and head for Punta Carenero. Once you have picked up Los Galafatos (the three rocks that look like turtles just breaking water), come around so that you keep Los Galafatos just to the north of Cerro Matlas, the site of the artillery observation post. Head for the rocks on a course of about 065° magnetic. As you approach Punta Carenero, head northeast; eyeball and feel with the sounding pole or leadline, working your way eastward.

The best water is close to the little island north of Los Galafatos—swing east and you are back in deep water. With care, 12 feet can be carried into the deep anchorage northeast of Cayo Jalovita. Throw the pick in anywhere and start exploring, fishing, and snorkeling on the outer reefs that form the south side of Ensenada Honda.

Eastern End of Vieques

You will need to check on the military situation before entering the eastern end of Vieques and anchoring in the wonderful harbors of the north coast. If a land line is available, call 865-5263 or 865-5266 and ask if the range is hot. Otherwise, you can use VHF and call "Vieques target" weekdays from 0800 to 1900. If you can't raise anyone on the radio, it probably means they are not firing, but keep trying. Another way to double-check is to focus your binoculars on the observation post. If a large red flag is flying, that means they are firing. If there is only the orange windsock and no flag, they are not. (Even if there is no firing, you may be warned not to enter this area, so remember that you do this at your own risk. We have never encountered any problems in eastern Vieques, and the anchorages are indeed splendid.)

When crossing Vieques Sound from Culebra to Vieques, the westerly set is very strong. In 1993, on the day we did it, the current was running at least two knots to the west. It set us so far to leeward that we ended up hard on the wind as we approached the eastern end of Vieques. It did not look like we would clear Punta Este, but suddenly, a mile off, we hit a back eddy. The current was running to windward at a knot and a half, possibly two knots, producing steep, breaking seas. It was rough going, but the ride sucked us up to windward and around Punta Este as if it were a vacuum cleaner. Once we were around the point, the current was again running to the west. What caused the eastward-flowing eddy north of Punta Este is beyond me.

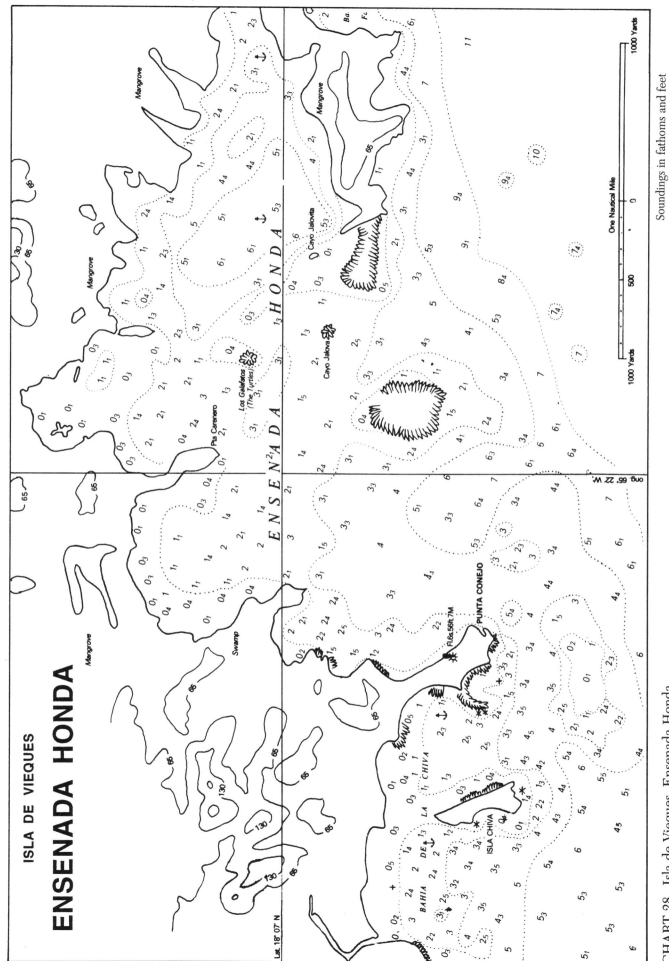

CHART 28   Isla de Vieques, Ensenada Honda

Soundings in fathoms and feet

BAHIA FANDUCA

East of Ensenada Honda, this bay does not seem to be deep enough to provide any shelter. I recommend skipping it.

BAHIA YOYE

(II A, A-1, A-13, A-131, A-2, A-23)

Exploring this area on foot, we decided that it looks excellent. Anchor in the northeast corner, and note that there are detached rocks off the southeast corner. (These rocks are not shown on the older Imray-Iolaire charts.) There should be good diving around the edges.

BAHIA JALOVA

(II A, A-1, A-13, A-131, A-2)

Here's another secluded bay with a white-sand beach. (We visited Bahía Jalova in a dinghy, not in *Iolaire*.) Feel your way in and anchor in the southeast corner in mixed sand and grass (the holding is somewhat iffy). There is excellent diving on the rocks on the east side and also on the island on the western side of the bay.

BAHIA SALINA DEL SUR

(Chart 29-30; II A, A-1, A-13, A-131, A-14, A-2, A-23)

No question, this is definitely one of the 10 best anchorages in the Eastern Caribbean, but be sure you have the all-clear from the military before you enter (see information above). Be sure you have the latest Imray-Iolaire charts, as the old ones are not correct for this bay. The reef on the south side of the harbor extends much farther west than the old chart indicates, so the harbor is even more sheltered than it seemed. The wind would have to go south of west before it could send a swell into the harbor. The reef only has a foot or so of water over it, so even in a southeasterly, all the swell would be broken. For the whole two days we were here in 1993, we encountered a small bobble, but since *Iolaire* is heavy and the mizzen was up, we were never uncomfortable. I suspect that lighter boats would want to minimize the roll by anchoring bow-and-stern in a southeast-northwest or a south-north axis.

The beaches cover the entire harbor, and there is excellent snorkeling on the reefs. The navy officially recommends that you not go ashore here, but if you do, be sure not to poke around any of the military debris you may find on the beach.

The best dinghy landing is just west of the small island on the north side of the bay. Swing in behind the island, drop the dinghy anchor, and run a bow or stern line from the dinghy to the seagrape trees ashore. You can leave the dinghy in perfect safety in calm water without having to pull it up onto the beach.

When we were here, we took a half-mile hike over to Bahía Icacos (see below), on the other side of the island. You can anchor in one bay and walk to the other, but it is hot, so be sure to carry water and wear shoes. (Yours truly, with his tough West Indian feet, did it without shoes, but Trich definitely needed hers.) You can also carry swimming gear and swim across to Isla Yallis, a beautiful deserted island with a fantastic white-sand beach on its eastern end.

We did aerial spotting of the harbors at the very eastern end of Vieques—on both sides of Punta Este—and all have beautiful white-sand beaches. Weather permitting, it certainly is worthwhile to hop in the dinghy from a secure anchorage farther west and go off to these beaches, where you can have complete privacy—there are no roads, so no tour bus is likely to show up suddenly with a horde of tourists.

BAHIA ICACOS

(Chart 29-30; II A, A-1, A-13, A-131, A-14, A-2, A-23)

Without a doubt, this is one of the finest anchorages in the Eastern Caribbean. The easiest entrance is from the west, on a course of roughly 142° magnetic on the 147-foot-high hill on the eastern end of Vieques. It's wise to have a good reef navigator at the helm. The entrance is narrow, but you can sail through. The last time we were here, the wind was way around in the south. We could not lay the channel, yet the heavy, old, engineless *Iolaire* tacked four times between the outer reef and Isla Yallis. We anchored in the middle of the bay.

Be forewarned that the old Imray-Iolaire chart does not correctly show the reef on the eastern side of Cayo Icacos; it extends much farther northwest toward Isla Yallis than the chart shows. This is excellent, in that it gives double shelter—two reefs to break any swell coming in from the north. We were anchored here when it was blowing a full 20 to 25 knots out of the north, and we had nothing but a small bobble in the harbor. We were on two anchors,

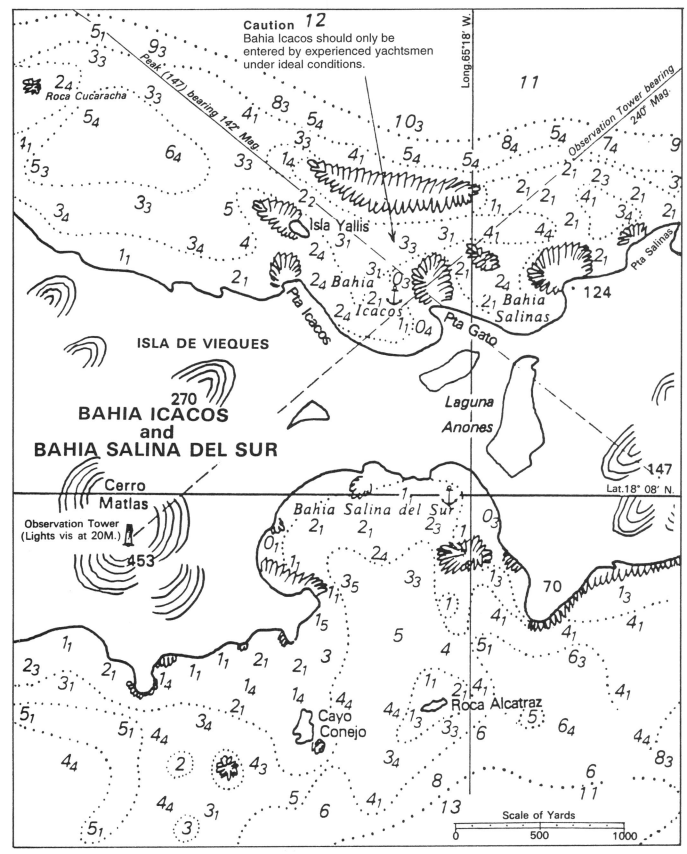

CHART 29-30 Isla de Vieques, Bahía Salina del Sur/Bahía Icacos   Soundings in fathoms and feet

and we did drag slightly before they set, but once set, all was well. Holding is good on a white-sand bottom, no grass.

It is possible to pass between Isla Yallis and Punta Icacos, but I estimate that the channel has only six or seven feet, whereas there was a full 14 feet through the channel north of Isla Yallis.

We did not sail or sound the eastern channel, but from the bosun's chair on *Iolaire*'s masthead, the water depths looked about right. I would not enter via the eastern channel, however, as it means running dead downwind. The only time I would do that is in the morning in light airs—on a boat with an engine.

Navigate with great caution along the eastern end of the north coast. We have explored the area in *Iolaire* and also by dinghy, and have updated the Imray-Iolaire charts accordingly. There are many hazards, some still uncharted. Sail only in good light, especially if you are using older charts. One particularly bad spot is the area west of Bahía Icacos, between Roca Cucaracha and Vieques, where there are numerous uncharted coral heads.

PUERTO DIABLO
(II A, A-1, A-13, A-131, A-14, A-2, A-23)

Iolaire did not go into this cove, but we explored it in the dinghy. Puerto Diablo is a one-boat anchorage only in summer, when the wind is out of the south. There is a nice sand beach.

PUERTO NEGRO
(II A, A-1, A-13, A-131, A-14, A-2)

I have not anchored in Puerto Negro and indeed have not even been able to find out whether it is a possible anchorage. If it is, it would be usable only in summer.

If you are heading westward from Vieques, it is dead downwind to Puerto Rico. The passage is discussed in chapters 1 and 6.

If you are going eastward to the Virgin Islands, take a break at one of the many anchorages in Culebra or Culebrita, and then slog your way eastward into Virgin Passage. Be prepared for some steep, high seas here, especially during flood tide, when the current opposes the tide. This is one of those times that comes to all sailors when you must pull your head in and slog it out. Remember, though, that you don't have to sail all the way to St. Thomas Harbor in one shot. As described at the beginning of this chapter, you can duck in and anchor in Airport Bay or behind Saba Island or at Buck Island, have a good night's sleep, and continue on to St. Thomas the following morning.

However difficult the return trip, I consider a cruise through the Passage Islands time well spent, especially for anyone who has become familiar with the Virgins and is casting about for new territory to explore. The people are friendly, the food inexpensive, the anchorages quiet and secluded.

NOTES

NOTES

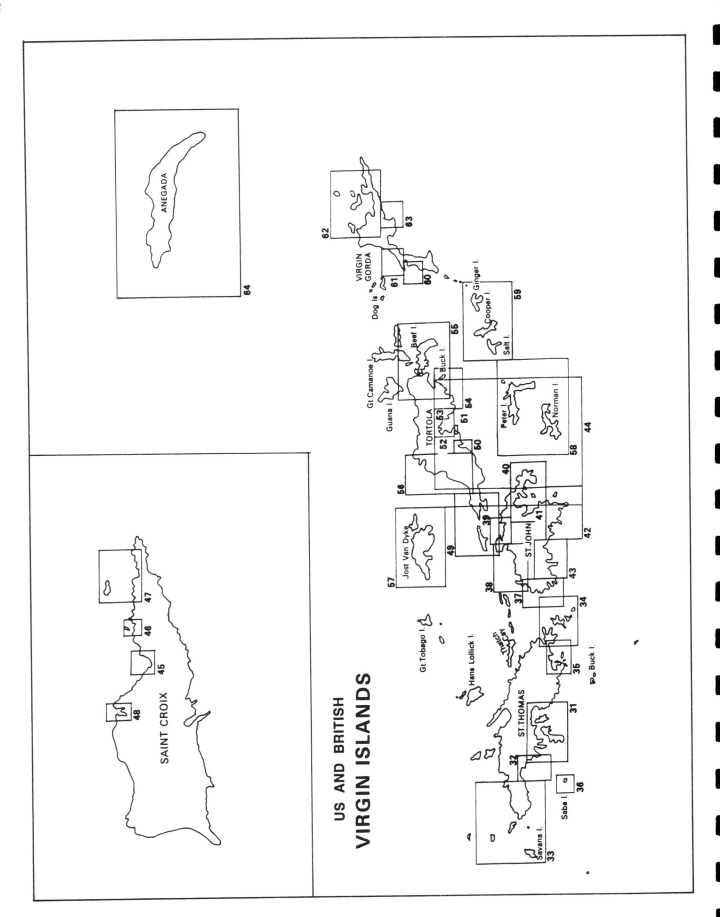

US AND BRITISH
VIRGIN ISLANDS

ANEGADA

64

SAINT CROIX

47

46

45

48

VIRGIN
GORDA

Dog Is.

62

63

61

60

Ginger I.

Cooper I.

Salt I.

59

Beef I.

Buck I.

55

Gt. Camanoe

Guana I.

TORTOLA

52

53

51

54

50

56

Peter I.

Norman I.

58

44

40

41

St. John

42

Jost Van Dyke

57

49

39

38

37

43

34

Gt. Tobago I.

Hans Lollick I.

Thatch Cay

35

Buck I.

ST. THOMAS

31

32

36

Saba I.

Savana I.

33

8

United States Virgin Islands

(Imray-Iolaire Charts A, A-23, A-231, A-232, A-233, A-234, A-235)

Thirty-five miles due east of Puerto Rico lies the group of islands commonly referred to as "the Virgins." They stretch from St. Thomas in the west to Anegada in the east and include St. Croix (even though it is 35 miles to the south). Except for St. Croix, all the islands are close to one another, offering excellent shelter from the ocean swell. But, because the islands lie on the same axis as the trades, these waters are not so protected that they break the force of the ever-present easterlies. While you may have to do a little more windward work than you might like—and you need to keep this in mind when selecting a boat for cruising in the Virgins—the islands are so close together as to afford numerous anchorages, all within easy sailing distance of one another. With many calm, comfortable anchorages and a steady, cooling breeze, it is hard to find better cruising grounds than the US and British Virgin Islands.

The three major US Virgins—St. Thomas, St. Croix, and St. John—are each discussed in separate chapters.

The United States purchased the Virgin Islands from Denmark in 1917 mainly as a defense measure; the navy needed another coaling port, and, more important, was afraid that Germany might acquire the islands. For many years, the islands were used strictly as a naval base, with the commanding officer of the base in charge of the whole operation.

Eventually the islands came under civil government, first with an appointed governor. Now the US Virgin Islands are frequently cited in the United Nations as an example of American colonialism. Although I have not seen it stated officially, I am sure that the US Department of the Interior would just as soon give the islands back to the Danes or grant them independence. This would save the US gov-

ernment a tremendous amount of time, money, and embarrassment.

These are the few remaining US possessions. They are part of the United States and pay whopping federal taxes. The total revenue, matched by subsidies from Washington, should produce an island paradise, but it doesn't. Why it doesn't could constitute a book in itself.

In fact, there happens to be such a book. For those interested in the background of how the US Virgin Islands were transformed from sleepy, pleasant little islands where everyone knew each other, to the present strife-torn areas they are today, I highly recommend Edward A. O'Neill's *Rape of the American Virgins.*

In the early and middle 1960s, my late wife and I would think nothing of wandering around St. Thomas late at night or in the early hours of the morning, walking into a West Indian bar, sitting down, and having a drink. In the early and middle seventies, however, radical black-power elements made themselves felt in St. Thomas and St. Croix. Despite the fact that the islands can only survive on tourism, some islanders became surly, arrogant, and downright dangerous. People were being robbed and stabbed in broad daylight. There were many areas in St. Thomas where even the police refused to go at night.

In earlier editions of the guide, I advised yachtsmen to take care of business in St. Thomas and get out immediately. Happily, however, things have changed. In recent years, the island government and the Tourist Board have mounted a massive drive to impress everyone in the islands that they need tourism and that tourists can only be attracted by a smiling face and a cooperative attitude. The campaign appears to be taking hold.

Admittedly, the crime rate is still high, and my experiences leave me with doubts as to the ability of the St. Thomas Police Department to maintain total law and order effectively. Nonetheless, the US Virgins are no longer the Vietnam-like no-man's-land that they were a few years ago—although you should still use common sense when wandering around at night.

The trades in the Virgins blow an average of 12 to 15 knots out of the east, but you must be prepared and rigged for a good deal more, since they often pipe up to 20 or 25 knots and howl for a few weeks. At other times, a front will blow through, attended by heavy squalls and plenty of wind and rain. The only thing to do, then, is to ride it out in a secure harbor for a day or two with a good book and a deck of cards. From December to April, the wind occasionally will sneak around to northwest. This is a slow process, so it can be detected easily. If it does occur, many of the customarily calm anchorages become lumpy, uncomfortable, and even dangerous. Be forewarned. Toward the end of April, the winds lighten and crawl southward, introducing what many consider to be the best cruising weather of the year. A comfortable, full-sail breeze usually remains steady through July. August through October, of course, is the hurricane season, with light and variable winds and a good deal of rain and humidity. The best way to proceed at this time is with plenty of stout ground tackle aboard, one ear tuned to the radio, the other ear tuned to local consensus, and both eyes on the weather map.

Note: Before considering cruising in the Virgins (or, for that matter, anywhere in the Eastern Caribbean) during hurricane season, be sure to read Reflections on Hugo, in the Foreword to this volume.

The temperature in the Virgins varies only slightly. In the summer and fall, the high is 90°F; in winter, it is 86°F. But as long as there is a breeze, it should never get really hot on board a boat.

The tidal rise and fall in the Virgin Islands is only about 18 inches, but this is not to be scoffed at. In some places—in narrow cuts or around the tips of islands—it can run very fast and significantly affect your course and sailing time. Generally, the tide floods in an easterly direction and ebbs in a westerly direction, so that if you are careful to watch the rise and fall on the shoreline, you can keep on top of the situation.

But it is not always so simple. During periods of heavy weather, with high winds from the east, the tide has been known to ebb (westerly flow) for as long as 24 hours, and when the weather turns calm again, the flow can be easterly for as long as 24

hours. In addition, the many juts and curves of the islands tend to alter the direction of the flow significantly, so it is essential to make a careful analysis in order to predict the strength and direction of the tidal currents at any given place and point in time.

A more complete description of wind, weather, and tides, along with a universal tide table, appears in chapter 6 of *Street's Transatlantic Crossing Guide and Introduction to the Caribbean.* This is the essential companion to each of the other volumes of this cruising-guide series, since it contains sailing directions for the entire Caribbean (including lists of navigational aids, radio stations, and times of weather broadcasts), plus information on entry and communications, provisions and services, chartering, yacht clubs and leaving.

Except during the hurricane season, most experienced yachtsmen in the Caribbean tend not to monitor weather broadcasts, because the standard forecast from November to June is winds east-northeast to east-southeast about 10 to 15 knots, higher in gusts. Even when the hinges are blowing off the gates of hell, 30 to 35 knots, they still will just say "higher in gusts."

But weather patterns, especially at the northern end of the Caribbean, have changed dramatically in the last 37 years, so weather broadcasts have become more important throughout the year. When I first arrived in the islands in the late 1950s, the weather fronts from the United States—the cold fronts—would push down through the Bahamas and stall on the western end of Hispaniola. As the years went by, these fronts began to push farther down until they finally spilled over to the western end of Puerto Rico. The only effect this had in the Virgins was to reduce the trades or once in a while produce a light wind out of the west. Eventually, though, the fronts started pushing themselves through Puerto Rico to the eastern end, and then sometimes on into the Passage Islands and even the Virgins. In February 1993, when we were anchored at Buck Island, St. Croix, facing northwest, we had pouring rain, fog, and a 25-knot wind from the northwest. Not only that, but the wind had been in the west for the previous two days!

Even though weather reports in the Eastern Caribbean can be pretty unreliable, it is wise to keep on top of them when cruising in the northern end of the Caribbean. El Oso, the English-language station (1030 AM, at seven to 10 minutes past the hour) in Puerto Rico, gives a fairly good weather analysis, but it is primarily for Puerto Rico and not necessarily viable in the eastern end of the Virgin Islands (remember that Anegada is 100 miles east of Puerto

Rico). Puerto Rico is a big enough island so its land mass can affect the overall weather.

WSTX (970 AM) on St. Croix provides a complete weather summary at 0735 and again at 0805, as well as a brief report three minutes after every hour.

WVWI (1000 AM) on St. Thomas gives weather at 0630, 1205, and 1715.

ZBVI (780 AM) on Tortola broadcasts weather at 1230, then again every hour on the half hour until 2300, when it closes down. It rebroadcasts BBC news at 1600 and 1900.

Virgin Islands Radio WAH in St. Thomas gives a brief weather report on channels 28 and 85 at 0800 and 2000, as well as very detailed weather reports covering the entire Caribbean and North Atlantic at 0600, 1400, and 2200. (Those times are approximate, as the weather report tends to come on five or 10 minutes after the hour.) That weather report is rebroadcast on SSB channels 401 (4357.0), 409 (4381.0), 604 (6510.0), and 1201 (13077.0).

VHF channel 3 carries a continuous NOAA Weather broadcast—with information updated regularly—24 hours a day. This is a great asset, as WAH on the top of St. Thomas can be heard almost all the way to St. Martin and the east coast of Puerto Rico. Within the Virgins are a couple of blank spots (such as Gorda Sound) where the broadcasts are obscured by mountains.

Radio Antilles (930 AM) and Radio Montserrat (885 AM) broadcast weather at 0655 and again at 0805. These reports are rebroadcast from Antigua's airport, which does not cover the US Virgins, but, being well to the east, it gives you an idea of what's happening out to windward and what might happen in the Virgins in a couple of days.

When discussing exact weather predictions in the Virgin Islands, I am reminded of the old Texas line: "Anyone who tries to predict weather in Texas is either a damned fool or a foreigner." My own best weather predictor seems to be my arthritic left toe. When it starts to hurt, I know a weather change is approaching—exactly what, I don't know, but we prepare for a change.

Some guides to the Virgins, and many bareboat-charter operators, maintain that the only chart one needs for cruising the Virgin Islands is NOAA 25641. This, in my view, is bad advice, because the scale is such that no details are shown for many of the favorite anchorages. Nor do I think much of some bareboat charterers' questionable practice of photocopying (without paying royalties) British Admiralty charts—which, in fact, often have not been completely corrected.

Imray-Iolaire charts now cover the entire Virgin Islands. One-half of Chart A-23 is St. Croix, and the other half shows the US and British Virgins, plus St. Croix—making it a passage chart for those who wish to visit St. Croix. Chart A-233 is printed on both sides and thus covers the entire area from the western end of St. Thomas to Anegada. Chart A-234 covers the northeast coast of St. Croix from Salt River to East End at a scale of 1:27,000. I advise yachtsmen to work with these Imray-Iolaire charts and forget about any of the other privately printed and government charts.

There has been tremendous growth in yachting in the US and British Virgin Islands. If you added up the number of boats cruising the islands—including bareboats, charter boats, and visiting yachts—I think the figure probably would top 2,000. Knowing this, you might figure it would be impossible to find a secluded anchorage. However, nothing could be further from the truth. If you want to cruise the Virgins and enjoy uncrowded anchorages, be sure to buy not only this guide but also all the other guides that are available. Circle in red all the anchorages listed in this guide that are not listed in the others. If you visit these circled harbors and anchorages, you will be almost guaranteed uncrowded anchorages.

Despite the growth in yachting in the Virgins, I still feel that the government of the US Virgin Islands is not especially "yachtsman friendly." For the last quarter-century, local politicians have been standing up and maintaining that yachts contribute nothing to the economy of the islands, but this certainly doesn't coincide with information from the USVI tax department. In 1988, the tax department analyzed how much tax money the charter-boat industry brought into the US Virgins, and the result was rather amazing—18 cents out of every dollar! And that was just charter boats, not counting the general yachting industry. That probably would have increased it to 22 cents on the dollar, probably making yachting one of the largest single tax sources in the US Virgin Islands.

After Hurricane Hugo and during the general worldwide recession in the late 1980s and early 1990s, the yachting population of the US Virgins began to decline. And the decline became even more precipitous when the British Virgins recognized the value of the yachting industry, revamped their regulations, and changed their attitude. Now the BVI government sends representatives to all the major boat shows to try to encourage yachtsmen to base their operations in the British Virgins. This is a far cry from the situation in St. Thomas.

In December 1992, the *Providence* (Rhode Island) *Journal* ran an article detailing how much money yachting contributed to the economies of both Rhode Island and Bermuda as a result of the Newport-to-Bermuda Race. The study found that the 10-day event altogether generated US$6 million. During the four days prior to the race, skippers and crews generated US$1.5 million in sales in Rhode Island, and at the end of the race, Bermuda picked up roughly US$1.3 million. In light of such statistics, one would think the USVI government would bend over backward to do everything possible for visiting yachtsmen. Unfortunately, that's not the case.

Nonetheless, the Virgin Islands boast some of the world's best sailing—particularly if you store ship and clear out to a secluded anchorage. So, in today's lingo—go for it! As Lord Nelson once said, "Ships and men rot in port."

NOTES

NOTES

9

St. Thomas

(Imray-Iolaire Charts A, A-23, A-231, A-233)

The harbor at Charlotte Amalie, St. Thomas, has been popular with sailors for hundreds of years. Originally, pirates of various nationalities favored it as an R&R site, but finally the Danes came in and established a modicum of control. I say "modicum" because they did not chase the pirates out, just asked that they behave a little better and keep their hands off Danish ships. The Danes made St. Thomas a free port, which meant that privateers (and the line between privateers and pirates is a fine one indeed) and warships of all nations could enter the well-guarded harbor and sell their legally and illegally acquired goods and ships.

St. Thomas had its heyday between 1790 and 1815, when there was almost continuous warfare in both the Old and the New Worlds, much of it at sea. Prizes and booty needed to be disposed of, and St. Thomas soon became a key market in this operation. Reading old accounts of the port in those years, it is interesting to follow the growth of business and the development of the population.

The total population of St. Thomas was barely 15,000 in 1780, while it was pushing 45,000 by 1815—a startling fact when you consider that the population in 1955 was again back at 15,000. With trade as the basis of its economy, the proportions of whites, free coloreds, and slaves were strikingly different from the other islands of the Lesser Antilles, which were strictly agricultural. It is true that sugar cane was grown on the steep hillsides of St. Thomas—witness the old ruins and windmill on Fortuna Hill—but the number of windmills does not begin to compare with the number of windmills on St. Croix, where the slave population was considerable.

During the long peace after the Napoleonic Wars, St. Thomas languished, and Denmark grew eager to sell the island to the United States. In 1867, some powerful senators were well bribed to ensure passage through Congress of a bill to purchase the island. However, newspapers got wind of it, and the situation soon became so hot that many senators felt that voting for the purchase would be tantamount to admitting receipt of a bribe. So the bill failed to pass.

During the next 50 years, the island became a major coaling and maintenance port, but the income earned was not enough to support the populace. Life was grim. Coal was loaded by women carrying hundred-pound basketloads on their heads; the wage was a penny per bag. Fortunately, conditions have improved a bit under American dominance.

The town of Charlotte Amalie—almost universally called St. Thomas—is quite fantastic. It is a free port frequented by as many as nine cruise ships a day. The shops are dazzling; an avid shopper in your crew could spend more than you could drop on a two-week charter. Anything can be purchased in Charlotte Amalie. As a rule, luxuries are cheap and essentials expensive. Calling St. Thomas a free port, however, is really a misrepresentation on the part of tourist boards and publicity agents; goods come into St. Thomas from all over the world, but that does not mean they are tax-free. There is a six-percent overall duty on everything that comes in to the island, plus an excise tax on what comes in from the United States, plus a gross receipts tax, plus local taxes. Frequently, these levies add up to more than the standard US duty!

There are some beautiful old Danish mansions on the hillsides and some picturesque old churches, plus one of the oldest synagogues in the Western Hemisphere; quaint little West Indian houses are flanked by gardens reached by a narrow alley or by a long, steep flight of steps. Happily, the slums of St. Thomas, which in the early 1970s were among the worst in the Caribbean, have largely been replaced by modern buildings.

A few aspects of St. Thomas may confuse the visitor. Although it is a US island, cars are driven on the left. After the United States purchased the island, driving on the right was instituted for a time, but it was not entirely successful. Frequently, a farmer, returning home in his cart in the wee hours of the morning, would fall asleep, and his donkey then would cross over to the habitual left-hand side. When a car came along at full tilt, the collision usually would kill the donkey, wreck the car, and disturb the sleep of the farmer. It was decided that it would be easier to instruct motorists to drive on the left than to retrain donkeys to walk on the right.

ST. THOMAS HARBOR (CHARLOTTE AMALIE)
(Chart 31; II A, A-23, A-231)

St. Thomas used to be one of the safest harbors in the Lesser Antilles. In all weather, it was completely sheltered except when the wind came straight out of the south, and even then it was not too bad. In those days, though, the harbor was neither bulkheaded nor dredged. The harbor channel entrance was quite narrow, so any surge that found its way into the narrow channel dissipated in the shoal, two-fathom harbor. In the 1950s, however, the harbor was bulkheaded. Waves came in and started ricocheting off the walls, creating an uncomfortable bobble, and at times a bad surge. As years went by, more and more of the harbor was bulkheaded, and more was dredged. Twice they dredged and widened the entrance channel, enabling big seas that came in from the south to pour right into the harbor and bounce off the harbor walls. At times, the surge builds up so much that boats even have to move away from the bulkheads and docks.

The mooring area for yachts is now drastically restricted, primarily because the cruise ships occupy so much of the harbor. (See the "anchoring prohibited" area on Chart 31.) The area where you are allowed to anchor is so jammed with yachts permanently based in St. Thomas that visiting yachts have almost no room. The options are to go alongside the Ramada Yacht Haven Dock, head west to Crown Bay Marina, or anchor by Elephant Bay.

In the past, the harbor patrol used to go around and tell yachts to move out of the ships' turning basin, but they've made themselves scarce. Perhaps they just collect their fees and don't bother to make their rounds—or perhaps their launches have broken down!

St. Thomas Harbor is one of the few in the Eastern Caribbean that is safe to enter at night. If you are unfamiliar with the area, use the main entrance only. A night approach through West Gregerie Channel can lead to difficulties on Porpoise Rocks, or, west of Lindbergh Bay, on the rocks off Red Point. Through the main entrance, it is simply a matter of following the range lights on Berg Hill until Rupert Rock's buoy lies abeam. Anchor off town and wait until morning to clear Customs. Incorrectly described on the 1972 chart, the range lights are green rather than red, the usual color for a range light. I suppose too many sailors climbed the hillside looking for the red-light district! If you are coming from the United States or Puerto Rico and have no need to clear Customs, head for the anchorage in Long Bay. But be careful: Long Bay has become a very crowded piece of water.

Another good anchorage is close under the hotel (Bluebeard's Castle) on Bluebeard Hill, with the hill bearing roughly due east magnetic.

When entering through the main channel during the day, you can see all the dangers clearly. In years gone by, we would save time beating to windward when coming into the harbor by passing to windward of Rupert Rock and cutting tight around West India Dock to tack up into the harbor. However, the West India Company has placed dolphins southwest of the end of its dock, so leave Rupert Rock to starboard when entering St. Thomas Harbor.

Similarly, if you are entering on the west side, all the hazards are visible by day, including an unlighted buoy on the western end of Lindbergh Bay, marking the shoal area south of Red Point. Once in West Gregerie Channel, be sure to pass north of the red flasher at Sandy Point. There is a very extensive shoal area between it and Water Island, and passing to the wrong side of this buoy has brought more than a few boats to grief.

The new Crown Bay Marina has been built just northeast of the cruise-ship docks. It was finished during the summer of 1990 and has all new docks with electricity and water. Showers are available—undoubtedly better than the horrible ones at Yacht Haven Marina (see below)—and I hope Crown Bay will follow the lead of Tortola's Village Cay Marina and install coin-operated showers. Fuel is available at Crown Bay, but there are not yet any repair facilities. However, within walking distance (or dinghy distance) are such facilities as Haulover Marine, Quartermaster Diesel, Banks Sails, and Island Laundry—as well as restaurants and bars. The address of

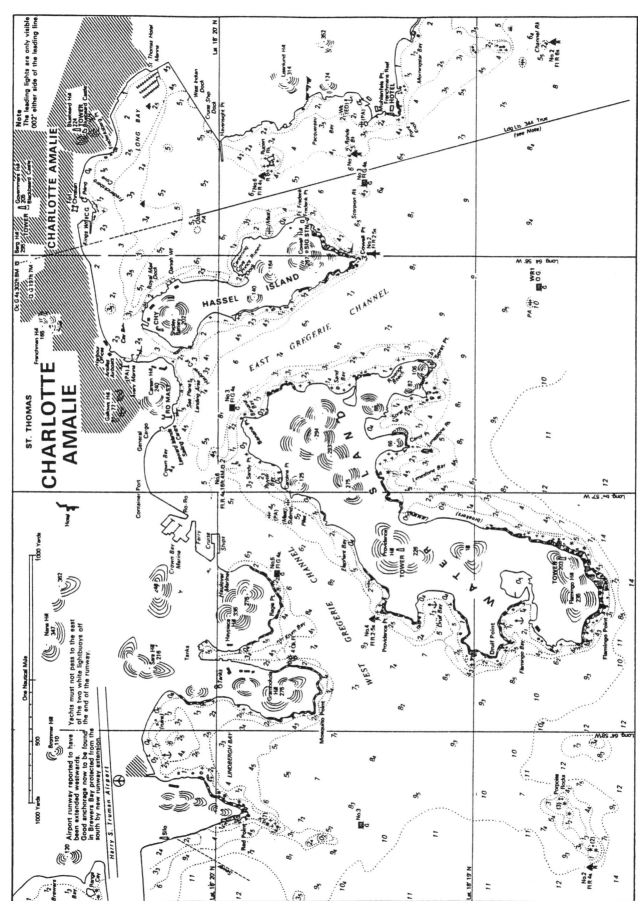

CHART 31 Charlotte Amalie

Soundings in fathoms and feet

Crown Bay Marina is P.O. Box 4398, St. Thomas, USVI 00803 (tel. 774-2255).

The old submarine base in St. Thomas is developing rapidly, so being stationed at the base is no longer the equivalent of an assignment in Siberia.

Haulover Cut has no more than nine feet of water, and even that may be pushing it. Any boat with more than an eight-foot draft should steer clear. Close-winded boats can sail through this passage, but they should enter on the eastern side, practically kissing the reef. Just when you feel that you have completely lost the wind, it will hook around the point of Hassel Island and you'll be home free.

Seaplanes used to land in St. Thomas Harbor, approaching through Haulover Cut. There was always the question of who had the right-of-way in Haulover Cut—a sailboat or a plane? I don't know. There was many a near-miss. A couple of runabouts were clobbered by the floats of one of the seaplanes, but luckily no one was seriously injured. The pilots picked up more than a few grey hairs on their heads, and many had extremely bad scares. All this became a bit of history when the seaplanes stopped flying in and out of St. Thomas, but in January 1994 there was talk of the service being reinstituted. Whether or not this will happen remains to be seen.

Once you are securely anchored in St. Thomas Harbor, if you are coming from a foreign country, you must clear Customs and Immigration. The office is at the western end of the waterfront, and thank goodness the former time-consuming procedure has changed. (Perhaps someone read the last edition of this guide, where I bemoaned the fact that you had to go to the Federal Building to clear Immigration—despite the fact that there was an Immigration office down on the waterfront!) You no longer have to go to the Federal Building for Immigration formalities—now everything is in a single location on the waterfront.

PACQUEREAU BAY
(Chart 31; II A, A-23, A-231)

On the eastern side of the main entrance to the harbor, this anchorage is excellent in most weather. There used to be two beautiful, white-sand beaches seldom used by yachts—but, alas, times do change. The Flamboyant Hotel, a group of round buildings built on five-inch naval gun mounts left over from World War II, is no more; in its place is Marriott's multistory Frenchman's Reef Beach Resort.

The resort's marina is small, but it does afford a place to tie up a dinghy, pick up water, and get to the hotel—with its shops, nightlife, restaurants, telephones, and so on. Furthermore, the water is clean enough for swimming, something you would not want to do in Long Bay.

Most important, there is a launch service all day from the marina to the waterfront in town. One of the nicest features about the launches that run from the Marriott to town (sometimes via Yacht Haven) is that they are superbly designed. Whoever designed these ferryboats really deserves compliments. Although they carry 20 to 25 people, their power is nothing but a Westerbeke 4/108. They chug along at six to eight knots, leaving a completely flat wake. What a contrast to the ferries at Isleta Marina in Fajardo, Puerto Rico! They create enough wake to capsize a dinghy and make everyone in the anchorage seasick.

LONG BAY
(Chart 31; II A, A-23, A-231)

This has been the traditional anchorage for cruising yachts since well before World War II, when the present Ramada Yacht Haven Dock was no more than a sunken barge. Since the early 1960s, Yacht Haven (tel. 774-6050 or 774-9700; fax 774-5935) has undergone a series of management changes—sometimes the new management straightened out everything and sometimes it fouled up everything. In practically every case, it went broke and sold out.

The complex used to be called the St. Thomas Sheraton, but now it is part of the Ramada chain, under its original name of Yacht Haven. The operation is run by Paul Drinkwine, his son Lawrence, and assistants. Many of the staff have worked on the dock for ages—such as Cartwright, who has been there for at least 30 years. Paul Drinkwine started his career as assistant dockmaster, endearing himself to management by saving money as a result of doing nothing! Well, almost nothing. He analyzed the costs of collecting dinghy landing fees—three staff members and a lot of aggravation—versus the amount of money that was collected. He then explained to the management that if they just stopped collecting the fees, they would save about $300 a week and all of the aggravation. So they did!

There used to be a major crime problem at Yacht Haven. The management tried all sorts of security measures but continued to have difficulties. Legitimate yacht owners kept forgetting their passes and would end up being locked out and unable to return to their boats. This, needless to say, caused a fair amount of consternation. But one thing led to another and the crime situation at Yacht Haven died down. The security gate has been removed and everything seems well controlled by the unobtrusive, plainclothes security guards who wander around the hotel and occasionally down on the dock.

The Bridge Bar is the gathering spot for all the yachties. It should be a goldmine, but evidently it isn't—perhaps because the service leaves a bit to be desired.

Within the Yacht Haven complex are a number of businesses: Reefco to take care of refrigeration, various charter organizations, yacht brokerage firms, and Flagship—which can arrange to take your mail and messages and fill your gas bottles. The excellent commissary not only has the basics but also all sorts of specialty items. The bar is convenient and cheap. You can buy a beer directly out of the cooler, sit at a table under an umbrella, and read the newspapers. Or you can pick up a fresh pastry at the excellent bakery and have an early morning coffee. (The bakery has bread delivered fresh every morning.) The Bosun's Locker, a division of Island Marine Supply (IMS), is run by two Frenchtown fellows, John and Dennis, who have been there since year one. It is friendly and carries most marine necessities. What they don't have they can probably get from another IMS store. (Needless to say, they stock Imray-Iolaire charts and Street guides.)

Between 1991 and 1993, the marina business was slow and dock spaces were going begging. In an attempt to fill them, Yacht Haven offered a very imaginative enticement—half of the dockage fee was given back in scrip, which you could then spend at any of the Yacht Haven shops. Thus, the dockage was half of the quoted rate.

Ramada Yacht Haven's single drawback is the shower facility, which is a concession operation. These showers have replaced the ones in Antigua as the worst ones in the Eastern Caribbean! Not only are they filthy, but they charge US$3 and half the time they are not operating! Why, oh, why doesn't Yacht Haven assume control of the showers and do what John Acland did in Tortola—install coin-operated showers? (The showers are available from Dick Morris, REMS Co., Ltd., Box 208, Pasea Estate, Road Town, Tortola.) Once John installed those showers and hired someone to clean them about five times a day, he was laughing all the way to the bank. Everyone in the Eastern Caribbean should follow his lead.

In past years, Yacht Haven was the ideal location, as all kinds of facilities were within walking distance: Repke's Power Products, a woodworking shop, Island Rigging and Hydraulics, and various other marine-oriented businesses. Power Products has moved to the Crown Bay Marina area and Island Rigging has moved to Haulover Marine. Others have moved over to Vitroco Park, which is easily accessible by going through the back of the gas station across from Yacht Haven. Here you'll find Proper Pitch (propeller servicing and reconditioning) and Lighthouse Marine (for used or new consignment items). It is also worthwhile to visit Skip Michele at Marine Warehouse—where you should be able to buy anything you can't find at the Bosun's Locker. Other facilities along the same street include a barber, electrical and electronic supply stores, supermarkets, Woolworth's, and so on.

A word of warning to skippers of charter yachts. If you are sending your stewardess to Pueblo's or one of the other supermarkets in St. Thomas to do a major reprovisioning, be sure to send along a hefty male crew member as well. The local hoods have figured out that stewardesses go to the supermarkets with large amounts of money, and they have carried out daring, daylight robberies in the supermarkets. The culprits, I might add, are seldom caught.

St. Thomas has so many marine-oriented businesses, and they change ownership and locations and names so frequently, that it is almost impossible for any guidebook to be on top of the situation. Thus, I suggest that you check the business listings in *Caribbean Boating,* the free regional newspaper distributed throughout the Eastern Caribbean. The rival paper, *Marine Scene,* covers only the United States and British Virgins, while *Caribbean Boating* is more comprehensive and covers the entire region.

St. Thomas is an ideal place to have your life raft inspected, as Frank Gazerik of Caribbean Inflatable Service (tel. 775-6159; fax 775-2017) runs an excellent operation. He is certified to check almost all of the commercially available inflatables used by yachtsmen. A word of warning, however: An entire book could be written on the subject of inspecting inflatables. When you need to have your inflatable checked, follow the same procedure as you would if you had to go to a strange doctor—look on the wall and check out the credentials. In the Caribbean, there are a number of life-raft inspection sites where the work definitely is not up to snuff. Jumping in your life raft, inflating it, and then discovering it has not been properly serviced is a gut-wrenching experience. An even worse experience is to pull the inflation cord, watch the life raft inflate, and then watch it deflate!

St. Thomas has such a massive parking problem that it is useless to take a car from Yacht Haven into town; you will have to drive out to the other side of town to park! Furthermore, the traffic jams are so bad that rowing into town in a good dinghy can be as fast as taking a cab; using an outboard is definitely faster.

This, however, entails various problems. First of all, when you get in the dinghy, you had better have life jackets or floatable cushions aboard or the Coast Guard will pounce and serve you with a summons and a fine for having no PFDs (personal flotation devices). Then, if you take your dinghy to town and tie it up at the pier between the Coast Guard dock and where the Harbor Department launches moor, it will probably smash itself against the stone seawall unless you have a breasting-out anchor. After all is secure, some urchins undoubtedly will come along and steal your cushions. And before you can get back to the marina to buy replacements, the Coast Guard will fine you for not having PFDs in the dinghy!

Latest news on this subject comes from Herb Payson in the May 1994 issue of *Sail*. The St. Thomas Harbor Department and the Coast Guard are strictly enforcing the PFD rule, PLUS they are requiring that all motorized dinghies—no matter how small—have a three-way (red, green, and white) light. At times it seems that the law-enforcement fellows in St. Thomas have it all backward. For example, it is perfectly legal to drive around St. Thomas with a beer in your hand; the police seem to think that as long as you are sober enough to stand up, you are sober enough to drive. On the other hand, if you drive out of a parking lot without wearing a seatbelt, you'll be in serious trouble. AND—those thieves who hold up the stewardesses at the supermarkets seldom get caught!! Who can figure?

Nor has the Harbor Department done much to help yachtsmen. For instance, there is a space east of the harbor office where they could build a dinghy-landing dock that would be near their own launches. Thus, they could keep an eye on the dinghies and minimize the theft problem. No attempt has been made to do this. The department is less than cooperative in other ways, too. A few years ago, my dinghy went adrift and was found many months later on the Harbor Department dock. I tried to repossess it but was told that before it would be returned to me, I had to have a sworn and notarized affidavit stating that I owned the dinghy. By the time I had compiled the documents, I discovered that someone had driven in with a truck, picked up the dinghy, and gone off with it.

Next we asked the Police Department to go after the Harbor Department employees to find out who took off with the dinghy. That approach went absolutely nowhere. A few nights later, I ran into an old

friend, and over a few drinks I discovered that he was on the Board of Governors of the Harbor Department, and that another mutual friend was a detective in the Police Department. With the aid of these two friends, I finally retrieved the dinghy. But what chance would a first-time visiting yachtsman have had? Actually, very little. I heard about one yachtsman who discovered someone trying to steal his dinghy. The yachtsman scared off the "visitor" by brandishing an unlicensed, allegedly unloaded gun. The "visitor" reported the incident to the Police Department, and the yachtsman spent almost a year in and out of court. Finally he got off with a suspended sentence, but he had to do many hours of social-service work in lieu of the jail sentence.

At least the situation has improved vis-à-vis the St. Thomas hospital's decompression chamber, which was nonoperational for nearly 10 years. Despite the fact that scuba diving is extremely popular in the Virgin Islands, there was no support for divers in emergencies. Happily, I can report that the chamber is now working and has performed yeoman service for the last four or five years. The divers to whom I have talked have had nothing but praise for the operation.

Anchoring off Sheraton Harbor in Long Bay is difficult. Since the turning basin for the cruise ships is being enlarged year after year—thus restricting the amount of space available for yachts—the inner part of the anchorage is always extremely crowded with permanently moored yachts.

I would not advise lying stern-to the waterfront under any circumstances, as there is just too much commercial traffic in the harbor. The wash is just too great, and there is every likelihood that your anchor rode will be severed.

FREDERICKSBERG COVE
(Chart 31; II A, A-23, A-231)

Between Fredericksberg Point and Kings Wharf, this area is being used more as the years go by. It is not a good spot when the wind goes around to the south, but during the winter, when the wind is in the north, it is excellent. Feel your way in carefully, and do not lie too close to shore in case the wind shifts.

CAY BAY—FRENCHTOWN
(Chart 31; II A, A-23, A-231)

This is also called Mud Hole. Until recently, the British chart (BA 2183) incorrectly listed Ballast Island as visible; it has been safely underwater for more than 40 years. There used to be a great advantage to lying in Cay Bay, as it had everything—restaurant, ice, market, taxi service, sail loft, etc.—but, unfortunately, Dick Avery's marina and boatyard is no more. Dick started off in a tiny boathouse on some land rented from the then-derelict Villa Olga. Over the years, the business grew like Topsy and expanded in a kind of unorganized fashion into a fairly large bareboat operation. He built a marine railway—the only "monorail" in existence—which may have looked crazy but worked. (Needless to say, it was not satisfactory if you were trying to avoid removing any keelbolts!) The marina had floating docks and a large building that housed a small-boat-repair shop, a charter office, and Nick Bailey's North Sails operation upstairs—the first true sail loft in St. Thomas. But differences of opinion with local government officials, and a variety of other problems, eventually caused the business to close. Dick is now back in his boathouse, down but not out, and I suspect he will rise, phoenix-like, in due course. Meanwhile, his wife, Marianne, still runs a very active crewed charter and bareboat operation.

EAST GREGERIE CHANNEL

(Chart 31; II A, A-23, A-231)

An anchorage that not many boats use is in the northernmost cove on the west side of Hassel Island, on the east side of East Gregerie Channel. It has room for only four or five boats and has no beach, but it has clean water and is a comfortable spot within dinghy distance of Frenchtown. About four times a day, however, the Tortola ferries use this route to get into St. Thomas Harbor, and since the speed limit is not enforced in the channel, you are likely to roll your guts out.

WEST GREGERIE CHANNEL

(Chart 31; II A, A-23, A-231)

The northwest side of Water Island has now become a very popular anchorage because of the overcrowding of the anchorage in St. Thomas Harbor. There is one disadvantage, however. If a navy ship is in and anchored west of Water Island, the navy launches will come roaring through West Gregerie Channel, kicking up a wash that will roll you enough to make you seasick and knock everything off the main cabin table (a good reason why every yacht should have a gimbaled table).

Opposite Water Island, more and more marine-

oriented businesses have set up shop in the section between Crown Bay Marina and just west of the cruise-ship dock. You'll find Haulover Marine, Banks Sails, Power Products, Crown Bay Maritime, and more. Supermarkets and shopping centers are nearby, as are numerous restaurants. Allegedly the crime situation in the Crown Bay Marina area is far less serious than in the Yacht Haven Marina area.

Haulover Marine (tel. 776-2078; fax 779-8426), run by Jean and Mary Kral, has been in operation since the early 1980s and is continually expanding. Until recently, their operation was run with the aid of a 100-ton crane, and they were hampered by lack of space for storing boats while they were being repaired. Now, because of the expanding commercial nature of the marine industry in the islands, and the lack of hauling facilities for megayachts and commercial tugs, Haulover Marine has installed a 450-ton drydock on the west side of West Gregerie Channel. The drydock is 90 feet long, with a 46-foot beam and 12-foot draft. The operation also includes a machine shop capable of doing aluminum and stainless welding and fabrication. Above the shop is the Banks Sails loft (tel. 774-8354; fax 774-8356, VHF channel 16), and on the same site are Island Rigging and Hydraulics, formerly Alan's Rigging (tel. 774-6833; fax 774-5024) and Offshore Marine (tel. 776-5432; fax 775-4507), which handles inflatables, Yamaha outboards, and cruiser engines. It's only a five-minute walk from Crown Bay Marina, but it's usually easier to take the dinghy.

Crown Bay Marina is trying like mad to establish itself, but it was finished just when Hurricane Hugo appeared and the era of massive yachting and megayachts was succumbing to recession in the Virgins. In November 1988, Yacht Haven was full, the anchorage in Long Bay was solid from Yacht Haven right over to Hassel Island, and Elephant Bay was full. Then came Hurricane Hugo, plus the recession, plus a rigid attitude on the part of the St. Thomas government. Result: Many bareboat-charter organizations have either gone belly-up or departed for the friendlier business climate of Tortola. The megayachts seem to have planted themselves firmly on Florida's east coast!

Crown Bay is having shower problems, but I'm hopeful they will follow the lead of John Acland of Tortola's Village Cay Marina and install coin-operated showers.

KRUM BAY

(Chart 31; II A, A-23, A-231)

An overhead power-cable crossing obstructs Krum Bay. The clearance is less than that marked on the chart, and this has been the cause of more than a few accidents. Best to avoid the bay entirely; it is noisy and foul. Leave the power company to its own devices.

The only way to enter Krum Bay is by dinghy, and the only reason to enter is to fill up your gas bottle. Tie up to one of the wrecked ships by the gas-bottle plant, carry your bottle over to the plant, wait while it is filled, and depart.

LINDBERGH BAY

(Chart 31; II A, A-23, A-231)

This is a good anchorage in normal weather, but avoid it if the wind is in the south or if there is a heavy ground swell from the north that somehow manages to hook around the west end of St. Thomas and sweep into the area. Also, heavy weather from the east-southeast can work up a terrific swell that has accounted for the loss of many boats, including my own *Iolaire*. In 1958, she was declared a total loss on the shore in front of the Caribbean Beach Hotel. I salvaged the wreckage, went on to rebuild her, and she is still going strong.

If you decide to anchor in Lindbergh Bay, do so bow-and-stern, facing south.

DRUIF BAY

(Chart 31; II A, A-23, A-231)

Locally known as Honeymoon Bay, Druif Bay is an excellent normal-weather anchorage on the west side of Water Island. In the late 1950s, I hooked into an antitorpedo net here, but that has long since rusted away. This used to be a deserted little bay where yachts anchored after various regattas to have beach parties, but it is no longer deserted. The beach is still very nice, and there is a beach bar, but you are likely to be surrounded by 15 or 20 boats in the anchorage. Nowadays, it's pretty tough to find a totally deserted anchorage in St. Thomas.

FLAMINGO BAY

(Chart 31; II A, A-23, A-231)

On Water Island, this bay is regarded as a private anchorage for the island, and visiting yachts are not welcome.

BREWERS BAY/AIRPORT BAY

(Chart 31, Sketch Chart 32; II A, A-23, A-231)

Brewers Bay was a seldom-used anchorage in years gone by, but it is destined to become more and more popular. As in Lindbergh Bay, you used to suffer from the swell coming in from the south, but when the airport runway was extended westward 1,500 feet, it created a beautiful all-weather anchorage north of the runway. If you don't mind the noise of jets (and they do not fly into St. Thomas at night, so you will be able to sleep), you can anchor in white-sand bottom near a white-sand beach that is virtually deserted during the week (but crowded on weekends). From the beach, it is only a 10-minute walk to the University of the Virgin Islands, where you can pick up a cheap but very slow bus ride into town.

Warning: At night you will see two small, white buoys with dim flashing lights off the western end of the runway. Stay west of them to keep clear of the airport approach lane.

I should report an amusing story about these two buoys. In April 1993, we had anchored in Brewers Bay after a long, hard day beating up from the Fajardo area of Puerto Rico. The next morning, we set off and started to sail inside the buoys, as no planes were approaching. Suddenly we heard a voice bellowing from the end of the runway: "Don Street, if you don't go outside those buoys, I am going to give you a big, fat fine!" We bore off and sailed around the buoys. My crew wanted to know how the man on shore knew my name. He was the Port Authority manager, George Cranston, whom I have known since 1956! When I first met him, he was a young boat boy on the 40-foot schooner *Sea Saga*, one of the early charter boats. He has come a long way since then! He enlisted in the US Navy and became a helicopter pilot, then he graduated from university under the GI Bill.

When anchoring in Brewers Bay, be sure to go right up on the shelf to 12 to 15 feet of water, as the bottom drops off very steeply. If you drag off the shelf, your anchor will be hanging straight down into 70 feet of water. Even though you are right next to the runway, you can sleep late, as there is very little early morning air traffic in St. Thomas. In March 1994, when we were there, only two small planes had landed before 0800—a far cry from Ensenada Honda on Culebra, where the commuting traffic to San Juan starts at dawn, and about a dozen planes take off before 0700. No need for an alarm clock for crew who have a tendency to sleep late!

I have been told that this bay is being ruined by a

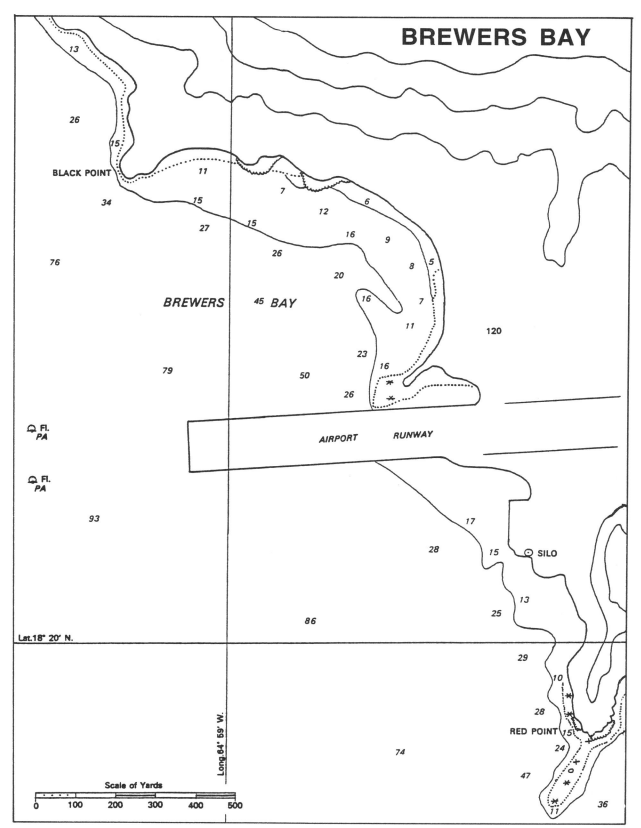

BREWERS BAY

13

26

15

BLACK POINT

34

11

7

6

12

15

15

27

16

9

26

8

5

20

76

45 BAY

16

7

BREWERS

11

120

23

79

16

50

26

🔔 Fl.
PA

AIRPORT   RUNWAY

🔔 Fl.
PA

17

93

28

15

⊙ SILO

13

25

86

Lat.18° 20' N.

29

10

28

RED POINT *15*

24

74

47

36

11

Long.84° 59' W.

Scale of Yards

0   100   200   300   400   500

SKETCH CHART 32   Brewers Bay

Soundings in feet

sewage problem. When the discharge pipe was built for the St. Thomas sewage system, it was not extended far enough westward into deep water, where the current would carry the treated sewage out to sea. Instead, in certain weather conditions, the current sweeps the sewage into Brewers Bay. Not only that, but the St. Thomas sewage-disposal unit very often is not working. Thus, much of St. Thomas's sewage is pumped into the sea in a raw state, and at times the current carries it into Brewers Bay.

MERMAIDS CHAIR

(Sketch Chart 33; II A, A-231)

Here's an excellent spot for one boat at a time— and only one—as long as the weather is calm. Use it only in settled conditions. Anchor in the cove west of Mermaids Chair; there is deep water close to shore, but no swinging room, so anchor bow-and-stern. There is a beautiful beach on a spit of sand. Cross over and enjoy the surf in Sandy Bay.

WEST CAY

(Sketch Chart 33; II A, A-231)

There is a fine anchorage in the small bay on the southwestern side of West Cay. Here, again, this should be undertaken only during the day and in settled weather, or when the wind is well to the north.

Although the chart does not show water in Big Current Hole, you can sail or motor through, as there is at least eight feet. From the north, it can be done on a beam reach. Otherwise, you will have to crank up the iron genoa and chug your way through until Little St. Thomas comes abeam.

Before you do this, however, be sure to check conditions. In 1960, we sailed *Iolaire* through, broad-reaching with a southgoing current, but in March 1993, when my mate Dale Mitchell and I were exploring the north coast of St. Thomas with Paul Drinkwine's Whaler, we ran into breaking seas in this cut. A sailboat either powering or sailing through in similar conditions would have been in serious trouble.

North Coast of St. Thomas

SANDY BAY

(Sketch Chart 33; II A, A-23, A-231)

Sandy Bay is totally useless during the winter

trades, since the beach is exposed to northern ground swells and the swell hooks around Botany Point. But during the summer, in a southeast wind, the bay should provide a good anchorage. Be wary of the holding, however. During our above-mentioned 1993 exploratory trip in the Whaler, we did not anchor, but we could see that the bottom was mixed sand and loose rock.

BOTANY BAY AND STUMPY BAY

(Sketch Chart 33; II A, A-23, A-231)

Botany Bay is a good anchorage with a sand beach, but, as with Sandy Bay, it is useless during the winter, and the holding is suspect. Nonetheless, as a summertime anchorage, it's a good place to get away from it all.

Amazingly, Stumpy Point, east of Stumpy Bay, does not give as much shelter as one would expect. There is no beach here, but it looks like good diving around the edges of the bay. Anchoring would be acceptable only in calm periods in winter (but remember the ground-swell danger), and in summer when the wind is south of east.

SANTA MARIA BAY

(Sketch Chart 33; II A, A-23, A-231)

Another instance of a summertime retreat where you can get away from everyone—no road (only a dirt track), no habitation. Few yachts have ever poked their noses into this area. We explored the bay in Paul Drinkwine's Whaler and found that it was only slightly rolly, despite a northeast swell (again, remember the northwest ground swell). There are two separate anchorages, off two separate beaches, plus huge coconut trees (too tall to climb). This is one of the few undeveloped beaches in St. Thomas, so it is a worthwhile stop in summer to get away from it all.

HULL BAY

(II A, A-23, A-231)

A favorite spot for surfers, Hull Bay is seldom visited by yachts, since it is open to the ground swell in winter. However, in summer, with the wind in the southeast, it is an acceptable anchorage. Eyeball your way in, as there are numerous coral heads and

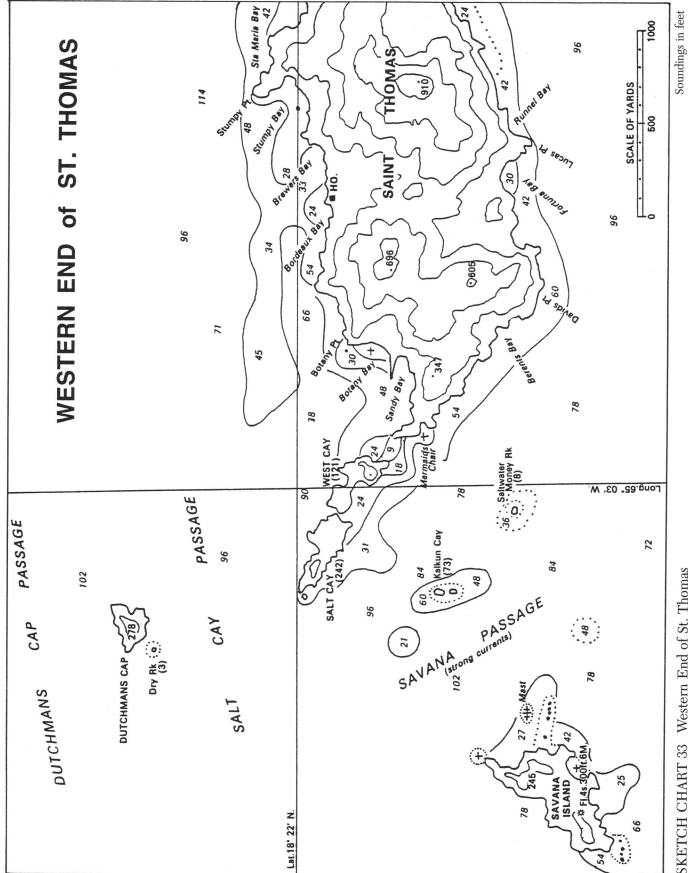

WESTERN END of ST. THOMAS

DUTCHMANS CAP PASSAGE

102

DUTCHMANS CAP

278

Dry Rk (3)

SALT CAY PASSAGE

96

Lat.18° 22' N.

Sta Maria Bay 42

Stumpy Pt

114

Stumpy Bay 48

Brewers Bay 28

33

HO.

Bordeaux Bay 24

34

54

96

66

71

45

Botany Pt

30

Botany Bay 48

Sandy Bay

347

WEST CAY (121)

24 9

18

Mermaids Chair

24

78

90

31

SALT CAY (242)

96

Kalkun Cay (73)

84 60 0 0 48

21

84

SAVANA PASSAGE (strong currents)

102

Saltwater Money Rk (8)

36 0

48

72

78

Mast

27

42

245

25

SAVANA ISLAND

Fl.4s.300ft.6M

78

54

66

THOMAS

910

SAINT

696

605

60

Davids Pt

Berents Bay

78

54

Runnel Bay

Lucas Pt

30

42

Fortuna Bay

96

96

24

42

42

Long.65° 03' W.

SCALE OF YARDS

0   500   1000

Soundings in feet

SKETCH CHART 33   Western End of St. Thomas

no detailed charts. My good friend Timi Carstarphen points out that the Frenchtown fishermen keep their boats in town in winter, but come April or May, they move them around to the north coast and work out of Hull Bay. Diving is good around the reefs. The beach ashore has a small bar and restaurant, and you can hitchhike or take a taxi to town from here.

MAGENS BAY

(II A, A-23, A-231)

If you are interested in checking out the north side of St. Thomas, Magens Bay makes a good stop for breaking up the trip, provided the ground swell is not coming in from the north. It is sheltered from all normal weather but completely open to the northwest, so keep an eye out for a changing sea. (Many years ago, there was a celebrated incident involving sharks and frogmen in this bay; one of the navy swimmers was killed.) The best anchorage is at the head of the bay in the easternmost corner in six fathoms of water. Be careful of the shoal at the head. It is easy to spot if the sun is high. Ornen Rock at the mouth is extremely difficult to see. To be sure of clearing it, favor Picara Point when making your approach.

From Picara Point to Redhook Bay, there is not much in the way of secure anchorages. The whole stretch is open to the prevailing winds, and little protection is afforded by St. John, which is three to five miles across open water.

MANDAL BAY

(II A, A-23, A-231)

This is not an anchorage, but west of the point is a small harbor, about six feet deep, that was dredged into the Salt Pond years ago by one of the prospective developers of Great Hans Lollick. Although I haven't been in there, I have been told that the harbor does exist, and it might be a possible jumping-off point for shoal-draft boats to explore Little Hans Lollick and Great Hans Lollick.

SAPPHIRE BEACH MARINA

(II A, A-23, A-231)

Behind the Sapphire Beach Resort, this new marina (tel. 775-6100) has been dredged out to about nine feet. There are 67 slips, and electricity, fuel, water, ice, and showers are available. Power-boaters—primarily sportfishermen—make up most of the clientele, because entrance (and exit) is almost due east. Going in, wind and sea are on your stern; going out, you are punching into the wind and, at times, a three- to four-foot chop. If the engine fails, you will have a catastrophe on your hands and end up on rocks.

REDHOOK BAY

(Sketch Chart 34; II A, A-23, A-231)

Lying north of Cabrita Point, this has become the second port of St. Thomas. Redhook is not the most attractive or comfortable anchorage, as it is open to the east, although it is partially sheltered by St. John, three miles away. When the winter trades pipe up out of the east, the chop can build up and make you seasick at the anchorage. When the wind goes northeast and funnels down the windward passage—there is virtually unlimited fetch—it gets so rough it is time to leave.

Further, the steady ferry traffic to St. John and to West End, Tortola, will cause you to rock and roll your guts out. The popularity of Redhook can be ascribed to its convenient location on the passage between the US and British Virgins. The permanent moorings here extend so far to the east that any visiting yacht has to anchor in an exposed location.

Although the marinas in the US Virgins charge resident yachts a dinghy landing fee (which apparently is reasonable, as I have not heard too many squawks about it), visiting yachtsmen can tie up their dinghies for free in several locations. Make sure, however, that you tie up your dinghy at a designated dinghy-landing spot and not where it is going to bash up a boat lying in the marina.

There are now three marinas in the Redhook area: American Yacht Harbor, the largest (tel. 775-6454; fax 776-5970); Sport Fishing Center (tel. 775-6500); and Vessup Point Marina (tel. 775-9964).

The Sport Fishing Center basically caters to sportfishermen, but sailboats are welcomed if slips are available. The marina is run by Neil Lewis, OWIH (Old West Indies Hand), who has been in and out of the charter business ever since he arrived here in the 1960s. Among other things, he commissioned the *Alexander Hamilton*—a 48-foot day-charter boat on the lines of a West Indian schooner—that was built on Nevis.

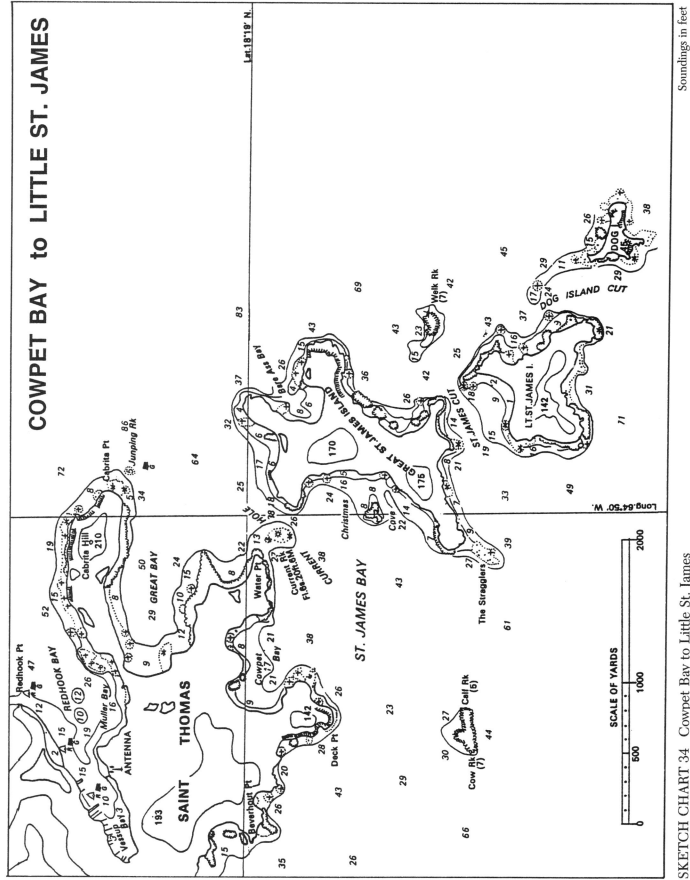

COWPET BAY to LITTLE ST. JAMES

113

Soundings in feet

SKETCH CHART 34 Cowpet Bay to Little St. James

At the American Yacht Harbor, slips have eight feet of water on the outer edge, less water as you get farther in. Facilities here include diesel, water, ice, sail repair, supermarkets, restaurants, shopping malls, marine hardware, post office, small-engine repairs, and good bus service to town. The bus passes by the Independent Boat Yard in the lagoon area, where there are even more repair operations.

During the boom times, before Hugo, all of these slips were filled and there was little room for visiting yachts, but this has changed. During the winter of 1992-93, there were always spare berths in all three of these Redhook-area marinas. They all stand by on channel 16, so call and reserve a berth. As mentioned above, anchoring out is not a good option, as you may end up halfway to St. John and have a very rolly anchorage.

Vessup Point Marina is popular with the big boats, as it has slips 15 feet wide and draft to 16 feet. The maxis have used Vessup Point as their base during race series in St. Thomas.

When Hurricane Klaus unexpectedly blew through St. Thomas in September 1984, the boats in the Redhook area fared quite well, as the wind came from the west, giving Redhook shelter from both wind and sea. However, in 1989, Hugo came from the east, and there was absolutely no shelter. Boats were stacked up four deep at the head of Redhook Bay.

GREAT BAY
(Sketch Chart 34; II A, A-23, A-231)

When passing from Redhook to Great Bay, give a wide berth to Cabrita Point. Jumping Rock is well offshore and hard to spot, although the Coast Guard has now marked it with a green buoy. If the buoy is in place, be sure to leave it to the west; if it is not there, give the point a wide berth. This hazard has nailed many a yacht over the years. I once talked to some divers who said the floor around Jumping Rock looked like a marine junkyard—shafts, props, and all kinds of other miscellaneous parts that had been knocked off passing boats.

Great Bay is not much of an anchorage, as it is a dead lee shore, but it has an attractive sand beach with a beach club. There is one good anchorage here: In the southeast corner, behind the reef, you can tuck in one boat in excellent shelter unless the wind goes well into the northeast. If it does, move on to avoid the chop.

COWPET BAY
(Sketch Chart 34; II A, A-23, A-231)

Beyond Current Cut, this is the home of the St. Thomas Yacht Club, and a fine spot it is for small-boat racing. But as a permanent anchorage, it is not especially good. It is on a lee shore only partially protected by Great St. James. The bottom is sand and good holding. There is always a rock and roll in this harbor, plus the St. Thomas-to-St. John ferries go by many times a day, and the wash can sometimes be strong enough to roll both rails under.

If the wind is in the east or north of east, it is not too lumpy. However, the St. Thomas Yacht Club fleet has expanded so much that it nearly fills the bay. Visiting yachtsmen have to anchor out clear of the permanent moorings, so this pretty much guarantees an exposed position.

Sometimes the wind swings south of east in mid-winter, instead of waiting for the usual April/May shift. This happened in 1987, for example. Immediately after the America's Cup races ended in Australia, we had to leave the anchorage at Cowpet Bay when a strong southeast wind built up. The wind stayed southeast for the rest of the winter, right up into spring and then on through the summer.

That the wind was truly southeasterly was evident from the fact that *Iolaire* headed south to Venezuela that year, and as we left St. Thomas Harbor, we found we could not lay the western end of St. Croix! We finally ended up in Venezuelan waters at Isla la Blanquilla! Further, racing in the Rolex, BVI, and Antigua regattas, going to windward, all boats were laying east and south, on port and starboard tacks. Bob Rice of Bedford, Massachusetts, the guru weather predictor for the Round-the-World and other races, reports that this happened because the upper-level intertropical conversion zone moved way north. He could not provide an explanation for why it did that, or when it is likely to happen again, but at least I can vouch for the fact that the supposed northeast trades can spend the entire winter in the southeast!

The St. Thomas Yacht Club is very hospitable and welcomes visiting yachtsmen from recognized clubs. Drop your anchor, go ashore, and introduce yourself to the club manager and to Wingrove, the long-term launch operator. The club has a good bar and restaurant but is open only during the day. (When it is closed, check out David's, right next door—an excellent restaurant.) You can back in, stern-to the yacht club dock, to pick up water and ice. Emergency electricity can be plugged in, but remember that this should be a one- or two-day stop, not a place for itinerant yachtsmen to spend weeks or months. After four or five days, you certainly will have overstayed your welcome at the ever-hospitable club.

The club runs a very active racing-cruiser program, with the year's highlight being the three-day Rolex Regatta. This is one of the premier events in the Caribbean Ocean Racing Circuit—one of the three legs in the spring series. (The other two legs are the Puerto Rico Regatta and the BVI Regatta.) The Rolex Regatta is always held Easter weekend. An impressive interdenominational service is always held on the beach at dawn on Easter Sunday.

The club also has a very active small-boat division racing catamarans, 420s, and Lasers. The small fry have a fine time in the club-owned fleet of Optimist prams. This is an ideal place for small children to learn to sail, as no matter what happens, they will blow right back onto a white-sand beach.

For moored boats there are dangers. The hotel on the north side of Cowpet Bay rents out Sunfish, and, as of 1993, they did not have bow fenders. One of them hit the fiberglass ocean racer *Uncle Sam* and knocked a hole right through her, which was very costly for the father who rented the Sunfish for his child. *Iolaire* was moored stern-to the yacht club dock and was pranged by a Sunfish, which can go through an inch of planking. Even though *Iolaire* has 1 1/2-inch planking, the encounter still made a large dent in her topsides.

NAZARETH BAY

(Sketch Chart 35; II A, A-23, A-231)

If you wish to spend the night in the area and have found that Christmas Cove at Great St. James is too crowded, sail around the corner to Nazareth Bay, where there is a beach north of Beverhout Point that is excellent in normal weather—as long as the wind is not south of east-southeast.

BRENNER BAY

(Sketch Chart 35; II A, A-23, A-231)

East of Long Point lies the Jersey Bay area, with a low, mangrove-covered lagoon to the west and Brenner Bay to the north. The entrance is east of Cas Cay. The only danger in Jersey Bay is a seven-foot spot, but there is no reason for a boat large enough to strike this shoal to be in the bay in the first place.

West of Rotto Cay is a privately marked channel leading off to the northwest and turning east-northeast as it nears Bovoni Cay. This channel leads into Brenner Bay, the home of a number of small powerboat yards and of the Independent Boat Yard, run by OWIH Peter Stoken (tel. 776-0466). It has a 30-ton Travelift and a large storage area. Basically, the yard hauls you on its lift and sets you down. Then you can either do your own work or hire one of the many organizations based in and around the yard. Here you will find Frank Gazerik (tel. 775-6159) and his Caribbean Inflatables—one of the best life-raft repair and check-out facilities in the Caribbean. He is licensed by almost all the major life-raft manufacturers and periodically goes back for retraining and recertification. Frank is very happy to let people stand by and watch when he does the check-outs, so you really get to know your life raft.

There are numerous small shops in and around the area. To find out exactly what is available, I suggest that you swing over to Timi Carstarphen's Fabian's Landing Bar and Restaurant, which opens at 0630 for breakfast. Timi, Peter Stoken, and the restaurant's customers will answer any questions about what facilities are in the Independent Boat Yard area—and, in fact, in the entire Virgin Islands. Timi has sailed aboard *Iolaire* with me on and off since the 1950s, and he also works with me in the marine-insurance business. From the yard, you can take a bus eastward to Redhook for shopping or westward to town (Charlotte Amalie).

The channel into Independent Boat Yard has been dredged to seven feet and is now buoyed. Peter Stoken reports that at the correct state of tide he has coaxed 8 1/2 feet into the channel. However, if your boat draws any more than seven feet, I advise sending the dinghy ahead to sound the depth. In any case, proceed slowly, as it is all soft mud, and you can back off if you run aground.

The lagoon to the west of Brenner Bay used to be full of fish, birds, and oysters. But as each year goes by, more and more of the mangroves are bulldozed away, leaving nothing but raw, scarred earth in preparation for yet another real-estate development.

Amazingly, it is possible to get seven feet (top of spring tides) into the anchorage south of Brenner Bay (see Sketch Chart 35). Follow the directions carefully. Pick up the range, which is Coculus Rock in line with the house with the sugar mill tower on Beverhout Point. As soon as they come in line, turn to port and run down the range, staying exactly on it. You will spot a sandbar extending north from Cas Cay. There is another shoal spot on the starboard side of the channel. Between them is the channel, no more than 30 feet wide and six feet deep. This approach should be made only in good light and ideal conditions. Once the shoal sandbar extending

116

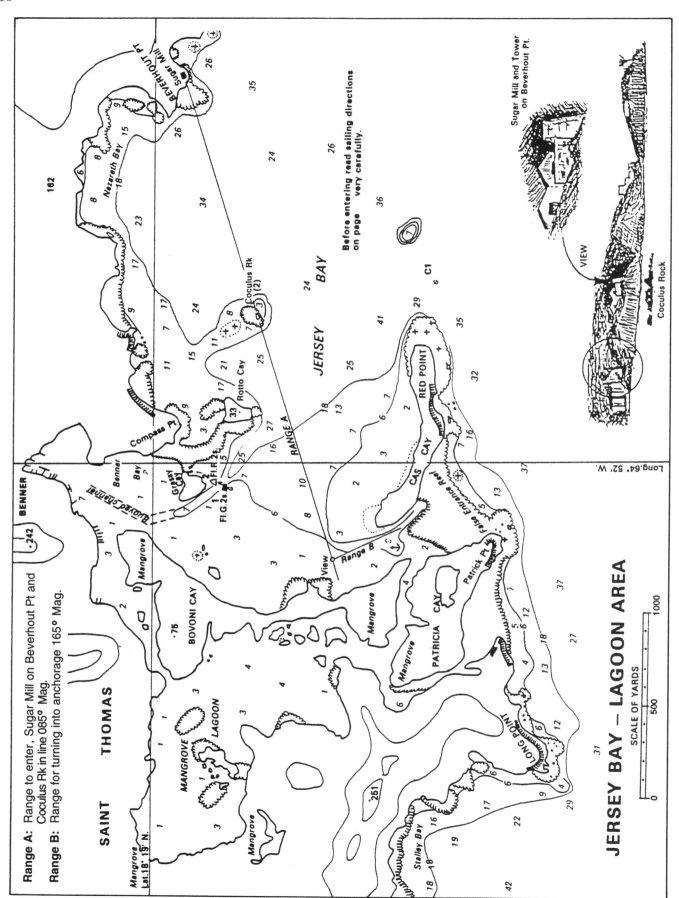

Range A: Range to enter, Sugar Mill on Beverhout Pt and Coculus Rk in line 085° Mag.

Range B: Range for turning into anchorage 165° Mag.

SAINT THOMAS

BENNER

Lat.18° 19' N.

Mangrove

Mangrove

BOVONI CAY

MANGROVE LAGOON

LONG POINT

Stalley Bay

Compass Pt.

Benner Bay

Grassy Cay

Rotto Cay

Coculus Rk (2)

Nazareth Bay

BEVERHOUT PT

Sugar Mill

JERSEY BAY

Before entering read sailing directions on page very carefully.

RANGE A

View

Range B

Mangrove

PATRICIA CAY

Mangrove

Patrick Pt

False Reef

Entrance Reef

CAS CAY

RED POINT

C1

Long.64° 52' W.

Sugar Mill and Tower on Beverhout Pt.

VIEW

Coculus Rock

JERSEY BAY — LAGOON AREA

SCALE OF YARDS

0   500   1000

SKETCH CHART 35   Jersey Bay—Lagoon Area

Soundings in feet

north from Cas Cay comes abeam, turn hard to port and anchor in 12 feet of water. (This information comes from Timi Carstarphen and my nephew Morgan MacDonald III, who did the sketch chart.) I would carefully run this channel first in a dinghy before taking the mothership in.

Small Islands near St. Thomas

SABA ISLAND

(Sketch Chart 36; II A, A-23, A-231)

This provides excellent anchorage in all normal conditions and is seldom visited by other yachts except on weekends. It is a great place to start up or wind down a cruise out of St. Thomas Harbor or Redhook—an ideal jumping-off spot when heading westward to the Passage Islands.

The ground swell has built up a sandspit beach between Turtledove Cay and Little Saba. Tuck up behind this spit and anchor; you will have plenty of wind sweeping unobstructed across the water, but the swell will be flattened by the sandspit. Make

sure to anchor bow-and-stern or with a Bahamian moor in case the wind dies out during the night and the swell begins to push you up toward the sandbar.

BUCK AND CAPELLA ISLANDS

(II A, A-23, A-231)

An excellent anchorage is in the westernmost cove of Buck Island. The cove is steep-to, and there is a full eight feet at the end of the ruined jetty. It has a rocky bottom, so don't anchor too far out, since you may have to dive your anchor out. If you must anchor off, rig a tripping line to the anchor crown. This is an excellent spot in all normal trade-wind weather. In late summer and fall, it is not recommended, since it is wide open to the west.

Another anchorage on the northwestern side of Buck is good only for daytime use. In the winter, the swells sweep around the point. But in the summer, when the wind starts swinging south, this is a pleasant spot. Use the southeast corner of the cove for anchoring.

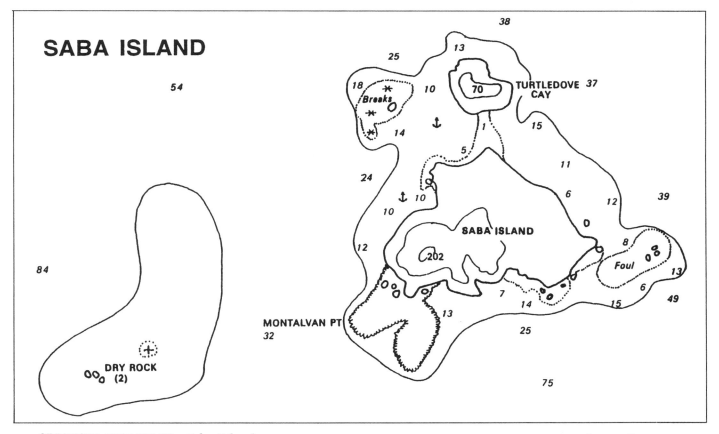

SKETCH CHART 36   Saba Island   Soundings in feet

GREAT ST. JAMES

(Sketch Chart 34; II A, A-23, A-231)

Of the two anchorages here, the best known and most popular is Christmas Cove. There is no problem in entering as long as you take care to avoid the reef extending northeastward from Fish Cay. There is 10 feet of water between the reef and the shore toward Great St. James. Elsewhere, the cove is plenty deep north or south of Fish Cay. North of the cay, a Bahamian moor is best, since you are likely to catch some of the current from the cut. This is an all-weather anchorage. Swimming and snorkeling are always good.

This anchorage is now moderately crowded at all times, as many people are living aboard their boats in Christmas Cove. They run across to leave their dinghies at the yacht club to commute to town or run their dinghies into Redhook (sometimes it can be a rough ride) and commute to town from there. However, it is usually possible to find an anchorage somewhere in Christmas Cove.

BARE ASS BAY

(Sketch Chart 34; II A, A-23, A-231)

An excellent anchorage for shallow drafts of five feet or less. The name does justice to its seclusion. If someone gets there before you, stay clear, since there is not enough room inside for two boats. Except when the wind is hard from the northeast, it is an excellent anchorage, but do not enter it unless you are familiar with eyeball reef navigation. Enter from the northeast, favoring the western side of the bay; round up behind the reef and anchor to a Bahamian moor. The bay is constricted, but it's well worth seeking out if you can be the first one there.

LITTLE ST. JAMES

(Sketch Chart 34; II A, A-23, A-231)

The NOAA chart does not post soundings in the passage between Great and Little St. James Islands. There is, in fact, ample water (more than 15 feet), as well as excellent snorkeling and diving, but beware of the strong current. The bottom used to be choked with lobsters, but they have been pretty well fished out. On the north side of Little St. James is a beautiful white-sand beach. Anchor in close, but be sure to use a Bahamian moor, since there is a strong reversing current that could cause you to drag or swing ashore.

Little St. James used to be quite deserted, but now a magnificent house has been built by a wealthy Dane. Reputedly, the house has 365 doors. No one quite knows the reason for this—perhaps he is superstitious and feels he should not pass through the same door twice in a single year.

GRASS, MINGO, LOVANGO, AND CONGO CAYS

(II A, A-23, A-231)

These do not afford overnight anchorages. Grass Cay has some little coves on the north side, but these are visitable only by outboard during the summer months. The coves have tiny, secluded beaches flanked by 100-foot rock cliffs.

Boats bound for St. Thomas Harbor from the north are likely to use Middle Passage. What is shown as an awash rock on the British chart and as a submerged rock on the American chart is in fact a rock under five feet of water that extends well to the west of the position marked on the chart. Beware! The passage between Mingo and Grass is not usable; you can use the passage between Mingo and Lovango, but the tide is very strong, much stronger than you find in Current Hole.

The anchorage between Lovango and Congo, off the small sand beach on Lovango, is good in settled conditions, with the wind in the southeast. Anchor by chain, since the bottom is stone and loose coral.

There are abandoned pens on Lovango Cay, where lobsters and turtles were stored in days gone by. When the pens were filled, the load was dumped on a boat and sailed full tilt over to St. Thomas before it could spoil.

Here's an interesting tale about this area—perhaps apocryphal. It seems that in the late eighteenth or early nineteenth century—when the port of St. Thomas was frequented by privateers, pirates, and naval vessels—the city fathers became tired of the goings-on between the sailors and the ladies of the night. They chased the ladies off St. Thomas and told them to establish their house of ill repute on an outlying island—henceforth known by the sailors as "Love an' go."

LITTLE HANS LOLLICK AND GREAT HANS LOLLICK

(II A, A-23, A-231)

Ever since the 1970s, a great deal of ink has been spilled on the subject of a big real-estate development on these two islands. I tend to discount this sort of Caribbean rumor until the first hotel graces the skyline.

There is an anchorage behind the reef on the southeastern side of Great Hans Lollick. This is viable only in moderate winds, since the reef does not provide adequate protection in heavy weather. Six feet is the most that can be taken inside this reef. Enter from the south, favoring the shore, and anchor anywhere inside away from the coral heads. Six feet will clear the sand bottom, but the scattered coral heads stick up a couple of feet.

The old Imray-Iolaire charts (and all other older charts) are wrong about this area. The reef between Little Hans Lollick and Great Hans Lollick has three to five feet of water over it, so it does not really break the swell. In calm conditions, you could anchor between the two islands, on a Bahamian moor, as the current will probably run eastward part of the time. (For additional information about tides, see chapter 6 in *Street's Transatlantic Crossing Guide and Introduction to the Caribbean*—the essential companion to all other Street guides.)

Any bird-watcher anchored here will have a field day, and the beach fans will find a beautiful, deserted beach on the southern tip of Little Hans Lollick. On the southwestern tip of Great Hans Lollick are some shelters that are used occasionally by day-trippers who come out from the small dredged harbor behind Mandal Point.

INNER BRASS ISLAND
(II A, A-23, A-231)

"Real-estate development" has been in the works here for many years. It's that same tired, old song, and I'll believe it when I see it. I advise not going to this island in the winter months because of the surge. At best, it may be worth a lunch stop in the quieter waters west of the island.

NOTES

10

St. John

(Imray-Iolaire Charts A, A-23, A-231)

Two miles east of St. Thomas lies the island of St. John, connected by ferry from Redhook on St. Thomas. Pillsbury Sound, between St. Thomas and St. John, can become very rough. With the strong north-running tide, the sea gets up against the wind, producing boxy, nerve-wracking, six-foot seas with six feet between crests.

St. John is unlike St. Thomas and St. Croix, since it has remained almost unpopulated for hundreds of years. When the Danes first settled on St. Thomas, many families set up second plantations on St. John to provide employment for younger sons. When it was discovered that St. John was more fertile and wetter than St. Thomas, the island soon prospered. The main town was in Coral Bay, which was fortified by numerous batteries, some of which are still visible today. A second port and a small fort were later established in Cruz Bay.

In the mid-eighteenth century, the slaves revolted and managed to kill everyone on the island except the few who tried to find refuge at the Durloe Estate, at what is now Caneel Bay. Durloe had built his manor house in the form of a miniature fort and mounted a number of cannons right inside the house. With these, the slaves were held off. Finally, troops were brought in from St. Thomas and Martinique, and the rebellion was put down. A large number of slaves chose to leap to their death in the sea off Mary Point, north of Francis Bay. The locals say that the moaning noise sometimes heard north of Whistling Cay is coming from the spirits of the dead slaves.

Although the slaves were defeated, the island never fully recovered. Many estates were allowed to go to seed, the Danes left, the squatters moved in, and peace and poverty reigned until the early 1950s, when the US National Park Service took over. Under the jurisdiction of the US Department of the Interior, staffers of the Virgin Islands National Park are busy preserving the island for the North American tourists. This has certainly been hard on the people who have lived on St. John for many years. In many instances, families have been dispossessed of their lands; others have been allowed to remain on their land until they died, with their children barred from inheriting it.

Besides its rich collection of harbors, St. John provides incredible opportunities for exploration on foot or by rental car or Jeep. Cars with drivers are also available. The roads are narrow and winding, and vary in quality, but there's an attractive beach around every corner.

Years ago, you were awakened early in the morning by the cries of peacocks—how anyone came to keep peacocks in Cruz Bay is beyond me. The only nightlife in those days was a small bar at Galge Point (called Gallows Point by the locals). The bar was always lots of fun, run by Duke Ellington—not the musician, but the one who wrote "The Fat Man" radio series back in the 1940s.

Besides the national park facilities and the ruins of the Annaberg sugar plantation, the most interesting attraction on St. John, to my mind, is the old fort marked "Government House" on the chart. Looking through the fort, you can see why pirate ships were able to seize the forts in the West Indies—the walls simply were not built high enough!

Virgin Islands National Park

The Virgin Islands National Park (operated by the National Park Service of the US Department of the Interior) occupies about two-thirds of St. John. The

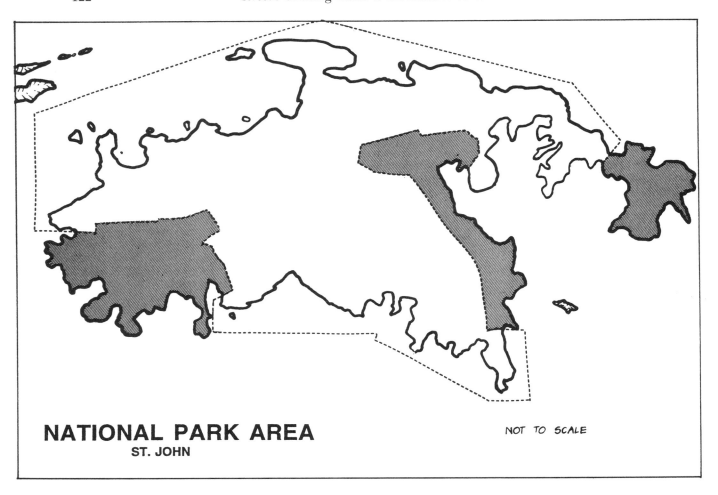

NATIONAL PARK AREA
ST. JOHN

NOT TO SCALE

underwater area surrounding much of the island is also under Park Service jurisdiction, as are Hassel Island on St. Thomas, Christiansted National Monument on St. Croix, and Buck Island Reef National Monument, off St. Croix. Make sure you obey the Park Service regulations, the most important of which is that anchoring is prohibited in certain areas to prevent damage to coral and seagrass. Even if some of the regulations seem illogical, most are very necessary and can be enforced by stiff fines—backed up, if necessary, by jail sentences.

In the early days of the national park, during the 1950s, the officials were more than a little heavyhanded. At that point, with a very small population in the US and British Virgins (St. John had maybe 600 residents when I first came to the islands), we felt that the national park unnecessarily intruded on the existing lifestyle. For instance, the first thing they did to protect the natural beauty of the island was to install chrome and aluminum picnic tables and outhouses on the beaches of St. John. Plus they established no-anchoring areas that

blocked off much of Trunk Bay. Yachts were forced to anchor so far out that they had to dinghy charter parties ashore rather than let them swim in. The famous Jack Carstarphen, one of the founders of the charter-boat industry in St. Thomas, was always in hot water because Shadow, his schipperke, would continually jump overboard and swim ashore, chasing Jack's charter clients. Once ashore, Jack would be greeted menacingly by "Smokey the Bear," the nickname given to a legendary Park Service ranger assigned there.

The charter skippers declared war on the Park Service and its new regulations. Among other harassments, the skippers took to annoying the officials by turning the underwater signs to face the wrong way, causing all sorts of confusion. One of the most amusing battles (won by the skippers) took place at the anchorage buoys in Trunk Bay. The skippers discovered that the buoys were held in place with nice, new Danforth anchors and chains—equipment 18 times larger than needed for the mooring buoys but just right for the smaller charter boats. The skippers liberated cement blocks from construction sites, collected some old, rotten line, and then sailed up to Trunk Bay. While their charter parties were entertaining themselves ashore, the skippers would dive down, set a cement block next to each anchor, and use the rotten line to connect the cement block to the buoy. Then they carted all the chain and anchors back to their boats.

After Park Service officials had replaced the blocks several times with new anchors, and had failed to find the culprits, they finally contacted the FBI office in San Juan. The FBI chief in San Juan was an intelligent fellow with a sense of humor, and he realized the difficulty of obtaining any convictions. So he flew to St. Thomas and spent a day or so wandering around the dock. After finding out the names of the leading lights of the charter fleet, he invited them all to the Yacht Haven bar for drinks on the FBI. Then he summarized the situation. He pointed out that they had all had a lot of fun (and a fair amount of profit) at the expense of the US government. Then he offered to let bygones be bygones as long as the chains and anchors were undisturbed in Trunk Bay. If there were more incidents, he promised that he would return in an official capacity and that heads would roll. Thereafter, anchors ceased disappearing from Trunk Bay, and the Park Service was there to stay. And so it remains to this day.

In retrospect, it is good that the Park Service did establish itself on St. John, as its presence has been critical to preservation of the island's beauty. None of us in the early days could even begin to contemplate the enormous expansion of the American Virgin Islands. Its population increased during one 15-year period from 30,000 to nearly 100,000. Had the national park administration not taken strong measures that at the time seemed to desecrate the natural beauty of the island, all undoubtedly would have been lost to developers more interested in making a buck than preserving the natural beauty of the island. There were a few landowners who did preserve the natural beauty, but they were few and far between—thus the necessity for National Park Service action.

If you plan to cruise in the national park area, be sure to obtain the latest information from the Park Service regarding anchoring areas (tel. 776-6201). Better still, stop in at the Park Service office in Cruz Bay and pick up a copy of the latest regulations. Since September 1993, for example, no anchoring has been allowed in Greater and Little Lameshur Bays, but there are mooring buoys—white with a blue stripe—five in Greater Lameshur and four in Little Lameshur. Boats up to 55 feet LOA are allowed to use the moorings.

Boats between 150 and 225 feet long can anchor only in Francis Bay and only in more than 30 feet of water. Boats over 225 feet LOA are not allowed to anchor in any park waters. It should also be noted that it is forbidden to use water-skis and Jet-skis within National Park waters.

There are many "no boat" areas marked by white buoys. This system keeps motorized craft away from swimmers and also marks such hazards as rock and coral.

Overnight stays within the Virgin Islands National Park are limited to 14 nights a year. How they enforce this, I cannot imagine. (Charter boats have a special commercial-use license issued by the National Park Service for unlimited entries.)

Trash barrels are stationed throughout the park, and it is absolutely essential that you use these for dumping your trash. There are stiff fines for disregarding this rule. Outside of the park area, it is sometimes difficult to find suitable trash sites, so it is wise to keep three trash cans in the galley—one for leftover food (for the fish); another for biodegradable paper, bottles, and cans (these can be dumped well out at sea if the bottles are broken and the cans punctured); and a third for plastic, which must be carried until it can be dumped ashore. Remember that there is an international agreement forbidding the dumping of ANY plastic at sea. The fine is a minimum of $50,000!

Pets are not particularly welcome in the park area, and they must always be leashed. The prime sea-turtle nesting season occurs between July and November, so dogs are not allowed on beaches during that time, as they excavate the nests and expose them to predators. Turtles are protected in all of the US Virgins. In the 1970s, the turtles would disappear the minute they saw a human, but now they are incredibly bold. In Cowpet Bay, for example, you can always look out shortly after dawn and spot a couple of turtles poking their heads up and inspecting the yachts.

Some of the other regulations seem rather overprotective, but they ARE the rules, so heed them. It is illegal to feed wildlife of any kind, so don't spread out crumbs for the birds ashore. It is forbidden to tie a dinghy painter to any vegetation ashore, so carry your dinghy anchor. This rule was enacted because too many yachtsmen were tying onto less-than-sturdy branches, and when storms would come up, the limbs would be broken.

There are, on the other hand, many good rules. For example, lobsters may be taken only if they are

9 inches long, and then only with a snare or by hand. No spearguns are allowed. Female lobsters bearing eggs cannot be taken, but it's too bad that they don't just legislate a closed season to ban the taking of lobster during the season when the females are carrying eggs. Do not take any queen conch; whelks can be taken only between 1 October and 31 March.

Fishing with a handline is legal on St. John and throughout the national park area except in Trunk Bay and Jumby Bay, where the fish are downright tame! They know they are protected and will practically eat out of your hands.

CRUZ BAY

(Sketch Chart 37; II A, A-23, A-231)

Cruz Bay is St. John's main port. Basic supplies—frozen meat, canned goods, bread, etc.—are available here, but it definitely can't be regarded as a place for stocking a boat. Better to hop a ferry to St. Thomas if you're in need of major provisioning.

Approaching Cruz Bay from the south, it is possible to sail between Steven Cay and St. John (Range A on Sketch Chart 37). However, this passage has numerous rocks, and caution is essential. Line up Carvel Rock (the rock east of Congo Cay) with the west hill of Jost Van Dyke island at 025° magnetic. Follow the range carefully (more so than your compass, since too many yacht compasses are inaccurate).

The rocks on the starboard side of the channel off Moravian Point have now been marked by a buoy. If the buoy is in place when entering or when passing through this channel north to south, favor the buoyed side of the channel. That will keep you clear of Skipper Jacob Rock. (I wonder who he was and what size boat he lost on that rock!)

Do not attempt to enter Cruz Bay, as it is just too crowded with boats, especially live-aboards on permanent moorings. The ferries are a law unto themselves, so stay clear of them. Their constant traffic makes you feel as if you were standing in the middle of Times Square at rush hour. If anyone gets in their way, tough!

If you insist on entering, anchor behind Lind Point and take the crew ashore via dinghy to clear Customs and Immigration. You are allowed to leave one person on board, preferably a US citizen. If you leave a foreign national aboard, you'll have to go back again and shepherd the boat-sitter through the inspection process. We discovered this one time when my wife, Trich, stayed on *Iolaire* while the rest of the crew went ashore to clear. Despite the fact that she was the skipper's wife and had sailed aboard *Iolaire* for 26 years, Immigration insisted that she be brought ashore and inspected.

Customs and Immigration officials are in the same room, but the procedures are no longer handled by one person—two to four people may be shuffling your papers. Clearance is not as simple as it used to be, but it is still easier than having to fight the traffic and go all the way downtown in St. Thomas.

Ashore in Cruz Bay, you will find an acceptable supermarket, a drugstore, restaurants, bars, and two attractive small shopping complexes (Wharfside Village and Mongoose Junction). Hop a taxi to the gas plant and have your bottles filled. There is also a good builders' supply store—St. John's Lumber—that carries a fair amount of marine supplies and has an excellent selection of tools.

Now that Cruz Bay has acquired the amenities of civilization, it also has a downside—the youth of St. John have gotten into "crack." Many of the young people have decided that working in the service industry is subservient, so they sit around on street corners, unemployed and unfriendly. It reminds me of a West Indian battle cry many years ago: "Tourism is whoreism." They feel that they are selling themselves while working for others. To anyone who says this, I reply, "What about Switzerland?" That country has been in the tourism business for untold generations, and there is nothing subservient about a Swiss bartender, waiter, waitress, or hotel owner!

A number of expatriates on St. John have bemoaned the fact that the troubles of St. Thomas have begun moving over to St. John; the atmosphere is less relaxed than in the past, and they no longer feel safe wandering around Cruz Bay at night.

It's a far cry from the early years when I was chartering *Iolaire*. We would check in at St. John rather than St. Thomas, as Customs and Immigration clearance was a one-stop, one-person operation that could be done in a matter of minutes. In those days, we also discovered a free telephone, which we dubbed "the phone that never was."

Here's the story. One day after checking in at Cruz Bay, I noticed a little wooden box attached to the tree at the head of the dock. I opened the box and found a telephone. This came as quite a surprise, since there were supposedly only three operating telephones on the island—one in the island administrator's office, another in the police station, and the third at Caneel Bay. This was a hand-cranked phone with two dry cells. I cranked it hard and my eyeballs lighted up—I was barefoot, and evidently there was a direct short to ground. So I went to the dinghy, dragged out the shoes I hadn't been

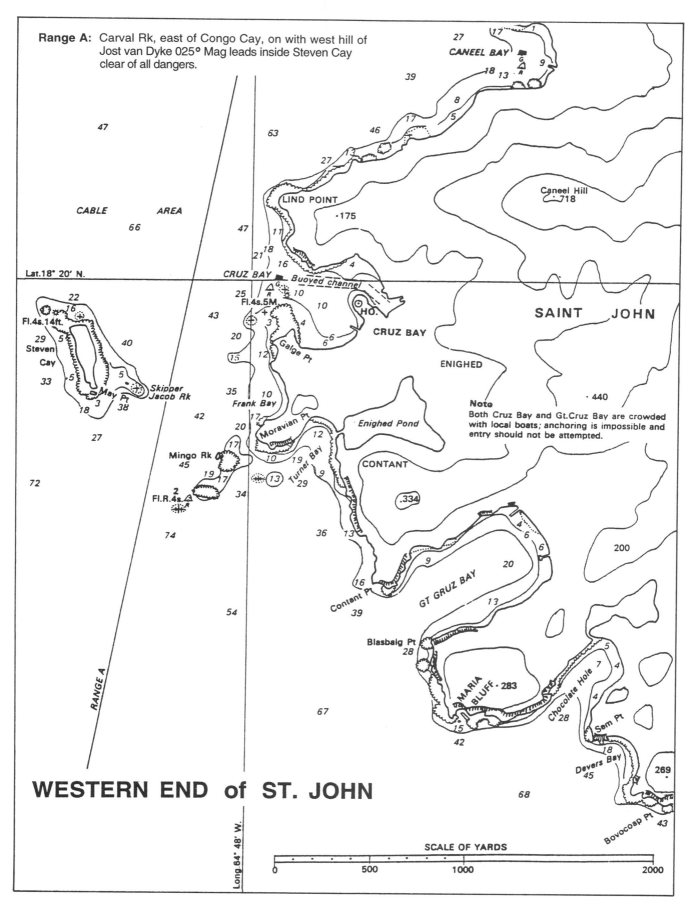

Range A: Carval Rk, east of Congo Cay, on with west hill of Jost van Dyke 025° Mag leads inside Steven Cay clear of all dangers.

27

17

1

CANEEL BAY

39

18 13

9

8

17

5

47

63

46

17

27

LIND POINT

Caneel Hill
·718

·175

11

Lat.18° 20' N.

47

18

21

16

4

CRUZ BAY

Buoyed channel

25

10

SAINT   JOHN

Fl.4s.5M

10

HO.

CABLE   AREA

66

43

3

4

CRUZ BAY

22

16

6

ENIGHED

Fl.4s.14ft.

20

12

Galge Pt

·440

29
Steven
Cay

40

15

Note

33

5

5

35

10

Both Cruz Bay and Gt.Cruz Bay are crowded
with local boats; anchoring is impossible and
entry should not be attempted.

5

May
Pt

3

Skipper
Jacob Rk

Frank Bay

18

38

42

17

Moravian Pt

Enighed Pond

20

Mingo Rk
45

17

12

10

19

Turner Bay

CONTANT

72

19

17

13

9

.334

Fl.R.4s.

2

34

29

74

36

13

54

9

16

GT GRUZ BAY

20

6

6

200

Contant Pt

13

39

Blasbalg Pt
28

MARIA
BLUFF ·283

5

Chocolate Hole

7

4

67

15
42

28

4

Sem Pt

18
Devers Bay
45

269

WESTERN END of ST. JOHN

68

Bovocoap Pt

43

RANGE A

Long.64° 48' W.

SCALE OF YARDS

0   500   1000   2000

SKETCH CHART 37   Western End of St. John

Soundings in feet

wearing, and tried the crank again. I heard, "Number, please?" So I gave a number in St. Thomas to arrange the next charter. The operator said, "Which telephone are you calling from, Caneel Bay?" I replied, "No." "The police station?" "No." "The administrator's office?" "No." "Well," she said, "that's impossible. You are in St. John and there are only three phones." I explained that I was standing on the dock speaking on a telephone that was fastened to a tree. "There isn't a telephone on a tree in St. John," she insisted. "Well," I insisted, "I'm talking on one."

After much arguing, she put the call through. Then I tried calling my father in the States collect, and again we had the same argument about the phone. But as long as it was a local or a collect call, the operator put the call through! This continued for at least two years, until I departed for the southern end of the Caribbean. When I next returned to St. John, both the tree and "the phone that never was" had disappeared. Civilization had arrived with coin-operated telephones—very efficient but not nearly as much fun!

There is a 30-ton Travelift that is basically owned by Caneel Bay Plantation, which also owns the yard. The yard is leased to Hugh Brown of St. John Watersports (tel. 776-6256). Hugh is also the local Hinckley dealer, so he obviously knows about troubleshooting and getting boats back in operating order. Hauling is pretty much a one-shot deal here, as there is no room to side-track. The yard is primarily for maintaining the Caneel Bay and Hinckley boats, but if an emergency arises, it is worth checking to see if there is space.

CANEEL BAY
(Sketch Chart 37; II A, A-23, A-231)

North of Cruz Bay, this is another excellent anchorage in normal weather, as long as the ground swell is not rolling in. This element should not be taken lightly; at times, the swell builds up to such an extent that it washes over the beach and literally laps at the ankles of guests in the hotel dining room. The whole area from Caneel Bay north to Hawksnest (sometimes Hogs Nest) is part of the Caneel Bay Plantation, a 170-acre resort developed by Laurance Rockefeller. This elegant place has been described as an ideal destination for "newlyweds and nearly deads." Nightlife ashore is virtually nonexistent; the doors are locked and bolted at 2200.

The Rockefellerian attitude toward yachts is difficult to ascertain. Sometimes it is very friendly, at other times it is icy. Perhaps it's related to the price of Exxon on the Stock Exchange.

The hotel here is like any number of other swank establishments on the island; for that reason, it leaves me cold. However, I am something of a traditionalist, and many people may like the well-groomed grounds and sophisticated atmosphere. In the back of the hotel are the partially restored ruins of the old Caneel Estate, once a sugar plantation. Like most ruins, they are well worth exploring. The plantation used to be heavily armed, and it was the one spot in St. John that held out against the slave rebellion in 1733. But a feel for the history of the sugar mill has been partially dampened by the addition of a snack bar on the top terrace, designed to take advantage of the spectacular panoramic view of the bay and the yachts lying in the area to the northwest.

You can anchor anywhere in the bay, but there are several large cruisers that use the dock, so I advise giving them plenty of room to maneuver. There is a space at the dock where you can tie up your dinghy, and the club asks that you use the dock rather than pulling up on the beach in the designated swimming areas, which are marked by buoys (an orange cross in an orange diamond).

HENLEY CAY
(Sketch Chart 38; II A, A-23, A-231)

An anchorage can be had off the beach on the south side, but currents sweep around both sides of the cay, making it insecure. This island was privately held and then sold to Caneel Bay. It now appears to be uninhabited, but I have been unable to ascertain its status.

HAWKSNEST BAY
(Sketch Chart 38; II A, A-23, A-231)

This is a good place to get away from the crowd at Trunk Bay, but unfortunately it is no longer completely deserted. Caneel Bay has expanded so much that parts of the shoreline here have Caneel Bay cottages, and the National Park Service has restricted anchoring to a small corner of the bay.

North and East Coasts of St. John
TRUNK BAY
(Sketch Chart 38; II A, A-23, A-231)

The only hazard in this area is Johnson Reef. The number of boats that have hit it is astounding, but how they manage to do so is mystifying. It is almost

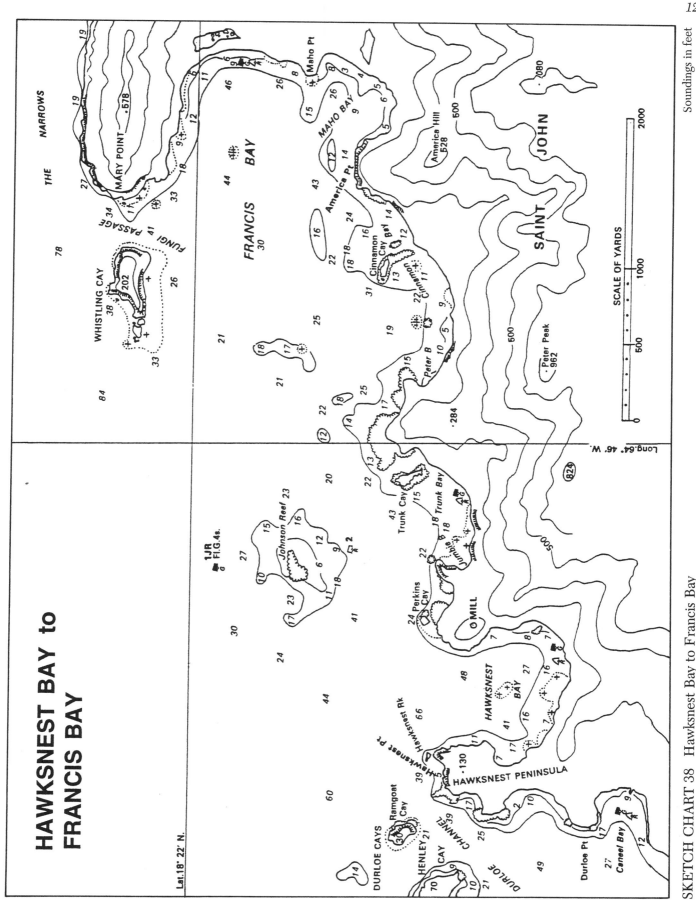

Soundings in feet

HAWKSNEST BAY to FRANCIS BAY

Lat.18° 22' N.

THE NARROWS

MARY POINT ·578

FUNGI PASSAGE

WHISTLING CAY 202

FRANCIS BAY

Maho Pt

MAHO BAY

America Pt

America Hill 528

SAINT JOHN

500

Cinnamon Cay Bay

Cinnamon

Peter B

Peter Peak 962

·284

·1080

Long.64° 46' W.

DURLOE CAYS

Ramgoat Cay

HENLEY CAY

DURLOE CHANNEL

Durloe Pt

Caneel Bay

Johnson Reef

1JR Fl.G.4s.

Trunk Cay

Trunk Bay

Jumbie

Perkins Cay

MILL

HAWKSNEST BAY

HAWKSNEST PENINSULA

Hawksnest Pt

Hawksnest Rk

·130

SCALE OF YARDS

0   500   1000   2000

500

SKETCH CHART 38   Hawksnest Bay to Francis Bay

always breaking and thus is easy to spot, plus it is marked by buoys. You can sail either north or south of it. The bay is an excellent daytime anchorage in the lee of Trunk Cay—provided, once again, that the northerly swell is not running. Because of the possibility of this swell making up, do not spend the night here. The beach is quite steep, so you can anchor close to shore. Try to arrive in the morning so you can have your swim and depart before the various tours from St. Thomas arrive and inundate the place. The beach is exceptional, and there is good snorkeling. A splendid feature is an underwater trail for neophyte snorkelers—complete with signs identifying the coral and the fish. Needless to say, spearfishing is prohibited. On the hill to the east of the beach is a modest lunch counter with a fantastic view.

I, for one, no longer visit this bay. There are many other less crowded bays that have not lost their natural charm under the good intentions of the National Park Service. Trunk Bay didn't used to be cluttered with picnic tables and aluminum outhouses. When the Bulon family owned it, there was only a vast stretch of natural beauty, and the charter skippers who anchored there took pains to keep it that way.

CINNAMON BAY
(Sketch Chart 38; II A, A-23, A-231)

This is not as nice as Trunk Bay, but that means it is a better anchorage. However, if the ground swell is rolling in, it will be uncomfortable. If spending the night, use a Bahamian moor. The shoreline is a combination of National Park Service and privately owned land. Before anchoring, check where the buoys are set and do not anchor in a forbidden area. There are camping facilities ashore, and light meals can be purchased, including breakfast. If you have too many sundowners and wake up in no mood to make breakfast, you can dinghy ashore and have breakfast prepared for you!

MAHO BAY
(Sketch Chart 38; II A, A-23, A-231)

A good anchorage in the summer, but uncomfortable in the winter with the swell. There's a nice, long, sandy beach that can be used by yachtsmen, but the area is private, so stay on the beach and don't go wandering around. The entrance is easy, but the bay is only six or seven feet deep. Boats drawing more can find water in the deep finger of the bay between America Point and Maho Point. Watch the color of the water carefully and set bow and stern anchors, since there is no room for deep-draft boats to swing. The holding is good on hard sand.

FRANCIS BAY
(Sketch Chart 38; II A, A-23, A-231)

An excellent anchorage in all weather—the best in northeast St. John. Whistling Cay evidently breaks the ground swell. But be absolutely sure your anchor is well set before going ashore. The bottom drops sharply from seven or eight feet to 50; if your anchor drags off the edge, it won't hold on the backside of the shelf no matter how much scope you have. Also, since the sand overlays the rock and coral, it is essential to double-check your anchor; in some places, it will bury in a few inches, hit rock, and fail to set. Dive down and check the hook; the extra precaution is well worth the effort. The holding here—despite what other guides might say—is NOT good. Before you make the decision to spend the night, check the no-anchoring buoys and figure out whether you are going to end up in a suitable position or anchor in water so deep that you will need a mile of line to get enough scope.

There is a good white-sand beach, and the swimming is delightful. Snorkeling, however, is rather fruitless, since there is nothing to see on the bottom but more white sand. On the southwest corner of Whistling Cay is an old Customs guardhouse from Danish days, placed there to prevent smuggling between the Danish and British islands.

The house overlooking Francis Bay was built many years ago by Mrs. Ethel McCully. As the story goes, she was on her way to Tortola aboard a local sloop, which tacked into Francis Bay to avoid the current in the narrows. Mrs. McCully decided on the spot that this was where she wished to live. The skipper refused to put her ashore, so she dove overside, swam ashore, found the owner of the land, and promptly bought it. She built her house in the early 1950s, when there was practically no ground transportation on the island. All the materials were sailed to Francis Bay, piled onto the backs of waiting donkeys, and toted up the hill. A book on the subject, *Grandma Raises the Roof*, should be of interest to those who want to know what St. John was like in those days. (Mrs. McCully had quite a sense of humor; her book's original title, which the publishers refused to accept, was *I Did It with Donkeys*.)

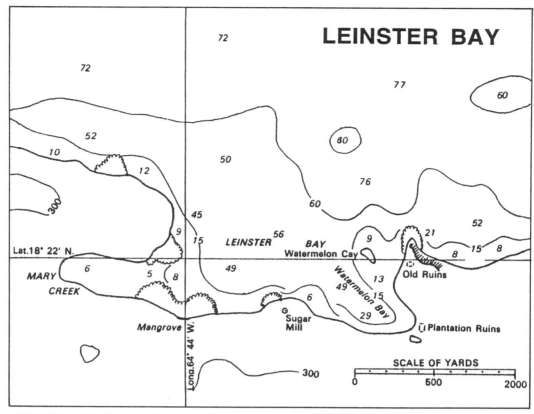

SKETCH CHART 39   Leinster Bay   Soundings in feet

WHISTLING CAY

(Sketch Chart 38; II A, A-23, A-231)

The "whistling" comes from the fact that if you are sailing downwind close aboard, you can actually hear the wind screeching through the high cliffs on the north side. The locals claim that this is the moaning of rebel slaves drowned below Mary Point. Rather than surrender, the slaves jumped to their death off Mary Point Cliff, sometimes called Bloody Point.

The shore between Francis Bay and Leinster Bay to the east is steep-to all the way. You can short-tack through the narrows against the current, but I strongly advise against it. When coming from the west, I prefer to go north of Great Thatch Island and back down through Thatch Island Cut.

LEINSTER BAY

(Sketch Chart 39; II A, A-23, A-231)

With its four separate anchoring spots, Leinster Bay is one of the favorites of this coast. The most commonly used anchorage is in the southeast corner, at Watermelon Bay; here there are no dangers.

Sail right in and anchor close to shore in deep water. The sand bottom is good holding, but avoid the several patches of grass. Trying to get your anchor to hold on grass is impossible. From this anchorage, a row ashore brings you to the ruins of an old lime-tree plantation. On the hill north of the bay is another old ruin, which at one time was used as a school. The view from here is superb.

On the southwest corner of Watermelon Cay is a fine anchorage. You can practically sail up to the beach, throw an anchor on the sand, and drop a stern anchor to hold you off. The island is completely deserted, with a good sand beach, shelling, and snorkeling. It is not too heavily frequented by boat traffic, so you may have the island all to yourself.

Directly north of the sugar mill in the middle of the bay, it shoals to six or seven feet. Shoal-draft boats can sail in and anchor right on the shoal. The point to the east gives ample shelter from the swell. Great Thatch Island to the north cuts the worst of the ground swell, and the wind sweeping across the water keeps the bugs away. A short dinghy ride will take you to a landing below the sugar mill.

At the westernmost edge of Leinster Bay, Mary Creek affords an excellent anchorage, but one that generally is thought too shoal for the average boat. However, a reliable reporter insists that six feet of water can be carried over the middle of the bar at low water. You must feel your way in. On the other side, it deepens to eight or nine feet. The sand is good holding. In the early morning, the mangrove cluster to the west is a bird-watcher's delight. Clams can be found in the shoals by the mangroves. In the Virgin Islands, wherever mangroves grow in mixed mud and sand, clams usually abound. Prior to World War I, clamming was a regular occupation in the Virgins, but now it seems to be monopolized by a few cagey charter skippers.

Although the wind sweeping Leinster Bay guarantees to make it bug-free, there is not enough fetch to build up a chop, so this is an excellent anchorage in all weather.

HAULOVER BAY
(Sketch Chart 40; II A, A-23, A-231)

Three and a half miles east of Francis Bay, Haulover Bay affords an excellent anchorage in the southeast corner off a white-sand beach. The bay takes its name from a practice of years gone by when in rough weather the local sloops—not wanting to round the eastern end of St. John—would sail to this bay, anchor, offload the cargo destined for Coral and Round Bays, and haul it across the lowland to dinghies waiting in Round Bay. The cargo sloop then would continue on to Tortola, Virgin Gorda, or Anegada. There is room for two or three boats in this cove, but no more.

Some charts of Haulover Bay show various rocks and trees that do not exist. The east side of the bay is steep-to with no isolated dangers. Sail in when the sun is high, drop a stern anchor, and sail in toward shore until you are just about aground; then drop the bow anchor. Moor bow-and-stern, but remember that the bottom drops off almost like a wall; make sure your anchor is well up in the shoal water. Some skippers, once anchored, pick up the bow anchor, run it right up onto the beach, and bury it in sand there. Not a bad idea.

NEW FOUND BAY
(Sketch Chart 40; II A, A-23, A-231)

The charts notwithstanding, there is nine feet of water at the head of the bay. The bay may be iden-

tified by an eight-foot-tall pinnacle rock on its south side. The rock is covered with guano and appears white at a distance. This is no anchorage for a novice—experienced reef pilots only. The entrance is from the northeast, midway between the reefs. Stand on in and round up, using a Bahamian moor, since there is very little swinging room. If a boat is already inside, do not enter; there isn't room for two.

PRIVATEER BAY
(Sketch Chart 40; II A, A-23, A-231)

West of Privateer Point is a satisfactory daytime anchorage when the wind is well in the north. You will find deep water right up to shore, a mixed sand-and-rock bottom, and a shingle beach. Not the best anchorage in the world, but a good spot to get away from it all.

ROUND BAY
(Sketch Chart 40; II A, A-23, A-231)

The nineteenth-century *Sailing Directions to the Caribbean* offers some interesting pointers for the Coral and Round Bays area. The leading mark for entering Coral Bay was described as a white-walled fortress on the hill above Moor Point. The town and Governor's House were described as half a mile inside Moor Point, which would put them in the northeast corner of Round Bay. This area is now totally overgrown, and I would not be surprised if ruins could be uncovered with a little machete work. Further exploration may be had on the wreck of the *Santa Monica*.

The wreck is easy to find. Line up the telephone pole in front of the stone house with the steps on a bearing of approximately 355° magnetic. Run along that bearing until the white house on the eastern side of the harbor bears 104° magnetic. That should put you right over the top of the ship. In January 1993, we found a buoy over the wreck but did not have time to check whether it was a buoy marking the wreck or a fish pot! Wrecks attract fish.

Thanks to Jill Tattersall—an author, historian, and artist who has lived on Tortola since the early 1970s—we have the story of the *Santa Monica*, a 36-gun British frigate that started life as a 25-gun Spanish frigate. In 1779, she was captured by the British when they took Gibraltar, after which she was repaired, put into service for Britain, and sent out to the West Indies station, based in Antigua. In 1782, when Admiral George Rodney heard that five

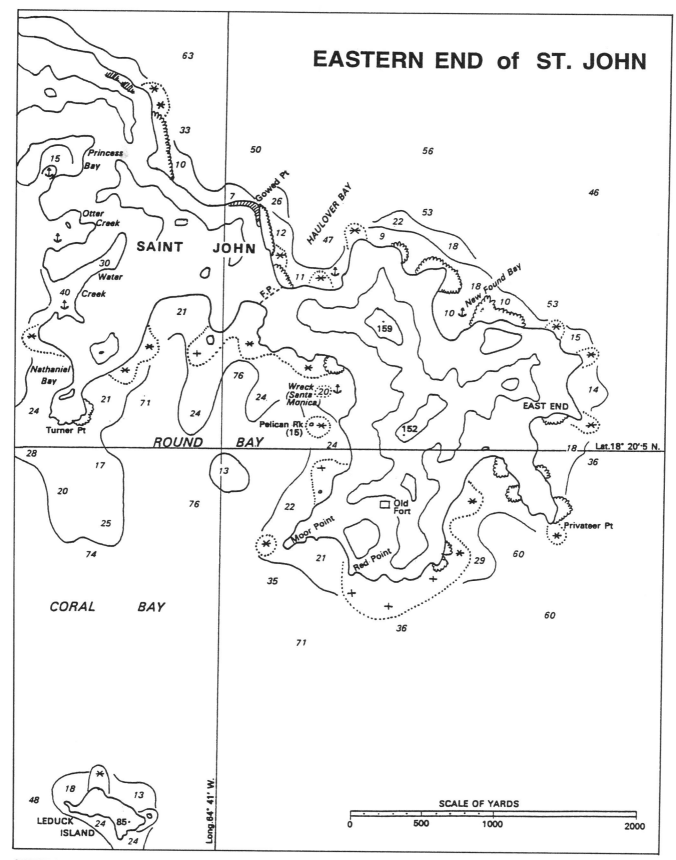

EASTERN END of ST. JOHN

63

33

50

56

15 Princess Bay

10

46

Otter Creek

SAINT JOHN

7 Gowed Pt *26*

HAULOVER BAY

22 *53*

12

47 *9*

18

30 Water

40 Creek

11

New Found Bay

18

10

10 *53*

21

159

15

Nathaniel Bay

76

Wreck (Santa Monica) *20*

14

EAST END

24

21 *71* *24*

24

Pelican Rk (15)

152

24

Turner Pt

ROUND BAY

24

Lat.18° 20′·5 N.

28

13

18 *36*

17

22

Moor Point

Old Fort

20

76

Red Point

25

21

29 *60*

Privateer Pt

74

35

CORAL BAY

36

60

71

Long.64° 41′ W.

18 LEDUCK *13* *48* ISLAND *24* *85· 24*

SCALE OF YARDS

0   500   1000   2000

SKETCH CHART 40   Eastern End of St. John

Soundings in feet

American ships were heading to the British Virgins to wreak havoc there—remember that sugar was tremendously valuable at the time—he dispatched the *Santa Monica* and three other ships to protect the islands and blockade Round Rock Passage. The *Santa Monica* left Peter Island heading south and bounced a number of times off what is now named Santa Monica Rock, south of Norman Island. Then she sailed west (downwind) to St. John for repairs. The crew sailed into Coral Bay but obviously didn't manage to beach her. She sank, probably when they were trying to warp her into shoaler water. Only one life was lost—that of a seaman who went below to retrieve his violin! Most of her gear was salvaged.

For more than two decades, the *Santa Monica* has been a bone of contention between archaeologists and the US and British Virgin Islands. In the 1970s and early 1980s, many artifacts retrieved from the *Santa Monica* ended up in the hands of the US Virgin Islands Archaeological Society. The British Virgin Islands Archaeological Society feels that since the *Santa Monica* was a British vessel, and first ran aground in British waters, the artifacts belong to them! Considering that she sank in US waters, the BVI case would appear to be fairly weak.

Just north of Moor Point are a few boats anchored on permanent moorings, plus the dinghy dock used by the landowners' association at Moor Point. This anchorage is a bit rocky and rolly; better to head north of the white guano-covered rock and anchor anywhere in the middle of that bay. The bottom is a mixture of sand and grass. Various odd currents circulate in the cove, and wind eddies come in from all directions, so I advise a Bahamian moor or two anchors in a Y-shape. I also advise diving down to check that the anchors are holding. When we were last there, it was blowing 20 to 25 knots, yet we were frequently tide-rode rather than wind-rode.

HAULOVER BAY SOUTH

(Sketch Chart 40; II A, A-23, A-231)

Surrounded by high hills, the next anchorage west of Round Bay can be dubbed Haulover Bay South, since it has no official name on the chart. Use a Bahamian moor to keep yourself from swinging every which way in the current. From here it is a short walk to Haulover Bay North, along a marked path, dead flat. It's only 100 yards from Haulover Bay South to the western edge of Haulover Bay North. Obviously this path was once used for transferring cargo that had come from Tortola to Coral Harbor, which formerly was the major port of St. John.

HURRICANE HOLE

(Sketch Charts 40, 41; II A, A-23, A-231)

North and west of Turner Point are Hurricane Hole and the small bays of Water Creek, Otter Creek, Princess Bay, and Borks Creek. The anchorages in these inlets are apt to be hot, airless, and, during the rainy season, quite buggy. But during the hurricane season, they can afford perfect shelter—as long as there are only a few boats in the area. The major problem now is that more and more boats have arrived in the US and British Virgins, and naturally they flock to the hurricane holes for shelter during hurricanes, causing major crowding. There are just too many boats and not enough hurricane holes.

Some boats put out three or more anchors so they can pivot into the wind. This technique is great in theory, but it takes up too much room. If everyone would moor stern-to (or bow-to) the mangroves and would lay out two, three, or four heavy anchors to deep water, literally hundreds of boats could be moored safely in the various hurricane holes. But no one has any authority (except perhaps the National Park Service) to go to the hurricane holes at the time of the warnings, assign specific moorings, and check that everyone is secured properly. The result of this is chaos—and potential disaster, such as what happened in Culebra during Hurricane Hugo in 1989. (The most organized hurricane hole seems to be Paraquita Bay and Lagoon, on Tortola's south coast.) Don't plan to camp out for weeks at a time in any of the hurricane holes on St. John. National Park Service launches check these areas regularly, and if you stay more than three or four days, you will be ordered to move on.

Before rushing to hide in a hurricane hole at the approach of a hurricane, read Reflections on Hugo in the Foreword to this volume.

CORAL BAY

(Sketch Chart 41; II A, A-23, A-231)

This is an excellent anchorage, but it has become so overcrowded with boats on permanent moorings that it is very difficult to find swinging room. The channel is marked, and you can carry a full 15 feet until the stone house on the spit of land on the north side of the harbor bears northeast; it gradually shoals to six feet at the dock, although knowledgeable locals tell me that they can get seven feet alongside. However, visiting yachts should plan to anchor outside the existing fleet, as it is just too packed to try to force your way in.

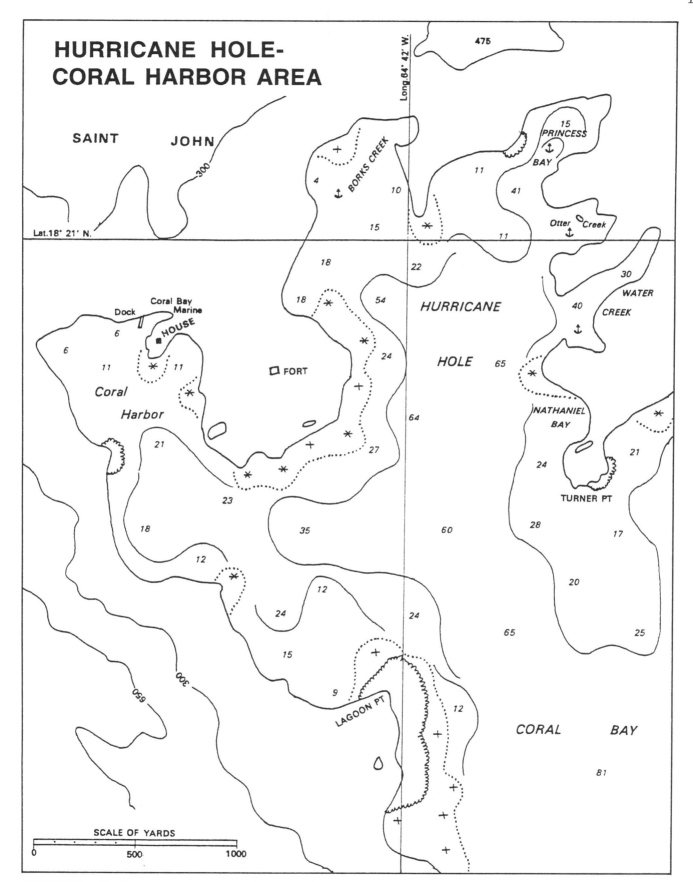

HURRICANE HOLE—CORAL HARBOR AREA

SAINT   JOHN

Long.64° 42' W.

Lat.18° 21' N.

475

BORKS CREEK

15 PRINCESS

4

10

11

41

BAY

15

Otter Creek

11

18

22

30

18

54

HURRICANE

WATER

Coral Bay Marine

Dock

HOUSE

24

40

CREEK

6

6

FORT

HOLE

65

11

11

Coral

NATHANIEL BAY

Harbor

64

21

24

21

27

TURNER PT

23

18

35

60

28

17

12

12

20

24

24

65

25

15

9

12

650

300

LAGOON PT

CORAL   BAY

81

SCALE OF YARDS

0   500   1000

SKETCH CHART 41   Hurricane Hole—Coral Harbor Area

Soundings in feet

At the head of the dock is Coral Bay Marine, run by Sandy and Alan Mohler (tel. 779-4994; fax 776-6922). In addition to selling ice and water, they do machine work as well as engine, electric, and refrigeration repairs. They also do rigging work and sail repairs and are an excellent general source of information. Alan likes to experiment: When we were there in January 1993, he was busy trying to develop an electric outboard!

Outboard fuel is not available here, so you'll need to hitch a ride into Cruz Bay with your gas tank. The same goes for propane, although it can sometimes be obtained here in an emergency in small quantities.

Joe's grocery store is about 400 yards down the road west of the dock. Or take the dinghy down to the break in the mangroves and run aground in mixed sand and mud about 50 feet from shore. Wade ashore, then walk 200 yards to Joe's. This store is about three categories higher than a West Indian rum shop, but it certainly is no supermarket.

About 100 yards up the road from Coral Bay Marine is the Sputnik Bar and Restaurant, a pizza source. The various other small restaurants in the area vary in quality and price. Check with local yachtsmen and take your pick.

Communications are good out of Coral Bay. Check with Coral Bay Marine or the Coral Bay office of Connections (tel. 776-6922; fax 776-6136), a Cruz Bay firm. Connections acts as a mail drop as well as a fax, telephone, and message center. The staff generally tries to be as helpful as possible to local and visiting yachtsmen.

Coral Bay is the Block Island Cowhorn capital of the Caribbean—perhaps even the world—as there are 10 or so of these small wooden craft (and illegitimate offspring). The true Cowhorns are designed and rigged like *Taurus*, the one Augie Hollen built in 1974, with two unstayed masts, a big lug foresail that overlaps the mainmast like a genoa, and no headsails. The illegitimate offspring are modeled on *Penelope*, built on Hassel Island, St. Thomas, by Les Anderson, a sailor and artist. Les installed a bowsprit, a main topsail, and a fisherman staysail, which meant a lot of strings to pull. For many years, there has been a friendly rivalry between the traditional Cowhorns and the revisionist ones.

Coral Bay also has its yacht club, which organizes a half-dozen or more races during various holidays. The club tries to keep the racing informal; protests are not appreciated. The races are always followed by parties that can only be termed memorable. Some aficionados claim, however, that they are NOT memorable, because they are so good you cannot remember a thing about them the next day!

Every real sailor will enjoy rowing around Coral Bay in a dinghy and checking out the many splendid boats anchored there. There is even an amazing number of very good-looking rowing dinghies, which obviously are used as intended, since their sterns are not desecrated with outboards!

Ashore, it's fun to poke around the old Emmaus Moravian Church and the remains of an old Danish fort on Battery Point. Some of the guns are below the fort at the water's edge. Farther above Battery Point, buried in the woods, is another fort that has not been restored. Why not? It seems to me that the National Park Service or the Virgin Islands government could cover the cost of restoration by using it as a tourist attraction.

LAGOON ANCHORAGE
(Sketch Chart 41; II A, A-23, A-231)

Below Coral Harbor, just at the mouth of Coral Bay, is Lagoon Point. Here the reef projects well out to sea to form a small, protected basin just beyond the point. There is six feet of water over a grass bottom, which is poor holding. The reason I mention this marginal anchorage is that from here it is only a short ride by dinghy to the reef on the windward side of the point, where experienced divers can find exceptionally good diving and spearfishing. Beyond the reef, the bottom drops off precipitously to 14 fathoms.

This anchorage used to be secluded, but, alas, it, too, has been discovered. When we were there in 1993, two dozen boats were riding on permanent moorings. Whether or not a visiting yacht could sneak in behind them and find shelter and anchoring room, I am not sure.

Between Lagoon Point and Ram Head to the south, there are no other anchorages. When passing south between Leduck Island and the St. John shoreline, favor the western shore, giving a wide berth to Eagle Shoal. The shoal is shown incorrectly on the government charts. It actually consists of three very narrow pinnacle rocks that are within about four feet of the surface. They are widely separated, two of them some 50 yards apart and the third about 200 yards to the northwest. Spread out like this, they cause no break in the swell and have spelled disaster for a number of boats heading from Sir Francis Drake Channel to Ram Head. You can avoid this shoal by keeping the southeastern end of Flanagan Island in transit to the extreme western end of Peter Island. This is an easy range to spot and will safely clear Eagle Shoal (see Range E in Sketch Charts 42 and 44).

South Coast of St. John

Beyond Ram Head lies the beautiful but seldom-visited south coast of St. John. There are nine or 10 good anchorages between Ram Head and Bovocoap Point alone—easily enough for a week's good cruising.

WARNING: None of the anchorages along the entire south coast of St. John—from Ram Head westward to Rendezvous Bay—is safe if the wind swings to the south. This is more apt to happen between early August and late November or early December, when the trade winds arrive, but there are exceptions. For example, in January 1973, it blew steadily south and southeast for weeks on end. And in 1987, the supposed northeast trades spent the entire winter in the southeast! Keep in mind that the south coast is best in the winter, while New Found Bay, Haulover Bay, and Trunk Bay on the north coast are better in the summer, when the wind is likely to be south of east.

RAM HEAD ANCHORAGE

(Sketch Chart 42; II A, A-23, A-231)

With the wind well in the north, an anchorage can be had anywhere behind Ram Head; anchor very close to shore, Bahamian moor or bow-and-stern. The bottom is loose rock and drops off very steeply. The beach is shingle and not appealing for those wanting to bask on white sand.

SALT POND BAY

(Sketch Chart 42; II A, A-23, A-231)

Northwest of Ram Head is the superb anchorage of Salt Pond Bay. It is easy to enter and deep enough for all but the largest boat, though somewhat restricted in space. Booby Rock is easy to recognize and avoid, since it is 35 feet high and plastered with guano. There are rocks awash at the entrance, with ample water to pass on either side. I think it best to leave them to starboard and round up on into the bay, carrying a full two fathoms of water to within 100 yards of shore. Deep-draft boats can anchor on a Bahamian moor; shoal-draft boats can stick a bow anchor into the sand and drop another anchor from the stern into deep water. Wind sweeps across the lowland between Coral Bay and Salt Pond, keeping the anchorage cool at all times. A short walk ashore will bring you to Salt Pond. During the dry season, large salt crystals frequently form around the pond's edge—free rock salt for the taking. Within the bay, the snorkeling is good fun, and experienced divers will enjoy the deeper water around Booby Rock.

KITTLE POINT BAY

(Sketch Chart 42; II A, A-23, A-231)

This bay is west of Kittle Point, which has a house on it. Connecting the house with civilization is a series of what appear to be large power poles and lines—installation of the poles must have cost as much as the house. The general depths in the bay are 30 feet, but there is room for only one boat. Deep water extends right up to shore. Obviously, the only way to anchor is to drop a bow (or stern) anchor and run a line ashore to the trees. There is one big gommier tree in the middle of the shingle beach that should provide a secure place to tie up. Of course, you'll need to avoid this bay when the wind is in the south. The bottom is sand, with very little grass, so the holding should be good. (Be sure to check in advance with National Park Service authorities; tying up to the tree may be prohibited here.)

Ashore, we found two rock cairns, one about six feet high and the other eight feet, both beautifully protected with 18-inch-high stonework around their bases. I have no idea who built these or why they were built.

The solitude of this anchorage should be complete, and the snorkeling around the shoreline superb.

CABRITHORN BAY

(Sketch Chart 42; II A, A-23, A-231)

This cove, unnamed on the chart, lies east of Cabrithorn Point. It is roughly 30 feet deep, with a white sand and rock bottom. There is room for only one boat to anchor. It is so deep that you will have to anchor on chain and ride on the chain or anchor and run a line ashore. However, we saw no obvious attachment point on shore. You might have to do what they do in the area around Cape Horn—drive rock-climbing pitons in between the rocks on shore and attach line to the pitons.

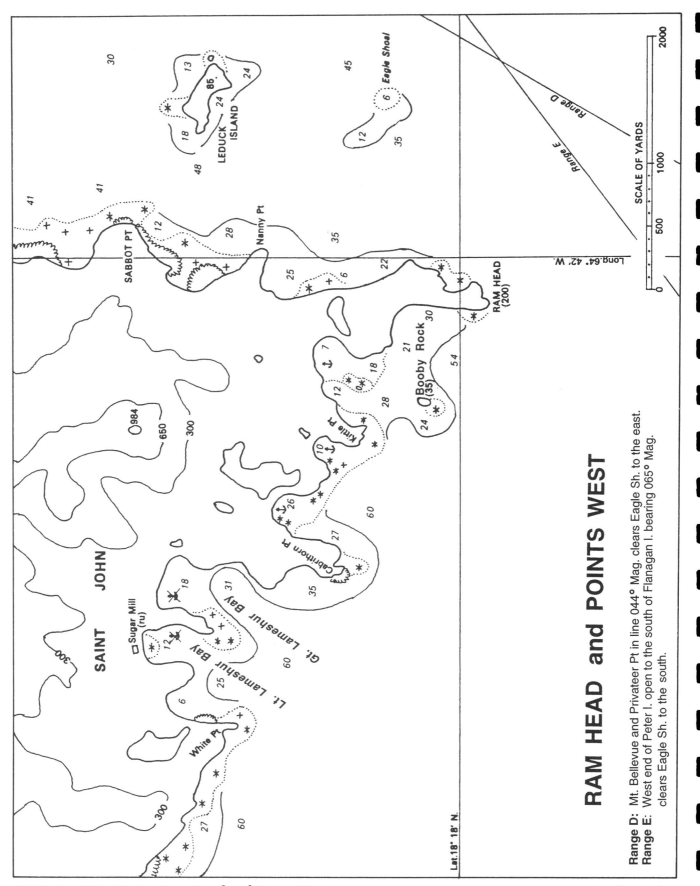

RAM HEAD and POINTS WEST

Range D: Mt. Bellevue and Privateer Pt in line 044° Mag. clears Eagle Sh. to the east.

Range E: West end of Peter I. open to the south of Flanagan I. bearing 065° Mag. clears Eagle Sh. to the south.

GREATER LAMESHUR BAY

(Sketch Chart 42; II A, A-23, A-231)

This bay once was the site of the Tektite Project, a NASA experiment in undersea living that was designed to test whether or not astronauts could exist in a confined environment for months at a time. Now the only remnants of the project are some semiderelict buildings, a dock in a state of disrepair, and a sign saying that visitors are welcome only by invitation of the Virgin Islands Environmental Resources Station (tel. 776-6721).

Greater Lameshur is a superb anchorage, with crystal-clear water and excellent snorkeling along the shoreline. In order to protect the seagrass beds here, the National Park Service has designated this bay as a mooring-only area, and five moorings (white with a blue stripe) have been installed. No anchoring is allowed! Lameshur would be sheltered unless the wind went all the way around to dead south. At the environmental resources building, there are large trash cans, but I am not sure whether or not they are emptied regularly. Stay away from the shoreline after 1630, as the sandflies come out with a vengeance. Relatively few boats stop here, and there is plenty of room, so this is definitely a superb spot.

LITTLE LAMESHUR BAY

(Sketch Chart 42; II A, A-23, A-231)

Yet another good anchorage with deep water right up to the shore. On the starboard hand are shoals to the head of the bay. There is a very nice white-sand beach, and swimming and snorkeling are delightful in the clear water. As with Greater Lameshur, the National Park Service has designated this as a mooring-only area, and four moorings have been installed. No anchoring! At the western side of the head of the bay are the ruins of an old estate.

REEF BAY

(Sketch Chart 43; II A, A-23, A-231)

The problem here is that the bay is wide open to the south. The point to the east does not hook far enough south, and a southerly swell—even a southeasterly swell—will wash right into the bay. However, a decent anchorage exists way up in the head of the bay. It's strictly a case of eyeballing your way in, following the deep water and anchoring in nine feet of water by the white buoy (installed by the National Park Service). Holding in this area appears good—sand with no grass—but if you begin to drag, you have very little room, so I would suggest anchoring and picking up the buoy.

The sea will break on both sides on the way in, but once you are in, it is sheltered unless the wind is southeast or south of southeast. The dinghy dock is up behind the reef and appears protected at all times. There is a very nice sand beach with picnic tables, but the tables are too close to the shrubbery. Although the beach during the day appears to be clear of sandflies, the table definitely is not.

The path heading inland leads to an old sugar estate with a rum factory, which is extremely interesting. I don't know when it was originally established, but certainly before the slaves were freed in the mid-1800s. Originally the mill was horse-powered, but in 1864 the management installed a steam engine that had been built in Glasgow in 1861. Sometime later, the factory must have become unprofitable, as the estate manager, William H. Nash, bought it at auction. He and his descendants continued operating the estate until 1916, when three hurricanes blew over St. Thomas and St. John. The storms flattened everything, destroyed the sugar crop, and damaged the factory so badly that it was not worth restoring.

That was a bad year for hurricanes—there were 14 of them in the Caribbean! The three that ruined the sugar estate were in mid-July, late August, and mid-October, and all three went pretty much right over the top of St. Thomas and St. John.

Historians tend to disagree about the timing of the collapse of the sugar industry in the Caribbean. Some maintain that it collapsed as soon as the slaves were freed, but this argument does not seem to hold water. During the 1870s, 1880s, and 1890s, sugar-refinery equipment continued to be shipped to the islands, and estate owners certainly would not have made these costly investments if their estates had not been profitable. I suspect that the truth is that the inefficient absentee-landowner plantations collapsed and died, while the locally managed ones continued to prosper. Perhaps they were not as fantastically profitable as they had been in the 1770s through the early 1800s, but they still were economically viable businesses.

A well-marked path up the hill through the woods leads to the Carib petroglyphs. It is a 30-minute walk along a beautifully shaded path, but I still suggest going early in the morning, when it is still cool. Along the way are many signs describing the interesting flora and fauna. Most intriguing are the miles of three-foot-high stone walls leading off into the bush. All are beautifully built and amazingly well

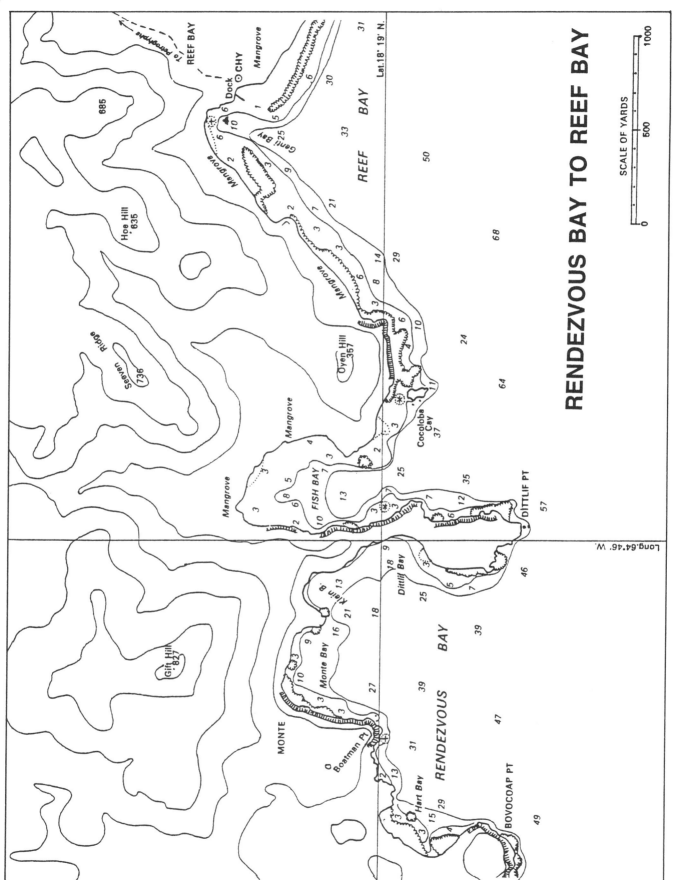

SKETCH CHART 43 Rendezvous Bay to Reef Bay

Soundings in feet

preserved—rather like Irish or New England walls deposited in the Caribbean.

When you reach the site of the petroglyphs, you'll find a series of pools and a small waterfall—probably nonexistent in the dry season, but quite a stream in the rainy season. The water in the pools is excellent, so carry along a bottle that you can fill when you get there.

Carib carvings are fairly prevalent in the southern islands of the Caribbean, but the Caribs only arrived in the Virgin Islands in the mid-fifteenth century. They conquered and killed the peaceful Arawaks, allegedly tossing most of them in a pot for dinner! Next they continued westward along the coast of Puerto Rico, and some of their raiding expeditions even reached the Bahamas. Apparently the Caribbean equivalent of the Viking raiders, they were wonderfully kind to their own people, but woe betide their enemies!

The rapaciousness of the Caribs was soon outdone by the Spaniards, who rapidly killed off everyone, leaving little trace of any indigenous civilization—Carib, Arawak, or anyone else.

FISH BAY
(Sketch Chart 43; II A, A-23, A-231)

Since the names given to West Indian shores often explicitly hark back to some specific incident or condition, it's a good bet that anything called Fish Bay is loaded with fish and oysters. But unless you're an avid fisherman, the bay, with its lowland to the east, impresses me as a poor stopover for the night. Since it's surrounded by mangroves, I suspect it would tend to be rather buggy. Fish Bay is shoal, but nine feet can be taken well up into it, provided you feel your way in carefully. In such marginal situations, remember that the Caribbean is lower in the spring and early summer than in the winter—sometimes substantially lower. The holding in Fish Bay should be good—our examination by dinghy showed that the bottom was sand with little or no grass, especially in the outer reaches of the bay.

RENDEZVOUS BAY
(Sketch Chart 43; II A, A-23, A-231)

There are practically no dangers in entering this seldom-used but excellent anchorage. Stand to the south, rounding Dittlif Point, and, keeping discreetly west of the reef alongside this point, round up into the bay. You can sail almost up to the shore before dropping your anchor. I am told there is good fishing and clamming here.

We were told on good authority that the best anchorage is in the northeast corner of the bay. Basically, you can anchor anywhere in the northern end of the bay, but be forewarned that the bottom is mixed sand and grass, not good holding. I advise using two anchors, and be sure to check them to be sure they are well dug in.

CHOCOLATE HOLE
(Sketch Chart 37; II A, A-23, A-231)

Chocolate Hole has had a reincarnation since I first visited it in 1958. At that time, I was in the land-survey business, and the company I was working for was trying to develop the area. The salt pond then was more open to the sea than it is now, and when it rained, the mud from the salt pond poured into the harbor—hence the name Chocolate Hole.

Chocolate Hole still has a salt pond behind it, but the little mud that comes out of it in very heavy rain tends to clear up within a few days. Generally the water is crystal-clear, with superb snorkeling off Maria Bluff and Bovocoap Point—favorite stops for St. Johnian dive boats. There is also good snorkeling all around the edges of the harbor.

In January 1993, we anchored in Chocolate Hole and felt secure, but Scott Burnett, who runs a boat-maintenance service (tel. 776-7360), came by to welcome us and warn that the holding was not very good. Abeam of us was an unused permanent mooring that we should have passed a line to, because a hard gust came through about 2200, the anchor pulled out, and we almost went across the harbor. Fortunately, we managed to get another anchor overboard and finally got some sleep with two anchors set.

The next morning, while checking the anchors, we discovered that they were only partially dug in, in mixed sand and grass bottom. We then ran a line out to the empty permanent mooring and picked up our anchors. If you decide to anchor here, I strongly advise setting two anchors, diving them down, and making very sure they are very well set. Scott Burnett reports that each winter one or two boats drag up onto the rocks and suffer fairly major damage.

If you pick up an empty mooring, go ashore immediately and look up Scott Burnett. You can find him by checking the house on the northeast corner of the harbor with a cupola on top. Or telephone him at the number above. There is nothing more aggravating to the owner of a permanent mooring

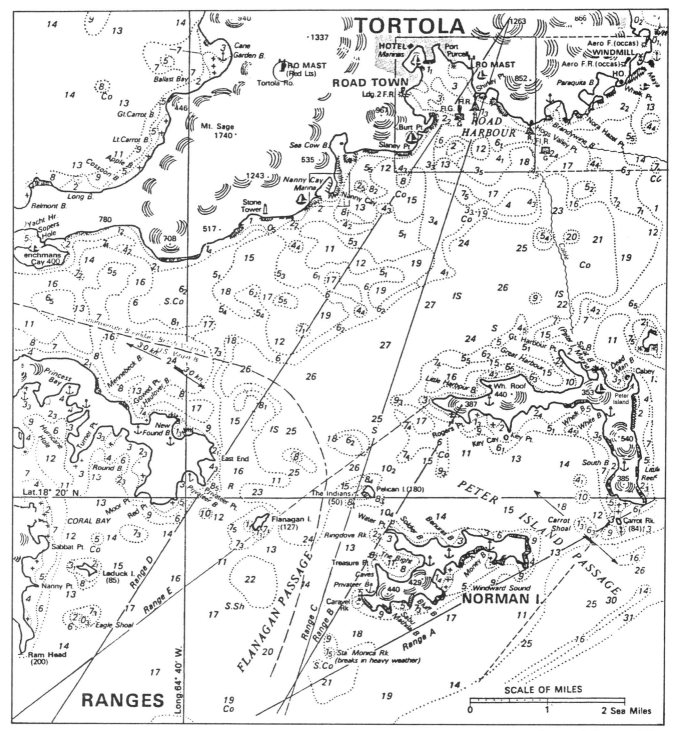

SKETCH CHART 44   Ranges, Eagle Shoal to Peter Island, British Virgins   Soundings in fathoms and feet

Range A: Southeast point of Norman I. in line with Carrot Rock bearing 074° Mag clears Sta Monica Rk to the south.
Range B: Hill on Peter I. in line with Water Pt 038° Mag clears Sta Monica Rk to the west.
Range C: Mt. Bellevue open to the west of Pelican I. 029° Mag clears Sta Monica Rk to the west.
Range D: Mt. Bellevue and Privateer Pt in line 044° Mag clears Eagle Sh to the east.
Range E: West end of Peter I. open to the south of Flanagan I. bearing 065° Mag clears Eagle Sh to the south.

than to sail home at dusk and find someone at his or her mooring. In fact, according to Herb Payson, in the May 1994 issue of *Sail* magazine, each permanent mooring here is privately owned and assigned to a specific boat, and it is now illegal to use one of these moorings without written permission from the owner. Bureaucracy gone wild!

GREAT CRUZ BAY
(Sketch Chart 37; II A, A-23, A-231)

This used to be an uncrowded anchorage, but since Cruz Bay has become very congested, Great Cruz Bay has attracted many more boats, including many on permanent moorings. These take up most of the worthwhile space; now you have to anchor outside the fleet of moored boats. This puts you out in the swell rolling your guts out. Needless to say, this is not a terrific anchorage for visiting yachts. The inner bay (where the permanent moorings are located) is settled in all normal conditions, but in abnormal conditions—such as during Hurricane Klaus, in 1984, when the wind came in from the southwest—it is a death trap.

TURNER BAY
(Sketch Chart 37; II A, A-23, A-231)

A good harbor only if the wind is north of east. Sand has been dredged from the bay for fill used elsewhere, so there's water, but entry demands careful eyeball navigation. If the wind comes south of east, it is best to move on.

When approaching from the south, there is no difficulty; coming from the north, I advise going outside the buoy off Moravian Point. A good reef navigator can pass inside the buoy and duck between the breaking rocks—the rocks break but there is deep water in between—but I advise against it.

One good reason to stop at Turner Bay is that it is within walking distance of Cruz Bay.

FRANK BAY
(Sketch Chart 37; II A, A-23, A-231)

In fair weather, this is a good refuge from the ferry wash in Cruz Bay, but it's choppy in bad weather and admits a swell in winter.

NOTES

11

⌒〜⌒

St. Croix

(Imray-Iolaire Charts A, A-2, A-23, A-231, A-234)

St. Croix, the largest of the Virgin Islands, at 82 square miles, lies approximately 35 miles due south of the other Virgins, separated from them by extremely deep water. Many people cruising the Virgins tend to skip St. Croix because of its relative remoteness, but it is an island well worth visiting. The main harbor at Christiansted is excellent; Buck Island, a morning's sail from Christiansted, offers superb snorkeling and diving; the yacht club in Teague Bay hosts weekend racing; the entire area inside the reef on the northeastern side of the island is a perfect place for small-boat sailing; and to the east of Teague Bay, the waters are completely sheltered and always calm, providing unparalleled snorkeling among coral heads.

Twenty-three miles long, St. Croix was, in its heyday, the most important of the Virgin Islands. St. Thomas was strictly a trading island that reached the zenith of its development toward the end of the Napoleonic wars as a free port, where privateers and naval vessels of all nations could bring in their prizes for auction.

In contrast, St. Croix owed its prosperity to the vast sugar plantations that covered the flat south coast and extended up into the hills. St. Croix survived as a profitable sugar island until it began to decline with the freeing of the slaves in 1848, but Christiansted remained the capital of the Danish Virgin Islands until the 1870s. (One of the most magnificent buildings in the Virgin Islands is the eighteenth-century Government House in St. Croix.) In the 1860s, St. Thomas rose out of the depression of the post-Napoleonic wars to become a major coaling port for transatlantic shipping. Thus, in 1871 the capital was moved from Christiansted to St. Thomas.

The whole lower section of Christiansted is a National Historic District in which the façade of buildings cannot be altered without official sanction. In my opinion, parts of this neighborhood constitute the most attractive area in the whole Lesser Antilles chain. The Danes were practical architects. The ground floors of their buildings were warehouses, while the second and third floors, housing counting rooms and living accommodations, were built out over the sidewalks, supported by tidy stone arches. As a result, in the lower part of town the sidewalks are shaded, making walking cool on sunny days and dry on rainy ones.

Not all of the buildings in Christiansted have been restored, but enough of them have to make it extremely attractive. Just walking around the town, with its uncrowded streets, is a pleasure. Fort Christiansvaern (Christiansted National Monument) has been restored and is maintained by the National Park Service. The courtyard of Government House has lovely gardens, and sometimes there are tours of the building.

If you happen to be on the island when the Landmarks League is conducting its tours of the old "great houses," be sure to join. These tours are only held a few days a year, and it's a once-in-a-lifetime experience—unless you happen to wangle an invitation to the Thursday-night buffet at the Tennis Club, where you might meet some of the landed aristocracy and wealthy expatriates who own these magnificent houses.

Some of the eighteenth- and nineteenth-century Danish planters became so wealthy through sugar and cattle that when they visited their homeland, they made a bigger splash in Copenhagen than did the king. As a result, the king of Denmark was embarrassed into enacting legislation that restricted the number of liveried servants and outriders who could accompany a coach through the streets.

Until the mid-1950s, St. Croix had an agricultural economy built on the three C's: cattle, cane, and cotton. Cotton was grown for the Sea Island cotton industry, and the cottonseed was used for cattle feed. Tourism trailed behind. In the late 1950s and early 1960s, tourism increased and the sugar industry collapsed. Then came Harvey Aluminum and Amerada Hess, bringing new industry to St. Croix. Fortunately the industry has remained on the south side of the island, but the social problems have not. Clashes between industry workers and local labor produced a rather horrific crime rate in St. Croix that only now is abating.

A special breed of cattle—the Senepol—was developed in St. Croix to withstand the dry, tropical climate, and the cattle industry remains highly profitable. If you tour the island by car, you will spot herds of these fat prime-beef cattle. In the 1950s, Stacy Lloyd introduced a herd of dairy cattle, a very successful enterprise. Today Island Dairies supplies fresh milk as good as any you can buy in the States. The other dairy in the Virgins, St. Thomas Dairy, supplies what people think is fresh milk, but it actually is reconstituted milk from the States.

The thriving beef and dairy industry in St. Croix makes one realize that Antigua could bolster its own flagging economy by raising cattle on the island's vast expanses of unused sugar acreage. When viable solutions exist, if only someone would pursue them, it is easy to lose sympathy for an Antiguan government that always claims it is broke. Antigua is no drier than the dry area of St. Croix, where cattle have been raised for centuries. With so much government-owned land available, Antigua could be the cattle kingdom of the Caribbean, exporting cattle to all the other islands and certainly supplying all of Antigua with fresh milk.

Even though tourism has increased in St. Croix, it still rests more lightly on the island economy than does the St. Thomas "cruise ship" brand of tourism. Few cruise ships come into Christiansted, and those that do are relatively small. At the height of the season in 1993, seven ships a month were coming into Christiansted—compared with seven a day in St. Thomas! Frederiksted sees more cruise ships, but few of the passengers get as far as Christiansted to do their shopping.

In St. Croix, tourism rests primarily on the expatriates who spend the winter here, plus tourists who spend five to 10 days or more on the island, so the contrast between shopping experiences in St. Thomas and Christiansted is truly amazing—and pleasurable. After spending a few days in St. Thomas fighting massive crowds downtown (includ-

ing passengers from the inevitable two or three cruise ships alongside the dock), the streets feel empty in Christiansted. It feels almost like a ghost town—a few customers, no hard-sell hustle or hassle, a place to browse in leisurely fashion and check out the shops and their wares. The shops are not as numerous as in St. Thomas, but they are more tasteful.

It's worth setting aside a full day for exploring the island. Rent a car (there are half a dozen rental agencies) and drive out of Christiansted heading west on Northside Road (Route 75). Follow that to Route 89, go a short distance, and turn left onto Route 78 (you'll need four-wheel drive for this part). Continue along Route 78—which offers magnificent views over to the south coast or north down toward the ocean—until you get to Hams Bay. If the last stretch of Route 78 is impassable, pick up Route 58 (Creque Dam Road) and head for Sprat Hall, one of the plantation "great houses" that has been converted to a guesthouse and restaurant. Sprat Hall is notable in that it has been lived in continually since it was built about 200 years ago; it is not a restored ruin.

At this point, you probably will be hot and ready for a swim, so park the car at any one of the many beaches on the west coast of St. Croix and have a swim. After lunch, head back to Christiansted via Centerline Road (Route 70—the old standby) or the new highway (Route 66), which takes you by numerous shopping centers with supermarkets equally as good as anything in the States. The selection of food in the supermarkets and shopping centers in St. Croix is head and shoulders above that in St. Thomas. Allegedly, everything is also 10 percent cheaper in St. Croix.

Larry Angus, head of St. Croix Marine, states that many of the big power yachts come over to St. Croix and load fuel via bunkers, saving as much as 20 cents a gallon over the list price. Then they do a major restock. The savings in fuel and food costs makes the trip to St. Croix well worth their while. The same would also hold true for boats heading north or going transatlantic in the spring.

I would not venture to guess who sells the cheapest bunker fuel in the Caribbean—at least half a dozen people have claimed they do. If you have a large power yacht, I suggest you ask around and find out the going prices for fuel in St. Thomas, and at Puerto del Rey Marina in Fajardo, on the east coast of Puerto Rico.

If you are following Centerline Road on your trip back to Christiansted, keep an eye out for signs for Estate Whim Plantation Museum, a beautiful, restored great house. The museum has fascinating exhibits on the various methods of grinding sugar cane.

When you look at the road map, you'll find wonderful names given to the old sugar estates: Prosperity, William's Delight, Betty's Jewel, Hope, Wheel of Fortune, and Anna's Hope. Some owners apparently were less sanguine about their enterprises, giving them such titles as Hard Labor, Solitude, Barren Spot, Little Profit, and, at the eastern end of the island, Slob.

St. Croix's main roads are well maintained, but many of the back roads, even though built in the 1950s, are unpaved and in bad shape. My Irish wife would describe them as nothing better than "boreens," yet they are all beautifully signposted. It is impossible to get lost in St. Croix if you have a road map.

During the 1970s, St. Croix had a serious crime problem that drastically slowed tourist development and caused many people to move off the island. Then the Cruzans established a special crime-prevention force—complete with four-wheel-drive vehicles, 24-hour radio coverage, and attack dogs—that apparently was instrumental in drastically reducing the crime level. (Police reported, off the record, that many of the "bad ones" had left for St. Thomas, where presumably the pickings were— and are—better and easier.) Then, as time went by, the drug situation began to get out of hand, and crime again skyrocketed. The worst crime situation in recent years was in 1989, in the aftermath of Hurricane Hugo. The looting of damaged buildings was so extensive that the local police department was incapable of controlling the situation. Military police had to be flown in to restore law and order.

I must add a note here about the media reaction to this in St. Thomas. The radio station management in St. Thomas heard the reports of the looting in St. Croix and quickly conferred with St. Thomas newspaper officials. They jointly decided to report nothing in St. Thomas about the St. Croix situation—in hopes that the looting idea would not spread. The newspaper and the radio station deserved a medal for their exercise of unbelievable self-control—and their decision was proven wise.

Interestingly, to the best of my knowledge, the crime problem that afflicts yachtsmen and their boats in St. Thomas has not spilled over to the yachts in St. Croix. Even after Hugo, there was no looting at St. Croix Marine—but that may be thanks to the singlehanded efforts of Stuart Ragland, then about 70. He found himself a broken chair and a big shotgun and sat at the gate, daring anyone to enter.

He held the fort against potential looters until reinforcements arrived in the form of boatowners and staff members. Anyone who knows Stuart would be able to understand this. He joined the Canadian Air Force in World War II and flew B-17s over Europe, after which he returned to college and became a doctor. Then he joined the US Navy and became a jet fighter pilot, flying off aircraft carriers at the age of 38. Quite a fellow!

In the more than three decades that I have been frequenting the Virgin Islands, almost everything has changed, but thankfully one old reliable has held out staunchly: Ted Dale's Comanche Club. Unfortunately, Ted no longer owns it, but the club still looks the same. The upstairs bar is cool and picturesque and the bartenders are friendly. Ted built the club back in the early 1950s, when there was no regular freight line between Puerto Rico and St. Croix. Ted fitted out his 72-foot Alden yawl, *Comanche,* as a cargo boat and carted all the construction material over from Puerto Rico.

When I first arrived in St. Croix, Ted was no longer using the *Comanche* for cargo hauling but rather for day chartering. He and his mate, Duke (who is even bigger than Ted), would sail the engineless yawl off the dock at the end of the club to Buck Island and back—just the two of them and a load of day-trippers.

The reason the *Comanche* had no engine was rather amusing. Ted told one of his crew boys to change the oil in the engine. The fellow was from down island, was a very good sailor, and had worked on local schooners, but he knew nothing about engines. He reported to Ted that the oil had been changed. Fine. The next day, they decided to use the engine to get off the dock and power out of the harbor. Halfway out of the harbor, the engine started belching smoke, seized up, and never ran again. The boy had changed the oil, but the only oil he knew about was linseed oil—which he had poured into the crankcase. Ted and Duke took the engine out of *Comanche,* put a chain on it, tossed it into the harbor, and rented it out to yachtsmen as a mooring.

The old *Comanche* finally died and was replaced by a schooner with two small mizzens. The schooner had an engine, but Ted hated to use it, so he put in the mizzens to make her handle more easily under sail.

The Comanche Club dock always used to look like it was about to give up the ghost, but it had looked that way ever since 1953, when it was built. Ted and Duke had banged the facility together in two weeks with 55-gallon drums, railroad iron scrounged from God-knows-where, a couple of sledgehammers, and a box of cigars for Duke. Everyone predicted that it wouldn't even last the first season—yet it lasted until 1989, when it was trashed by Hurricane Hugo.

The club also boasts a tower fashioned by Ted and advertised as a honeymoon cottage. It's often available as a cheap room even if you don't happen to be traveling with a bona-fide bride. Sitting on top of the tower as the moon comes up, with the yacht harbor spread out at your feet and a cool drink in your hand, is one of the Virgin Islands' not-to-be-forgotten experiences.

Ted and Duke were quite the sailors. They used to sail the old 72-footer off the dock, around the harbor, and back and forth from Puerto Rico without engine or winch. I found the story hard to swallow until one day I asked Duke to haul me to the top of *Iolaire's* mast, and I pointed to the winch. He just laughed. He hauled me up hand over hand so fast that when the halyard two-blocked, I almost kept going into space like a moon rocket!

Ted also has a predilection for outlandish small craft. At one point, he even had a genuine Venetian gondola in which he rowed around the harbor. In the late 1980s, he was still sailing a Carib war canoe whose rig consisted of five Sunfish lateen masts—the only five-masted lateen schooner in existence. He now lives at Pull Point, on the island's north coast, surrounded by a collection of his outlandish boats.

St. Croix hauling facilities and marine supplies are good. St. Croix Marine was founded by Bill Chandler in the early 1960s and then sold to the Knutsons of Knutsons Shipyard in Hailsite, Long Island. They in turn sold it to Larry and Ginny Angus. It is now part of the Island Marine Supply outfit, which has stores in St. Thomas and Tortola. The chandlery is excellent, and facilities include a small bar and restaurant, showers, a 60-ton Travelift, and a 300-ton railway. Draft is limited to 11 feet on the railway and eight feet on the Travelift. The railway caters to large yachts as well as to the big US Coast Guard boats and the patrol boats of the independent Caribbean nations.

The people at St. Croix Marine have developed a good reputation for excellent work, but it is a little on the expensive side. They have a machine shop and excellent welding equipment for both stainless and aluminum, and they can do electrical and refrigeration repairs, but save your radio and electronics repairs for St. Thomas or Tortola. It is wise to remember that St. Croix Marine is basically a commercial yard that handles yachts—not a yacht yard that does some commercial work.

When we were here in January 1993, there was ample slip space available at St. Croix Marine.

In recent years, the area around the marina has developed rapidly, so you can find most of what you need within walking distance. Admittedly, to do major shopping, it is necessary to go out of town via taxi or rental car to Pueblo's or Grand Union. The order can be delivered if you wish; check with Ginny Angus beforehand. Edwina Ragland, who has lived in the marina for several years, has her life so well organized that she only has to do a "big shop" once a month.

Ice (cubes and blocks) is available from St. Croix Marine; laundry is within spitting distance. While we were there in January 1993, a new communications company, Answer Plus, was being set up to offer such services as faxing, phone message center, photocopying, secretarial work, and DHL.

Right outside the yard is the shop of James Langton, a highly skilled shipwright who served a seven-year apprenticeship in England. One service difficult to find in St. Croix is sailmaking. There are various people who do emergency sail repairs, but they come and go. You'll need to ask at St. Croix Marine or at the yacht club to see who is doing sail repairs.

The easiest way to get to town from the marina is to take the dinghy; there are various docks in town, but most of the yachties use the floating dock of the Stixx Hurricane Bar and Restaurant. I recommend that you not walk back from town to St. Croix Marine at night.

In the past, before Green Cay Marina was built, mooring facilities for visiting yachts in Christiansted Harbor were in short supply. That meant that Gallows Bay, Welcome Bank, and the anchorage west of Protestant Cay were always overcrowded. Ever since the construction of Green Cay Marina (150 slips, 10-foot draft in the channel; tel. 773-1453; fax 773-9651), the pressure has been off. There is now plenty of room to anchor on Welcome Bank, but be warned that when it blows hard, the sea breaks on the reef and flows over the reef into the harbor. The water then pours out through the channel, sometimes attaining a speed of two to three knots!

In January 1993, when we arrived in heavy weather (having sailed from St. John to Christiansted—35 miles—in five hours, a seven-knot average under staysail and mizzen only), the current was pouring out of the channel at a good, solid three knots. We tried to anchor into Welcome Bank and were tide-rode, so we moved over to the eastern side of the harbor southwest of Port Louise Augusta.

Most older charts are wrong about the depth of

the channel, which has been dredged to 18 feet through the old schooner channel. This created deep water right along the eastern side of the harbor. Even the latest chart given to me by the Harbour Department in early 1993 showed an extensive shoal off Altona Lagoon, but we sounded near shore in the dinghy and ascertained that within 75 feet of shore, there was still nine feet of water. Exactly how this happened, no one seems to know. One story is that the dredging company needed a place out of the traffic lane to store their equipment, so they dredged right up to the shore of Altona Lagoon but never reported it, as they didn't want any arguments from the Environmental Protection Agency!

When anchoring in this area, go as close to shore as possible (but beware of the wrecks of sunken barges), because waves come pouring across the top of the reef during heavy weather, and the water goes rushing out of the harbor mouth.

Unless you have a very shoal-draft boat—five feet or less—do not try to anchor west of Protestant Cay. The area is completely filled with local boats on permanent moorings, and there is NO room for visiting yachts. If you do draw less than five feet, you can run down behind Protestant Cay, staying very close to shore, round up, and anchor behind (i.e., to the west of) the anchored fleet. Be sure to use a Bahamian moor, as sometimes the current will run to the east 24 hours a day; at other times, it will run to the east at each change of tide and swing you around your anchor twice a day.

The yacht club at Teague Bay has some facilities for visiting yachts, but the area off the club is quite shoal.

There is a small marina in Salt River, but entrance is not easy, and draft into the marina is restricted to six feet. Once there, you are 25 minutes from town by car. Salt River will never develop as a yachting center until a deep, 12-foot channel has been dredged and marked. This major operation must be a government-sponsored project. Unfortunately, the Virgin Islands politicians have never been blessed with foresight when it comes to development, despite the massive amounts of money that yachting has brought to St. Thomas and the British Virgins.

To the south of St. Croix Marine, you can find the commercial harbor with the harbormaster's office, plus Immigration and Customs offices. Contrary to the well-worn rumor, you do not have to go to the airport to clear. Sometimes you have to wait for a Customs official to come from the airport, but that's all. Anchor and then go ashore with crew lists, etc., in the usual way.

The best chart for this area used to be Imray-Iolaire Chart A-23, and it is still good, but new Chart A-234 is a detailed chart (1:27,000) that covers the northeast coast from Salt River to the eastern tip of the island.

You can sail directly from St. Thomas to St. Croix (course 173° magnetic; distance 35 miles, sea buoy to sea buoy), but you will be making leeway and facing a weather-bow current of one-half to one and one-fourth knots, which would necessitate steering a course between 160° and 163°, depending on the leeway made by the individual boat. (Remember that many of the bareboats make a tremendous amount of leeway, and if you're sailing a real sand barge, you would do well to steer closer to 150° magnetic.) If the wind is southerly, it will mean that you will be hard on it, making for a rough all-day sail. Chances are you won't get there until twilight, and you should not enter Christiansted at dark under any circumstances.

From St. Thomas, it is better to leave from Buck Island, since that will shorten the distance by four miles. Head for the well-defined notch east of Christiansted. As you approach the island and pick up the town of Christiansted, do not head directly for it, since the town is well west of the harbor entrance. Continue heading for this notch until you pick up the radio tower on Fort Louise Augusta (WIVI, 970 kHz), and bring that to bear on 173° magnetic, which will lead you through the channel. There is a range into the channel, but it is difficult to pick up. The radio tower used to be even easier to pick up—it was a giant structure that was visible way out to sea—but it, too, was done in by Hugo. The replacement tower is tall and thin and supported by guy wires (how they build one of those things and install it is beyond me), and it's not quite as distinctive as the old one.

You can also depart from Norman Island or the eastern end of St. John. The advantage of the latter is that you will not have to go through Customs and Immigration upon arrival, which you will have to do if you come from Norman Island. The course from Salt Pond Bay is 180° magnetic; from the western end of Norman Island, 196° magnetic (distance: 32 miles). Both courses should result in a beam or broad reach with little leeway being made; you will only need to reckon with the set of the current.

In leaving Norman Island, avoid Santa Monica Rock by holding to 180° magnetic until the south tip of Peter Island appears from behind Norman; then you will be safely south of the rock. (Sketch Chart 44 gives ranges for this area.) Santa Monica Rock is marked 1 3/4 fathoms on the chart, but it can still be hit by the average draft, since a yacht can drop on it in a swell, and frequently the rock causes waves to crest and break.

When approaching St. Croix from Norman or St. John, again head for the saddle between the two hills east of Christiansted until the city itself comes into view. Immediately upon discerning the city, head for its eastern edge to pick up the radio tower; if you continue too far east, the range from the saddle will lead over the western edge of Scotch Bank. This bank breaks in heavy seas and has shoals with as little as a quarter of a fathom over them. Continue heading for the eastern part of Christiansted until the radio tower at Fort Louise Augusta bears 173° magnetic, then follow directions below.

Be aware that Scotch Bank breaks along its entire length in heavy weather, especially when the ground swell is coming in from the north. The US and Imray-Iolaire charts are correct in showing only two to three feet of water in the shoalest spots. Despite this, however, some guides and privately printed charts show minimum depths of eight or nine feet. Disregard these, since it is just as shallow as the US and Imray charts indicate.

In the old days, when *Iolaire* was chartering out of St. Thomas, we regularly visited St. Croix on our two-week charters. We would leave St. Thomas and work our way eastward to the British Virgins. Then, after nine or ten days, we would take off from the BVI and sail directly to Christiansted, where we would restock with food and ice and spend a day touring the island by car (as described above). Then we'd daysail out to Buck Island and head back to St. Thomas. Doing it in this fashion, we were guaranteed a glorious reach in both directions.

CHRISTIANSTED HARBOR

(Chart 45; II A, A-23)

Enter Christiansted Harbor only by day. At night, the lights are confusing—and they get changed regularly; even the latest Light List is likely to be out of date, and it is easy to run hard aground. Coming into the harbor, stay absolutely in the channel, with the radio tower placed squarely between the buoys at 173° magnetic—red to starboard when entering. Scotch Bank shoal will be to the east, Barracuda Ground and shoals (also called Long Reef) to the west. Don't forget that various parts of Scotch Bank are covered by only two feet of water, and the whole bank is covered with breaking water in periods of heavy weather.

Rather than sail the turns inside, stand on in di-

rectly to Fort Louise Augusta until flashing green buoy number 7 is brought abeam; then bear off to a course of 205° magnetic, leaving the red-and-black buoy to starboard. Gradually bear off to the west, following the new 18-foot schooner channel. Anchor anywhere you want between Fort Louise Augusta and St. Croix Marine, remembering that the closer inshore you are, the smoother your anchorage will be and the fewer problems you will have with the aforementioned northgoing current that sometimes pours out of Christiansted Harbor. If you continue down onto Welcome Bank to be near St. Croix Marine, beware! There is a six-foot spot northwest of the marina. It is definitely there, as we bounced on it twice in 1984 and saw it again in 1993.

Make sure you are out of the channel, as island freighters go chugging in and out at all hours of the day and night—and woe betide anyone anchored in the channel. Plus, the Amerada Hess oil barge periodically comes into the harbor and down into Gallows Bay to bunker cruise ships. The barge and tug are very unmaneuverable, so any yacht anchored in or near the channel could easily get wiped out.

The charts show seaplane landing areas, but as of January 1994, the seaplane service between St. Thomas and St. Croix had not been operational for four years. In 1994, a large political fight was underway about who would get the landing rights and when service would resume. It's anyone's guess what will happen.

If you try to enter this harbor at night—which I strongly suggest you don't—you must be certain of your range and buoys before proceeding. Innumerable yachts have mistaken the lights and come to grief on Barracuda Ground and Round Reef. Don't enter the harbor until you have picked up and positively identified the leading lights and/or the radio tower at Fort Louise Augusta. Come in on a range of 173° and hold that range until you are about to pile up on Fort Louise Augusta; then bear off, keeping land close aboard. Once inside the harbor, round up and anchor. Wait until dawn to proceed further—and reread the introductory notes above before you select an anchorage.

GREEN CAY MARINA

(Chart 46; II A, A-23)

A mile-and-a-half east of Christiansted, Green Cay Marina is superbly sheltered. The dredged marina is protected by two stone breakwaters with a very narrow channel between them. During Hurricane Hugo in 1989, boats inside the marina suffered

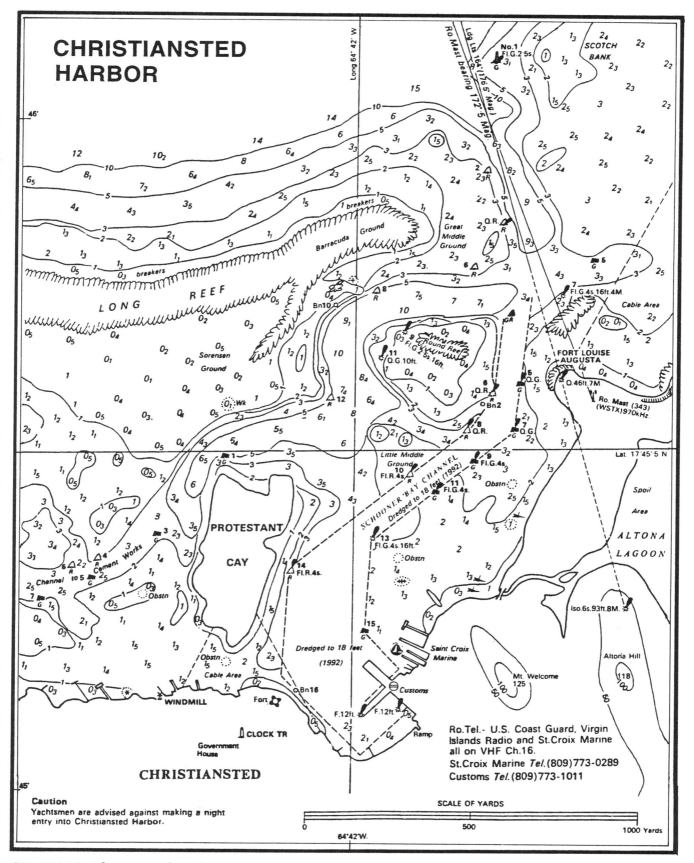

CHRISTIANSTED HARBOR

Long 64° 42' W.

Ldg Lts 164°(176.6° Mag.)

Ro Mast bearing 172.5° Mag.

No.1 Fl.G.2.5s. G

SCOTCH BANK

2 Q.R. R

Great Middle Ground

Round Reef Fl.G.5s.16ft.

11 Q.G.10ft.

8 Q.R.

Bn10.Q.

Bn2

6 Q.R.

7 Q.G.

9 Fl.G.4s. G

5 G

7 Fl.G.4s.16ft.4M.

Cable Area

FORT LOUISE AUGUSTA

Q.46ft.7M. Ro.Mast (343) (WSTX)970kHz.

LONG REEF

Sorensen Ground

Barracuda Ground

breakers

breakers

Wk

12 R

Little Middle Ground 10 Fl.R.4s.

11 Fl.G.4s. G

13 Fl.G.4s.16ft.

Obstn

Obstn

SCHOONER BAY CHANNEL

Dredged to 18 feet (1992)

Lat 17° 45'.5 N

Spoil Area

ALTONA LAGOON

PROTESTANT CAY

Cement Works

Channel to 5

7 G

Obstn

14 Fl.R.4s.

Dredged to 18 feet (1992)

15

Obstn

Cable Area

Saint Croix Marine

Customs

Mt. Welcome 125

Altoria Hill 118

Iso.6s.93ft.8M.

WINDMILL

Fort

CLOCK TR

Government House

CHRISTIANSTED

Bn16

F.12ft. F.12ft. Ramp

Ro.Tel.- U.S. Coast Guard, Virgin Islands Radio and St.Croix Marine all on VHF Ch.16.
St.Croix Marine *Tel.* (809)773-0289
Customs *Tel.* (809)773-1011

Caution
Yachtsmen are advised against making a night entry into Christiansted Harbor.

SCALE OF YARDS

0   500   1000 Yards

64°42'W.

CHART 45   Christiansted Harbor   Soundings in fathoms and feet

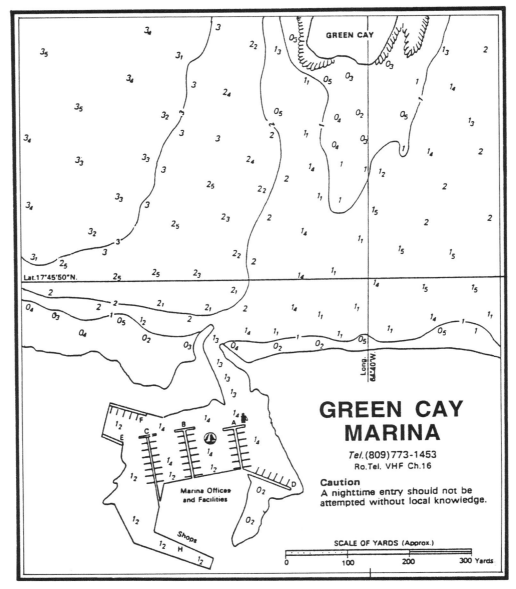

CHART 46 Green Cay Marina

Soundings in fathoms and feet

little damage—mainly dings and dangs, easily re-paired. In contrast, Christiansted Harbor was a com-plete disaster, with boats scattered all over the place.

Green Cay Marina has been a popular place for live-aboards (provided they have a car) and for those who need to leave their boats for a long period of time. The car is crucial, as the marina has only an administrative office, a bar and restaurant (closed Mondays), and a dive shop—no commissary, marine gear, etc.

If you need marine supplies, jump in the dinghy and go to St. Croix Marine. Tie up and go to the chandlery at the marina. Or hop in the car and do the same. Green Cay Marina is not a particularly

good spot for visiting yachts—for the above-men-tioned reasons as well as for the fact that there are few empty berths. Be sure to ascertain well in ad-vance whether or not there is berthing space. (For sailing directions to Green Cay Marina, see direc-tions to Buck Island, below.)

BUCK ISLAND
(Chart 47; II A, A-23)

Four-and-a-half miles northeast of Christiansted, Buck Island provides an excellent daysail. Take off in

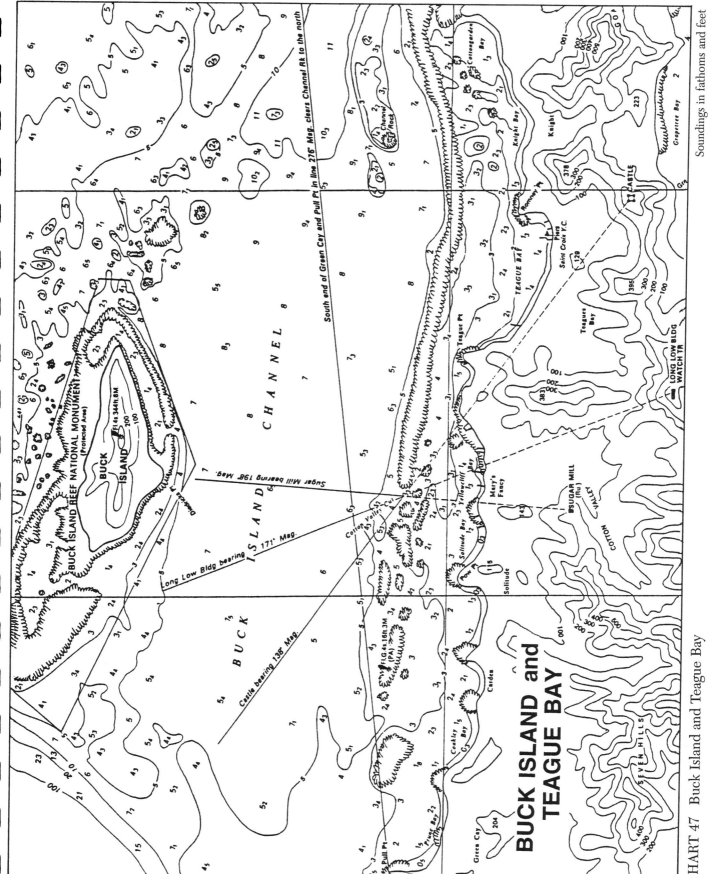

Soundings in fathoms and feet

BUCK ISLAND and TEAGUE BAY

CHART 47   Buck Island and Teague Bay

the morning and beat to windward in calm seas. Spend a few hours exploring the island and its magnificent reefs, and then enjoy a nice, easy run home before dark.

Many years ago, Buck Island (not to be confused with St. Thomas's Buck Island) was given to the government with the stipulation that it never be developed, thus creating a wonderfully wild park for Cruzans and tourists. (Its official title now is Buck Island Reef National Monument.) Charter skippers were diligent in cleaning the area before they left, and every so often the members of the St. Croix Yacht Club would come over to tidy up the beach, plant trees, and maintain its unspoiled beauty. Somewhere along the line, the National Park Service decided to improve on nature by erecting picnic tables and outhouses and labeling all the coral for the benefit of literate scuba divers. Well, better that than a 40-story hotel and a lot of "No Trespassing" signs.

When sailing to Buck Island from Christiansted, do not tack inshore inside buoy number 7 off Fort Louise Augusta, since there are two shoal patches here that have already nabbed plenty of boats. Once clear of these shoals, it is best to hug the shore as closely as possible to gain the shelter of Shoy Point and Green Cay. There is 10 feet of water between Green Cay and the "mainland," but you will find it only if you have a local pilot on board. The consensus seems to be that the deepest draft that should be taken between Green Cay and the mainland is seven feet. The last time I sailed to Buck Island, we watched St. Croix Yacht Club boats sail through there on one leg of a race.

East of Green Cay, eyeball navigation is necessary in the area between Green Cay and Pull Point, as there are numerous coral heads with deep water in between. Hug the St. Croix shore, where the water is deepest. Venture into this area only in good light; don't try it if the light isn't really good.

An anchorage can be found behind Green Cay. If the wind is north of east, anchor off the southern tip; if the wind is south of east, anchor toward the northern end of the island. The water is clear and the snorkeling is good, but there is only a gravel beach. Be careful on the southern end of the island, as the sandbar comes and goes with every ground swell, so no chart can be totally accurate.

When you are clear of Green Cay, hug the shore until you can lay the west end of Buck Island, then stand out toward Buck. The white-sand beach on the western end of the island offers the best anchorage. Sail right in toward the shore. Shoal-draft boats can actually get close enough to have someone jump ashore with the bow anchor, but be sure to set a stern anchor to hold the boat off.

Veteran rock-dodgers can sail eastward along the island to a gap in the reef marked by two stakes. Five-and-a-half feet of draft can be taken through the gap, but it is strictly a case of eyeball navigation—the buoys are not well placed. Power through the gap and run northeastward behind the reef, which is above water and forms a natural breakwater. Inside the reef, over the white-sand bottom (no grass), you can find six to nine feet of water. At the northeast end of the island are the marked underwater trails.

If your boat draws more than five-and-a-half feet, anchor at the western end of the island by the white-sand beach and take the dinghy around to the underwater trails. If too many people are on the trails, head for the western end of the reef. Diving and snorkeling are good anywhere along the reef. A lot of the local dive- and charter-boat skippers maintain that in calm conditions, the best diving is on the reefs north of Buck Island.

Another point to remember is that if you are careful, you can circumnavigate Buck Island in your dinghy, finding all sorts of wonderful driftwood and small beaches (usually shingle rather than sand) on the north side of the island.

In settled weather, it is possible to anchor off Buck Island for the night, but if anchored close to shore, be sure to have a stern anchor out, as the ground swell is likely to come in and swing you up on shore. You only have to look at the white-sand beach on the southwest corner of Buck Island to realize that the area is subject to ground swells.

Buck Island will never become overly crowded, because a number of years ago, the National Park Service started issuing permits for commercial operations that carry day-trippers and divers to the island. The permits were issued in the name of the boat and its capacity. Basically, the only way anyone can go into the Buck Island day-charter business is to buy out an existing operation and acquire the seats. I am told that this is the reason that excursion boats badly damaged in Hurricane Hugo were rebuilt: The boats carried the permits, rather like the taxi-medallion system that exists in various parts of the United States.

Ashore at Buck Island are toilets, trash cans, barbecue pits, and a good dinghy dock (on the south side of the anchorage area, east of the main anchorage). Posted on a shed east of the dinghy dock are the regulations covering the island, plus information and photographs of all the marine life found in the vicinity.

There is also a nature trail across the island; en route you'll see a variety of Caribbean flowers, cacti, trees, and birds. Be sure to wear shoes and carry drinking water. The trail starts from the western end of the island and includes Lookout Point, with a splendid view of the sea's contrasting hues. Make your way back down the south side, which has a panoramic view of St. Croix.

If you don't feel like taking your own boat to Buck Island, sign up with one of the local excursion boats (including multihulls) in Christiansted. There are half-day and full-day snorkeling tours; the full-day trips include rum punches and a barbecue on the beach. In the old days, one of the boats was skippered by a local character named Bomba—an old-time Cruzan and a gentleman of the highest order. Bomba was an institution of a man, with the sunniest smile and the biggest feet in the entire Antilles. Unfortunately, he is no longer with us, having departed to the sailors' Valhalla. The St. Croix Yacht Club has a special race and trophy in memory of Bomba.

Bomba was an excellent seaman and very much a hero to the young Cruzans of the early 1960s; many of them followed in his footsteps and became day-charter skippers. Originally they used converted West Indian sloops, but then the boat of choice became Dick Newick trimarans that fly between Christiansted and Buck Island. Now middle-aged, these skippers still demonstrate excellent seamanship—which we observed more than once when we were anchored at Buck Island in January 1993.

TEAGUE BAY

(Chart 47; II A, A-23)

Teague Bay, at the northeast end of St. Croix, is the base of the St. Croix Yacht Club. Completely sheltered by a barrier reef, it is a superb place for small-boat racing. It's also a glorious spot for sailing cruising boats; there's not much room, but the water is smooth and there is always plenty of wind whistling in across the reef.

To enter Teague Bay, make your way east past Green Cay and Pull Point. The entrance to the bay is marked by the dry sandbar north-northeast of Green Cay Estate. The bar was completely washed out in Hurricane Hugo, but it is slowly rebuilding and probably will be above water again by the time you read this book. (If the bar isn't visible, watch for a sandy shoal just under the water west of the 16-foot-high beacon mentioned below.) Once past the sandbar, stand eastward until the mill at Coakley

Bay bears south, then tack southward. Enter midway between the reef to the east and the dry sandbar to the west.

The reef on the eastern side of the main entrance is marked by a black dolphin with a four-second flashing green light, 16 feet high, marked "1" and visible three miles. Work your way eastward, favoring the inshore side. There is plenty of water but also plenty of coral heads.

East of this entrance are two small red-and-black, privately maintained (by the St. Croix Yacht Club) buoys marking another entrance east of the main entrance just described. The gap—locally named Cotton Valley Cut—bears 138° magnetic from a castle; 171° magnetic from a long, low building with a watch tower on its eastern end; and 198° magnetic on a sugar mill above Mary's Fancy. The gap between the buoys is no more than 30 feet. Plus, once you have passed through the gap, you have to turn to port (normally, heading up, or to starboard bearing off) to clear a large patch of shoal water southeast of the entrance channel. Once clear of the shoal, it's just a matter of tacking eastward, using eyeball navigation. Depth in the cut is 12 feet, but the cut is so small that I would definitely not go through it in a boat longer than 50 feet.

The history of this cut is rather amusing. During World War II, one Sergeant Paris, an Oklahoma farmer, was stationed in St. Croix. He looked at the lay of the land, noticed that Cruzans were raising cattle profitably on the island, and realized that St. Croix was no drier than Oklahoma. So, when he got out of the service, he took his mustering-out pay, returned to St. Croix, and bought the old Cotton Valley Estate from the government. He paid something like US$5 an acre for a thousand or so acres. He squawked like mad to avoid buying the ruins—insisting that he couldn't raise cattle on ruins—but to no avail. He bought the estate—ruins and all—and established a herd that made him a tidy profit in the 1950s and 1960s.

Ex-Sergeant Paris was also an avid fisherman, so he kept a boat at Cotton Valley Estate, but he didn't like making the run of a mile to the west to clear the end of the reef before he could go fishing. Being an old military sort, he was discussing this one weekend with some army buddies who were visiting him, and they all decided there was an easy solution. They went out with a pile of dynamite, created a hell of an explosion, and Cotton Valley Cut was born.

When the Rockefeller group decided they wanted Cotton Valley Estate because of the wonderfully preserved ruins, Sergeant Paris sold out for a considerable sum. He then bought a big sportfisherman, but it was too big to use in the little channel he had blasted, so he left the new boat in town. Nowadays, the channel is used regularly by St. Croix Yacht Club boats.

If you use the main entrance to Teague Bay, there is plenty of water, but watch out for isolated coral heads. It's best to do this when the sun is high. Good anchorage can be had anywhere off the yacht club, but do not try to get too close to shore, as the water shoals to five feet fairly far off.

When anchoring, be sure the hook is well buried, because there are occasional patches of grass, and holding in them is precarious.

The St. Croix Yacht Club is extremely active, organizing Sunfish and cruising-boat races. It is open Wednesday through Sunday, is extremely hospitable, has excellent facilities, and extends guest privileges to yachtsmen who are members of other recognized yacht clubs.

In mid-October, the St. Croix Yacht Club runs the Mumm's Champagne Regatta, a new race that is becoming increasingly popular. About a hundred boats show up for three days of racing and fun.

Depth alongside the yacht club dock is limited: About seven feet can be squeezed in along the end of the dock. When finding your way from the anchorage area to the end of the dock, make sure you either have a local pilot on board or first feel your way with a dinghy and sounding pole. Water and electricity are available alongside the dock, but no fuel.

Once at the yacht club, you are a 20-minute drive from Christiansted. There is no shopping in the area, but it is easy to hitch a ride to town.

Yachts can continue east of the yacht club—as proved by John Burr, who used to anchor his seven-foot-draft *Iolanthe* off his home at the eastern end of the island—but extreme care is required. It might be easier to get into your dinghy and take it east to a secluded spot for some snorkeling, swimming, and sunbathing.

SALT RIVER BAY
(Chart 48; II A, A-23)

This is the only other harbor on the north coast of St. Croix. When proceeding westward, be sure to stay outside White Horse Reef, which breaks even in normal weather. Before setting out for Salt River, it is advisable to check with local yachtsmen regarding conditions in the area. Sometimes the ground swell from the north creates extensive shoaling just inside the entrance.

To enter the Salt River if coming from the east, pick out White Horse Reef. (Older charts show a Sealab buoy moored off the entrance to Salt River. It's gone, so don't bother looking for it.) Continue westward until you pick up a white buoy (privately maintained) at the eastern end of the submerged reef. Leave this buoy close aboard to port and line up the gazebo heading 173° magnetic. Pass eight feet to the right of the green buoy northwest of the central coral formation and continue heading toward the gazebo on 173° magnetic. When the tower on the abandoned hotel bears 128° magnetic, alter course to port to 170° magnetic so as to pass 10 feet to the east of the red buoy. Then head toward the gazebo on 180° magnetic; when the Salt River Marina office bears 068° magnetic, head toward the marina. If your vessel draws six feet or more, contact the Anchor Dive Center on channel 16 (call sign Buoyancy Mobile), and they will send someone out to lead you in. The Anchor Dive Center is open daily from 0800 to 1700.

Some say the best thing to do is round up as soon as you pass the white buoy at the end of White Horse Reef, anchor, and send the dinghy ahead to check the depth. Once inside the reef, the controlling depth seems to be a maximum of six feet.

Salt River Marina (tel. 778-9650; fax 778-0706) has 36 slips, six-foot draft, cistern water, bar and restaurant, small commissary, dive shop, and the Gold Coast Catamarans shop. Gold Coast Catamarans has developed an enviable reputation for designing daysailing cats—42 to 65 feet—to US Coast Guard specifications. Evidently the firm is very successful, as they have built 25 catamarans and also have had four built under license in Venezuela.

I am not a great admirer of cats (neither the four-legged ones nor the sailing multihulls), but I must admit that if you are in the day-charter business, the only way to make a profit is to use a PPM (profitable people mover)—i.e., a catamaran or a trimaran.

Salt River is an excellent hurricane hole. During Hurricane Hugo in 1989, very little damage was done to the boats here, except for the ones that were nailed by a NOAA barge used as a support vessel for the Sealab buoy. NOAA never properly secured the barge, which went adrift and swept through the anchored fleet, doing massive damage. I doubt that any of the boatowners succeeded in collecting compensation from NOAA—another reason for having insurance. In any case, before you decide to head for a hurricane hole, reread Reflections on Hugo in the Foreword to this volume, and give the whole situation careful thought before making a decision.

I feel strongly that the government should dredge

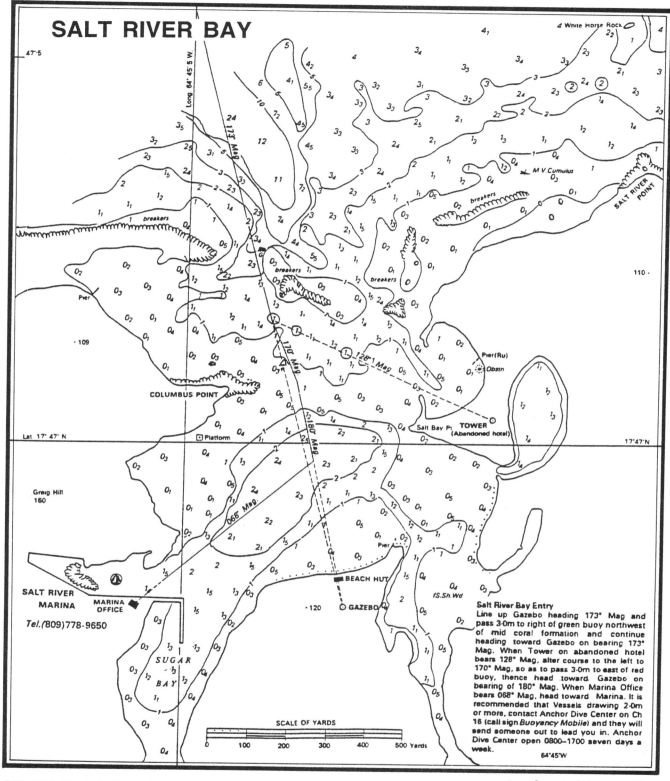

SALT RIVER BAY

Salt River Bay Entry
Line up Gazebo heading 173° Mag and pass 3·0m to right of green buoy northwest of mid coral formation and continue heading toward Gazebo on bearing 173° Mag. When Tower on abandoned hotel bears 128° Mag, alter course to the left to 170° Mag, so as to pass 3·0m to east of red buoy, thence head toward Gazebo on bearing of 180° Mag. When Marina Office bears 068° Mag, head toward Marina. It is recommended that Vessels drawing 2·0m or more, contact Anchor Dive Center on Ch 16 (call sign *Buoyancy Mobile*) and they will send someone out to lead you in. Anchor Dive Center open 0800–1700 seven days a week.

64°45'W

SALT RIVER MARINA

MARINA OFFICE

Tel. (809)778-9650

SUGAR BAY

SALT RIVER POINT

TOWER (Abandoned hotel)

COLUMBUS POINT

Greig Hill 160

BEACH HUT

GAZEBO

White Horse Rock

M.V. Cumulus

SCALE OF YARDS
0   100   200   300   400   500 Yards

CHART 48   Salt River Bay

Soundings in fathoms and feet

and mark a 10-to-12-foot channel into the inner part of Salt River. Until this is done, Salt River will never realize its tremendous potential as a yachting area.

WEST COAST OF ST. CROIX

(II A, A-23)

This area is seldom visited by yachts, since it is dead to leeward of all other anchorages in the island and is completely open to the ground swell. Besides, the shelf is small, and the bottom drops off so steeply that it is difficult to find an anchorage.

The latest rumor is that a marina is being planned for the west coast, but seeing is believing. Any marina built here would have to have an incredibly strong breakwater to protect it from the ground swell and any hurricane-generated swells. Just for a start, the main commercial dock that was ruined by Hurricane Hugo was not replaced for several years.

The town of Frederiksted lies on the west coast. It used to be a listless place with few signs of commercial activity, but now, with the infusion of industry on the south coast and the influx of cruise ships, the town has a new lease on life. It is not as attractive as Christiansted, but there are a number of old buildings with a great deal of charm, and Fort Frederik is worth exploring.

Strand Street has some magnificent buildings, including the commercial buildings that preserve the old architecture. One eyesore stands out, though, both here and in Christiansted: The Bank of Nova Scotia buildings are completely at odds with the surrounding architecture. One wonders why the local planning commission ever allowed the buildings to be built.

Don't try to anchor near the southwest tip of the island, since the swell sweeps around the point and the current is very strong.

SOUTH COAST OF ST. CROIX

(II A, A-23)

The south coast of St. Croix is not used by yachts, as it is heavily commercial. Limetree Bay is the home of Harvey Aluminum and Amerada Hess—obviously not a good yacht anchorage. Yachts could possibly find shelter up in the eastern end of Kings Bay, but why would anyone want to anchor to leeward of a major oil refinery?

East of Limetree Bay are some anchorages that look promising when the wind is well into the north. Kit Kapp on *Fairwinds* did some extensive exploration on the south coast of St. Croix with seven feet of draft and reported that every time the tide went out, he found himself aground. One must conclude, therefore, that the south coast is open to exploration only by boats drawing five feet or less.

NOTES

NOTES

12

British Virgin Islands

(Imray-Iolaire Charts A, A-2, A-23, A-231, A-232, A-233)

The British Virgin Islands comprise the two major islands of Tortola and Virgin Gorda; the six minor islands of Norman, Cooper, Peter, Ginger, Jost Van Dyke, and Anegada; and cays, islets, and rocks too numerous to mention. This small archipelago east of the US Virgins is one of the last few outposts of the once-vast British empire.

Perhaps it has been thanks to this fact that the crime rate has been comparatively low in the British Virgins. Even though the islands have a local legislature, the British government is still responsible for internal law and order as well as external defense. Until recently, murders have been rare and robberies few. In this regard, it is perhaps significant that Tortola still has a gallows. Two people convicted of murder were hung in the early 1980s. In the late 1980s, when the British governor commuted a death sentence, the locals rioted to such an extent that the governor was replaced. Honesty in the British Virgins until recently was such that if you borrowed a car and asked for the keys, the usual reply was, "In the ignition—where else?" Unfortunately, times have changed: Cars are still left unlocked, but keys are no longer left in the ignition.

In recent years, there have been a number of murders—all drug-related, because the British Virgins became a transfer point for drugs being smuggled from Colombia to Puerto Rico and the United States. The British government stepped in, sending out police officers, British-trained Customs officers, and police launches. Also, an arrangement with the US Coast Guard allows it to board vessels in Tortolan waters. Whether or not these measures will stop the drug smuggling remains to be seen.

The laws are enforced zealously, even by Tortola's police launches. Visiting yachtsmen should take pains to keep everything above board. If the police catch a visiting yacht with a store of illegal drugs, they certainly will impound the boat, put the crew in the cooler, and sell the yacht at auction. A few such seizures and they should easily be able to afford all the police launches they desire. They already seem to be more than willing to slap fat fines on yachtsmen who do not even realize they are breaking the law.

The smaller islands are still sparsely populated, but development is well underway. I hope the powers-that-be have taken note of what happened to St. Thomas and St. Croix and will learn from their mistakes.

Luckily, the British Virgins have traditionally maintained what might be called a one-class economy, in that there has been no landed plutocracy controlling everything for itself. Some people own more than others, to be sure, but there is no particular ruling class, as exists in many other small islands of the Lesser Antilles.

To try to prevent damage to the fragile coral, the British Virgins have instituted a buoyage system for divers. A red buoy indicates a mooring for daytime use only; no diving is allowed. A yellow buoy is for commercial diving only; a white buoy is only for amateur diving, on a first-come, first-served basis, with a 90-minute time limit. A blue buoy is for dinghies only.

When I first arrived in the British Virgins in 1957, electricity was available only in Road Town, the capital. A small generator serviced Government House, the hospital, and a few houses along the waterfront. Fort Burt on Road Town Harbour, then the only hotel, existed on kerosene lanterns and kerosene refrigeration; the lantern they used to hang out on the patio was more visible at sea than the rudimentary battery-powered light marking Burt Point. Telephones were nonexistent. Radiotelephones occasionally worked, but more often they did not. Virtually all intra-island commutation was by boat, since the longest paved road was then one mile. Anyone who wished to visit the incomparable beaches on the north side of the island was obliged to hire a horse in Road Town and follow a path over the mountaintop. So few people did this, however, that the mountain long remained a favorite place to grow sugar and brew illegal rum. Unfortunately, this local practice is one of the casualties of progress on Tortola.

The mountain was also the home of people who grew "grass" and cultivated "magic mushrooms," which evidently induced quite a high. This area is now Sage Mountain National Park. Although it is not strictly a tropical rain forest, Sage Mountain has the largest trees on the island, and a reforestation program is underway on the mountain.

The island is now crisscrossed with paved roads connecting Road Town with the two villages of West End and East End. Judging from the capital's name, thoroughfares have been on the minds of islanders for some time. But it was not until about 1960 that there was a road between Road Town and West End. The Public Works Department built one, declared it open, and invited the administrator to drive his Land Rover over it. The trip was so bad that he left his vehicle in West End, returned to Road Town by boat, and ordered Public Works to improve the road and retrieve his Land Rover. Thanks to the sensitive seat of this gentleman's pants, you can now drive over the road in relative comfort.

There is electricity now throughout the British Virgin Islands, even in the outlying areas, but this has been a mixed blessing. The power comes at one of the highest prices in the world—caused by the expensive installation that required running cables underwater and crisscrossing them over rugged terrain. In addition, the total installation cost had to be paid off in what many people felt was too short a time period. When power first came to Tortola, individuals were not allowed to compete with the government and have their own generators, but power has already become so scarce on the island that citizens are being encouraged to install their own generators to make their own electricity.

In the early 1970s, a telephone system was installed to tie together all the British islands in a worldwide system. For a while, it was one of the best systems in the Caribbean, but as the islands expanded exponentially, the phone operations went downhill. Now, however, the system has been given a major overhaul, phone booths have been installed all over Tortola, and everything operates quite efficiently. In fact, this can be considered one of the better systems in the Eastern Caribbean—almost on a par with the United States. One of the nicest features is that you can use your Visa or MasterCard to call anywhere in the world. You can also use the USA Direct system with an AT&T card. There are also special phones designated for Caribbean phonecards—plastic cards sold in various denominations that can be inserted in a slot to prepay calls.

Outboard motors have arrived in the British Virgins, scuttling in their wake some 100 Tortola sloops that were actively used in the 1950s but now have disappeared entirely. I look upon this loss to the sailing world with mixed emotions. It was embarrassing to beat to windward in a modern cruising yacht and discover that a tired old Tortola sloop with a baggy sail could keep right up with me. I always wondered how they could be so fast until I discovered that their rapid progress was due not to inherent boat speed, but rather to the skipper's knowledge of local wind shifts and currents.

Road Town is the only bona-fide town in the British Virgin Islands. Although Road Town shopping cannot compare with St. Thomas, it is busy playing catch-up. In the past, this was largely a tourist economy based strictly on bareboats, but it is now expanding rapidly into the cruise-ship business. Availability of food has progressed immeasurably, and there is a wide range of shops, particularly in the Road Town area. They range from the locally owned rum-shop-cum-grocery-store to Peter Haycraft's Rite-Way chain of supermarkets located throughout the island. The main market in Pasea Estate rivals the supermarkets in St. Thomas. Another well-stocked Road Town supermarket is Bobby's, at Wickhams Cay I. For those who can afford it and want the highest-quality (and highest-priced) items, check out the Ample Hamper emporia in Road Town and West End. There is also gourmet shopping on Virgin Gorda, but in every case you had better take along a bucket of money.

In 1992, the British Virgin Islands government began a user-friendly campaign to try to encourage yachts and charter boats to move to and operate out of the British Virgins. Their success has been even greater than they expected! The anchorages were becoming so crowded that boats were continually swinging into each other during wind shifts, or when the wind died out at night. That problem, however, has been largely solved, because the most popular anchorages now have well-maintained Moor Seacure buoys—permanent moorings for boats 50 feet or less—that can be picked up. The nightly fee—

US$15 in 1994—is payable at a designated local bar or restaurant.

The influx of charter boats has been a major boost to the local economy, and the marine-oriented businesses have received a major shot in the arm. As a result, they are expanding their services and inventories. Among the operations are Island Marine Supply (which has branches in Road Town and Fort Burt in Tortola (tel. 494-2251); at Redhook, Yacht Haven, and Sub Base in St. Thomas; and in St. Croix); Golden Hind at Wickhams Cay II; Nanny Cay Chandlery; and Cay Marine Chandlery at Wickhams Cay I (tel. 494-2992; owned by Ulrich Corea, the former head of Golden Hind). In addition, there is the marine supply store at Virgin Gorda Yacht Harbour. As a result of all this entrepreneurship, you can find just about anything you need for a yacht—paint, varnish, books, and so on. If it is not on the shelf, they will order it quickly from all over the world. A number of the above-mentioned operations claim that they will be opening branches in West End, but seeing is believing.

Parts for engines, generators, and refrigerators are available at Parts and Power in Tortola, founded by my old friend Jon Repke, refrigeration expert extraordinaire. In fact, back in the early 1960s, he was the first person to make refrigeration work reliably on yachts. He installed systems that were so good you could run your engine only an hour a day and still have no problems with your refrigerator and deep freeze. He designed and installed the Rolls-Royce of refrigerator systems—Rolls-Royce quality and also Rolls-Royce price! You pretty much held out your right arm and asked him where he wanted to lop it off for payment!

Parts and Power is now run by Tom Gerker and his wife, an efficient and cheerful couple who gave up trying to make a living on the east end of St. John and moved to Tortola.

All of the major outboard manufacturers are represented in Tortola, and there are a number of good machine shops. Nautool Machine (tel. 494-3187) at Wickhams Cay II has built up an excellent reputation for doing superb stainless-steel work, and they can weld stainless and aluminum. On the road to the main commercial port is Tony Edwards's T&W Machine Shop (tel. 494-4252). BVI Marine Management is at Nanny Cay (tel. 494-2938). Last but not least is Mike Underhill (tel. 495-4280), who has a combined home and machine shop in the "bush" of West End (ask the locals to point out the path to his place; it's easier to go that way than to take the road). Mike has been doing superb machine work on *Iolaire* for more than 30 years.

Cay Electronics is also at Wickhams Cay II (tel. 494-2400; fax 494-5389). Not only can they do electronics work but also handle refrigeration, watermakers, and the like. The firm has other branches in Newport, St. Thomas, and Antigua.

Tortola has changed enormously from the days when it was a sleepy little island with minimal hauling facilities. Elmer Bouchelle used to love the slipway in Baughers Bay because for a small fee and a couple of bottles of rum, they would haul the boat and scrub the bottom, then go off to the rum shop and leave Elmer there to do the work. A couple more bottles of rum, then back in the water. The other hauling facility was the marine railway at Beef Island. That used to be the most inaccessible spot in the British Virgins. The only way to get to and from Beef Island other than by boat was a long walk over to the ferry, which was hauled back and forth on an endless line, then a long ride on the wooden bench of a spring-less bus on a dirt track leading from West End to Road Town. Thus, if you hauled at Beef Island and discovered you needed gear that the slipway did not have, you had to go all the way to St. Thomas. For maybe two or three missing bolts, it became a very expensive ordeal—a three-day journey to obtain the parts while you sat on the slipway being charged a per diem. A long and humorous book could be written about hauling experiences at Beef Island.

Now the bareboats and charter yachts are taken care of easily, as there are large hauling and storage facilities at Nanny Cay, Tortola Yacht Services, and Virgin Gorda Yacht Harbour. These three organizations together have five Travelifts with capacities that range from 20 tons to 70 tons. (Tortola Yacht Services just installed the 70-tonner in 1992.) Large yachts up to 200 tons can be hauled on a railway at West End Slipway.

In the spring of 1993, there was a West Indian equivalent of war over the West End Slipway. The combatants were the Smith family (who owned the land around the slipway), Morgan Sanger (who was leasing and operating West End Slipway), and Bill Coffman (whose sparmaking shop was adjacent to the slipway). After the dust settled in November 1993, Sanger and Coffman had departed and the Smith family was operating the yard—with the help of many expatriates of various nationalities. The yard is trying hard to maintain its reputation of doing excellent restoration and repair work on wooden boats. Only time will tell how well they succeed.

On the northeast corner of Sopers Hole is a woodworking operation that always seems to have one or two major wooden rebuilds underway. In addition, there are a number of freelance shipwrights—both locals and expats—floating around the island. Ask around. Of the locals, I can recommend Edwin Titley (tel. 494-2130), who was one of the shipwrights helping us rebuild *Iolaire* in 1958 after she had gone up on the beach at Lindbergh Bay in St. Thomas.

Sail repairs are no problem in Tortola or Virgin Gorda. Manassel Phillips (tel. 494-4982), near the police station in Road Town, repairs sails and makes awnings—as does Elmer at Elm Sail, above the Tortola Marine Management office at Road Reef Marina. Bob Phillips of Doyle's Sails (formerly Hood) has a large, up-to-date loft in Wickhams Cay I. He makes new sails, repairs old ones, sells secondhand sails, and also has a good supply of high-tech rigging gear, winches, and so on. Next Wave, at Virgin Gorda Yacht Harbour, also repairs sails.

Richardson's Rigging Services (tel. 494-2739), 300 yards south of the main commercial ferry dock in Tortola, has an amazing collection of marine hardware—undoubtedly one of the best supplies of yacht rigging, winches, blocks, and roller-furling systems east of Miami. They also have another branch at Tortola Marine Management, Road Reef Marina. Most important, the owner, Al Richardson, promises 24-hour service. He and his wife live alongside the shop, so you can call at any hour if you have an emergency. Al will surface and immediately try to solve your problems. Golden Hind (tel. 494-2124), at Tortola Yacht Services, also does rigging work, so you have two choices.

NOTES

NOTES

13

⌒◝

Tortola and Nearby Islands

(Imray-Iolaire Charts A, A-2, A-23, A-231, A-232, A-233)

In 1994, Tortola was still a great place to visit, but will we be able to say that in 10 years—or even five years? Unfortunately, the lure of the cruise ship has influenced the thinking of some of the politicians and businessmen in Road Town. They have now built a US$3 million cruise-ship dock on the west side of Road Harbour—a project that has been vigorously but unsuccessfully opposed by a large number of people. The costly dock will only increase the island's debt burden. It has been an exercise in futility for the local harbor pilots, who have pointed out that the existing commercial dock could easily be extended at minimal cost (in comparison to the new dock) without encroaching on the Road Town waterfront.

The new dock is bound to bring major changes. What island needs a steady stream of cruise ships? Look how they have ruined St. Thomas and St. Martin. Not only that, but the businessmen and politicians have also turned their attention to the Beef Island Airport.

One reason yachting development was held up for many years in the British Virgins was the difficulty of getting there. The runway at Beef Island was only built by the British Army Royal Engineers in 1968, and it took some time before airlines began flying in and out of Beef Island. Now the airport is served by numerous small airlines, and there is little or no difficulty in obtaining flights from Tortola to San Juan or St. Thomas, where you can then change for direct flights to almost anywhere in the world. But this hasn't satisfied the entrepreneurial types. In December 1992, a firm was given US$300,000 to study the feasibility of expanding Beef Island Airport. They are planning to extend the runway to 7,000 feet to accommodate big jets, but does a small island like Tortola really need the international traffic this will

generate? Do they have enough hotel rooms and the infrastructure to support the increased activity? Everyone doubts it. This project is estimated at US$20 million—which, on top of the megamillions for the cruise-ship dock, will create an impossible debt burden for an island with a tax base of 20,000 people. Not only that, but the arrival of jets is bound to ruin the Trellis Bay and Marina Cay anchorages and drive out the private and charter yachts.

The bareboat industry is not a growth industry in Tortola—it's an explosion industry. From a few scattered bareboats based in the British Virgins in the early 1970s, the number has grown to the point where a dozen companies operate whole fleets of bareboats out of Tortola. Probably one of the major reasons why the British Virgin islanders have maintained their independence, helpfulness, and charm has been the fact that the major tourist expansion in these islands has come via the bareboat industry rather than the hotel industry. Tourists staying at hotels require large numbers of waiters, bartenders, floor sweepers, cooks, and maids—service jobs for which the local Tortolan is neither trained nor psychologically prepared. The bareboat industry employs people to prepare, stock, and repair boats—jobs that encourage pride of workmanship and promote self-esteem.

So many bareboat operations moved into the British Virgins during the 1970s and early 1980s that in 1982 the government declared a moratorium on new companies. However, that went by the board, and now the government is encouraging the companies. This means that Darwin's Law prevails—survival of the fittest—and, as a result, several firms have gone belly-up, including the old, established Caribbean Sailing Yachts, which was the first large bareboat organization to operate out of the Eastern Caribbean. (Who knows what will happen to the CSY marina facilities in Baughers Bay? Perhaps it will be under new management by the time you read this.)

Fortunately, the bareboat explosion does not mean that every anchorage has become overcrowded. Bareboat charterers seem to have a lemming instinct, and they tend to cluster together in favorite anchorages. Also, most of the guides to the area are written by and for the bareboat industry, so they tend to emphasize the harbors that are easy to enter and exit. They don't mention many of the good but obscure, seldom-visited anchorages that are discussed in this guide. Be assured that there are still places where you can find privacy.

Along with the explosive growth of the bareboating industry, marinas in and around Tortola have developed rapidly. The Wickhams Cay area is now lined with marinas. Village Cay Marina, with 106 slips on the Wickhams Cay I side, was managed for many years by John Acland, one of the smartest marina operators in the Caribbean, and the person who first installed token-operated showers. He went from having a shower operation that was driving him crazy and costing him money to a system where customers purchased tokens, inserted them in a machine, and a limited amount of water came out. If you ran out of water, you inserted another token. The result was that the shower operation went from being a money-losing scheme to one that turned a nice profit. The showers are open from 0600 to 2200, and someone comes in six times a day to clean them. Why doesn't every marina in the Eastern Caribbean switch to this system? (A few of them have, and they have basically solved their shower problems.)

On the northern and eastern side (Wickhams Cay II) is the marina operated by The Moorings—150 berths and expanding. Originally, no one was allowed to anchor in the basin at Wickhams Cay, but now there are so many boats anchored in the basin that it is all but impossible for a visiting yacht to avoid fouling someone's anchor.

Careening Cove, the old mangrove lagoon under Fort Burt, is no more. It is now solid concrete walls, the home of Road Reef Marina (including Tortola Marine Management) and the police launch jetty. The yacht club is building a clubhouse on the eastern side; Roosevelt Smith has built the Fort Burt Marina on the western side. There may no longer be much space for visiting yachts.

Getting into this basin requires care, as the channel is no more than eight feet deep (see details below in Road Town section).

The Prospect Reef Hotel has a small, usually very crowded marina. Entering and exiting is not easy, and I suggest you try it only in a boat of 40 feet or less, in calm conditions, and under power. Do not even consider sailing into or out of this marina.

At Sea Cow Bay, on the western side of Road Town, considerable dredging has been done, and it is now a good anchorage. I suspect that a marina will appear here one of these days. At Nanny Cay, a fine marina was developed, but it has had its problems in the past several years. In West End, there are two marinas: Sunsail (formerly Stevens Yachts) and the Sopers Hole Marina.

The marina in Maya Cove is strictly for Tropic Island Yacht charters, but you can anchor out if it is not too crowded.

Tortola is expanding so fast that it is impossible to name all of the repair facilities and suppliers. Some recommended ones are listed in chapter 12, but you should also check *Caribbean Boating*, the annual directory of the Marine Trades Association, and the local Yellow Pages. If you are in Road Town, ask Dennis MacDonald at Island Marine Supply in the Fort Burt Marina—he knows what's going on around the island and can offer helpful advice. (Any book that tries to list all the services at any given time is bound to be out of date before it is printed, so be sure to check the above sources.)

If you need to ship anything in or out of Tortola, the most economical way of doing it is to contact John Drealey, Box 540, Road Town, Tortola, BVI; tel. 496-0775. Or write him at Box 8309, Cruz Bay, St. John, USVI. Or look for him moored at Sopers Hole Marina. His arrangement is excellent: He runs a shuttle service between Tortola and the US Virgins and sends everything via UPS from St. John, which cuts the cost to one-fourth of what it would be for normal shipment from Tortola.

Thankfully, you can now have your gas bottles filled by Texaco. I say thankfully because for many years it was impossible to fill aluminum gas bottles in Tortola. After an aluminum bottle exploded in Trinidad in the early 1980s, the order went out to all Texaco stations in the Caribbean that no more bottles were to be filled. Everyone in the Eastern Caribbean ignored the order except Texaco in Tortola. So, for many years, filling bottles here was a time-consuming and expensive ordeal. You had to take them all the way out to Fat Hogs Bay, look for Mr. Charwell opposite the school, and have the bottles filled from 100-pound cylinders. If you happen to be in East End, you can still go to Mr. Charwell, but now it's a breeze just to go to Texaco—as long as your propane bottle has a test date less than eight years old. If it is older than that, they will not fill it, and I have found no one in the Eastern Caribbean who can hydrostatically test propane bottles and put a new date on them.

All is not lost, however. Go to the TICO liquor shop (combined with the Bon Appetit Deli) at the entrance to Wickhams Cay II, where one of their employees fills gas bottles the same way Mr. Charwell does. And he is not concerned about test dates.

Laundry is no problem. In West End, there is an excellent laundry about one-fourth mile from Sopers Hole; in Road Town, Silvia's laundry is located at the traffic circle by the Rite-Way intown store. There are other laundry services scattered around the island, but Silvia's has taken good care of us for longer than I can remember.

When in Tortola during the winter, especially if the ground swell is running, it is worth renting a car for the day and driving over the mountains to the north-side beaches. Here you'll find beautiful white sand for sunbathing and rolling surf that's great for surfboarding or body-surfing. All major car-rental agencies are represented here. In West End, Denzil Clyne has an agency only one-fourth mile from Sopers Hole—very convenient for picking up or leaving cars if you are anchored in Sopers Hole.

If you are going back to Road Town, drive up to the SkyWorld restaurant, on one of Tortola's highest peaks. It is a great place to sit looking west down through the Virgin Islands and to watch for the green flash as the sun sets. If you plan to stay for dinner, be sure to take along a jacket or sweater or heavy shawl, since it gets chilly as soon as the sun goes down.

A small point of interest to stamp collectors: Tortola is the only place in the world that offers British stamps printed in England with the queen's imprint on them that carry US currency designations.

WEST END

(Sketch Chart 49; II A, A-2, A-23, A-231)

Sopers Hole makes an excellent spot to enter or clear, as it has superb shelter for all normal directions. Unless the wind comes in from the west—which it very seldom does—you should be fine. Only a hurricane (or once in a while a major North Atlantic storm) will produce a west wind. This did happen in December 1992, when the edge of a big North Atlantic storm reached the Virgin Islands, producing three days of strong westerlies.

When anchored in West End, remember that there are high hills on both sides of you that funnel the wind down through the anchorage, giving you a cool, bug-free spot. You can sit in the anchorage afraid to go to sea because it is blowing so hard, yet once you leave, you discover it is blowing nowhere near as hard outside as inside.

Anchoring at West End presents a few problems. It is 60 to 70 feet deep, so you have to put out at least 200 feet of line. When the wind dies out during the night, everyone starts swinging around in huge circles. The next thing you know, you are wrapped around your neighbor. Basically you have four choices:

1. Anchor well to the west of the Customs dock, and you will have enough swinging room, although you will be quite a distance from everything else.
2. Move up to the middle of the harbor, pick up one of the Moor Seacure buoys, and pay the rental fee.
3. Find a berth at either Sunsail or Sopers Hole Marina.
4. Go right up to the head of the harbor, drop the stern anchor out, run your bow up onto the beach, and jump off. Then run your anchor up on shore and bury it. (This is why it is useful to carry a spade on board so you can dig a deep hole in which to bury your anchor!) If you choose this option, make sure you anchor well over to the south or north. Leave the center free for the tug that comes in pushing a sand barge.

Once secured, you'll discover that Sopers Hole is a pleasant anchorage with many facilities. You can clear Customs and Immigration above the ferry dock. The office opens at 0830. If you are in a hurry, get there early, as the line builds up rapidly and clearance can take an hour or more.

Garbage disposal is free on the north side of Sopers Hole, where there is a public garbage bin; the fee is US$1.50 a bag on the south side (at the Ample Hamper).

You can take ferries from Sopers Hole to Jost Van Dyke, Cruz Bay, St. Thomas, or farther east in the British Virgins. So many ferries go in and out, with ever-changing schedules, that you'll need to get the latest information at the ferry dock.

Across the street from the ferry dock are two small West Indian-style grocery/restaurant/bars that sell block ice. On the south side of Sopers Hole, the Ample Hamper—stocked with expensive goodies—also sells ice. If you take the dinghy out through the cut (be forewarned that the current can run almost six knots under the bridge in heavy weather), you'll find two small "supermarkets" that also are outdoor

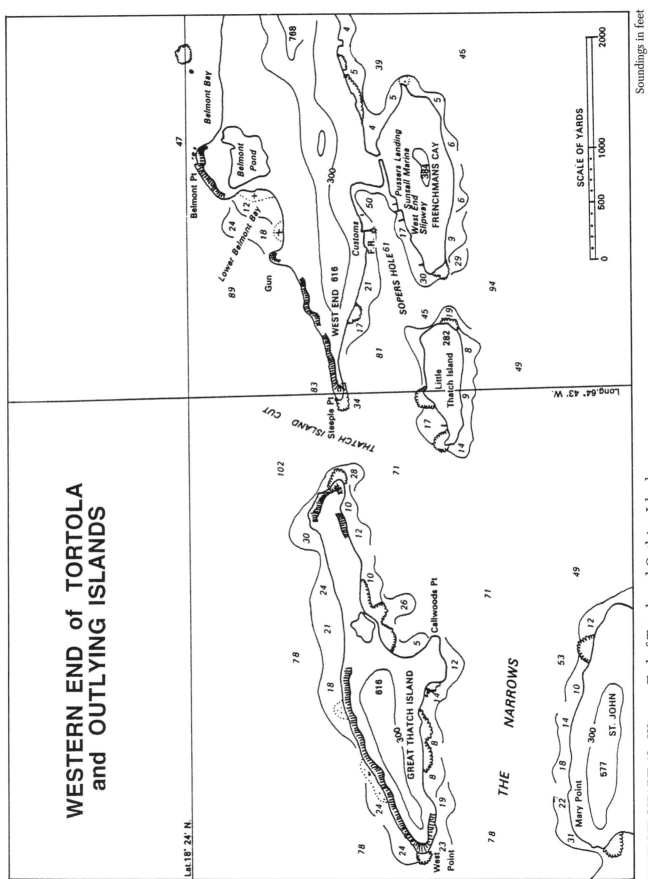

WESTERN END of TORTOLA
and OUTLYING ISLANDS

Lat.18' 24' N.

Belmont Bay

768

4

5

39

45

Belmont Pt.

Belmont Pond

5

5

47

5

4

Lower Belmont Bay

12

24

18

Gun

89

300

Pussers Landing

Sunsail Marine

West End Slipway

381

FRENCHMANS CAY

6

6

9

Customs

50

1

F.R.

17

SOPERS HOLE 61

30

29

WEST END 616

21

17

45

94

17

282

19

8

81

Little Thatch Island

9

14

17

49

83

Steeple Pt

34

THATCH ISLAND CUT

Long.64° 43'.W.

102

28

71

10

12

30

10

24

26

21

5

Callwoods Pt

12

78

18

616

12

300

GREAT THATCH ISLAND

8

8

THE NARROWS

71

49

53

12

24

19

14

10

8

18

300

ST. JOHN

577

Mary Point

22

18

West 23 Point

24

31

78

SCALE OF YARDS

0   500   1000   2000

Soundings in feet

SKETCH CHART 49   Western End of Tortola and Outlying Islands bars. This is a great place to relax, cooled by the breeze. In winter, you can be blown out, but in summer, when it's hot in Sopers Hole, the breeze in an open-air bar is very welcome.

Phones are available at the ferry dock and between Sunsail and the Baskin in the Sun diving operation, but if you are using the latter phones at night, take along a flashlight.

Marine supplies are available at the West End Chandlery, up the hill near Frenchman's Cay, but the selection is small; it's mostly fishing gear. Cay Chandlery claims it will be opening a marine hardware store in this part of the island, but no guarantees.

Water is available at Sopers Hole Marina; fuel is available from the fuel dock by Sunsail. As mentioned in chapter 12, there are woodworking, machine shop (Mike Underhill), and hauling facilities in West End.

West End is the home of the ever-popular Pusser's Landing, which has museum-quality ship models worth admiring, as well as walls lined with fine prints. The open-air bar and restaurant is a popular gathering spot for local and visiting yachtsmen, and the store is loaded with beautiful goodies, but they will put you into the poorhouse! I nearly fell through the floor when I saw the price on what was described as a classic "Gladstone" bag—practical and classic, yes, but for US$750? No way. I went back to admiring the ship models.

On the north side of the harbor, west of the ferry landing, is the Jolly Roger, another popular restaurant and night spot.

There is a dinghy passage between Frenchman's Cay and the "mainland." I am told that late in the evening and early in the morning, there is good fishing in the flats at either end of the passage. However, pelicans are often interested in fishing lures, so be careful. A pelican puts up a good fight at the end of a light tackle. Furthermore, trying to help the creature by removing a hook from its mouth is a good way to lose a finger. The current runs very strongly to the west through this passage—you definitely need an outboard to get through it, not a rowing dinghy. A small restaurant/bar on Frenchman's Cay can supply basic grocery needs.

A couple of years ago, at my suggestion, Sunsail switched from charging a flat fee for showers (after having difficulty collecting the fee and failing to convince people they shouldn't use 50 gallons of water to take a shower) to coin-operated showers. As with Village Cay Marina, this solved their problem. Why don't more marinas heed this advice? Unfortunately, there is still a fixed charge for electricity at Sunsail.

The small boat or a boat like *Iolaire* that uses minimal electricity is overcharged, and boats that use a lot of electricity are undercharged! They need to put in meters so that boats are charged for what they actually use.

East of Sopers Hole, some charts show a shoal half a mile off the ruin midway between Fort Recovery and Nanny Cay. In truth, the shoal is only about 200 yards offshore, but there is little reason for a boat to come up on it anyway, since the best place to get out of the adverse current when working eastward is on the St. John shore.

NANNY CAY
(Sketch Chart 50; II A, A-2, A-23, A-231)

For many years, Nanny Cay developed slowly, but in the early 1980s the operation was bought out by the Guinness Group, which then poured in great quantities of money, making Nanny Cay a full-service marina with restaurants, plenty of dock space, a Travelift that can haul 50 tons, room to store boats out of water for long periods, a machine shop, a chandlery, an electronics repair shop, and a sail-repair loft. Although Nanny Cay Marina has been plagued with mismanagement, the fellows in the yard continue to be superb. They could not be nicer or more cooperative.

Situated on a low point of land where the wind sweeps across, the marina is cool, airy, and relatively bugless most of the year. The marina even has hot showers! The Peg Leg Landing bar/restaurant, which often features a steel band or a film, is at the end of the marina overlooking the water.

Transportation into Road Town used to be a problem, but now there are so many ferries in and out of West End that there is regular bus service between West End and Road Town. A bus will pick you up or drop you off at the entrance to Nanny Cay. However, if your boat is all the way down by the end of the dock by Peg Leg Landing, you will have about a half-mile walk from the entrance to the boat—a long distance to lug a heavy load of groceries. This same problem exists when you are berthed near Peg Leg Landing and need something from the chandlery or the shipyard. Years ago, I urged the Nanny Cay management to buy bicycles and rent them to people using the marina—I am sure they would recoup their investment quickly, and even end up making a handsome profit. (Hans Lammers has done this at Jolly Harbour Marina in Antigua.) Riding a bike a mile is quick and easy; walking a mile can be time-consuming if you need something in a hurry.

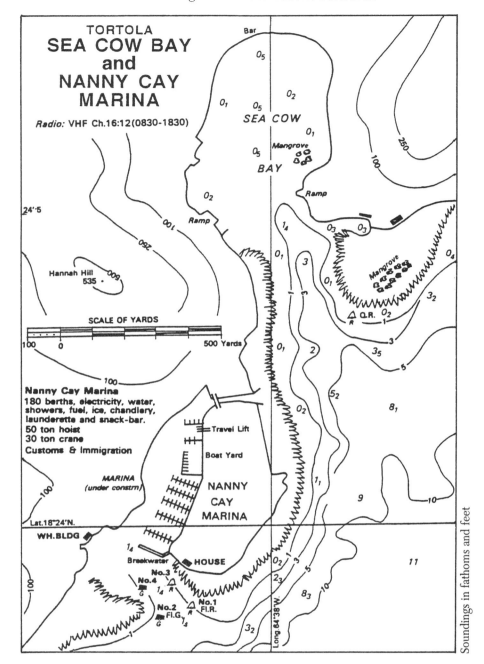

SKETCH CHART 50   Sea Cow Bay and Nanny Cay Marina

Nanny Cay filed for bankruptcy but continues to operate under the management of its main creditor, Barclays Bank. Unfortunately, however, the bank types are sitting there in fancy offices and paying themselves high wages. Any money left over goes to Barclays—none is reinvested in the marina. These guys know nothing about marina management, so Nanny Cay may be headed downhill. Perhaps someone will come along and buy the place—properly

run, it could be one of the nicest marinas in the Eastern Caribbean. (A lot of suppliers were left hanging with unpaid bills when the marina went into receivership. I had just sent a big shipment of Imray-Iolaire charts and was unable to get either the money or the charts! Most frustrating.)

When entering Nanny Cay, the outer channel, with nine feet controlling depth, is well buoyed, but make sure as you pass the dock that you hug the eastern side, as the channel has been dredged only on that side. It is possible for shoal-draft boats (five feet or less) to anchor on the mud flats, but there is room for no more than two or three boats.

SEA COW BAY

(Sketch Chart 50; II A, A-2, A-23, A-231)

A mile to the east of the entrance of Nanny Cay, this is an interesting bay, as it provides a sheltered, uncrowded, bug-free anchorage with easy access to the main road between West End and Road Town. A row or a short dinghy ride to the northern end of the harbor leads to a dock and launching ramp, where you can leave your dinghy. Nearby is Struggling Man's Place, a friendly local establishment with reasonably priced meals, roti, beer, ice cream, and a telephone. A short walk down the road leads to the ubiquitous West Indian rum-shop-cum-grocery-store.

Peg Leg Landing in the Nanny Cay Marina is also a dinghy ride away, although the return trip may be a bit wet in rough weather. At Nanny Cay, you can hire Windsurfers and practice your skills in the area behind the reef in Sea Cow Bay.

The bay first came to our attention as a place where Robb White, who wrote *Our Virgin Isle*, first settled. The book is the story of his and his wife's search for an island paradise in the 1930s. When they lived in Sea Cow Bay, it was shallow, hot, airless, and buggy. Subsequently, the Whites went to Marina Cay, where they wrote the book (which is now in print as *Two on the Isle*). A movie made from the book in the mid-1950s boosted the economy of the charter-boat industry, as all of the charter boats were leased to accommodate the film crew. Local charter skippers and their wives and girlfriends all were stand-ins and extras in the movie. Now there is even talk of a remake of the film!

In the 1970s and 1980s, various development projects in Sea Cow Bay sparked interest in dredging, and now this is an excellent anchorage. It's guaranteed to be uncrowded for a few more years, as this is the first guide to mention it as an anchorage.

On entering, hug the red buoy on the eastern side of the harbor. Round up behind the reef, which shoals suddenly from 20 to 10 to two feet. Nudge as close to the reef as you dare, drop your bow anchor, and back off, veering plenty of line, because you are anchoring on the backside of the shelf. In periods of calm weather, drop a stern anchor to keep yourself from swinging up on the reef if the wind dies out or

switches to the northwest at night when the cold air flows down from the mountain.

Seven to eight feet can be carried to within 200 yards of shore to an east-west line and the apartments on shore. North of this line, the depths shoal quickly to six feet, then to five and four feet. The majority of the inner harbor averages five feet. It is all sand, so no damage is done if you run aground. You should be able to do some good fishing in the mangrove roots around the edges of the shoal mangrove area.

Upon leaving the bay, keep the red buoy close to port, then head for the very pointed peak at the west end of Norman Island, bearing approximately 180° magnetic. Hold this course until you are clear of Nanny Cay, then bear off to the west. If heading east, it is all deep water once you are clear of the red buoy. Start tacking eastward, favoring the shore, and short-tack up the Tortola coast to avoid the current and sea.

PROSPECT REEF HOTEL AND MARINA

(Sketch Chart 51; II A, A-2, A-23, A-231, A-232)

This complex is located half a mile southwest of Burt Point. Its marina, though small and not easily approached, provides complete shelter and ready access to hotel, bar, restaurants, showers, and so on. The entrance is restricted, the basin shoal. I would not try entering the marina in a boat more than 45 feet LOA or in one that draws more than five feet.

ROAD TOWN HARBOUR

(Chart 52, Sketch Chart 53; II A, A-2, A-23, A-231, A-232)

I advise strongly against entering Road Town Harbour at night, as range lights may or may not be working. Even anchoring on the southwest corner of the harbor can be difficult, as far too many yachts anchor in this area without anchor lights. Plus you want to make sure not to anchor in the 12-fathom hole east of Road Reef. Not only would you then need tons of line, but the edges of the hole are full of sharp rocks that will cut through an anchor line in very short order.

In daylight, stand out into the harbor and then decide which anchorage you want. If anchoring off town, run in on 302° magnetic and anchor 100 yards off the Customs dock. The anchorage off the main dock tends to be rough, and the bottom is loose sand and weeds. Do NOT under any circumstances go

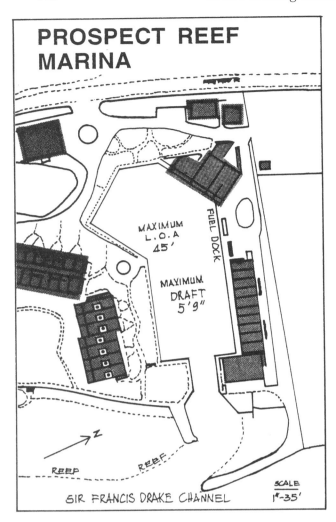

PROSPECT REEF MARINA

MAXIMUM
L.O.A
45'

FUEL DOCK

MAXIMUM
DRAFT
5'9"

N

REEF   REEF

SIR FRANCIS DRAKE CHANNEL

SCALE
1"-35'

SKETCH CHART 51   Prospect Reef Marina

alongside the dock. You are bound to suffer damage from the surge or from the ferries and freighters. Further, it is not advisable even to take a dinghy alongside that dock, since the swell will bang it to pieces.

If you are headed to the Fort Burt area, don't be misled by the fact that a couple of boats are moored right on top of the shoal spot there—they are multihulls and shoal-draft boats. A few boats drawing five feet are moored on the eastern edge of this shoal. As long as you do not stray west of 188° magnetic on the Fort Burt Hotel, you will be able to avoid the shoal.

For yachts desiring to sail in and out of Road Town, the anchorage under the Fort Burt Hotel is by far the best. Northeast from the sandspit, under Fort Burt, the bottom drops off steeply into a hole. If you hit the hole, be prepared for anchoring in 70 feet of water. Make sure you have a minimum of

four fathoms of chain on your anchor (if you don't, shackle two lengths of chain together), since the bottom is coral, mud, and sharp rocks.

Notice, too, that even though there is nine feet of water 60 yards off the dock of the old Moorings Marina, there is only four and a half feet alongside. And the Fort Burt Marina, on the Paradise Pub dock, has a bare seven feet of water alongside the outer dock; it shoals rapidly at the inner slips. In April 1994, these docks were undergoing reconstruction.

With care, you can get seven feet of draft inside the Fort Burt area. In years past, this was a beautiful, mangrove-lined cove with complete shelter in hurricanes. It was also a wonderful bird sanctuary. Now it is all gone. The point is stripped bare and the entire inside of the lagoon is wall-to-wall concrete. It is the home of Tortola Marine Management (TMM), VISAR, the police launch dock, Roosevelt Smith's Fort Burt Marina, Dennis MacDonald's very efficient branch of Island Marine Supply, and the new clubhouse for the British Virgin Islands Yacht Club. Other projects are developing almost daily.

VISAR, by the way, is Virgin Islands Search and Rescue—the local equivalent of the Royal National Lifeboat Institution (RNLI)—which is basically the brainchild of Barney Crook of TMM. He and some friends managed to raise enough money to purchase a huge semirigid rescue craft and the equipment to go with it. They also financed training sessions taught by instructors brought out from the RNLI, and some VISAR people have gone to England for additional training.

This magnificent organization has done extremely successful rescue work. It is on call 24 hours a day, and the service is completely free. They help with salvage if possible; they will cart injured people off yachts and transport them to the hospital; and they have gone to assist yachts with problems. VISAR is the anchor to windward for charter yachts. Before it was established, there was no backup for help after closing hours. VISAR's performance has made the US Coast Guard in the US Virgins look absolutely sick. Visiting yachtsmen—even though they should hope not to need VISAR's services—really should contribute a few dollars to them to help support this worthwhile organization. As Barney Crook has said, "If every person who visits the British Virgins on a bareboat would contribute a dollar to VISAR, the organization's financial problems would be alleviated, although perhaps not solved." I feel that a ten-dollar bill thrown into the pot for every week that a group does a charter would certainly help VISAR! (Donations would be just as welcome from private cruising yachts visiting the area; many shops on the island have collection boxes.)

Whatever facilities eventually appear after all the building and renovating in the Fort Burt area, I am sure that the Paradise Pub (formerly Sir Francis Drake Pub) will remain in business. This cheerful pub/restaurant is a popular gathering spot for local yachtsmen and visiting yachties. A small grocery store can supply all essentials for yachtsmen.

If you prefer to moor in the Wickhams Cay area at Village Cay Marina or The Moorings Marina, stand north into the harbor, leaving Harbour Spit buoy to port. Then swing to a course of due north until you spot the stakes marking the channel. Now run on 303° into the inner basin of the harbor north of Wickhams Cay (see Sketch Chart 53).

Although the channel reputedly is 11 feet deep at low water (I suspect it is only 10 feet in the summer), there is a very small rock in the channel with nine and a half feet of water over it. We know—we hit it hard with Warren Brown's *Tar Baby* when we were at the BVI Regatta in the spring of 1990. Upon inquiring, we discovered that a number of other boats had hit the same rock. No one seems to know exactly where the rock is, but the general view is that if you hug the port side of the channel going out (starboard side going in), you will avoid it. Some say it is in the middle of the channel, others say it is one-third of the way out from the starboard side of the channel when entering. Considering that there is a big dive organization operating out of The Moorings, and the Royal Navy has stopped by at various times, why haven't they gotten together and blown that rock out? Rumor has it that the channel will be dredged to 15 feet, but seeing is believing. Deep-draft boats are strongly advised to send a dinghy ahead to check the depth of the channel and the basin before entering.

Once inside Wickhams Cay, to starboard you will find Wickhams Cay II. This has the Moorings Marina with the Moorings fleet and berths for visiting yachts, plus the Golden Hind, Tortola Yacht Services, and a complex of marine-oriented businesses—sailmakers, life-raft servicing, plumbing supplies, Parts and Power, outboard suppliers, Cay Electronics, the Ample Hamper, and so on. There's also the Moorings Marina bar/restaurant and a swimming pool.

On the port side is Wickhams Cay I, with Village Cay Marina and its extensive shopping complex. Whichever marina you choose, you'll probably find that everything you want is in the other marina. For example, the Moorings Marina is convenient to the Rite-Way supermarket and the major marine repair facility, but to get to the center of town you have to take your dinghy over to Village Cay Marina or take a long taxi ride around the lagoon. Why doesn't an enterprising young Tortolan pick up a rundown Boston Whaler, slap an outboard on it, and operate a water-taxi service back and forth between Wickhams Cay I and II? They do this in St. Georges, Grenada, and it's a real boon.

If you go into Village Cay Marina, you probably will be shuttling back and forth to the other side. But at least Cay Marine Chandlery is at Wickhams Cay I.

Down the road, in Pasea Estate, is Tortola's largest supermarket—Rite-Way, owned by Peter Haycraft, who started his career in the islands as captain of the first modern interisland ferry, *Youth of Tortola*. The supermarket is also rather picturesque, with the butchers wandering around in traditional British costumes of straw boaters and striped shirts.

Nowadays you can buy frozen fish in the supermarket and occasionally get a fresh catch from a passing fisherman, but buying fish in Road Town used to be a wonderful morning occupation. The Anegada sloops—some equipped with the wet-well usually associated with the Bahamas rather than the Virgins—would anchor alongside the pier. People clambered on board and peered down into the wet-well, shouting, "Dat one, mon; dat one, mon; dat one, mon," as they pointed out the specific fish they wanted. If the fisherman didn't grab the fish his customer meant, he'd have to throw it back into the wet-well and try again.

PORT PURCELL

(Chart 52; II A, A-2, A-23, A-231, A-232)

This is the main commercial dock, not to be used by yachts unless they are in the 100-feet-and-over category. In case you do have a megayacht, there is plenty of water at the dock, even at low tide.

BAUGHERS BAY

(Chart 52; II A, A-2, A-23, A-231, A-232)

On the east side of Road Town Harbor, Baughers Bay is an excellent anchorage, protected in all but a southerly wind. Be careful when anchoring in this area, however, as there are some scattered coral heads that stand eight feet above the bottom.

Caribbean Sailing Yachts used to have its marina here, but it has gone belly-up, and I have no idea what happened to its moorings. If you find a moor-

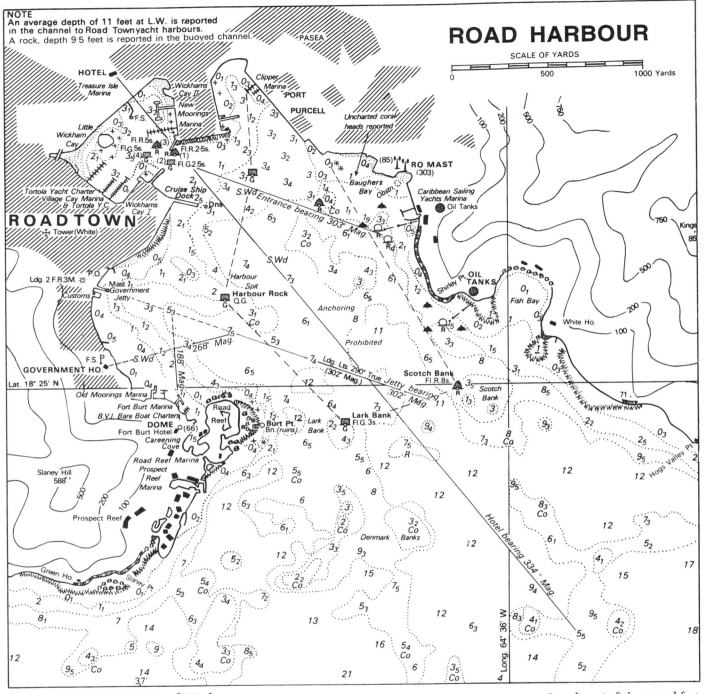

CHART 52   Road Harbour

Soundings in fathoms and feet

ing here and pick it up, I recommend that you dive down and check on it, as it may not have had any maintenance for many years.

FISH BAY

(Chart 52; II A, A-2, A-23, A-231, A-232)

Fish Bay is too shallow for most boats except shoal-draft multihulls. For those who can fit in, it can be private and beautiful, as long as you keep your eyes on the bottom and avoid the oil tanks on shore.

BRANDYWINE BAY

(Chart 54; II A, A-2, A-23, A-231, A-232)

The British and American charts of Brandywine Bay differ from each other so much that I wonder if the surveyors took the name of the bay to heart while going about their appointed task. (When making our Imray-Iolaire charts, I regarded the American chart as the more accurate of the two.) This is a good anchorage when the wind is north of east. Ashore is the superb but pricey Brandywine Bay Restaurant, specializing in Northern Italian cuisine.

PARAQUITA BAY AND LAGOON

(Chart 54; II A, A-2, A-23, A-231, A-232)

Private property surrounds Paraquita Bay and Paraquita Lagoon. There is obviously an entrance to the lagoon, but whoever knows about it has kept silent. Looking in from Sir Francis Drake Channel, you will probably see the mast of a sailboat rising above the low shoreline. Do not be deceived. It is indeed a sailboat—a shoal-draft centerboarder. The lagoon is shallow. I have been told that the Royal Navy blasted a five-foot channel into the lagoon several years ago, but I have never seen the results of its work. Nevertheless, the lagoon is navigable by dinghy. You can fish among the mangroves, or bird-watch, or dig clams in the mud. Tortola-based boats use the lagoon as a hurricane hole.

MAYA COVE

(Chart 54; II A, A-2, A-23, A-231, A-232)

Shown on the charts as Hodges Creek, this anchorage is covered best by Imray-Iolaire Chart A-231.

The channel to Maya Cove is not shown on the charts, but it is easy enough to enter. However, sailing out to windward through the narrow opening can be more than exciting. From Sir Francis Drake Channel, Maya Cove can be seen at quite a distance. West of Buck Island, on a promontory about 100 feet high, there is a conspicuous white house with a windmill tower to the east of it and a white-pillared house to the northwest of the windmill tower. The cove is beneath this little complex.

To enter, run down the range formed by the windmill and the passage between Ginger and Cooper Islands. The range is 312° magnetic to the windmill. Given the usual easterly trades, you probably will find yourself running broad off. Take a good look with the binoculars before entering, as you may discover that the cove is so crowded that there is no anchoring room.

As you approach Maya Cove, you will notice red and green buoys marking the outer entrance to the cove. Pass between the buoys and bear off to port, which probably will require a jibe if you are under sail. A large basin will open up to starboard. Anchor wherever there is room. To anchor, bear off to starboard to give yourself plenty of room inside the reef, and then round up and drop the hook. Sheltered no matter what the wind and sea conditions are, you are nevertheless cooled by a gentle breeze that sweeps across the low reef and drives off any mosquitoes. There is at least 10 feet of water throughout the basin, and the channel reportedly has a depth of eight feet.

Maya Cove is the home of Tropic Island Yacht Charters, and there is a friendly restaurant/bar on the western side of the harbor that has its own dinghy dock. The Pelican Roost management not only is happy to let you tie up your dinghy to its dock but also takes messages for you in your absence. Getting to Road Town from Maya Cove is no major problem, as the bus service to East End goes by. Besides, hitchhiking is still an acceptable mode of transportation in Tortola.

Maya Cove is an excellent place from which to sail a small boat. You can sail inside the reef over to Paraquita Bay or eastward inside Buck Island to East End (marked Fat Hogs Bay on the charts), and then on through the passage between Tortola and Beef Island to the small bays and coves on the western end of Beef. All told, there is a six-mile strip of coast that can be traversed in complete safety in a small dinghy.

In April 1994, a dredging and filling project was underway in the western corner of the cove, but I was not able to find out why.

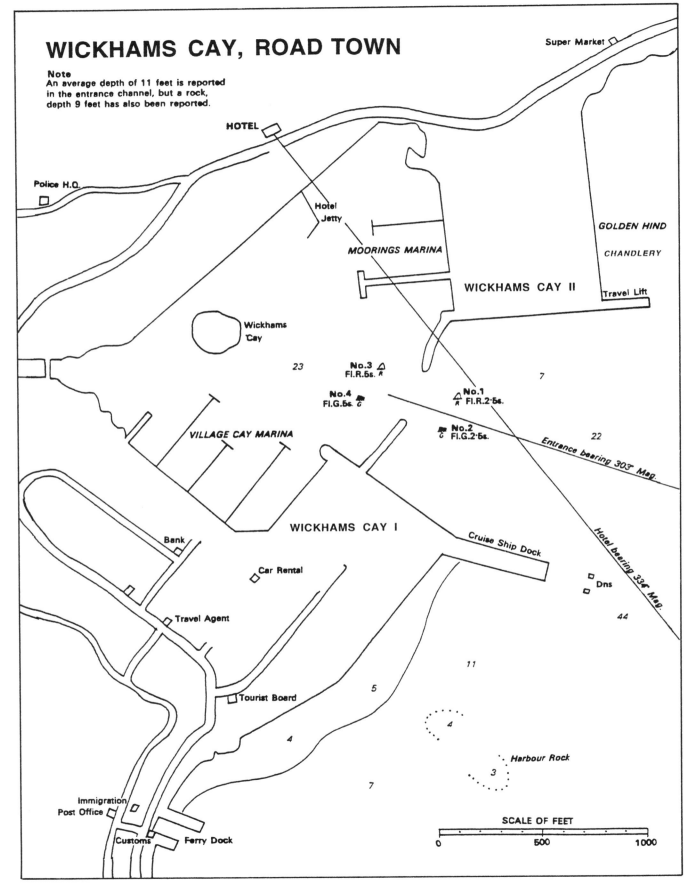

WICKHAMS CAY, ROAD TOWN

Note
An average depth of 11 feet is reported
in the entrance channel, but a rock,
depth 9 feet has also been reported.

Super Market

HOTEL

Police H.Q.

Hotel
Jetty

GOLDEN HIND

CHANDLERY

MOORINGS MARINA

WICKHAMS CAY II

Travel Lift

Wickhams
Cay

23

No.3
Fl.R.5s.

7

No.1
Fl.R.2·5s.

No.4
Fl.G.5s.

No.2
Fl.G.2·5s.

VILLAGE CAY MARINA

22

Entrance bearing 303° Mag.

WICKHAMS CAY I

Bank

Cruise Ship Dock

Hotel bearing 334° Mag.

Car Rental

Dns

44

Travel Agent

11

Tourist Board

5

4

4

Harbour Rock

7

3

Immigration
Post Office

SCALE OF FEET

Customs   Ferry Dock

0   500   1000

SKETCH CHART 53 Wickhams Cay, Road Town

Soundings in feet

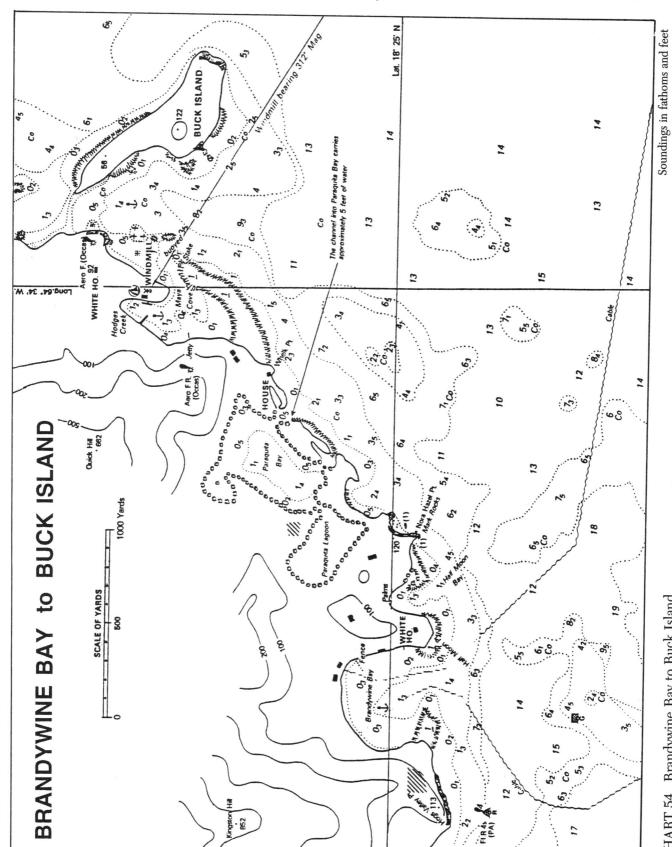

BRANDYWINE BAY to BUCK ISLAND

Soundings in fathoms and feet

CHART 54 Brandywine Bay to Buck Island

BUCK ISLAND

(Chart 54, Sketch Chart 55; II A, A-2, A-23, A-231, A-232)

Why no one ever anchors behind Buck Island is beyond me. It is completely sheltered unless the wind swings to the southeast, which happens so infrequently that it is not a real danger. A cool breeze usually blows over the lowland. Beaches and bottom are sand. The area offers good shelling and the romance of a deserted island. Buck Island was the original site of the airport serving Tortola back in the late 1940s. It has a crosswind runway and a rough grass strip. The pilots must have been superb.

Buck Island was also the home of Buck Island Bucks. Years ago, the island's owner minted coins that were similar in size to US silver dollars. Everyone thought it very humorous—except the US government. They nearly threw him in jail for counterfeiting, although he pointed out rightly that he was merely creating his own currency, and that if someone was fool enough to accept his currency, more power to him. The federal government still did not see the humor of the situation, and Buck Island Bucks soon passed out of circulation.

FAT HOGS AND EAST END BAYS

(Sketch Chart 55; II A, A-2, A-23, A-231, A-232)

Fat Hogs Bay used to be the home of many native Tortola sloops and cargo schooners. Alas, the last time a sloop or schooner was built here was in the early 1960s. A walk along the shore today reveals nothing but skeletons of sailing days past.

The entrance to Fat Hogs Bay is easy, in that the eastern reef is marked with a light. Then use eyeball navigation and stay in the deepest water. Work your way eastward and anchor in a suitable depth. Don't go too far east of the light unless you have a shoal-draft boat—in April 1993, *Iolaire* scoured out a new, seven-foot, six-inch channel! A good way to knock the barnacles off the bottom of the keel.

A few years ago, it looked as though this bay would develop, because Go Vacations established its base here, built a marina and hotel, and brought in a large fleet of bareboats. The operation folded, and for a while everything stagnated. Then the owners of the Go Vacations boats banded together and formed Seabreeze Charters, but this seems to be a continuing business, not an expanding one.

North Coast of Tortola

Along the north coast of Tortola are miles of isolated beaches. Long stretches of beautiful, soft, white sand have been piled up by the relentless ocean swell. The coast is exposed to the full force of these swells, and there are no harbors that offer real protection or safety. It becomes impossible—except by land—to visit the beaches in the winter, when the swell has built up. In the summer and occasionally in the early fall, when the wind tends to come more out of the south, you can anchor off these beaches, but at no time would I regard these as overnight anchorages.

BELMONT BAY

(Sketch Chart 49; II A, A-2, A-23, A-231)

Belmont Bay is on the extreme western end of the north shore of Tortola, and I have been told that there is a good anchorage in behind the eastern arm of the reef. Although I have not checked them myself, depths are reported to be 10 feet.

CANE GARDEN BAY

(Sketch Chart 56; II A, A-2, A-23, A-231)

Some people regard Cane Garden Bay as the most beautiful in the Virgin Islands. The ruins of some old buildings and a rum distillery can be seen, and a small, modern hotel and good restaurant are on the south shore. Cane Garden Bay is no longer as isolated as it was in the past. Now it is only 15 minutes by road over the top of the mountains and down into Road Town (and vice versa). The road, however, is such that you might have a heart attack before you reach Road Town.

When entering Cane Garden Bay, favor the north side of the bay and then swing in behind the reef and anchor. In the winter, this is a lunch stop only. A swell can build up to unmanageable proportions with little warning. More than one Tortola cargo schooner has ended up high and dry on the beach as a result of an unexpected swell. Despite this, Cane Garden Bay has become a popular yacht anchorage—but I would still avoid it in the winter.

Nonetheless, more and more boats are going to Cane Garden, even in winter. If you go in and anchor, pick up one of the Moor Seacure buoys, which are well installed, well maintained, and suitable for any boat up to about 50 feet. If all the moorings are in use, be sure you are on a good Bahamian moor, as

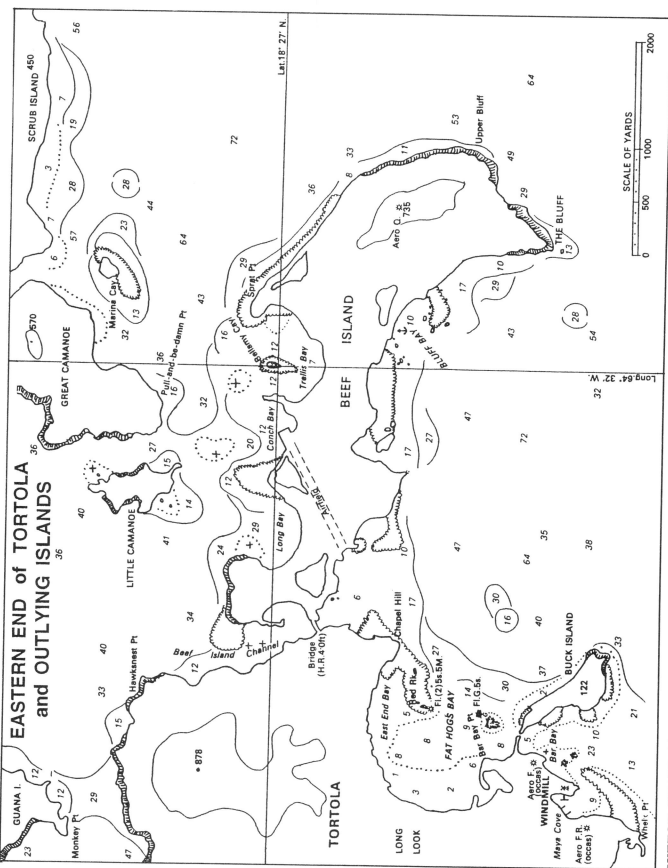

179

SKETCH CHART 55   Eastern End of Tortola and Outlying Islands

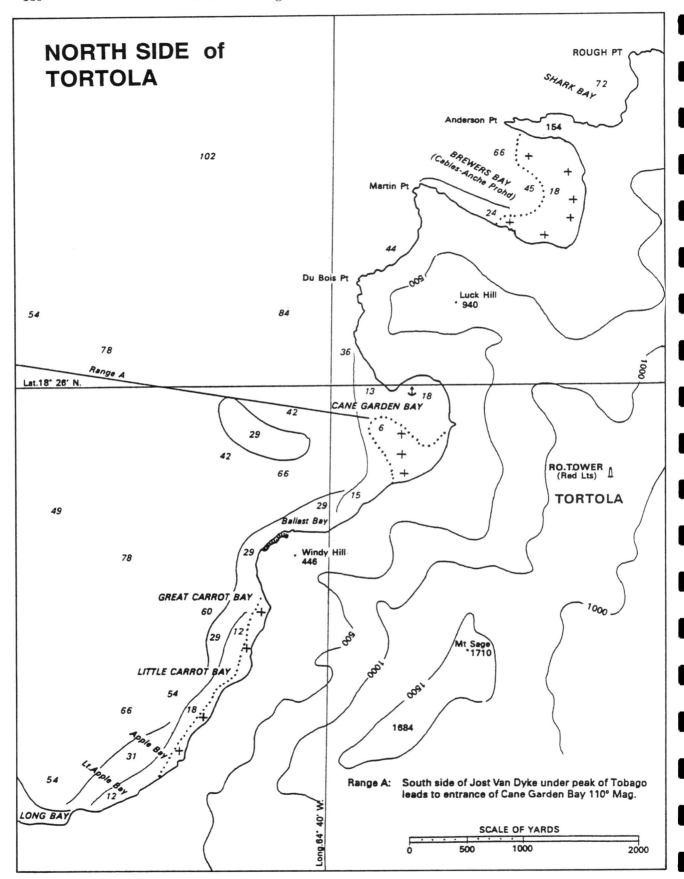

NORTH SIDE of TORTOLA

ROUGH PT

SHARK BAY   72

Anderson Pt   154

102

66   45   18

BREWERS BAY
(Cables-Anche Prohd)

Martin Pt   24

44

Du Bois Pt   600

Luck Hill
• 940

54   84

78

Range A

Lat.18° 26' N.   36

42   13   ⚓ 18

CANE GARDEN BAY

29   6

42   RO.TOWER
(Red Lts)

66   **TORTOLA**

15

29

49   Ballast Bay

78   29   • Windy Hill
446

1000

GREAT CARROT BAY

60

29   12

LITTLE CARROT BAY   Mt Sage
•1710

54

66   18   1600

Apple Bay   31   1684

54   Lt. Apple Bay

12

LONG BAY

Range A: South side of Jost Van Dyke under peak of Tobago
leads to entrance of Cane Garden Bay 110° Mag.

Long.64° 40' W.

SCALE OF YARDS

0   500   1000   2000

SKETCH CHART 56   North Side of Tortola

Soundings in feet

the ground swell can come in during the night when you are sound asleep. The first thing you will notice is a bump as you bounce on the bottom, and before you are out of your bunk, you will feel the second and third bounces. You will be up on the beach before you have time to do anything.

Despite all the warnings about swells in Cane Garden Bay, it has become one of the popular yacht anchorages. Thank god for reliable weather broadcasts and Moor Seacure buoys!

It should be noted that the ground swells of November and December 1991 cleaned everything out of Cane Garden. Bars and restaurants that had been standing there for years were completely washed out—so much so that all they could do was drive a bulldozer through and start rebuilding from scratch. I would hate to have been anchored in the bay when the swell came in.

Several boats have somehow mistaken Little Carrot Bay, to the south of Cane Garden, for Cane Garden Bay, and have found themselves in serious trouble. When approaching from offshore, put the south side of Jost Van Dyke directly under the peak of Tobago Island, at 110° magnetic. This range will lead to the entrance to Cane Garden Bay. Then you must eyeball it, following the buoys—if there are any.

If you are anchored elsewhere on Tortola, Cane Garden Bay is a pleasant place to go by rented car for lunch and a swim. There are three restaurant/bars on the beach: Rhymer's, Stanley's, and Quito's Gazebo. You can also tour the Callwood Rum Distillery, and sample the potent stuff produced there. Do *not* go to Cane Garden Bay when cruise ships are docked in Road Town. On those days, you will wait all day for lunch.

BREWERS BAY

(Sketch Chart 56; II A, A-2, A-23, A-231)

Brewers Bay used to be my candidate for the most beautiful bay in the British Virgin Islands. It was seldom visited by yachts, as sailing into the harbor is extremely difficult. There are radical windshifts, plus hard williwaws blasting down off the hills interspersed with periods of flat calm. Further, the chart shows an anchoring-prohibited cable area, although that ban was not observed or enforced. The smart skipper always anchored with a tripping line on his anchor so that if he hooked the telegraph cable, he could trip his anchor up from under it.

The beach was soft, white sand and completely deserted, so it made a good lunch stop if there was no ground swell. It was never used as an overnight anchorage, as in those days there was no way of predicting a ground swell. Now, in periods of no ground swell (generally the summer months), it does make a good anchorage, but be sure to rig a tripping line on your anchor. The beach is no longer deserted, as there are a few small restaurants, a bar, and a campground.

Proceeding eastward from Brewers Bay along the north coast of Tortola, there are no dangers; the shoreline is all steep-to. During periods when the ground swell is running, it is rather spectacular, as the sea hits the cliffs and the spray sometimes rises 100 feet in the air—truly magnificent.

When the wind is in the south, the ground swell is not running, so you should be able to find a daytime anchorage off the beautiful sand beaches on the north side of Tortola. When we sailed along this coast in late March 1993, the wind was out of the south, there was no ground swell, and it was a perfect time to anchor off these almost completely deserted beaches. There is some habitation on these beaches, but absolutely no development. Just remember, however, the ground-swell warning.

It's no problem to pass between Guana Island and Hawks Nest Point. You can beat through there with no difficulty, as there is deep water up to shore on both sides. However, as you approach Little Camanoe and the Long Bay area, you must be extremely careful, as many boats have bounced off the rocks here, and a few have been lost. At times, this area has been privately buoyed by the bareboat companies, but the buoys are very unreliable—sometimes they are there, sometimes not. None were in place in March 1993. If you keep your wits about you, you should have no problems.

See the Trellis Bay section, below, for information on the hazards in this area. Also, do not try to sail between Great and Little Camanoe, as flukey winds funnel between the islands. Even *Iolaire* has not been able to sail through this passage.

Beef Island

Beef Island is due east of Tortola, to which it is connected by the Queen Elizabeth II Bridge—an imposing name for an unimposing structure. There used to be an arduous though navigable channel between the two, but the bridge, although once opened, is now closed permanently. The clearance is four feet, which effectively bars the route for masted vessels. The last time I recall its being opened was during a Round-Tortola Race a number of years ago. One of the starters made private arrangements with the operator to have the bridge opened at a specific time. He breezed through the channel, the bridge was opened, and our friend shortened his distance by many miles. An uproar ensued—not so much because he had taken a shorter route, but rather because the bridge, once opened, was jammed in that position for several hours, and the traffic to the Beef Island Airport was backed up most of the way to Road Town.

Alan Batham, the original owner of Marina Cay, kindly helped with the directions for this channel, which is of interest primarily to launches and powerboats. At the southern end of the cut, there is about five feet at high tide. (The bridge clearance, as mentioned, is four feet.) When approaching from the north, the channel is complicated by a reef, with the entrance at the west side, close to the Tortola shore. The channel runs from this entrance southeast behind the reef toward a single mangrove tree at the water's edge. It has been blasted cross-current through sand, and it may well silt up again. Before blasting, the depth was three feet. Close to the mangrove tree, the channel goes toward the bridge and deepens.

Coming from the southern end, with the mangrove tree astern and traversing the main channel in a northwest direction, there are three peaks visible in the skyline. Steer on the right-hand one, and, when this sinks behind the others, you can make the turn to starboard. Don't try this at night!

If a heavy swell is coming in from the north, and particularly when the tide is setting against it, do not approach the Tortola shore on the north entrance. Come in squarely to the reef from well to seaward, and keep the reef as close on your port hand as possible, the face of it being quite sheer. The water is 12 feet deep at this point. The same applies going out in the reverse direction. There are reefs off the Tortola shore that are dangerous in a heavy sea.

Traveling south from the bridge, the channel heads southwest of the big rocks at the mouth. The shallowest water—five feet—is just inside off the end of the reef, which stretches out on the starboard hand. Once clear of the gap, there are no further hazards to the south.

BLUFF BAY

(Sketch Chart 55; II A, A-2, A-23, A-231, A-232)

Located on the south coast of Beef Island, Bluff Bay was a seldom-used anchorage; everyone was convinced that only six to eight feet could be carried inside the bay. Then veteran charter skipper Ross Norgrove, in *White Squall*, drawing nine feet, made it one of his favored anchorages.

Sail toward Beef Island, working your way cautiously into the shelter behind the high hill at the southeastern end of the island. A reef extends along the south shore of Beef; look for a low white rock, which, on closer inspection, you will see to be covered with guano. About 300 yards before Whale Rocks, you will see a gap in the reef. The axis of the channel leading inside is approximately northeast magnetic. Sail in on starboard tack. Once past the eastern reef, turn to starboard and anchor in 12 feet.

One afternoon, Norgrove, lying at anchor in Bluff Bay, watched a bareboat sailing toward him. It was late afternoon and the sun was low in the sky. Despite the poor visibility, the boat confidently zigzagged its way up the bay and anchored beside *White Squall*. Amazed to find a bareboat skipper with the ability to make such a tricky anchorage in poor light, Ross invited the newcomers over for a drink. Several rums later, it came out that these fellows had seen *White Squall* anchored comfortably in the bay, and they had just sailed right in, never suspecting that there was a reef between them and the anchorage. Some people just live right.

TRELLIS BAY

(Sketch Chart 55; II A, A-2, A-23, A-231, A-232)

Trellis Bay, on the north side of Beef Island, was formerly the main anchorage for Beef Island. Facilities included a marine railway, a hotel, and a powerboat dock. Exactly why Vladic Wagner built a slipway in this most inaccessible spot beggars the imagination—but he did. For many years, it was the major shipyard in the British and US Virgins. Now the railway and the hotel have been abandoned, but the dock is still used for launch service to Marina Cay.

To enter Trellis Bay, you can sail in either east or west of Bellamy Cay. It's strictly eyeball navigation, and this is no place for deep-draft boats. Despite what other guides say, maximum depth at the entrance is only 15 feet, shoaling to 12. Most of the bay is about 10 feet, shoaling to five or six feet around the edges. If you make a mistake, most of the bottom is just plain sand. *Iolaire* has been "parked" there more than once. At night, you should not be in this area at all, as it is not lighted. The light shown on Bellamy Cay in the charts hasn't worked in years. This is a good anchorage in all weather. No sea ever reaches into the bay, and the holding ground is good.

DO NOT anchor in line with the airport runway—a plane could run into your mast, with disastrous consequences. Even if you are *not* moored exactly in the runway flight path, you are likely to give yourself and the pilots heart attacks!

Bellamy Cay boasts The Last Resort, a popular restaurant-cum-nightclub featuring excellent cooking and piano entertainment by Tony Snell. Some years back, he ran a similar establishment on the western end of Little Jost Van Dyke, until it burned down. Everyone who has been entertained by Tony says that it is not to be missed. Many people don't realize that Tony was a Spitfire pilot who was shot down in World War II. He was captured and then escaped a number of times. A book has been written about his brilliant escapades.

For 12 years, Jeremy Wright has run Boardsailing BVI in Trellis Bay with tremendous skill and enthusiasm. I can vouch for the fact that he is a fine instructor—he taught my son Richard, then 12, to sailboard in one day. Jeremy is also an excellent raconteur, full of stories about his early days in the Caribbean during the mid-1970s. More amazingly, even though he has lost most of his hair, he has lost none of his enthusiasm for boardsailing.

Beyond Boardsailing BVI is De Loose Mongoose, a café/bar that serves three meals a day (even banana pancakes for breakfast) in a relaxed setting.

Believe it or not, even though there are Customs and Immigration officials at the airport—within spitting distance—Trellis Bay is not a port of entry. When we arrived in Trellis Bay in 1993, trying to take advantage of favorable winds, we were told at the airport that we had to go all the way to Road Town to clear! The BVI government claims to be yachtsman-friendly, but the Customs officials apparently haven't got the word yet. They threatened us with a US$10,000 fine, seizure of our boat, and a jail sentence. We ended up shelling out US$120 in fines. Do not play games with Tortola Customs.

You can rent a car at the airport, but the cars there are much more expensive than in Road Town. I recommend that you hitch a ride to town and hire a car there.

WARNING: There are two dangers in this area. There is a middle ground, with three feet of water over it, two-thirds of the distance between the southwest tip of Great Camanoe Island and the rock pile that is visible on the Beef Island shore at the eastern end of Long Bay. Since this middle ground is hard to spot, hug the northern side of the channel and you will clear it. The second danger is a rock 100 yards northeast of the westernmost arm of Trellis Bay. Again, use the north side of the channel and you will be safe. In years gone by, this rock was a great support to the boatyard at Trellis Bay. Boats would haul, go back into the water, start to run down the channel, and hit the rock. They would then turn around, go back to the yard, and haul again.

Despite what you may have heard or read, the above two reefs are NOT BUOYED and probably never have been. I cannot figure out why Tortola officials install buoys in places where they are not needed—such as Great Harbour on Jost Van Dyke—but do not put them on rocks that boats have regularly bounced off for at least a century. It beats me.

Marina Cay, the Camanoes, and Guana

MARINA CAY
(Sketch Chart 55; II A, A-2, A-23, A-231, A-232)

Marina Cay lies one mile north of Trellis Bay and offers one of the most comfortable anchorages in the Virgin Islands—no sea, no current, just a continual cooling breeze. There is room for 20 boats, and it is so sheltered that not the slightest chop will build up, no matter what the wind direction.

In the early 1960s, Alan and Jean Batham developed a resort hotel here, a thriving business in a six-acre island paradise. They built several cottages and a main house with a dining room and an open-air bar. Attempts to expand to Beef Island proved unsuccessful, but their son, Michael, with his wife, Terry, took the family business successfully to Great Camanoe Island. Alan and Jean ended up buying Ross Norgrove's *White Squall* and then set out for New Zealand, where they now live. Marina Cay has since gone through several owners and managements; the present owners are working hard to revitalize the business.

Marina Cay certainly has changed since the days when Jean was cooking on a kerosene wick stove and Alan was out shooting fish to serve for dinner. Now it is a busy modern operation—fuel, water, ice, showers, and laundry are all available at Marina Cay. Needless to say, there is a restaurant—plus an open-air, honor-system bar, a legacy from the days of the Bathams. In 1994, management changed again: The Pusser's Rum corporation (which owns the bar/restaurant/store complexes in West End, Road Town, and Leverick Bay) took over the lease on Marina Cay.

Marina Cay Harbor is easy to enter. From the west,

you can sail right in. (But be wary of the two hazards described under Trellis Bay, above.) From the southwest (Sir Francis Drake Channel), begin by staying well off Beef Island. The tide makes it sloppy near shore, and you will lose your wind under the cliffs even on the windward side of the island. There are no hazards coming from the east or northeast; it is easiest to pass north of Marina Cay. There is good water to the north, right up to the conspicuous long rock (six feet high) on the northeast tip of Marina Cay Reef. To enter the anchorage, run down between Marina Cay and Scrub Island; then round up, douse sail, and pick up a mooring. This is also the best route for leaving Marina Cay if you are heading east, because it keeps you out of the channel between Beef Island and Marina Cay, with its strong tide and steep chop.

Another entrance to the Marina Cay anchorage is from the north between Great Camanoe and Scrub Islands. There is ample water, but the channel is restricted and should not be attempted unless you know what you are doing. Reefs on both sides of the channel are visible when the sun is high.

The current runs through this channel at a great rate, especially during springtides. In November 1993, when we sailed *Iolaire* through here, the current was running south at such a rate that even though we were doing two and a half knots, we were only inching over the bottom! It took us a good half hour of carefully nursing the sails to get us through.

Once in Marina Cay, there are Moor Seacure moorings available for visiting yachtsmen. The eastern buoys have seven feet of water under them and the western buoys have 12; the buoys cover the entire shelf. If you try anchoring on your own, you will be in 30 to 40 feet of water, so I recommend that you pick up a mooring buoy.

The whole area between Great and Little Camanoes and Beef Island is marked with privately maintained buoys, but they do go adrift. Characteristics can be changed to the extent that neither the charts nor this guide will describe the buoys. If you keep your eyes open and sail in good light, the locations of the buoys in reference to the shoals should be obvious to you. (See the Trellis Bay section, above, for information about the two local hazards.)

LITTLE CAMANOE ISLAND
(Sketch Chart 55; II A, A-2, A-23, A-231, A-232)

Although it is possible to land a dinghy on Little Camanoe, the island offers no anchorage for the average cruising boat.

GREAT CAMANOE ISLAND
(Sketch Chart 55; II A, A-2, A-23, A-231, A-232)

In the summer, when the ground swell is not running, there is a good anchorage in Lee Bay. There is deep water close to shore, so use a Bahamian moor or anchor bow-and-stern. If you decide to try anchoring here in the winter, do not get too close to shore. If you were on a single anchor and the ground swell came in during the night, you would be on the beach before you even knew what was happening.

In light weather, I have seen boats anchored on the eastern side of Great Camanoe, just north of Scrub, but this is primarily a calm-weather anchorage. My friend Jon Repke tells me this is actually a good anchorage for a shoal-draft boat in all but heavy weather, as you can enter at the south side of the cove and sail north behind the reef, which breaks the swell. It doesn't stop the wind, so you are guaranteed a cool, bug-free anchorage. Do not try this, however, unless you are an experienced reef pilot and draw less than five feet.

In order to avoid the rocks south of Great and Little Camanoe, many boats opt for the passage *between* these two islands, but I do NOT recommend it unless you are under power. We tried it in *Iolaire* in December 1993 and finally turned around—the wind just bounces around too much.

GUANA ISLAND
(Sketch Chart 55; II A, A-2, A-23, A-231, A-232)

Guana Island is owned by the Bigelows and the private Guana Island Club. The houses are up on the hill and there are no facilities for visiting yachtsmen. However, they seem perfectly happy to have yachts stop at White Bay and use their beach. There is no way to get up to the club other than by foot, and it is a long way, all uphill. Although the beach is attractive, White Bay is not a particularly good anchorage. It is difficult to find water that is shallow enough for anchoring and yet far enough offshore that it prevents your swinging into coral heads when the breeze dies down at night. For this reason, I advise mooring bow-and-stern. Usually the small swell hooks around the point, and it is most comfortable lying east-and-west, so that the boat meets the swell with either the bow or the stern.

The beach in White Bay is spectacular, with beautiful white sand, but that is why it is a rocky, rolly anchorage. The better anchorage is tucked in west of Monkey Point, at the south end of Guana Island. You still have access to an excellent beach: Row your dinghy ashore, climb over the low rocks on the point, and you will find a lovely beach on the eastern side.

Jost Van Dyke

Jost Van Dyke is a small, relatively unspoiled island, slightly off the mainstream of island progress. Until recently, there were no cars or roads—only tracks suitable for horses—and the only settlement was the port of entry at Great Harbour. But the idyll has not lasted, although the area is still good.

I think *Iolaire* was the first yacht ever to clear in and out of Jost Van Dyke. In 1957 or 1958, I realized that Jost Van Dyke sloops did not go to West End to clear. We wanted to go to Marina Cay without having to stop at Road Town, so we ducked into Jost Van Dyke and inquired whether we could clear. There we found Albert Chinnery, then a young man who could barely read or write but who was the Queen's representative empowered to enter and clear us all at one time. One sheet of paper, one crew list, no fees! Albert retired in 1992, and today you'll find a typical West Indian anomaly: The Customs and Immigration office opens at 0800, but the officers who do the paperwork do not arrive until 0825, when they come over from Tortola on the first ferry.

Civilization has arrived on Jost Van Dyke: The onetime donkey-track roads are now paved, and they zigzag over the hills with grades so steep that any American civil engineer would have a heart attack if he saw them. He would insist that such roads couldn't be built, and even if they could be, cars could not possibly drive over them. However, non-islanders fail to understand West Indian construction methods—or West Indian drivers, who, given a four-wheel-drive vehicle, would happily drive up a vertical cliff. Telephones and electricity have also arrived, and there are even streetlights in Great Harbour. The grocery situation leaves a little to be desired, however. There is just the usual island-style rum shop—carrying butter, bread, rum, and a few odds and ends.

GREAT HARBOUR
(Sketch Chart 57; II A, A-2, A-23, A-231)

For many years, the only place offering meals and entertainment on the island was the Tamarind Restaurant and Bar, at the east end of the beach in Great Harbour. Run by Feliciano Callwood (known

far and wide as "Foxy"), it started out as a lean-to affair—a few palm branches thrown over a couple of packing cases in which were stored the ingredients for a really fabulous rum punch. Now known as Foxy's, this has now become one of the most famous entertainment spots in the Lesser Antilles.

Over Foxy's bar in 1974, a few of the owners of wooden boats started discussing a race open just to wooden boats. Foxy put up a suitable prize—some liquid refreshment—and the race was held on Labor Day Weekend. It drew five boats. The next year, it snowballed—more than 60 wooden boats appeared for the race. One of the outstanding entries was Dr. Robin Tattersall's *Galatea,* a beautiful little Herreshoff Nereia ketch. Since then, the annual Wooden Boat Regatta has been averaging 80 competitors, plus lots of spectator boats. Now other races also finish in Jost Van Dyke, including the Hook-In-and-Hang-On boardsailing marathon. Great Harbour might well be described as the party capital of the British Virgin Islands.

Rudy Thompson (no relation to the famous St. Thomas sailor) has also opened a Great Harbour restaurant. Called Rudy's, it has an excellent reputation for its barbecues. Other small bars and eateries have sprung up all along the beach. These come and go like the seasons, so there is not much point in trying to list them.

Great Harbour is normally sheltered, except when the wind veers well to the south. The northern end of the bay is reef-encumbered. East of the reefs on the northwest side of the bay, there is an anchorage in 12 feet of water about 300 yards offshore. To reach the Settlement dock, row your dinghy east until the dock bears 010° magnetic. A gap through the reef will lead you ashore. The village is very small, with no supplies except some good "informally distilled" white rum. (There's a way of spotting the really good home-distilled white rum. Drop an ice cube into a glass of it. If the cube sinks to the bottom, you know you are dealing with a potent brew.)

WHITE BAY
(Sketch Chart 57; II A, A-2, A-23, A-231)

West of Great Harbour lies what was once a beautiful, deserted, white-sand beach. It is not so deserted anymore. Entrance can be gained around the western end of the reef or through a break in its center. This break was difficult to spot until the Myricks—who used to own Sandcastle, the small hotel here—placed a range over their beach bar.

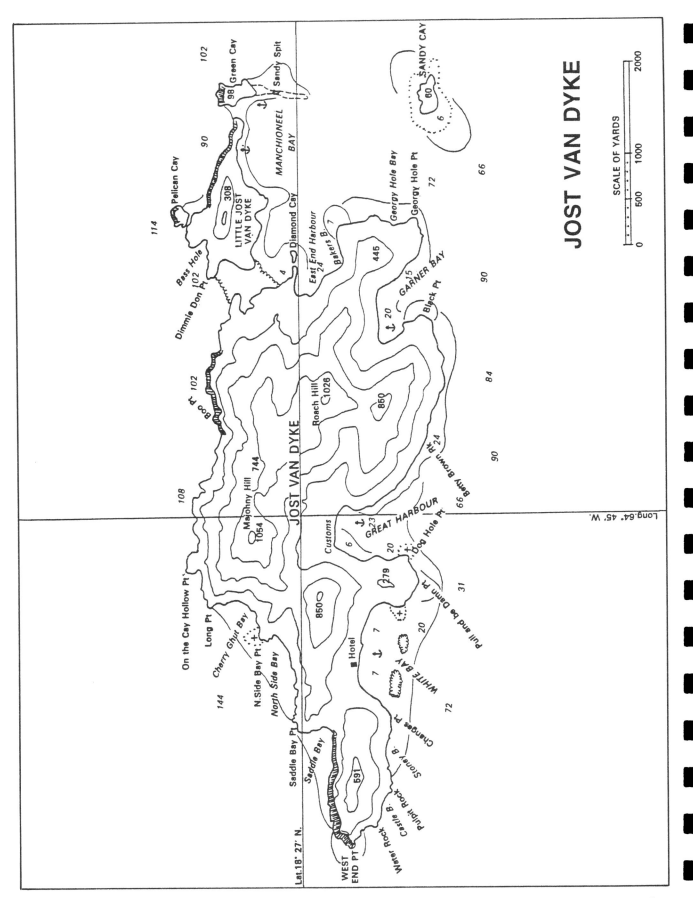

JOST VAN DYKE

SCALE OF YARDS

0   500   1000   2000

Long. 64° 45' W.

Lat. 18° 27' N.

Green Cay 102
98 Green Cay
Sandy Spit
MANCHIONEEL BAY
SANDY CAY 80
6
90
Pelican Cay
LITTLE JOST VAN DYKE 308
114
Bass Hole
Dimmie Don Pt 102
Diamond Cay
East End Harbour 24
Baker's B. 7
Georgy Hole Bay
Georgy Hole Pt 72
66
445
GARNER BAY 90
Black Pt 15
20
Boo 102
JOST VAN DYKE
Roach Hill 1026
850
84
Berry Brown Rk 24
90
Majohny Hill 744
1054
On the Cay Hollow Pt
GREAT HARBOUR
Dog Hole Pt 99
Customs 6
23
20
Long Pt
Cherry Ghut Bay
N. Side Bay Pt
North Side Bay 144
850
79
Hotel
WHITE BAY
7
7
7
20
Pull and be Damn Pt
31
Saddle Bay Pt
Saddle Bay
591
Changes Pt
Stoney B.
Pulpit Rock B.
Castle Rock B.
Water Rock
WEST END PT
72

SKETCH CHART 57   Jost Van Dyke

Soundings in feet

Now the palm trees have become so overgrown that the range is no longer visible, but the new owners have marked the break in the reef with red and green buoys. In 1993, I checked out the channel with the help of Jerry Reed, mate of *Mikado;* we found nine feet through the channel and 10 feet in the basin inside, but the basin is so small that I certainly would not take in any boat that is more than 45 feet long. A good anchorage can be had outside the reef in the northeast corner of the bay, northwest of Lower Flat Rock, where there is 10 to 15 feet of water over a sand bottom. The surge sometimes makes White Bay uncomfortable, but the place has nonetheless become popular among the bareboat crowd. (Part of the attraction may be the Soggy Dollar Bar, reputed to be the home of the original Painkiller, a smooth but potent local concoction.)

GARNER BAY (LITTLE HARBOUR)
(Sketch Chart 57; II A, A-23, A-231)

Also known as Little Harbour, Garner Bay lies east of Great Harbour. Although it is open to the southeast and very deep, it is a little more sheltered than you would expect. This is a picturesque spot with hills on three sides rising abruptly from the water. Anchoring here is extremely difficult, as the center of the harbor is very deep—60 or 70 feet. The three- or four-fathom shelf around the edges is completely taken up with Moor Seacure rental buoys. So either you anchor in deep water or you pick up a buoy and pay the fee. The water is crystal clear. In the western corner of the harbor, there is 30 feet of water right up to the beach. Here there are two restaurants, Harris's Place and Sidney's Peace and Love, right next to each other. On the east side of the harbor is Abe's Little Harbour, another small eatery that puts on a pig roast one night a week during the season.

EAST END HARBOUR
(Sketch Chart 57; II A, A-23, A-231)

East End Harbour, south of Diamond Cay, is wide open to the east. By all counts, it should be a hopeless anchorage, but for some reason its northwest corner is usually good—cool and breezy, with only a slight swell. Since it is on a dead lee shore, I advise using a two-anchor rig, making sure that each is firmly set. Put them out ahead of you in a Y config-

uration, and, wearing a face mask, swim down and make sure they are holding.

North of Diamond Cay is another anchorage that is well sheltered when the wind is coming from the south. The anchorage is close aboard the north side of Diamond Cay. Dredging is currently underway here, so the anchorage area will expand and become even deeper.

Along the north coast of Jost Van Dyke, the cliffs drop vertically into the sea. There are one or two shelves along this coast, making those areas a lot shoaler than the charts show. No one has closely investigated this stretch, but Saddle Bay, North Side Bay, and Cherry Cut Bay (south of Long Point) may have possibilities as daytime anchorages *in summer only.*

Under no circumstances should you approach the north shore of Jost Van Dyke in the wintertime. The Atlantic swell rolls and crashes against the cliffs, sending waves of solid water a hundred feet high. In the old days, when the people of Jost Van Dyke fished for a living, each winter two or three people were knocked from their perch on the cliffs by extra-large waves.

Little Jost Van Dyke, Green and Sandy Cays, and Tobago Island

LITTLE JOST VAN DYKE
(Sketch Chart 57; II A, A-2, A-23, A-231)

On the south side of Little Jost Van Dyke, there used to be a small hotel/restaurant where honky-tonk music could be heard until the wee hours of the morning. But it is no more—a fire razed it, and no one is sure when or if it will be rebuilt. Nonetheless, the dock is still there, with eight feet of water alongside; it has been expanded tremendously, so something may be in the works. A few years ago, rumor had it that a Canadian consortium was planning to develop the island and build roads, plus a bridge connecting the island to Jost Van Dyke, but nothing came of that. Now we'll wait till the next rumor surfaces.

There are actually two docks on the south side of Little Jost Van Dyke. The anchorage is west of the easternmost dock; there is no water west of the western dock.

At the eastern edge of Little Jost, on the southern side under the hill, you will spot an old cistern. Here you can anchor, with the cistern bearing northeast. It is an excellent anchorage, with a sandy bottom and good shelter except when the wind goes well to the south. Unless the wind is practically due south, Green Cay and its seasonal sandspit to the south provide excellent protection for this anchorage.

GREEN CAY
(Sketch Chart 57; II A, A-2, A-23, A-231)

Due west of Green Cay's sandspit is an exceptional anchorage that is very well protected from the sea. The wind sweeps across the bar to make it cool and comfortable. No need for a Bahamian moor here, since the wind will keep you off. It is best to come up close and anchor on the bar. The depth increases sharply to 10 fathoms as you move away, and should your anchor drag any distance, it might fall right off the edge. During the winter, the ground swell manages to wend its way between Green Cay and Little Jost Van Dyke, making the spot occasionally untenable as an overnight anchorage.

In March 1993, I ran into my old friend Hans Hoff of the big motorsailer *Mikado*. He told me he had spent a day and a night anchored in the lee of Green Cay—and he has done it many other times. He cannot understand why that is not one of the most popular anchorages in the Virgin Islands.

The sandspit extending south from Green Cay has been extended drastically over the years. It has been aided and abetted by this region's version of Johnny Appleseed—i.e., the irrepressible Rudy Thompson, who has been busily planting coconut palms on the sandspit. This appears to be making the spit grow and extend southward every year, providing more and more shelter as time goes by.

SANDY CAY
(Sketch Chart 57; II A, A-2, A-23, A-231)

East of Jost Van Dyke, Sandy Cay offers a fine beach and good snorkeling. If the wind is in the southeast, anchor off the northwest corner of the island. If it is in the northeast, anchor off the southwest corner. This is strictly a daytime lunch spot; the beach should not be missed. Eyeball your way in and anchor in a suitable depth.

If the ground swell is running, do not try to land your dinghy in Sandy Cay. In December 1992, a charter boat tried to land in rough weather; they got ashore all right, but on their way back to the boat,

they dumped the dinghy. Several crew members landed in the hospital—evacuated courtesy of VISAR (Virgin Islands Search and Rescue). Be careful: A dinghy, a beach, and surf can be a very dangerous combination.

TOBAGO ISLAND
(II A, A-2, A-23, A-231)

Tobago Island is seldom visited, but it does provide an anchorage for one yacht at a time—as long as the ground swell is not running and you are sure it will not be coming in. This is in a small cove close under the cliffs off the sand beach on the western side of the island.

There is an amusing story about this anchorage. Jon Repke of Parts and Power had an excellent mechanic who owned a boat and had a beautiful girlfriend. Periodically, the mechanic would become tired of St. Thomas and working and would disappear. If Jon was desperate for him, he would send out a radio message. Someone usually would respond and tell Jon where the mechanic was, and Jon would then take off in his plane and look for him. When Jon found him, he would circle over the boat a few times and often drop a streamer with a message indicating where the mechanic was needed.

If Jon sent out a message and no one knew where the mechanic was, he always flew directly to Tobago Island, where he knew he would spot the fellow's boat tucked up into the cove, moored bow-and-stern. Pretty hard to hide from your boss when he owns an airplane!

There are three hazards in the vicinity of Tobago Island. One is Mercurius Rock, east of the island. With approximately six feet of water over it, it crests and breaks in heavy weather. Another is King Rock, south of Tobago, which, though just under the surface, seldom breaks. Watson Rock, west of Tobago, rises steeply from seven fathoms with a shelf dropping 20 to 25 fathoms on its western side. It has excellent diving and can be reached easily from the Tobago Island anchorage.

Great and Little Thatch Islands
GREAT THATCH ISLAND
(Sketch Chart 49; II A, A-2, A-23, A-231)

Few yachts visit Great Thatch, although I know several that have anchored comfortably just west of

Callwood's Point. Here you can lie parallel to the beach, sheltered from the ground swell. It's a good idea to set a second anchor to the southeast to prevent a southerly shift in the wind from swinging you ashore. The snorkeling is excellent, and, if you are lucky, you may pull in a lobster or two.

Doug White of *Stormy Weather* is one of the few people I know who has explored Great Thatch Island. He warns of the wreck of a local sloop sunk right about the middle of the anchorage area.

Once on the beach, there is an old Customs house that is badly overgrown and hard to spot. If you are the exploring type, there are ruins atop the ridge behind Callwood's Point. Don't try going there, however, unless you have heavy shoes, heavy trousers, a long-sleeved shirt, a hat, a water bottle, and a sharp machete. Hack your way inland, heading north or northeast toward the ridge. If you are lucky, you will find the remains of an old road that leads to the ruins at the top of the ridge. The ruins comprise a large house with several outbuildings and a well-preserved cistern. From here, there is a wonderful view of western Tortola. Folklore has it that in the late nineteenth century, the island was inhabited by a cattle rancher who one day went a little bonkers, burned the whole place, and departed.

LITTLE THATCH ISLAND
(Sketch Chart 49; II A, A-2, A-23, A-231)

The home of what I call the "on-again, off-again Finigon Hotel." The Finigon was the first small hotel on the western end of Little Thatch. Since 1954, the hotel's owners and managers have come and gone with great frequency. The only stable residents of the place seem to be the mountain goats. The island is without a good anchorage, and this has detracted from its commercial success. One anchorage off the northwest corner is good only for the summer months. During the winter, the ground swell rolls in through Thatch Island Cut, producing a turbulence that can be dangerous at times. Before searching for the Finigon, check at West End to find out whether or not it is open for business.

In April 1994, there was a flurry of activity on the island: Work was underway on the main building and the houses on the beach were freshly painted. These houses are particularly attractive—traditional West Indian style, with peaked roofs and wide porches all around. With this sensible design, you can just install an overhead fan and forget about air-conditioning.

Norman Island

Norman Island is reputed to be the island that Robert Louis Stevenson had in mind when he wrote *Treasure Island*. It is entirely possible, since there are several anchorages that seem to fit into the scheme of that classic adventure. Seven anchorages are scattered around the island (clockwise from the western end): Privateer Bay, Treasure Point Caves, The Bight, Miner/Carstarphen Cove, Benures Bay, Money Bay, and Windward Sound. Treasure hunting is still much bruited about. As recently as 1972, a gold doubloon supposedly was found in one of the caves on the island.

PRIVATEER BAY
(Sketch Chart 58; II A, A-2, A-23, A-231, A-232)

Augie Hollen reports that with the wind in the southeast during the summer months, the anchorage in the southern end of Privateer Bay is excellent. It is a short swim to Caravel Rock, where there is good snorkeling, spearfishing, and underwater spelunking. You can watch the pelicans soar above the cliff, fold their wings, and plunge into the water with the force of a cannonball. The beach is rock. A Bahamian moor is advisable here to keep from swinging ashore, since the wind will continually box the compass. For strong swimmers and experienced spearfishermen, there is some good fishing, albeit in rough water, south of the southwesternmost point on Norman Island.

This is one of the better anchorages in Norman Island, as you can sail on in, late in the afternoon, bury two anchors in shoal water (or ashore), and drop a stern anchor out. The area south of you, off Treasure Point Caves, will be crowded with charter yachts and cave visitors, but come 1700, they will all depart for The Bight or other anchorages, and you will have peace and quiet for enjoying your sundowner on deck. In the morning, if you want to get up for an early morning skinny dip, fine—no one will be there and no one is likely to be visiting the caves before 0900, by which time you can be ready to pick up your anchor and go sailing.

TREASURE POINT CAVES
(Sketch Chart 58; II A, A-2, A-23, A-231, A-232)

A common stopping place on Norman Island is off the caves, which are about 300 yards south of Treasure Point. Many different stories are told about the

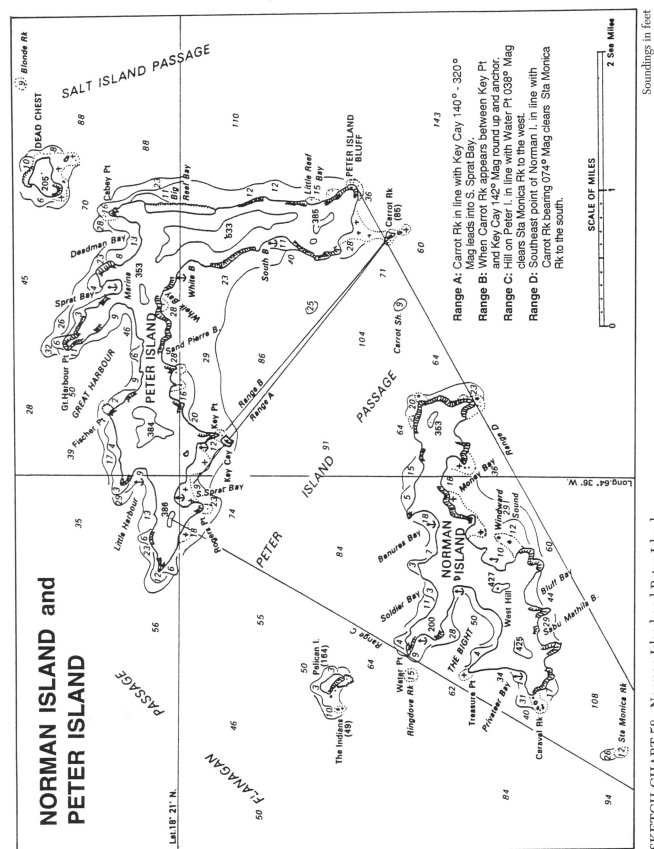

NORMAN ISLAND and PETER ISLAND

Range A: Carrot Rk in line with Key Cay 140° - 320° Mag leads into S. Sprat Bay.

Range B: When Carrot Rk appears between Key Pt and Key Cay 142° Mag round up and anchor.

Range C: Hill on Peter I. in line with Water Pt 038° Mag clears Sta Monica Rk to the west.

Range D: Southeast point of Norman I. in line with Carrot Rk bearing 074° Mag clears Sta Monica Rk to the south.

SCALE OF MILES

Soundings in feet

SKETCH CHART 58   Norman Island and Peter Island

treasure found in the southernmost cave. I don't think anyone knows the whole truth, but you can hear some interesting tales from the older folk around here. At this anchorage, the bottom is deep. The wind loops over the hill, and you will lie stern-to the shore; but you are pretty exposed, and I advise against spending the night here. All three caves can be explored by dinghy. Snorkeling is good all along the shore.

THE BIGHT
(Sketch Chart 58; II A, A-2, A-23, A-231, A-232)

The Bight is the largest and best anchorage on Norman; the best place in The Bight is on the shelf in the extreme northeast corner. Feel your way in with a leadline, because if you miss the shelf, you will be anchoring in seven or more fathoms of water. The bottom is sand and the holding good. Gusts of wind may blow down off the hills, but there will be no sea. The beach ashore is fair, but watch out for sea urchins. There are ruins to explore ashore, and coins, pottery, and tile fragments abound. Finally, be careful of the livestock. They seldom see humans and are anything but friendly.

When anchored in The Bight, you don't even have to cook on board. Just get into your dinghy, go over to the *William Thornton,* a Baltic Trader converted to a floating bar and restaurant, where you can have your sundowner, listen to music, and order a meal. Then return home via dinghy.

MINER/CARSTARPHEN COVE
(Sketch Chart 58; II A, A-2, A-23, A-231, A-232)

Named for the yachtsmen who popularized this anchorage, it lies southwest of the northwestern arm of The Bight. As in the Treasure Point Caves anchorage, the wind loops over the hill in Miner/Carstarphen Cove, so you will lie with your stern toward the shore the entire time. The bottom is mixed sand and rock in about five fathoms. If you have a yawl or ketch, it is best to leave your mizzen up to prevent the boat from waltzing around and fouling your anchor or your rode on the rocks on the bottom.

BENURES BAY
(Sketch Chart 58; II A, A-2, A-23, A-231, A-232)

On the north side of Norman Island, an anchorage in Benures Bay offers protection when the wind is in the south. Anchor as close to the white-sand beach as you dare. The bottom is sand and provides good holding. Above, the wind whistles between the two 250-foot-high hills, guaranteeing a cool and bug-free anchorage year round. I am told that there are ruins of an old estate on the ridge to the west.

MONEY BAY
(Sketch Chart 58; II A, A-2, A-23, A-231, A-232)

With the wind well into the north, Money Bay provides a calm anchorage and still another beautiful white-sand beach. The chances of finding another boat here are slight, and, in any case, there is only room for two or three boats. To conserve swinging room, I strongly recommend a Bahamian moor or bow-and-stern anchors. It is a deep harbor, and, with proper scope out, the swinging radius on just one anchor will be considerable. If possible, tuck yourself up in the northeast corner, where it is the quietest. From Money Bay, you can take your dinghy three-fourths of a mile to Windward Sound.

WINDWARD SOUND
(Sketch Chart 58; II A, A-2, A-23, A-231, A-232)

Windward Sound is a reef-sheltered anchorage— only for the courageous. To enter, it is best to put a person in the rigging. There is ample water once inside, but the channel itself is only six or seven feet deep, narrow and zigzaggy. It leads diagonally from the northeast to the southwest, and there are breaking reefs on both sides. The harbor will take only one boat at a time, and it is small enough to explore by swimming off your boat. Don't bother to launch your dinghy.

Peter Island

LITTLE HARBOUR
(Sketch Chart 58; II A, A-2, A-23, A-231, A-232)

Of the numerous anchorages on Peter Island, Little Harbour is the one most often visited by yachtsmen. It is easily identified from a distance by the white roof of the house once owned by Sir Brundel Bruce. Sir Brundel was well known for an effective method of curing litterbugs of their bad habit. Anyone who threw trash overboard in the harbor would receive several bullet holes in his mainsail—a rather drastic but effective remedy for a major problem.

Entering Little Harbour presents no problems.

Sail in, drop your hook, and you will be secure in normal trade-wind weather. Tortola blocks any ground swell that might upset the harbor, so the only risk would be from a northwester, which comes on in the winter with a slow, gradual shift.

More of a threat is overcrowding. Little Harbour is extremely popular due to its proximity to Road Town and its picturesque setting. To control swinging here, use a Bahamian moor.

The area ashore used to be owned by Percy Chubb III, who bought the land to "get away from it all." Mr. Chubb was the head of Chubb & Son, one of the largest yacht underwriters in North America. Sitting on his porch, he watched the antics of the bareboat charterers sailing through the Virgin Islands, and his observations had much to do with his firm's reluctance to insure bareboats and charter boats in the Antilles. If fewer people complained about the difficulty of obtaining insurance and more people improved their anchoring techniques, we might be able to straighten out the current insurance situation in the islands.

When Percy Chubb died several years ago, the house was sold to the Amway Corporation.

GREAT HARBOUR
(Sketch Chart 58; II A, A-2, A-23, A-231, A-232)

The next bay east of Little Harbour is Great Harbour, which is also sheltered in all normal weather. It is deep—so deep, in fact, that unless you have a tremendous quantity of line, it is difficulty to find a suitable anchorage. On the south side, midway between the mouth and the head of the harbor, there is a three-fathom shelf. Don't anchor here. Rather, drop your hook in the north side, one-third of the way up the harbor, where there is another three-fathom shelf. To use the southern anchorage is to make enemies of the local fishermen. Every afternoon, the fish come in along this side of the harbor, and any boat lying there—even just a dinghy running around—is likely to spook the entire school and send it back out to sea, leaving a group of frustrated, indignant fishermen. Similarly, they have passed the word not to use outboards anywhere in Great Harbour. These people have been making a living for more than 150 years by net fishing in this harbor, and it would be regrettable to spoil their livelihood.

If you look up on the eastern hillside in the afternoon, you will spot a watchman looking out to sea for the arrival of the fish. When he signals that the fish are in, a net is run out from shore, around the school, and back to shore. The net is slowly drawn tighter and the fish are driven into a large penned area, where they are kept alive until they are taken to market. If the catch is a good one, you can buy fresh fish at a reasonable price. Once they have finished their work, you can sail right up to the beach, drop a stern anchor, and throw a line ashore. The fishermen will tie it to a seagrape tree. Make sure your stern anchor is well set, and you will be moored for the night. No dinghy is needed. You can jump ashore dry-shod from the bowsprit.

SPRAT BAY
(Sketch Chart 58; II A, A-2, A-23, A-231, A-232)

East of Great Harbour, Sprat Bay is not shown on the British and American charts. In fact, I think *Iolaire* was the first yacht ever to anchor inside Sprat Bay, as everyone thought it was too shoal. We sailed in and discovered that if we anchored right in the center of the harbor on a Bahamian moor, all was well for our draft (seven feet six inches), but if we were not in the exact center, we bottomed out at low tide.

As the years went by, more and more boats began to use this harbor. Finally, the Norwegians bought most of Peter Island and started a massive land-development program—creating the Peter Island Resort. Now Sprat Bay has a marina, docks, water, fuel, electricity, and ice. Space sometimes is available, but check with the dockmaster via VHF before entering. (Anchoring no longer is allowed.) When docking, it is a case of powering on in, dropping your anchor, backing in, and tying up stern-to.

When entering, the deepest water is the eastern side of the channel; the western side shoals gradually.

The luxurious resort was devasted by Hurricane Hugo in 1989, but it reopened in 1991—every bit as elegant as it had been before. Jackets used to be required for dinner, but I am not sure that is still the case. Check upon arrival.

The harbor here is always windswept and cool. Snorkeling, especially along the eastern edge of the harbor, is excellent. A short walk to the east along a new road that crosses the saddle of the two hills brings you to Deadman Bay (see below).

DEADMAN BAY
(Sketch Chart 58; II A, A-2, A-23, A-231, A-232)

Deadman Bay is a wonderful daytime anchorage, but it is not comfortable at night. The swell usually sweeps around the eastern point and hooks into the harbor. The seas are rarely large enough to be dangerous, but even the small swell hitting you on the beam tends to make you roll.

The best anchorage is in the extreme southeast corner. The palm-fringed beach is superb—beautiful white sand—and the snorkeling is excellent. For those who like to go for big fish, swim around the northeastern point of the bay and you will find plenty, including some large tarpon.

Unfortunately, the bay is not deserted, but at least there is a beach bar where you can have a drink or a late meal without having to dress for the occasion.

SOUTH BAY

(Sketch Chart 58; II A, A-2, A-23, A-231, A-232)

South Bay is not the best anchorage on Peter Island, but it is a place to stop. There is no beach, but there are plenty of shells, and probably plenty of whelks. Moor close to shore with bow and stern anchors, since the wind coming over the 450-foot cliffs will haul in from the west to blow you onshore.

WHITE BAY

(Sketch Chart 58; II A, A-2, A-23, A-231, A-232)

White Bay is named for its gorgeous white-sand beach and its frothy surf. Although the ground swell from the north is mostly broken up by Tortola and the other islands, some of the surge still sneaks in here, building up the beach. Again, there is deep water suitable for anchoring close to shore, but the holding is not especially good. Be sure to rig bow and stern anchors or a Bahamian moor, since the high hills tend to suck the wind in toward the beach.

WHELK BAY

(Sketch Chart 58; II A, A-2, A-23, A-231, A-232)

The beach here is shingle and loaded with whelks. Ross and Minine Norgrove of Tortola offer good advice about whelks: "Always remember that they can hear you. When you make a noise, you can see the whelk move a few inches, but those few inches will be just enough to put him under a rock and out of view. So do not use a motor to go ashore, do not beach the dinghy roughly, do not run along the shingle beach, and do not talk—in no time, you will have a bucket of whelks. Whelks are delicious when properly cooked. Put an inch of water—half salt water,

half fresh—in the bottom of a pressure cooker, throw in the whelks, and put the pressure cooker on the fire. Bring the pot to full pressure and then start timing. Cook for 45 minutes at full pressure. At the same time, prepare a sauce of melted butter, lime juice, and your favorite spices. Whelks can provide a fabulous free meal, and when correctly prepared, they can hold their own with escargots."

KEY POINT

(Sketch Chart 58; II A, A-2, A-23, A-231, A-232)

There is an excellent anchorage west of Key Point. To enter, stand in on starboard tack, heading northeast toward the high hill on Key Point. By the time Carrot Rock disappears behind Key Cay, you should be fully prepared to drop your hook or you will come to a sudden stop. Immediately upon resighting Carrot Rock, round up, douse sail, and anchor. Here you are protected in all weather, and a gentle breeze blows in from between the cay and Key Point, keeping the anchorage cool at all times. There will be good snorkeling within swimming distance of the boat.

SOUTH SPRAT BAY

(Sketch Chart 58; II A, A-2, A-23, A-231, A-232)

Another cozy anchorage on the south coast of Peter Island. Inside, there is 10 to 12 feet of water and room for only one boat. The entrance is narrow. The entrance bearing brings you onto a broad reach or a run, so watch out not to get going too fast. Head northwest, pointing for the western peak of Peter Island. When Carrot Rock begins to close in behind Key Cay, turn to 320° magnetic and run down this line of bearing with a lookout posted forward or in the rigging. As soon as the reefs are spotted, alter your course to pass midway through the gap in the reef, round up, and anchor on a Bahamian moor, which will be good insurance against swinging onto the reef at night. This is a small bay, so be careful.

DEAD CHEST ISLAND

(Sketch Chart 58; II A, A-2, A-23, A-231, A-232)

Northeast of Peter Island lies the island where the pirate Edward Teach (a.k.a. "Blackbeard") is supposed to have stranded a group of recalcitrant crew members. He left them with a cutlass, a bottle of rum, and no hope of getting ashore, since they didn't know how to swim.

There are no good anchorages on Dead Chest Island. Blond Rock, between Peter and Salt Islands, will scare the living daylights out of you if you pass over it. There is roughly eight feet of water over it, so stand clear unless you have a shoal-draft boat or you wish to join the ranks of Edward Teach's abandoned crew. You might try snorkeling near it. Since it rises sharply out of 70 feet of water, it should be alive with fish.

Salt Island

SALT POND BAY

(Sketch Chart 59; II A, A-2, A-23, A-231, A-232)

A number of years ago, a light was established on the northwest corner of Salt Island—a 10-second flashing red light, 174 feet high, visible 14 miles. However, often when I crossed Anegada (Sombrero) Passage, I was unable to find this light. In the spring of 1984, it finally dawned on me that the light is obscured by hills to the south and east of it. Exactly what sectors are obscured, I cannot confirm authoritatively, but it seems to be obscured from 057° magnetic clockwise to 197° magnetic. No one understands why the light was established where it is, since you would think the Ginger Island Light would be sufficient. Once it was established, why didn't the powers-that-be announce the sectors in which the light is obscured?

Salt Island is a good place for a lunch stop, but don't spend the night here. The anchorage is off the settlement in three fathoms, but it is exposed and the water is rough. Ashore, the locals make their living by gathering salt from the pond behind their village. The pond is community operated but technically owned by Her Majesty the Queen. Each year, the commissioner of the British Virgin Islands comes to the island and accepts an annual rent of one sack of salt. Most of the residents have now moved to Road Town so that their children may benefit from the school system there. However, several older folk remain, staving off boredom by showing visitors around and consuming quantities of "the big drink"—which means any alcoholic beverage that they can con from a sympathetic visitor.

Some Salt Islanders must have made some money somewhere, and prosperity may be starting to spill over to Salt Island. In March 1993, when we sailed along the beach, we noticed a very nice new (and expensive) house. Also, some of the old shacks had

been refurbished, and quite a few boats were pulled up on the beach.

Sailing close to the northwest end of the island, you will see a perfect silhouette of the British rampant lion gazing northward. It makes a dramatic photograph in the late-afternoon sun.

The wreck of the steamer *Rhone* can be found in Lee Bay, her stern section lying in 45 feet of water west of Pinnacle Rock. If you want to dive on the *Rhone*, it is best to anchor north of Pinnacle Rock. You really need scuba gear to see anything, and currents in the area of the wreck are *very strong*. Back in the early 1950s, an English frogman lost his life diving on the *Rhone*. It has also been reported to me by experienced local divers that the diving conditions are best—least current and clearest water—before noon. Usually around noontime, a strong current springs up, making diving difficult if not impossible. In fact, it seems a bit foolhardy to dive on the *Rhone* unless you have as a guide one of the local divers familiar with the wreck and the currents in the area.

The *Rhone* was sunk on October 29, 1867, by one of the worst hurricanes to come through the Virgin Islands. It is a fact to remember when heading south to the islands that you can get caught in a late-October hurricane if you are not careful. Leaving the East Coast of the United States in mid-October is dangerous. It is a mistake that has cost the lives of more than one of my friends.

THE SOUND

(Sketch Chart 59; II A, A-2, A-23, A-231, A-232)

On the east coast of Salt Island, between Groupers Nest and Salt Island Bluff, The Sound seems to be completely obstructed by a shallow reef. I have never explored it by boat, but from the air it appears to have only two or three feet of water over the reef, with plenty of water inside. While flying overhead, I remember thinking that someone should blast a channel through the reef, since the harbor would make a perfect anchorage—wind sweeping in over the reef, a deep sandy bottom, and a white-sand beach. One of the charter skippers reported seeing a 35-foot boat—undoubtedly a centerboarder—at anchor there. Evidently there is a gap in the reef on the eastern side of The Sound that Dr. Benjamin Spock of *Carapace* (35 feet long, drawing four and a half feet) used regularly when the conditions were good. I have been told that if you really know your way and can thread a hawser through the eye of a needle, you can take six or seven feet into The

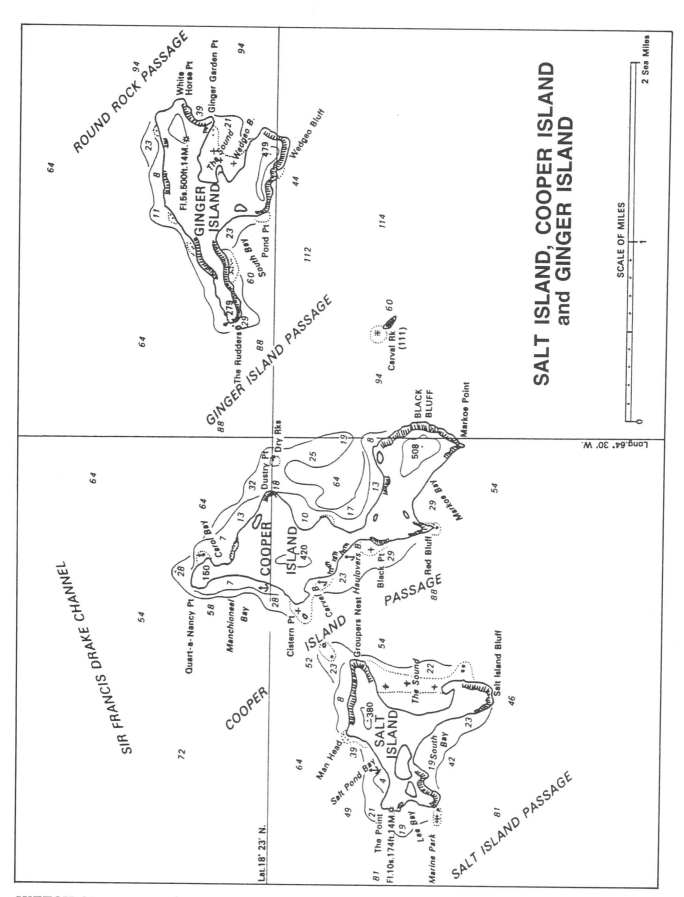

SALT ISLAND, COOPER ISLAND and GINGER ISLAND

SCALE OF MILES

2 Sea Miles

Long.64°.30'.W.

ROUND ROCK PASSAGE

GINGER ISLAND

White Horse Pt
Ginger Garden Pt
The Sound 21
Wedgeo B.
Wedgeo Bluff
Fl.5s.500ft.14M.
Pond Pt.
South Bay
The Rudders
GINGER ISLAND PASSAGE

Carval Rk (111)

BLACK BLUFF
Markoe Point
Markoe Bay

SIR FRANCIS DRAKE CHANNEL

Dustry Pt.
Dry Rks
COOPER ISLAND
Carol Bay
Quart-a-Nancy Pt
Manchioneel Bay
Cistern Pt.
Carval B.
Groupers Nest Haulovers B.
Black Pt.
Red Bluff
PASSAGE

COOPER ISLAND

Lat.18°.23'.N.

Man Head
Salt Pond Bay
The Point
Fl.10s.174ft.14M.
Lee Bay
Marine Park
SALT ISLAND
The Sound
Salt Island Bluff
South Bay
SALT ISLAND PASSAGE

SKETCH CHART 59   Salt Island, Cooper Island, and Ginger Island

Soundings in feet

Sound at high tide. Once inside, you can tuck yourself into the southeast corner among the mangroves and find yourself in a perfect hurricane hole.

the two hills, and there is always a breeze from across the point.

LEE BAY
(Sketch Chart 59; II A, A-2, A-23, A-231, A-232)

Do not try anchoring in Lee Bay. Anchoring would be difficult, and you would damage the coral. Rather, if you want to dive on the wreck of the *Rhone,* I strongly advise that you come here with one of the local diving organizations. If you are not with one of these groups, pick up one of the permanent moorings that have been established by the British Virgins National Parks Trust, do your diving, and move on.

SOUTH BAY
(Sketch Chart 59; II A, A-2, A-23, A-231, A-232)

As long as the wind is east or north of east, a good anchorage can be found in South Bay. Seldom used, it is a place where you can get off by yourself.

Cooper Island

MANCHIONEEL BAY
(Sketch Chart 59; II A, A-2, A-23, A-231, A-232)

This is Cooper Island's northwesternmost bay, with a grove of palm trees, a good beach, and an excellent small restaurant. Anchoring is basically impossible here, as the shelf is covered with permanent Moor Seacure moorings. Pick one up and pay the fee ashore at the bar. If you try to anchor clear of these moorings, you will be in 60 feet of water. I, for one, do not enjoy hauling up the couple of hundred feet of line needed in this depth. In fact, most bareboats don't even carry enough line to anchor in 60 feet of water, so just pick up a mooring and be done with it.

The bay has crystal-clear water and good snorkeling at the northern and southern ends. Take the dinghy around the corner, where you will find all sorts of excellent dinghy anchorages to use while diving or snorkeling along the west coast of the island.

There are a few small cottages here, built by some sun-worshiping Continentals. The southernmost of these is interesting, since it has been established on the ruins of a colonial estate. From a distance, it looks hot and airless, but a closer look reveals that the planters were no fools; the wind eddies around

CARVEL BAY
(Sketch Chart 59; II A, A-2, A-23, A-231, A-232)

This bay makes an excellent anchorage when the wind is in the north. The water is deep right up to the shore. Its possibilities were first recognized by Ross Norgrove, formerly of *White Squall* and *White Squall II,* who put in during a very heavy blow out of the northeast, expecting to spend no more than a couple of hours. It was such a nice spot and so well sheltered that he spent the night there and then used the anchorage regularly after that. As a rule of thumb, when the wind is south of east, anchor north of Cistern Point, in Manchioneel Bay; if it's north of east, anchor south of the point, in Carvel Bay.

The southern half of Cooper Island is rocky and exposed. There are no anchorages. But if you visit the area in a dinghy, you will discover good fishing.

Ginger Island

East of Cooper Island, Ginger Island (Sketch Chart 59) is uninhabited and without beaches or harbors. There used to be an erratic and practically invisible light on the island, but it has been replaced by a good white light, 500 feet high and flashing every five seconds. It is visible 14 miles out to sea from all quadrants that a yacht would use to approach the British Virgins.

(When crossing Anegada (Sombrero) Passage, coming from the east and heading for the British Virgins, it is best to lay off a course that passes eight to 10 miles south of Ginger Island because of the unpredictable current in the passage. Then, when you pick up the light on Ginger Island, you can alter course to enter the BVIs via whichever passage you want. As I mentioned in chapter 1, my preference is Round Rock Passage, between Round Rock and Ginger Island.)

Northeast of Ginger Island is Round Rock, the highest and southernmost of the rocks south of Virgin Gorda. It has no habitation or landing. North of it is a series of rocks awash, called The Blinders. And north of these is Fallen Jerusalem, so-called since it was thought to resemble the ruins of Jerusalem after the Roman conquest.

A temporary calm-weather anchorage can be

found off the beach on the north end of Fallen Jerusalem. It may be a little rough, but you will have complete privacy, since few boats stop there. The snorkeling is excellent and the spearfishing is reputed to be good.

Area Between Round Rock and Virgin Gorda

This entire area is very poorly charted and extremely dangerous. I am surprised that more boats have not been lost here. There are numerous discrepancies among the various charts. NOAA 25243, for example, shows a rock with six feet of water over it between Round Rock and the southernmost Blinder; no such rock appears on the British chart. Flying over the area, I have spotted a few other uncharted rocks sticking out of deep water.

In short, do not attempt the passage north of Round Rock except in ideal light conditions, in calm weather, and with a crew member in the rigging. The current runs strongly here, the sea is choppy, and it is almost impossible to make this passage against the current if the wind is blowing hard against you.

The passage between Fallen Jerusalem and Virgin Gorda can be used as long as it is not blowing hard out of the east. There is deep water along the entire route except for The Blinders, which break in all states of tide. Needless to say, if you are beating to windward, do not attempt this passage without the engine running unless your boat is really good on this point of sailing. Running downwind through this passage is no problem as long as you are careful about The Blinders, which you can pass either to the north or to the south.

NOTES

14

Virgin Gorda and Nearby Islands

(Imray-Iolaire Charts A, A-2, A-23, A-231, A-232, A-233)

Virgin Gorda, second largest of the British Virgin Islands, used to be refreshingly backward, with only a few people living there on the barest necessities. Time has brought development, but the unique charm of Virgin Gorda can still be found just a short walk inland, away from the marinas and other marks of the modern world.

Electricity has arrived in Virgin Gorda, too—a boon to the mariner. On a clear night, the lights of the island sometimes can be seen as much as 30 or 40 miles to the east. This should reduce the number of vessels lost in the Anegada area, but it will not eliminate all of the losses. If the visibility is not perfect, you can hit Horse Shoe Reef before you see the lights. (Witness the freighter that hit the reef and was a total loss in the spring of 1973. Many vessels have faced the same fate since then—at least one a year, and sometimes two or three a year.)

An airport has also been built on Virgin Gorda. It has a crosswind runway guaranteed to test the skills of a pilot. Some don't pass the test. On the day of the airport's inauguration ceremony, the first plane to land on the new strip crashed, killing the pilot and four passengers. It was reported that the plane had hit the wire holding up the welcome sign and had spun out of control.

The western shore of Virgin Gorda is well known for its beautiful beaches. But if you are willing to do a little exploring, there is also some wonderful scenery on the east side of the island. Equip yourself with sturdy shoes, long trousers, shirt, and hat, and walk east over the hills in the direction of Africa. There is no land between that continent and Virgin Gorda, and, if the trades are blowing, the seas that have built up over the vast expanse of ocean crash spectacularly against the rocks.

A walk farther along the shore toward the north leads to Copper Mine Point and an abandoned copper mine that reaches far out under the floor of the ocean. Every time the price of copper goes up, there is talk of reopening the mine, but as yet nothing has come of it. The bays and reefs north of Copper Mine Point provide excellent snorkeling and spearfishing for those who are accustomed to rough water. However, these bays are only accessible by land. Being on the windward side of the island, they are too exposed to risk bringing a boat into them. Of course, there is always the exception. One yacht sailed across the Atlantic, became lost, bounced over the reefs outside of Taddy Bay, and came to rest in one piece within the bay. Later, she was towed out in calm weather and continued on her way.

THE BATHS
(II A, A-2, A-23, A-231, A-232, A-233)

The most popular part of Virgin Gorda is a beach along the southwestern tip of the island known as The Baths. It is so called because of the huge boulders—larger than most houses—that time and the elements have tossed helter-skelter on top of one another. Waves wash in among them and create a series of pools of crystal-clear water, made even more beautiful by the sun filtering through openings in the rocks. Warmer

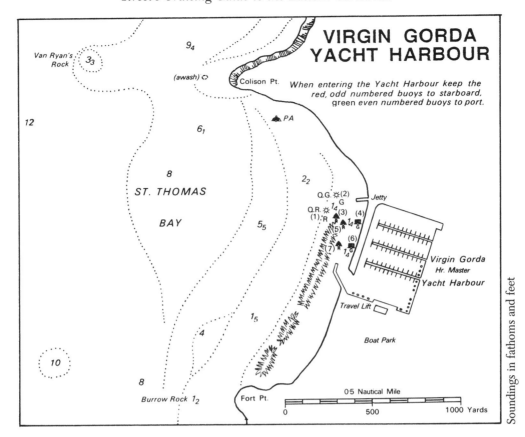

VIRGIN GORDA YACHT HARBOUR

Van Ryan's Rock

3₃

9₄

(awash)

Colison Pt.

When entering the Yacht Harbour keep the red, odd numbered buoys to starboard, green even numbered buoys to port.

12

6₁

PA

8

ST. THOMAS

BAY

2₂

5₅

Q.G. ✳(2)
G
Q.R. ✳(3)   (4)
(1) R
(5)
(6)
(7)   1₄

Jetty

Virgin Gorda
Hr. Master
Yacht Harbour

Travel Lift

Boat Park

1₅

4

1₅

10

8

Burrow Rock 1₂

Fort Pt.

0·5 Nautical Mile

0   500   1000 Yards

Soundings in fathoms and feet

SKETCH CHART 60   Virgin Gorda Yacht Harbour

than the ocean water outside, the pools are far more enticing than a suburban bathtub.

To reach The Baths, anchor off the second beach up from the southern tip of Virgin Gorda. Once ashore, work your way south. You can't miss the passageway. Try to get there very early—I mean 0700—as all the day charter boats start coming in by 0900, as do the island's hotel guests. A small bar and a barbecue are set up with a table on the beach. Spend a half hour exploring The Baths, then go back to the boat for a late breakfast and clear out before the area is inundated with other boats.

If you are anchoring directly off The Baths, be very careful. The bottom drops off steeply, and there are submerged rocks directly off the beach that have only six feet of water over them. This group of rocks is on a line drawn between the westernmost rocks of Virgin Gorda and the high point of Fallen Jerusalem.

Do not anchor overnight off The Baths. Even in the daytime, it is best to leave someone on board, because the ground swell can build up

quickly and pivot you around stern-to the beach in a short time. There is always a swell, so it is advisable to leave your mizzen up so that the prevailing easterlies will blow you directly offshore and keep you there. Ordinarily, with care, a dinghy can be taken through the surf, but sometimes it is impossible to land. The snorkeling around the rocks is excellent. There are many small, brightly colored fish—pretty but too small to spear.

Unfortunately, the popularity of The Baths has changed things so drastically that not only has the shoreside view been spoiled, but there have also been a number of robberies of boats left unattended at anchor. Evidently, the thieves have swum out to the boats while the crews were ashore and made off with large sums of money. No one seems to know who has been responsible for these incidents. The residents of Virgin Gorda took measures some years ago to stop the thievery, but I still hear occasional reports of trouble. You are well advised, here and elsewhere, to guard valuables carefully and not to leave cash on board.

VIRGIN GORDA YACHT HARBOUR
(SPANISH TOWN)

(Sketch Chart 60; II A, A-2, A-23, A-231, A-232, A-233)

The old settlement of Spanish Town, at the south end of St. Thomas Bay, has pretty much disappeared. It has been swallowed up by Virgin Gorda Yacht Harbour and the Little Dix Bay resort, which used to be owned by RockResorts, the Rockefeller holding company. This complex has everything—dockage, water, electricity, grocery store, boutiques, banks, telephones, Travelift for boats up to 50 tons, and a well-stocked chandlery. The yard has considerable space, so this has become a popular place to lay up boats during the hurricane season. Virgin Gorda Yacht Harbour draws a crowd, so be sure to contact the harbormaster on channel 16 before entering, as frequently there are no berths available.

Enter from the north end of the reef behind Colison Point and turn southward from the Little Dix dock, the large dock at the north end of St. Thomas Bay. Pick up channel buoys (international buoy system), stay directly in the 10-foot (reported) dredged channel, and swing on into the basin.

If you anchor outside St. Thomas Bay, remember that it is open to the northwest ground swell. The best anchorage is up in the northeastern corner behind Colison Point, but there are three dangers:

1. The ground swell can come in at night if you are anchored on a single anchor, and you can be high and dry on the beach before you can react. Over the years, numerous vessels have been lost in just this fashion.
2. The wind loops across Cow Hill, and the back eddies will swing you around on your anchor. It will probably break out, so anchor on a good, secure Bahamian moor.
3. Finally, although the general depth is 12 to 15 feet of water once you are up on the shelf, there are coral heads that project six to eight feet from the bottom, so only enter this anchorage in good light, or you may find one of those coral heads.

LITTLE DIX BAY/SAVANNA BAY

(Sketch Chart 61; II A, A-2, A-23, A-231, A-232, A-233)

These harbors are beginning to become popular as anchorages, but keep in mind that both are completely open to the northwest ground swell. Although the charts show offlying barrier reefs, these are not high enough to effectively block the swell, which sometimes will break all across the entrances.

Inside the reef, you'll find two fathoms of water, but only two feet over the reef itself. The entrance is unmarked and requires eyeball navigation. If you do go in, don't stay the night. There is little shelter from the northerly swell. Rather, enjoy your stay here but allow plenty of time in the afternoon to sail out to a secure anchorage. In fact, the best way to get to Little Dix Bay is to anchor in St. Thomas Bay and take a taxi over the hill.

Savanna Bay is strictly a summer or calm-weather anchorage. The winter swell rolls over the reef and can break across the entire entrance channel; again, clear out before evening. In the summer months, however, Savanna Bay can be a secure anchorage. Enter 30 yards north of Blowing Point and continue eastward, following the reef around to port. Favor the reef side of the bay, since the beach side is littered with obscured coral heads. Anchor with the lowland between the hills bearing southeast. The wind usually sweeps in through this gap, keeping you cool and bug-free. Once anchored, hop in the dinghy and explore north to Pound Bay, Maho Bay, and Tetor Bay. They all provide excellent snorkeling and spearfishing.

The remainder of the western coast of Virgin Gorda is beautiful but without good anchorages. It is continually exposed to the rollers from the northwest, and there are no barrier reefs for shelter north of Tetor Bay.

ANGUILLA POINT

(Chart 62; II A, A-2, A-23, A-231, A-232, A-233)

In the summer, when there is no danger of a ground swell, there is an excellent anchorage directly west of Anguilla Point with good snorkeling on the reefs in the southwest corner of Mosquito Island. From here, you can visit Gorda Sound by dinghy. The anchorage is beautiful and cool, with wind sweeping through the gap between Mosquito Island and Anguilla Point.

While snorkeling in this anchorage in 1983, Olaf Harken found a hundred-dollar bill sticking up out of the sand. He made another dive and came up with four 20-dollar bills. That's all he and his crew found in a frantic afternoon of searching, but it was enough to finance one hell of a party ashore. Olaf said he lost money, however, because the dinner

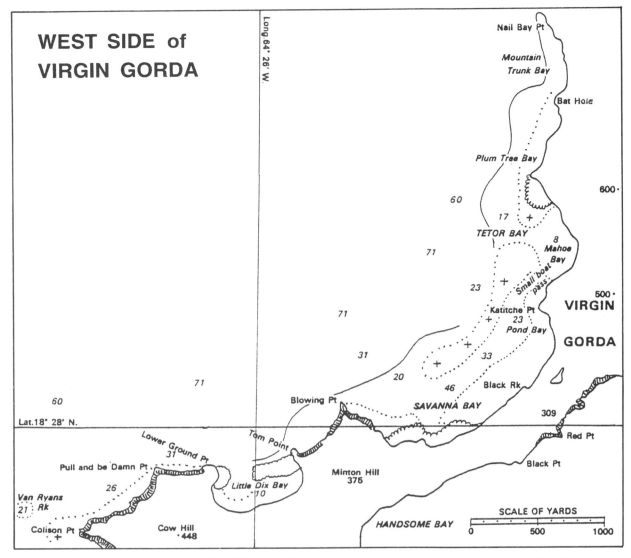

SKETCH CHART 61   West Side of Virgin Gorda

Soundings in feet

ended up costing him a lot more than he had found while snorkeling!

Don't anchor off Anguilla Point in the winter because of the ground swell, and don't anchor there on summer weekends, because the Puerto Rican Navy comes charging in from St. Thomas and Puerto Rico. They power flat-out between Mosquito Island and Anguilla Point, causing huge wakes that will roll both rails under.

GORDA SOUND

(Chart 62; II A, A-2, A-23, A-231, A-232, A-233)

On the northern end of Virgin Gorda, Gorda

Sound provides yachtsmen with many good anchorages that are protected in all weather. The main entrance to the sound is between Colquhoun Reef off Mosquito Island and the reefs off Cactus Point on Prickly Pear Island. Both reefs are visible at all tides. To be sure that you can make the entrance with ease, tack well to the north of Mosquito Island on your approach. The entrance itself is closer to Cactus Point than to Mosquito Island, and the course through the hole in the reefs is southeast, 145° magnetic. Some careful navigating is called for here.

Each year, a number of boats entering Gorda Sound end up on Colquhoun Reef, and even though it is now marked by buoys, it is still tricky. The problem is that leeway and current combine to drive a

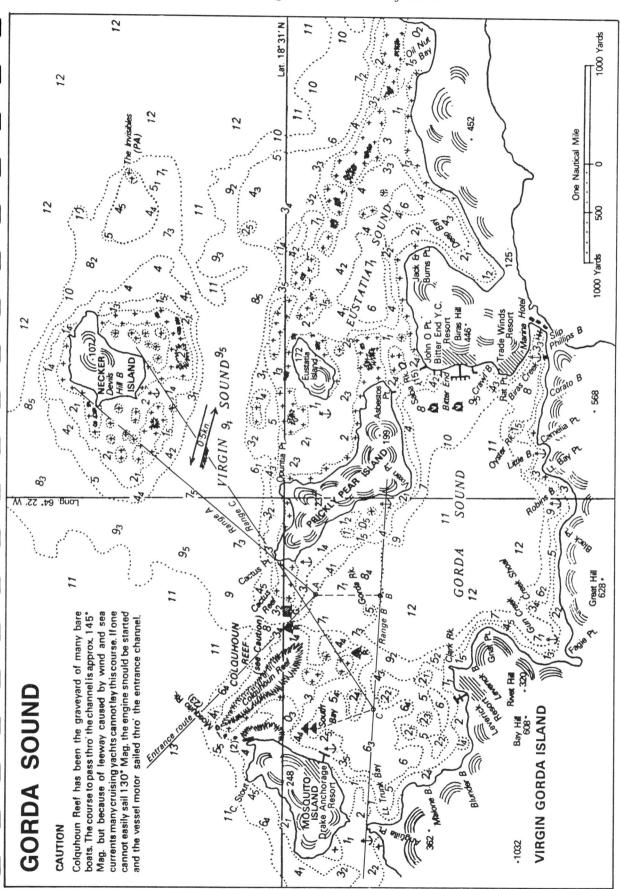

GORDA SOUND

CAUTION

Colquhoun Reef has been the graveyard of many bare boats. The course to pass thro' the channel is approx. 145° Mag. but because of leeway caused by wind and sea currents many cruising yachts cannot lay this course. If one cannot easily sail 130° Mag. the engine should be started and the vessel motor sailed thro' the entrance channel.

Soundings in fathoms and feet

One Nautical Mile

1000 Yards   500   0   1000 Yards

VIRGIN GORDA ISLAND

CHART 62   Gorda Sound and Surrounding Islands

boat down on the reef. So, although the range up the channel is 145° magnetic, you should be able to sail a course of about 130° magnetic to counteract the forces pushing you to leeward. If you can't make 130°, turn on the engine, furl the jib, and motorsail through the entrance.

You are by no means home free after getting through this first opening. When Bert Kilbride ran Mosquito Island in the 1970s, he counted 50 groundings in one year in the tricky channel to the western end of Gorda Sound. So I urge you to follow the directions below carefully. They are complicated, but, I hope, foolproof.

The course through the entrance is southeast, 135° magnetic; maintain this course until Necker Island (off to port) disappears behind Cactus Point (Range A, point A).

Alter course to due south, 180° magnetic. (Do *not* turn west of south, and do *not* turn and head for the dock on Mosquito Island.)

Continue south, looking off to starboard. Eventually you will be able to see Seal Dog Rocks in the channel between Mosquito Island and Anguilla Point (Range B, point B). When the Seal Dogs disappear behind Anguilla Point, you have the whole of Gorda Sound before you. But to reach Mosquito Island from this imaginary point B, you still cannot turn directly for the dock.

From point B (Range B), turn west to a course of 285° magnetic. You should be heading directly for Anguilla Point. If Seal Dog Rocks reappear, you are too far north. Head farther south, and keep the rocks just hidden behind Anguilla Point.

Continue on 285° magnetic until you see Necker Island appearing off your starboard quarter from behind Cactus Point (Range C, point C). When the whole of Necker Island is visible, turn northward and head toward South Bay and the anchorage off the dock at Mosquito Island. You will be well protected there, for even though a small chop can build up, no sea can find its way through the small entrance to Gorda Sound.

Off the dock, you will find Moor Seacure buoys, which are everywhere in the British Virgins. These can be used for the night at a rental charge; pay the fee ashore at the bar on Mosquito Island. (Mosquito Island is private, the home of Drake's Anchorage Resort Inn, but visitors are welcome at the bar and restaurant.)

As you walk up the dock, the flagpole is the aluminum mast from Huey Long's 53-foot wooden yawl *Ondine*, on which I cut my offshore sailing teeth. As a college student right after the Korean War, I went

to Bermuda as a paid hand aboard *Ondine*. When Huey fired the skipper, I ended up as captain—but at a paid hand's wage! Subsequently, we parted company, and *Ondine* later sailed up on Anegada Reef, where she was a total loss. After the crew abandoned her, I went up to Anegada on *Iolaire*, anchored well offshore, and went all the way around the island in a 10-foot dinghy. I salvaged massive amounts of gear from *Ondine*, including a 29-foot mizzenmast, which we transported in the dinghy and which is still on *Iolaire*'s stern. The mainmast became the Mosquito Island flagpole.

When I later met Huey Long in Bermuda, he said, "How did you get all those fittings from *Ondine* when my crew couldn't?" I replied, "I put them on, so I should have known how to get them off!" He said, "Let's have a drink on that one!" And we did.

There is a fine view of Gorda Sound from the top of the hill on Mosquito Island. A path on the north side of the island leads you to the top. Wear sneakers, since there are prickly plants. The swimming off the Mosquito Island beach, the snorkeling on Colquhoun Reef, and the piña coladas at the open-air bar—all are most enjoyable.

The second entrance to Gorda Sound is between Mosquito Island and Anguilla Point. This narrow channel is frequently used by locals and others sailing in small boats. It saves you considerable distance and keeps you out of rough water when the trades begin to pipe up. Enter in midchannel, a third of the channel's width away from Anguilla Point, but once east of Anguilla Point, swing to the south and steer about south-southeast magnetic (157°). More than anything else, it is a question of using your eyes and aiming for the narrowest section of the sandbar. You should be able to carry seven feet through the channel safely. Fergus Walker of *Poseidon* assured me of this, and *Te Hongi*, which draws seven and a half feet, has used this passage without trouble. However, I advise against using the Anguilla Point entrance to Gorda Sound if there is a large ground swell running, since the swell breaks completely across the channel. In the winter of 1978-79, this caused the total loss of one of The Moorings' Gulfstar 50s.

Under ideal conditions, *Iolaire*, drawing seven and a half feet, has many times sailed this entrance, passing both eastward and westward. But it was always done on a springtide and in the summer, when there was no ground swell. In December 1992, when we went out in a dinghy with a leadline and sounding pole and rechecked this route, we came up with the least depth of eight feet.

PRICKLY PEAR ISLAND
(Chart 62; II A, A-2, A-23, A-231, A-232, A-233)

As you enter Gorda Sound through the northwest entrance, instead of following the preceding complicated directions all the way into South Bay, there is a small, beautiful, secluded, white-sand beach that offers an ideal anchorage for one boat. It is along the shore of Prickly Pear Island, on the port hand as you come in. Two words of caution, however: In the afternoon, it can be oppressively hot, so bring something for shade; and don't eat the fruit that looks like a crabapple—it is poisonous.

Just west of the land marked on the chart as Vixen Point or Observation Point, there used to be an absolutely idyllic anchorage where you could run right up on the beach and bury the anchor. Now, however, a parasailing operation has been set up here, and, needless to say, parasails and tall sailboat masts don't mix. There is also a beach bar catering to the small cruise boats that visit Gorda Sound. Scratch this from the list of attractive anchorages.

The south and southwest coasts of Prickly Pear offer swimming, diving, and exploring as good as you can find anywhere. An anchorage can also be had due west of Saba Rock. Use a Bahamian moor, since the reversing current can be tricky. Make sure you are in shoal water and your anchor is well buried, as the bottom drops off very steeply in 12 to 14 feet to 50 feet. If you are not secured in shoal water, you will be trying to anchor on the backside of the slope, with no likelihood that the hook will hold.

SABA ROCK
(Chart 62; II A, A-2, A-23, A-231, A-232, A-233)

In the middle of the entrance to Gorda Sound, on Saba Rock, is the home of Bert Kilbride, probably the greatest wreck expert in the British Virgins. In 1992, at the age of 77, Bert married 39-year-old Gayla, and the two of them run Saba Rock as a bar and short-order restaurant. It's an absolutely great, informal place to have an evening sundowner, meet other yachties, and chat with Bert about the "good old days" in the Caribbean. He first came to St. Thomas in 1954, in the construction business, and he has really seen changes!

Despite his age, Bert is still "King of the Divers." If you want to go diving, why not go with the best? His operation is excellent, and he is a great raconteur about diving experiences. When we saw him in late 1992, he discussed his plans to go to Salt River in St. Croix and retrieve the anchor that Columbus lost there when he stopped by in 1493. Then he'll go

down to Portobello, on the east coast of Panama, where he and salvager Mel Fisher have located Sir Francis Drake's lead coffin. (Drake died of malaria as he was preparing to lay siege to Panama, and he was buried in a lead coffin.) Bert and Fisher have received permission from the Panamanian government to retrieve the coffin and transport it to England so that Drake can be interred in Westminster Abbey.

BITTER END
(Chart 62; II A, A-2, A-23, A-231, A-232, A-233)

Bitter End Yacht Club and Marina, located on John O Point, is one of the most popular bareboat stops in the British Virgins. The sailing-oriented operation has dozens of Windsurfers as well as Rhodes 19 daysailers, J-24s, Express 29s, and more. Bitter End is tied in with *Yachting* magazine and North Sails and runs sailing clinics and match races. The sailing program is run by Nick Trotter, who arrived in the Caribbean as a young kid in the mid-1970s. After 18 years in the Caribbean, he aged about five years. He is still easygoing, very personable, and competent—and he looks about 25.

You can pick up a guest mooring here (and pay the fee) or anchor on your own. Anchor between Saba Rock and Prickly Pear Island, as otherwise you will be in 50 to 60 feet of water. You'd have to put out so much scope that you would be likely to foul boats on permanent moorings when the wind died at night.

There is a morning trash pickup service for US$1.50 per bag. (Carry a couple of large garbage bags, as the fee is the same, no matter what size bag you have.) Water, ice, and fuel are available. If you are tied up to the dock, you can have a television plugged in, but otherwise, you can pay a visit to the bar, where you'll find satellite TV. Other facilities include a delicatessen, a commissary, and of course a restaurant. Hotel rooms can also be rented. In short, you can find just about everything here.

Bitter End was founded by Basil Symonette when there was nothing but bush on the end of the island. Basil and his friends hacked away the bush and built a small guest house and bar that they dubbed "The Last Resort." (Needless to say, they named it for its remote location.) Eventually, Basil sold out to Myron Hokin, who had visited the area in his big motorsailer *Allianora*. Now the entire end of North Point is owned by the Bitter End Yacht Club.

The one problem with being anchored here on the shelf between Asbestos Point and John O Point is the fact that when it is blowing hard, the boardsailors from the yacht club use this as a speedway. In December 1992, we sailed in and anchored, even though it was blowing 25 to 30 knots. Then a boardsailor came screaming up to us, collapsed his sail, and yelled, "Hey, you can't anchor here; you're in our speedway." The response we gave him was not exactly polite. For the next three days, we did have a lot of fun watching the speed demons go back and forth. The good ones were doing an easy 25 knots.

BIRAS CREEK
(Chart 62; II A, A-2, A-23, A-231, A-232, A-233)

A good anchorage can be had in Biras Creek, south of John O Point, since the wind sweeps over the low saddle of land between Biras Creek and the ocean to keep the cove cool and bug-free. Ashore at Biras Creek is one of the most attractive hotel/restaurant complexes in the Lesser Antilles. There is a small marina at the head of Biras Creek; on the south side of the harbor is a facility that has fuel, water, and ice. The small railway is strictly for the use of Biras Creek and Bitter End boats, as the slip is uninsured, so they are unwilling to haul yachts.

When entering Biras Creek from the west, watch out for Oyster Rock, which has four feet of water over it at low tide. It is mischarted on the older Imray-Iolaire charts, where it is marked for a depth of 11 feet. The rock is north-northeast from Camelia Point; stay well to the north and you will avoid it.

GUN CREEK
(Chart 62; II A, A-2, A-23, A-231, A-232, A-233)

Gun Creek was a wonderful backwater that changed little from the arrival of the first yachts in the early 1950s until the late 1960s. However, a road has now been put through from the south side of the island, and the picturesque little village has pretty much disappeared.

Launch services from Bitter End and Biras Creek come into Gun Creek, where you transfer to a bus or taxi to Virgin Gorda Yacht Harbour for launches to Tortola or flights out of Virgin Gorda Airport.

I have had reports that Pancho, the senior launch driver for Bitter End, has a very nice pub up the hill in Gun Creek. It's not fancy, but it offers good, inexpensive West Indian meals, a pool table, and a friendly bar—a very entertaining change of pace.

LEVERICK BAY RESORT
(Chart 62; II A, A-2, A-23, A-231, A-232, A-233)

Leverick Bay is developing rapidly under the influence of another Pusser's Rum store. The moorings off Leverick Bay—like the other Moor Seacure moorings—must be paid for by the night, but when you first arrive in the bay and pick up your mooring, you receive a free bottle of Pusser's rum. Not a bad marketing technique!

Despite what some other guides say, this is not a 40-boat marina. I would say you could fit in no more than eight or 10 boats (40-footers). There are a number of offlying moorings, plus a dinghy landing. Leverick Bay is a worthwhile stop, as ashore you will find one of the two free showers in the entire Caribbean. (The other one is in St. Barts, but there the water is cold.) Not only is the shower free here, but the water is hot! There are also laundry machines, a delicatessen, and a bar and restaurant. You can buy fuel, water, and ice (although it's only cube ice; block ice is available at Bitter End).

If the wind is south of east, Leverick Bay can be fine, but if it begins to blow up out of the east or north of east, remember that there is roughly two miles of fetch across Gorda Sound. Thus, in winter when it is blowing hard, this is not a comfortable anchorage. Although I have never anchored in Leverick Bay in heavy weather, I have been told that you can get seasick sitting on the mooring.

On summer weekends, you will find the same problem as at the anchorage west of Anguilla Point: The Puerto Rican Navy comes roaring through, and you will roll your guts out.

When leaving Gorda Sound via the western entrance, go over to the Virgin Gorda shore by Blunder and Malone Bays, head northwest, and point to the western end of Mosquito Island. Once Anguilla Point comes abeam, turn southwest. This course will keep you clear of the reef and any breakers that may be building up on the reef on the southwest point of Mosquito Island.

EUSTATIA SOUND
(Chart 62; II A, A-2, A-23, A-231, A-232, A-233)

This is a great place for diving and exploring. The area is sheltered enough to anchor close aboard any of the reefs, so you can swim directly off the boat without launching a dinghy. The channel between Saba Rock and Biras Hill is seven feet and requires careful eyeballing. Make sure the sun is high, and don't return any later than 1500. There is no way

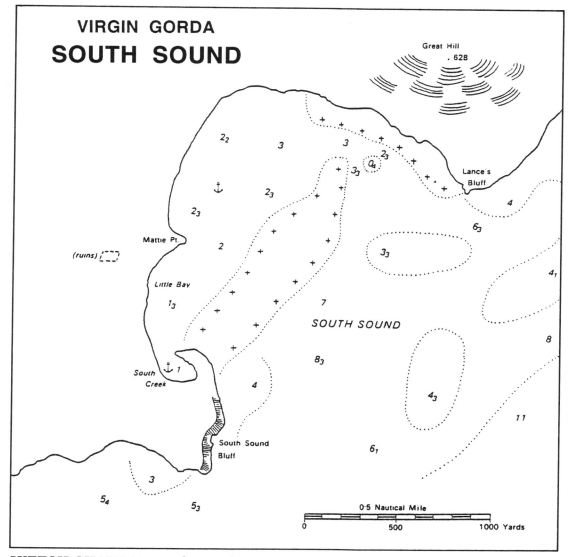

VIRGIN GORDA
SOUTH SOUND

Great Hill
. 628

Lance's
Bluff

Mattie Pt.

(ruins)

Little Bay

South
Creek

South Sound
Bluff

SOUTH SOUND

0·5 Nautical Mile

0   500   1000 Yards

SKETCH CHART 63   South Sound

Soundings in fathoms and feet

you can make it back to Gorda Sound with the sun in your eyes. If you have stayed on the Eustatia side past 1500, you can get out to the north through a wider and deeper passage between Prickly Pear and Eustatia Islands. Or you can go around and spend the night in Deep Bay, a nicely protected, bug-free, and breeze-cooled summer anchorage east of Bitter End. I am told that clams are plentiful there.

Northwest of Eustatia Island is a good anchorage between the island and the reef. It's a fabulous spot for shoal-draft boats, but do not use it overnight except during the summer. The winter ground swell makes the area untenable. It is impossible to leave after 1600. If the swell builds up, you are trapped.

Eustatia Island is private and well built up. There

is one ugly house on the top of the ridge, but if you take the dinghy around to the western side of Eustatia Island, you will notice some handsome houses built out of natural stone—some of the most attractive of that type I have seen anywhere.

In November 1992, we explored the area east of Eustatia Island/Eustatia Sound in a Boston Whaler lent to us by Nick Trotter of Bitter End. We came to the conclusion that this is an excellent place to get away from everything, as the reefs are shoal enough at the eastern end of Eustatia Sound to form an absolute breakwater. One could anchor out behind the reefs and dive directly from the boat without even having to put the dinghy in the water. It would be a breezy and bug-free anchorage. When anchoring in this fashion, I would definitely anchor bow-and-stern; during the night, if the wind dies out, the current running across the reef could swing you right onto the reef.

Shoal-draft boats can work their way all the way east into Oil Nut Bay, where you would be absolutely guaranteed to be alone, as there is no vehicle access to the bay.

NECKER ISLAND
(Chart 62; II A, A-2, A-23, A-231, A-232, A-233)

Necker Island used to be uninhabited, but now it is owned by Richard Branson, who operates it as the ultimate resort for the ultra-wealthy. It is the "in" place for the beautiful people, including members of the Royal Family. When the royals are here, you are likely to run up against Scotland Yard officers patrolling in small boats and chasing everyone out of the anchorage. At other times, it is permissible to anchor here but not to go ashore.

To get here, head eastward across Virgin Sound until the hill on the southwest corner of the island is bearing due north magnetic. Stand on in, heading north and favoring the land. Be sure you do this in good light, as the approach must be eyeballed. When the high peak bears east-southeast, you should be able to find about 10 feet of water. Put down a proper moor and you will be well set for the day. The anchorage should not be used overnight except in summer. Even then, make sure you are moored well before dusk.

SOUTH SOUND
(Sketch Chart 63; II A, A-2, A-23, A-231, A-232)

The most secluded anchorage in Virgin Gorda is South Sound, on the south coast. It has proved excellent in any weather for a skillful seaman who has boat enough to beat the six and a half miles from Round Rock to South Sound. Remember, when you are attempting this feat, that there will be nothing between you and Africa, and the Atlantic swell will have become short and steep. The windward side of Virgin Gorda in normal conditions is rough in the extreme.

To enter South Sound, head for Lance's Bluff with a crew member aloft to guide you. As you approach Lance's Bluff, bear toward Great Hill, bringing that to bear approximately due north magnetic. As you approach the coast, you will spot a gap in the reef no more than 50 yards wide. In the middle of the gap is a shoal spot; there is plenty of water north and south of the shoal spot. Ross Norgrove advises staying south of the shoal and swinging northwest around the end of the reef before running due south. The reef gives complete protection, and the snorkeling is fine. Fifteen feet can be carried as far down as Mattie Point, but there is some argument about the water depth south of Mattie Point. If you draw more than six feet, it is best to anchor north of Mattie Point, get in the dinghy with a leadline or sounding pole, and feel your way before trying to sail farther. If you get down into South Creek, you have found an ideal little hurricane hole—*for one boat only.*

NOTES

NOTES

15

⌒⌒

Anegada

(Imray-Iolaire Charts A, A-2, A-23, A-232, A-233)

Anegada, lying 15 miles to the north of Virgin Gorda, is a flat island whose reefs are strewn with the wreckage of more than 500 ships. It is so low that it was appropriately listed on the old charts as Drowned Land. The highest point of elevation is just under 30 feet, and it is surrounded by reefs, so for many years—until quite recently, in fact—the main source of revenue on this island was from the salvage of wrecks. In bad weather, you can run aground on Horse Shoe Reef (Anegada Reef) long before there is any possibility of seeing the island of Anegada. This was even more true in years gone by, when the only lights in The Settlement in Anegada came from kerosene lanterns.

Even now, scarcely a year goes by that some yacht or local interisland freighter isn't wrecked in this area. The 100-fathom curve is only a mile or so offshore, and there is a full eight fathoms right up to the reef, which is basically a vertical wall. On the north shore, the bottom comes up to the top very rapidly.

In 1960, the wooden yacht *Ondine* found all this out the hard way. She was coming from Bermuda, planning to make a landfall on Sombrero Island and then run down to St. Thomas. It was a fast trip, but they had taken no sights for 48 hours. She was to leeward of the course at four o'clock one morning when there was a godawful crash. She hit the outer reef, bounced over, and ended up in the pool inside the outer reef. The crew members were unable to get her off, so they stripped *Ondine* of as much as they could and then abandoned her. (As I related in chapter 14, I had worked aboard *Ondine* during my university days, so I knew her well, and after she was abandoned, I managed to salvage her mizzenmast and mizzen boom—both of which are still on *Iolaire*—and about a ton of deck fittings.)

In the early 1980s, Norrie Hoyt on *Telltale* came within an ace of piling up on Horse Shoe Reef. He was heading for Tortola from Bermuda, had overcast conditions, and had been unable to take sights. He had allowed for a westerly set of the current, not realizing that there frequently was an easterly set north of Anegada. Norrie had the scare of his life when his wife, Kitty, quietly said, "Norrie, I think you had better do something; there's a nice white-sand beach in front of us." Poking his head out of the hatch, Norrie almost had a heart attack, but then he quickly bore off and passed around the western end of Anegada.

Boats have piled up on Horse Shoe Reef when running downwind from Antigua, St. Barts, St. Martin, and Anguilla. When running downwind, most skippers tend to sail high of the course, plus they forget that the current on the approach to Anegada is likely to be running due north rather than west or northwest. This puts them north of the course and right smack onto Horse Shoe Reef.

Fortunately, there is now an eight-mile light on the western end of Anegada, and the eastern end of Virgin Gorda has a 16-mile light at Pajaros Point. In addition, the streetlights on the road that leads over the mountain from Gun Creek to Spanish Town on Virgin Gorda are high and bright. On clear nights, you can usually see the lights of Virgin Gorda 20 to 25 miles out at sea. As long as the visibility is good, these two lights should keep yachts from piling up on Anegada. However, undoubtedly some people, through bad navigation and on a rainy, squally night, will end up, much to their horror, finding Anegada the hard way—by piling up on it.

Electricity has also arrived in Anegada. The glow produced by the island's three hotels and The Settlement allows Anegada to be visible six to eight miles off—except, of course, on a squally night, when visibility may be reduced to a quarter of a mile.

The charter companies used to bar their clients from going to Anegada, as the only anchorage was off The Settlement, anywhere from a half mile to a mile offshore (depending on draft). Further, even anchoring a mile offshore meant threading through a mile of coral heads—not a terrific idea for the average bareboater.

I have always wondered why The Settlement is where it is, rather than farther west, where there is deep water much closer to shore. The most logical response I have heard is that the village was located near the freshwater wells—the rest of the island has no water at all, except what can be collected during rain.

Today, most bareboat companies allow their charterers to go to Anegada, as there are now three hotels, the anchorage for the two easternmost hotels is buoyed, and there is a good range for the anchorage off the westernmost hotel. As long as you approach the anchorages around noon, and keep your wits about you, you should have no problem finding a good spot in normal settled conditions.

Why go to Anegada? Many reasons. The water is crystal-clear, miles of reef provide superb snorkeling, and the local hotels specialize in fish and lobster dinners—lobster is still plentiful in Anegada. The 11-mile-long island has more than 22 miles of white-sand beach! If you want isolation, it is just a matter of walking far enough away from everyone so you can shed your clothes and your inhibitions. If you prefer not to walk, just hop in the dinghy. You can virtually circumnavigate the island inside the reef and select the perfect beach. Anchor the dinghy off in two or three feet of water and wade ashore.

Anegada Reef Hotel, the easternmost of the hostelries, is the best known and most popular. It is run by Lowell (Lu) and Vivian Wheatley, a local family. They serve three meals a day and provide a trash-pickup service for US$2 a bag (consolidate small bags into a big one). Be sure to have the trash ashore by 0830. The hotel staff can arrange sportfishing and diving excursions, as well as tours or taxis to the isolated beaches on the north side of the island. The hotel's small boutique/gift shop is one of the most attractive I have seen throughout the Virgins—many of the items in the shop are locally made.

Just west of the Anegada Reef Hotel is Neptune's Treasure, run by the Soares family. Originally from Bermuda, the Soareses had been commercial fishermen for generations, and they headed for the Virgins when they heard about the great fishing there. They originally settled in Jost Van Dyke but decided

that it was too close to St. Thomas and civilization. In the early 1970s, they moved to Anegada, where they fished and lived in tents for three years—apparently it took that long to get a building permit! Things move slowly in the West Indies. Everything was so primitive in the early days that the family even had to transport its water from Road Town to Anegada.

The fishing business was successful, and the Soares family eventually established the little Neptune's Treasure hostelry here. The Soareses have raised six children—some have left the island, some have stayed, and some have left and then returned. One daughter married a man from Saba—a mountainous island with no beaches—who decided he preferred low-lying Anegada with its miles and miles of sand. There are now 17 Soares grandchildren, many of whom have been raised in Anegada.

I strongly recommend taking a dinghy down to Neptune's Treasure, putting your feet up, and having a chat with Mrs. Soares, who is full of fascinating information on Anegada, the Virgins, and Bermuda. She is the one who usually holds the fort here, because her husband and sons-in-law are out fishing for a week at a time, and the chances of catching them ashore are pretty slim. If you do, however, you'll find that they, too, have lots of good stories about the islands and fishing.

The third hotel here, the Pomato Beach, was built in 1989 by Anegada native Wilfred Creque. He still remembers sailing on the Anegada fishing sloops that combed the reef, kept the fish alive in wet-wells, and sailed down to Road Town to market the catch.

The hotel has a room set aside as a small but interesting museum that includes a wide array of artifacts collected by Mr. Creque on land and at sea. Among the items is an old chart of the Virgins done by Mr. Laurie, part of the firm that still makes the Imray-Iolaire charts.

It is now possible to fly into Anegada from Virgin Gorda and from Tortola's Beef Island Airport. In the spring of 1994, there were three flights a week. Who knows what it will be when you arrive! (The Speedy's Delight boat service also makes day trips from Tortola to Anegada. Check in Tortola for the schedule.)

The history of flying into Anegada is rather interesting. The first airstrip was built in the 1950s to help service the shark fishery, which was trying to make a go of it. When the fishery fell through, the airstrip was abandoned. In the early 1960s, the British government doctor in Tortola had a private plane, and he wanted to fly to Anegada for his visits rather than use the unreliable (and some said unsafe) government launch. He inspected the airfield from the air, decided it looked OK, and managed a perfect touchdown. All went well until halfway down the runway, when he hit an 18-inch-deep ditch across the strip, shearing off his landing gear! It seems that one of the locals had decided to dig a drainage ditch across the runway! Such was aviation in the islands in the 1960s. Luckily, the pilot was not injured and the plane was not too badly damaged, but it did have a bent-up prop and no landing gear.

The aircraft insurance company figured it had a total loss on its hands—obviously, the plane could not be repaired in Anegada and flown out. However, a fellow named Jack Curtis heard about the problem, called up the insurance company, and offered to get the plane out. The skeptical company offered him a fair chunk of money—on a no-cure, no-pay basis—but couldn't figure out how he would accomplish the feat. But he did. Jack chartered a small tug and a small barge, towed the barge to Anegada, and then summoned every able-bodied man on the island (labor was cheap in those days). They literally picked up the aircraft, put it on their heads, walked it across the island, and manhandled it onto the barge. The locals then had a good rum party, after which Jack paid them off, departed with the plane, and earned himself a good bit of money. Naturally, the insurance company was equally happy.

The next aviation adventure came in the late 1960s, when the supersonic Concorde began making flights. A group of entrepreneurs figured there would be many Concordes, so they secured a lease on virtually all of Anegada from the BVI government. They figured that the planes could land on Anegada and disgorge their passengers, who would then transfer to smaller planes that would service the other islands. Plus there were to be a whole series of resort hotels built on Anegada—a giant development project. Plans were well underway for a monstrous airstrip (running almost the entire length of the island) when everything fell through, the developers were paid off, and Anegada reverted to its quiet old self. It turned out that the BVI government had sold land that it didn't own. Most of the land was Crown property, even though a lot of it over the years had become locally owned freeholdings.

Anegada has reached the twentieth century—but just barely. The total population on the island is about 150, and except for the three hotels and The Settlement, the island is virtually deserted. It's a real haven for yachtsmen who enjoy exploring.

ANEGADA
(Chart 64; II A, A-2, A-23, A-232, A-233)

To reach Anegada, remember that it is a 16-mile run from Gorda Sound, so start early in order to arrive no later than 1300. The course from Gorda Sound to the Setting Point anchorage is 007° magnetic, but take back bearings, because the current can be setting to the east, even though it normally is a westerly set. A back bearing of 013° magnetic on Gorda Peak will lead you to the channel entrance to the Setting Point anchorage or the anchorage off Pomato Point.

From the deck as you approach Anegada, head toward West End—tall palm trees will appear; alter course to about north magnetic until you pick up the two hotels between Pomato and Setting Points.

At this point, if you have an old Imray-Iolaire chart, or an old guide, the bearings for the channel are wrong, as the channel and the buoys have been moved farther to the southeast. A bearing of 060° magnetic on the easternmost of these two hotels leads to the outer end of the channel. In April 1993, we found the axis of the channel to be 082° magnetic on the eastern end of the white-sand beach east of the commercial jetty—the end of the beach where the mangroves start. Remember, however, that ground swells and hurricanes will alter the bottom, and buoys will also be moved. You must rely on eyeball navigation. We carried 10 feet through this channel, but remember that it could be as much as 18 inches shallower in May, June, and July.

The channel buoys here are privately maintained and not very large, so they can be very difficult to spot. The day we arrived, there were three red and two green buoys; two were moderate size and three were about the size of a fishing pot buoy. The anchorage is mixed sand and grass and the holding is not particularly good. If the wind is from the southeast, you will have a fair degree of fetch. I recommend using two anchors and diving to make sure they are well set. The deepest water for anchoring—10 or 11 feet—is near the commercial jetty. As you swing farther west to the Moor Seacure buoys, it shoals to seven and then six feet.

If you wish to go to the Pomato Point Hotel's restaurant and bar, continue past Setting Point, heading toward West End, until the hotel in the middle of the beach bears 050° magnetic. Run in on that line of bearing on the center of the building. There is 10 feet in the outer anchorage, shoaling gradually. Anchor in suitable depth. You will discover that the reefs off Pomato Point provide good shelter once you are tucked right up into the head of the harbor.

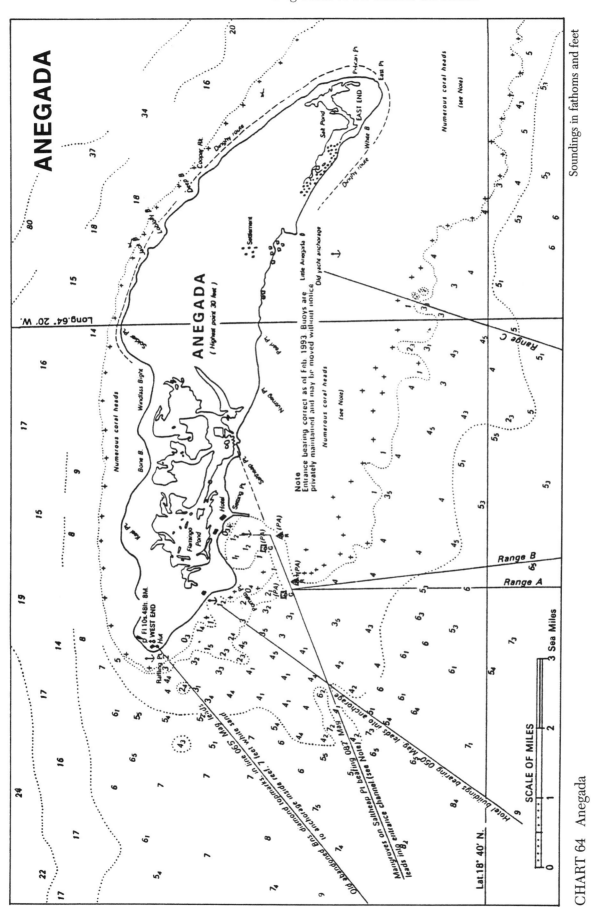

CHART 64 Anegada

Soundings in fathoms and feet

Range A: Back bearing on Gorda Peak 013° Mag leads to Setting Point anchorage channel entrance.
Range B: Back bearing 007° Mag from Gorda Sound entrance leads to Setting Point anchorage channel entrance.
Range C: Back bearing on Gorda Peak 033° Mag leads to anchorage near Little Anegada.

From the Pomato Point anchorage, you can either walk the mile-long beach to Raffling Point or take the dinghy inside the reef and anchor off.

Departing from the Setting Point anchorage is a lot easier than entering. When leaving the anchorage, pick up the buoys, and when well clear of the last buoy, set your course for your next destination.

The last anchorage is off Raffling Point, at West End. You can carry six feet inside the reefs, but it is a tight squeeze and is best left to experienced navigators. Avoid it in winter, when the ground swell can build up and push you ashore or trap you inside the reef. Despite the potential hazard, yachtsmen like this spot—there is a good beach away from it all.

On Raffling Point are two telegraph poles stuck in the sand, with a diamond on top of one of them. These poles, lined up on 065° magnetic, provide a range that leads inside the reef to where the barges used to offload heavy equipment to build a huge airstrip that never saw the light of day. Use this range, but also eyeball the route.

Between Raffling Point and Pomato Point, the water is roughly nine feet deep, but the sand can hump up with surprising suddenness to five or six feet. We found that out the hard way while exploring here in *Iolaire* in April 1978. We parked hard on a sand hump, but with the aid of our old faithful Wilcox-Crittenden anchor (copy of a Herreshoff) and two big winches, we were able to crank her around and sail her off. Obviously, you should not explore this area except in ideal conditions. Subsequently, we found an anchorage behind a reef that formed an almost-perfect breakwater, although I must admit that the holding was not very good.

That night, we also discovered that despite opinions to the contrary, there is at times a very strong easterly current in the Anegada area. We woke up at 0330 to discover that this current had swept us up to windward and onto the reef—despite the fact that our big awning and mizzen were rigged. With the wind still blowing 10 knots, we were tide-rode, not wind-rode. We quickly set an anchor off to the west, pulled her off, rigged a Bahamian moor, and all was well.

You can actually take a dinghy around Raffling Point and up inside the outer reef on the north side of the island.

No matter where you are in the vicinity of Anegada, if you anchor behind a reef, either use a Bahamian moor or anchor bow-and-stern. Beware of poor holding in areas where there is either grass or sand that covers dead grass. No anchoring or fishing is allowed on Horse Shoe Reef itself—the western edge of the reef is marked by orange buoys—so stay away from this area.

SOMBRERO ISLAND
(II A-2)

Forty-five miles east of Necker Island Channel and 28 miles north-northwest of Anguilla lies tiny Sombrero Island, with one of the major lighthouses in the Eastern Caribbean. It was also one of the earliest ones, although not the oldest: The French established a light on Désirade in 1828 and another one on Petite Terre in 1835. Unfortunately, although the British lit Sombrero, they failed to light the other dangers in the area—namely, Anguilla, Anegada, and Barbuda. In the days of vague navigation, ships that missed the Sombrero light frequently ended up on Anguilla or Anegada and sometimes Barbuda. Among them, these three islands have claimed roughly 800 wrecks.

Not many yachtsmen stop at Sombrero. Jol Byerley on *Ron of Argyll* was here back in the 1960s, but he was unimpressed and reported, "Don't bother." However, Dr. Robin Tattersall stops there frequently, and he feels it is one of the more interesting islands in the area. It rises sheer out of the sea, with 40-foot cliffs, almost like a permanently moored aircraft carrier. Its surface is pockmarked like the moon, and there are ruins of old buildings and an old railway line, left over from the days when the island boasted a phosphate mine.

It seems (throughout the Caribbean it is very difficult to separate fact from fiction) that when the British arrived to establish the light on Sombrero, they discovered New England Yankees illegally occupying the island and mining phosphate, which they shipped back to New England for use as fertilizer. Needless to say, the British chased off the American squatters and went into the phosphate business themselves in a big way. Exactly when the mining operation died out is lost in the murk of West Indian history.

The light on the island is tended, and the lighthouse keepers are quite happy to see visitors. They probably will offer to show you the lighthouse, which has a fantastic view from the top. About the only regular caller here is a small steel freighter that transports the keepers' supplies from Anguilla.

The anchorage is on the west side of the island, directly under the ladder landing marked on the chart, in 12 fathoms of clear water with a white-sand bottom. Though deep, it is good holding. In calm weather, you can run a line over to a ring set in the rock and hold off with an anchor set to the west.

Be sure to avoid the two rocks marked Paynes Landing on the chart; they are just awash north of the anchorage. The only way to scale the cliffs is via the ladder, which the lighthouse keepers will lower, from the steps cut in the cliffs.

A number of people have reported on anchoring at Sombrero, and all concur that the lighthouse keepers are welcoming to visiting yachtsmen. I have talked to some divers who say the place is alive with lobsters—more than they know what to do with— yet I have had other reports that there are plenty of fish but no lobsters. The fishermen advise bringing a good, heavy speargun.

Index